Pelican Books
Explosion in a Subcontinent

D1330072

Explosion in a Subcontinent

India, Pakistan,
Bangladesh and Ceylon

Edited by Robin Blackburn

Penguin Books
in association with *New Left Review*

Penguin Books Ltd, Harmondsworth, Middlesex, England
Penguin Books Inc., 7110 Ambassador Road, Baltimore, Maryland
21207, U.S.A.
Penguin Books Australia Ltd, Ringwood, Victoria, Australia
Penguin Books Canada Ltd, 41 Steelcase Road West, Markham,
Ontario, Canada
Penguin Books (N.Z.) Ltd, 182–190 Wairau Road, Auckland 10, New Zealand

This selection first published 1975
Each chapter was first published separately in *The New Left Review* and
subsequently revised for Penguin Books, except for the Introduction, first
published here, and 'Imperialism and the Growth of Indian Capitalism',
which is a revised version of an essay first published in *Studies in the Theory
of Imperialism*, edited by E. R. J. Owen and R. B. Sutcliffe, Longman, 1972.
We thank the editors and publishers for permission to reproduce it here.
'Introduction' copyright © *The New Left Review*, 1975
'India: Emerging Contradictions of Slow Capitalist Development' copyright ©
The New Left Review, 1970, 1975
'Imperialism and the Growth of Indian Capitalism' copyright © E. R. J. Owen
and R. B. Sutcliffe, 1972, 1975
'Politics and Society in Bengal' copyright © *The New Left Review*, 1973, 1975
'The Ceylonese Insurrection' copyright © *The New Left Review*, 1971, 1975
'Speech to the Ceylon Criminal Justice Commission' copyright © *The New
Left Review*, 1974, 1975
'The Economic Structure of Pakistan and Bangladesh' copyright © *The New
Left Review*, 1971, 1975
'Pakistan and Bangladesh: Results and Prospects' copyright © *The New Left
Review*, 1971, 1975

Made and printed in Great Britain by
Cox & Wyman Ltd, London, Reading and Fakenham
Set in Intertype Plantin

Contents

Introduction
Robin Blackburn

The essays collected together in this book seek to identify and analyse the major social and political forces at work in the contemporary history of the subcontinent. The dramatic events of 1971 threw into sharp relief the underlying crisis of the social order that dominates all four subcontinental states.

The savage repression of the revolt by peasants and youth in April 1971 brought into view the acute contradictions of Mrs Bandaranaike's Ceylon – notably its inability to sustain a social democratic Asian welfare state in a context still dominated by imperialism and capitalism. That Mrs Bandaranaike's government was forced to rely on lavish assistance from nearly every major power, and internally on slaughter and imprisonment on a mass scale, so soon after a sweeping electoral victory, underscored its extremely precarious position. Fred Halliday explores the causes and consequences of the revolt in a broad survey of the recent economic and political development of Ceylon.

In the 1960s Pakistan was touted as a success story for the application of the strategies for economic development elaborated by the World Bank and Ford Foundation – Pakistan was a show-case which proved that a large Asian country could sustain a genuine and thoroughgoing industrialization without breaking with capitalism. Richard Nations demonstrates that the highly lopsided and qualified industrial development achieved in West Pakistan was based upon the systematic subjugation and exploitation of East Pakistan, which was converted into a virtual economic colony: a source of cheap raw materials and a

5

convenient tied market. The emergence of a strong nationalist movement in East Bengal, as Tariq Ali indicates, has undermined the whole basis of the Pakistani 'miracle'. It threatens to release social revolutionary forces within West Pakistan itself since the attempt to ape a full-scale imperialist power led to a crushing débâcle which has seriously discredited the ruling political forces. Tariq Ali also examines the problems of the Bengali national movement, neglected by most sections of the Communist Left and condemned to the timid and demagogic leadership of Mujibur Rahman and the forces of petty-bourgeois nationalism. Already Mujib's régime has found it necessary to promote strong measures against student and worker opposition and a spate of political murders has been committed by private armed gangs linked to the Awami League.

Throughout 1971 and into 1972 the government of Mrs Gandhi received the resounding ratification of victory both in the domestic electoral arena and in war against the country's traditional antagonist. Mrs Gandhi was able to present herself as the triumphant champion of social and national liberation. However, as the studies in this book by Prabhat Patnaik, Meghnad Desai, Premen Addy and Ibne Azad show, this edifice of political victories has been built on very shaky social and economic foundations. Prabhat Patnaik analyses the different factors which slow down and compromise India's attempt to achieve an independent and self-sustaining process of industrial growth. Meghnad Desai focuses on the problems of agriculture and the contradictions of the 'Green Revolution'. While significant advances towards more rational capitalist social relations are taking place in a number of rural areas selected for special development, it is also clear that this very process unleashes social contradictions which the traditional structure of rural social relations was adept at containing. Thus while agricultural output is somewhat increased, the increase in the potential for social upheaval is ever greater because the benefits of development are extremely unevenly distributed.

Premen Addy and Ibne Azad give an account of the national movement in Bengal which highlights the social roots of the national movement and the limitations of its ideology. Set against the more general studies this essay scrutinizes the logic of political developments in one of the most advanced provinces of India, an industrial enclave which was the original base from which British imperialism extended its domination over the subcontinent. It is here that Mrs Gandhi encountered some of her most severe difficulties. In the end these were only resolved through imposing presidential rule on West Bengal and conducting vigorous repression of the local Communist Party (the CPI(M)) which dominated the province's United Front government. In the course of the campaign of repression several hundred trade-union activists and Communist Party militants were physically eliminated by hired thugs.

Although such methods allowed Mrs Gandhi to retain control of the situation in Bengal in the short run, there are already signs that in India as a whole the effect of her double triumph has been dissipated with remarkable speed. Following her victory in the elections Mrs Gandhi sought to establish Congress governments in eight states which would be responsive to the Central Government. By June 1973 she had been forced to prop up these governments by imposing presidential rule in four of the provinces, and there were severe problems on the horizon in the remaining four. Meanwhile the distant thunder of rural unrest in the thousands of villages rumbled away in the background, distracting attention from the panoply of near-imperial power which Mrs Gandhi seemed set on reconstructing in New Delhi. Scarcely one year after wholesale endorsement at the polls in March 1972 the government of Mrs Gandhi was more beset than ever by indications of the crisis of slow capitalist development: renewed strike waves, student riots, separatist agitation, police revolts and harvest failure. Faced with these intractable problems the familiar crisis in the balance of payments and the exchange rate was almost reassuring.

Introduction

India was the launching pad of the industrial revolution in capitalist Europe. It furnished capital, raw materials and an enormous captive market for Britain, the first industrial capitalist power. But the capitalist penetration of India, far from leading to autonomous capitalist development, led to de-industrialization, disinvestment and the strengthening of many archaic and regressive social relations, an area in which political independence has so far not led to any fundamental change. It is this historical context, combined with the pressure of a world capitalist market structured and dominated by imperialism, which creates the impasse of capitalism on the subcontinent today. There is every reason to believe that the failure of capitalism in India could only have profound consequences for the imperialist metropolis itself. The region which played such a prominent part in the birth of capitalism could well prove to have a prominent part in its downfall.

R.B. 1973

The essays collected together in this book were completed prior to the deepening of the crisis of the world capitalist economy following the outbreak of the Arab–Israeli war in October 1973. The boom in the prices of some primary commodities, which was already under way at this time, led to an improvement in the balance of payments position of some Third World countries. However, this was not at all the case for the different states of the subcontinent. Their export prices rose very little, while there was a sharp increase in the prices they were paying for imports. (See Angus Hone, 'The Primary Commodities Boom', *New Left Review* 81, October 1973.) This situation was very much aggravated by the steep rise in oil prices. And, since the Green Revolution led to dependence on oil-based fertilizers, the inflationary pressure has affected agriculture as well as industry. Indeed, towards the end of 1974 it was clear that there had been an appalling deterioration in the living conditions of the great mass of urban and rural poor in the subcontinent. In India and Bangladesh there were famines on a scale not witnessed since those in China in the nineteen-thirties. This great accumulation of human misery will surely visit a terrible vengeance on the social order which has permitted it: on the local possessing classes, on their associates in the advanced capitalist countries and on the corrupt and demagogic régimes which defend capitalism and imperialism.

The states of the subcontinent are now more than ever dependent on the major imperialist powers. Domestically the crisis has revealed the governments of the subcontinent to be more subservient than ever to the interests of the rich farmers, the grain merchants, the money-lenders and indigenous capitalists. Wherever workers, agricultural labourers, poor peasants and students have organized to defend themselves their democratic rights have been ruthlessly trampled upon. The wholesale repression of the railwaymen's strike by Indira Gandhi in March 1974 was an ominous further step towards establishing a Bonapartist régime in India. But time is running out for the possessing classes of the subcontinent. The ravages of the economic crisis are simultaneously undermining the traditional mechanisms of domination which keep the rural masses in thrall to the local notables and exposing the demagogy and pseudo-socialist phrase-mongering of the politicians. In the countryside many poor peasants are being forced to sell their tiny plots of land and swell the ranks of a rural proletariat as yet unprotected by even the most minimal trade union organization. In the towns the corruption of Congress administrations and their complicity with those who are enriching themselves in the midst of devastating misery are making them the target of vigorous popular upheavals, as in Maharashtra and Bihar.

The only source of consolation to the beleaguered régimes of the subcontinent is the evident disarray of the left-wing parties – explored in a number of the essays in this book. Due to the baneful influence of Stalin the various currents of Indian Communism have been prone to believe that socialist revolution is not on the agenda in the subcontinent, and that something less than an untrammelled assertion of workers' and peasants' power is capable of completing the unfinished democratic revolution. This now seems more than ever an illusory prospect. Those who still maintain that any significant section of the indigenous bourgeoisie have a progressive role to play must confront the grisly record of repression which the new rulers of the subcontinent have established since Independence. Moreover the régimes which have resorted most blatantly to populist rhetoric have also suppressed most violently any sign of popular unrest. There is, of course, every reason for revolutionaries in the subcontinent to use to the full all remaining opportunities for legal organization or agitation, to encourage unionization and the development of class-struggle tendencies within the unions, and to propagate the need for socialist revolution in elections. But the spirit that will be needed to challenge successfully the structures of oppression and exploitation on the subcontinent is that to be found in the eloquent Defence Speech by Rohan Wijeweera. Revolutionary intransigence of this sort, wedded to the struggles and aspirations of the masses, can alone break the arrogant and arbitrary power of the new Raj. The clash in Ceylon in 1971 came before the JVP had established a revolutionary democracy based on peasants' and workers' committees. It seems likely that the new generation of revolutionaries emerging on the subcontinent, of whom Wijeweera is a leading representative, will be better prepared next time.

R.B. 1974

India: Emerging Contradictions of Slow Capitalist Development
Meghnad Desai

A socialist revolution in India would be an event of fundamental significance to the development of world history. An immense population of 550 million whose rural and urban masses are plagued by abysmal misery and unemployment make India one of the great potential storm centres within world capitalism. Yet the simple fact that India's peasants and workers are massively exploited and oppressed is not enough to guarantee a revolutionary solution since the history of the subcontinent has accumulated a formidable series of devices for containing and controlling the impulse to popular revolt. These range from religious antagonisms which have murderously divided the masses to powerful political machines which yoke them together with their class enemies; from archaic survivals of feudal social relations to the most modern strategies of imperialist penetration. Recently this whole system of domination appears to have strikingly consolidated itself just when serious strains and contradictions were appearing within it.

From the mid sixties Indian capitalism seemed to be in major trouble. Following defeat in the 1962 border war with China and the indecisive clash with Pakistan in 1965, the Indian Government greatly stepped up its military spending so that the military budget nearly quadrupled within the decade. In both 1965–6 and 1966–7 there were famines which impelled the government to import large quantities of wheat from the United States. Inflation accelerated and the balance of payments deficit soared. Under international pressure the rupee was devalued in 1966. In the General Election of 1967 the

Congress Party emerged with a small majority of 46 seats after twenty years during which it had enjoyed a majority of nearly two thirds in the Lok Sabha. The Congress Party was replaced by coalitions of opposition parties of the Left and Right in many of the states. By the end of 1967, 330 million out of a 550 million population were being ruled by anti-Congress coalitions. Two years later Congress was riven by a bitter national split, with many important Party bosses opposing Indira Gandhi. At the same time as this crisis in the bourgeois political order there were growing signs of popular revolt. A peasant uprising flared up in the Naxalbari district of West Bengal in 1967, to be followed by a peasant guerrilla movement in the Srikakulam district of Andhra Pradesh under Maoist influence. In Calcutta the formation of United Front Government led by the Communist Party of India (Marxist) was accompanied by the most vigorous strike wave India had ever seen.

The year March 1971 to March 1972 seemed to resolve these different crises in a peculiarly favourable fashion for the established order in India. This was, in fact, an *annus mirabilis* for Indira Gandhi, the dominant wing of the Congress Party and the India they represented and led. In the March 1971 mid-term elections, Indira Gandhi's Congress Party was returned with a two thirds majority over all her antagonists. The faction which had opposed Mrs Gandhi was virtually eliminated. In Srikakulam, centre of the Naxalite revolt, a candidate for Mrs. Gandhi's Congress was elected with a large majority in a high turnout. Following her electoral victory Mrs Gandhi was able to score an even more impressive military victory over Pakistan, leading to the establishment of Bangladesh and the dismemberment of India's traditional antagonist. This was all achieved while defying the hostility of India's major creditor country, the United States, and by adroitly using the support of the Soviet Union. With such famous victories behind her Mrs Gandhi was able to inflict another electoral defeat on her opponents and, notably, to oust the CPI(M) from its dominant position in West Bengal. Meanwhile, sectarian warfare between CPI(M) militants and CPI(ML) – Naxalite – militants was used as a cover and an excuse by the government to deploy police and private strongarm squads to break the left movement in Calcutta. A *mélange* of murder, torture and arrests in the cities and in the countryside succeeded in 'pacifying' West Bengal, stamping out most of the peasant unrest and braking the impetus of the working class movement. The Maoist leader, Charu Mazumdar, was arrested and subsequently died in prison.

With her own internal rivals destroyed and India's external foe decisively humbled, Indira Gandhi appeared to have established an impregnable position for herself. In any moderately stable social system a string of such brilliant successes would suffice to consolidate the political order for many years to come. In the case of India such a prospect does not seem likely. The diplomatic, military and electoral triumphs of 1971–2 certainly reflected a temporary strengthening of Indian capitalism's economic position. But, as we shall see, the long-term prospects for Indian capitalism remain bleak, and the very forces which helped to give Indira Gandhi room for manoeuvre in this period will confront her Government with grave problems at a later date. The electoral reversal of 1967 had followed two famines and a period of rapid inflation. Consumer prices in 1967–8 were 75 per cent above their level in 1960–61, and food prices had risen by 97 per cent. Only in 1968–9 did the price level fall for the first time in many years. On the agricultural front, food-grains output rose after famine and surpassed the previous highest level of 89 million tons (1964–5) in 1967–8 (95 million tons); this level was maintained in the following year and then rose again in 1970–71 to 107 million tons. The increased food output meant a reduction in imports of wheat from the United States. This, together with the increase in exports following the rupee devaluation of 1966 reduced India's balance of payments deficit in 1968–9 to a half its level in the previous two years. This meant a breathing space from her foreign creditors for the first time since large-scale foreign aid started in 1956–7. Meanwhile increased food output naturally alleviated some of the domestic problems confronting the Indian government. An important ingredient in the good harvests of this period was the 'Green Revolution', whose contradictory impact on Indian society we shall discuss below. It was against this background that Indira Gandhi was able to reshape the Congress Party and regain its mass support.

Indira Gandhi was to be blessed not only by economic recovery but also by the blunders and failures of her political opponents. The ruling military clique in Pakistan did its best to create an invaluable ally for her in the shape of a powerful Bengali nationalist movement. Domestically, the parties which came to power in the provinces after 1967, whether they were on the Right or on the Left, proved equally incompetent either in defending the interests of the ruling class or in generating massive transformation of the economic or social structure. We shall analyse concretely the record of the CPI(M)-led United Front in West Bengal below. Suffice it to say that it failed to consolidate the proletarian upsurge or use it to launch a wider revolutionary process. It was then forced to face Indira Gandhi's repression at a time when its popular support was ebbing and its strategy in disarray.

The favourable conjunction of good harvests and confusion among her political opponents gave Indira Gandhi just the opportunity she needed to rediscover the original momentum and mythology of the Congress Party. In order to find out whether the hopes and expectations rekindled in 1971–2 are likely to meet the same fate as those which attended India's birth as a state will require an investigation of the underlying economic and social developments since Independence. In this way the fundamental dilemmas of Indian capitalism can be seen in proper historical perspective and its future destiny appraised.

Economic Relations

In the post-Independence period, the Indian Government relied mainly on state planning to achieve economic growth. Large areas of economic life were naturally beyond the planners' control, and their plans were in any case mainly concerned with preparing blueprints rather than implementing them. In effect, what went by the name of planning are various schemes for mobilizing private and public savings to accumulate capital by taxation, monetization and credit creation. The failure of successive plans to achieve serious growth, inflationary pressure that arose after 1964 and the bad harvests of 1965–6 led to postponement of the Fourth Five Year Plan which was to have started in 1965–6. There had been repeated talk of revamping the Fourth Plan, reordering the priorities towards higher employment and eradication of poverty. The Planning Commission itself was reorganized in 1967, but the Fourth Plan never got off the ground. The result has been that the limit of growth of per capita income has been on the average one per cent per annum. But there have been great fluctuations. Per capita income went *down* during the two famine years of 1965–6 and 1966–7. It was only in 1969–70 that per capita income exceeded its previous highest level of 1964–5. Table I overleaf summarizes the record since 1951.

Per capita food availability started from the extremely low level of 13.5 ounces per day in 1951. Food-grains output grew up to 1960–61, stagnated for the next three years and rose in 1964–5; then a famine situation developed in 1965–6 and 1966–7, when output fell below 1961 figures. It was probably back to the 1961 level by 1971. It should always be remembered, of course, that the per capita figures hide the true abyss of poverty of the Indian masses, because of the great inequalities in the distribution of income and wealth. The food-grains record can be seen from these computations: (see tables 2 and 3).

Meghnad Desai

TABLE I
Per Capita Income at 1949 Prices in Dollars

1952	52·21	1961	61·16	
1953	53·34	1962	61·39	
1954	55·53	1963	61·20	
1955	55·86	1964	62·81	
1956	55·86	1965	65·92	
1957	57·49	1966	62·95	(39·84)
1958	55·76	1967	62·57	(39·71)
1959	58·13	1968	64·27	(40·79)
1960	58·24	1969	63·75	(40·46)

(Figures in brackets for 1966–9 refer to post-devaluation
equivalents. The rupee was devalued in June 1966 from
US $20.86 to $13.20 per Rs. 100).

TABLE 2
Per Capita Availability of Food-grains (ounces per day)

1952	13·53	1961	16·46
1953	14·51	1962	16·27
1954	16·10	1963	15·55
1955	15·66	1964	15·82
1956	15·17	1965	16·72
1957	15·74	1966	14·19
1958	14·39	1967	13·96
1959	16·49	1968	16·10
1960	15·78	1969	14·72

Growth of industrial production has been more rapid than
growth of agricultural production, but has also been very
uneven from one year to the next. The industrial sector at the
time of Independence was extremely small. In 1950–51, mines
and large-scale industrial enterprises employed only 2·7 per
cent of the labour force, while small enterprises and railways
employed 9 per cent. In the twenty years since then, the preponderance of agriculture has been reduced from 48 per cent of
the Gross Domestic Product to 40 per cent.

TABLE 3
Index to Food-grain Production (1950 = 100)

1950	100·0	1962	140·3
1951	90·5	1963	133·6
1952	91·1	1964	136·5
1953	101·1	1965	150·2
1954	119·1	1966	120·9
1955	115·0	1967	123·8
1956	115·3	1968	159·0
1957	120·8	1969	157·5
1958	109·2	1970	168·6
1959	130·6	1971	182·7
1960	127·9	1972	182·0
1961	137·1		

TABLE 4
Index of Industrial Production (1960 = 100)

1951	52·0	1961	109·2
1952	61·1	1962	119·7
1953	59·8	1963	129·7
1954	59·3	1964	140·9
1955	69·7	1965	153·7
1956	77·0	1966	152·4
1957	80·2	1967	151·4
1958	82·9	1968	160·9
1959	98·9	1969	172·4
1960	100·0	1970	180·8
		1971	186·1

Planning has led to the growth of a state sector, whose role to a large extent has been to build up a cost-free infrastructure for the Indian bourgeoisie by undertaking risky and expensive investments. This sector now produces steel, machine tools, heavy electrical equipment, locomotives and aircraft. There is also a state monopoly of railways, telecommunications, and some road transport. The state sector, which currently accounts for 40 per cent of all paid-up company capital, has thus created much of the heavy machine-making industry that India lacked at the time of independence.

The private industrial sector is highly concentrated. Twenty family groups controlled 20 per cent of total private capital in 1951. This had increased to 33 per cent by 1958. In 1965, the Monopolies Commission found out that 75 leading business groups owned 47 per cent of the assets of all non-Government companies. These groups are the Big Bourgeoisie in India. Their investments span trade, finance and commerce. In 1958, the two largest family groups, Tata and Birla, owned 20 per cent of total private capital stock in Indian companies. Their ownership of banks (until the recent nationalization) gave these dynasties substantial control over smaller and regional institutions set up by the Government, to provide industrial capital, and by the publicly owned Life Insurance Corporation, both of which regularly invest in the companies of these groups. It should be said that, in some respects, its high degree of concentration is a symptom of the ultimate political weakness of the Indian Big Bourgeoisie, not its strength. Compared with medium and small business at the regional level, and compared with the interests of rural property, Indian big business has a narrow social base. The degree of capitalization of companies in the modern sector is low: the twenty peak groups control about 1,000 companies with total share capital of Rs. 3,500 million. Diversification of interests means that in each industry the monopoly power of any one group is not very high, but the existence of joint ventures gives these groups collective control over the economy.

The growth of the state sector has been accompanied by the nationalization of credit and financial institutions. Starting with the government takeover of the largest foreign-owned commercial bank – the Imperial Bank of India – in the early 1950s and of all commercial banking in 1970, this growth of the 'public sector' has been claimed as evidence of 'socialism' or a 'socialist pattern of society' by the ruling party. What it has really meant is the elimination of obstacles to the growth of the regional bourgeoisie, and the encouragement of an immense growth of government bureaucracy in many regulating activities such as industrial licensing, import licensing, foreign exchange control, state trading, etc. In 1969 the public sector, comprising the federal and state governments as well as their enterprises (excluding railways), employed 10 million people, compared to the organized private sector which employed about 7 million. Between 1961 and 1969, the total number of employees in the public sector grew by 50 per cent – about $3\frac{1}{2}$ million people. One aspect of Indian 'socialism' is job-creation for the petty bourgeoisie.

A related and much-publicized aspect has been an attempt to control Big Business. This is less spectacular than it sounds. The government has carried out inquiries into the affairs of Big-Business houses such as the Birlas and the Dalmia–Sahu–Jain houses. These are both among the ten largest companies. By nationalizing the banks and creating a public image of hostility to Big Business, the government has been able to give an impression of radicalism to the petty bourgeoisie and the poor, while at the same time making clear that their credit and licensing policies will foster the growth of all but a few of the largest business houses. This policy and the emergence of linguistic states in the 1950s (on which see below) have meant the growth of regional entrepreneurs, who, while being large, do not carry the stigma of being Big Business (and who resented the monopoly control of bank credit exercised by the Big Bourgeoisie). In a sense, one could describe the policies of the Indian government since Independence – setting up heavy industries, nationalizing credit, and policing the growth of the Big-Business houses and of international companies – as designed to remove the fetters on the growth of capitalist relations. The Big-Business houses were an obstacle to the government as well as to the growth of smaller business. Congress 'socialism' was a compromise designed to further the interests of the politically influential rural notables as well as of the bourgeoisie. The contradictions of this policy are severe and will become serious in the future. The rural property-owners want high agricultural prices and lavish Government assistance to agriculture: the urban Big Bourgeoisie wants low agricultural prices and restrictions on state expenditure. The urban petty bourgeoisie are interested in job-creation for themselves, rather than the economic growth and accumulation that concern the Big Bourgeoisie.

Many government policies are inimical to accumulation. The costs of government inefficiency, wastage and bureaucracy are paid in terms of inflation and increased taxation which finance the government's budget deficits. It is the rural and urban poor who bear the burden of these policies but do not benefit from the jobs. The Indian state reflects the interests of the rural bourgeoisie and regional business, since the Big-Business houses are not big enough to control the state. (They are not big compared to, say, the Zaibatsu in Japan before the Second World War, nor do they have the same close economic and social links with the government that the Zaibatsu enjoyed.) This makes the state adopt contradictory policies towards economic growth, aiding some sections of the bourgeoisie with credit and cheap infrastructural inputs, but hemming in other sections with controls, licences, threats of nationalization, and a wasteful bureaucracy.

If state industrial policy since the fifties has generally strengthened the bourgeoisie, the aim of its agrarian policy has been to promote capitalist relations in agriculture. Government credit, fertilizer and procurement programmes have always favoured the rich peasant. Their goal has been to ensure a large marketable surplus for the towns by assisting the rich peasants who are the main suppliers. This has meant a concentration not on increasing output from all farms, but only from those large farms which can generate a substantial surplus. This drive has been accompanied by a growth of sharecropping and of the enormous mass of landless labourers, due partly to land-owners' desire to counter land-tenancy reform and partly to the slow growth of the urban sector, which has swelled the number of rural unemployed.

As yet, the predominant mode of production in agriculture is small peasant production. Government land reforms and the land reform programmes of the Left concentrate on ending rent exploitation of tenant farmers, but have done little to counter wage-exploitation. There is a distinct tendency now towards capitalist agriculture not only in the agriculturally advanced region of Punjab but all over India. A study of large farmers in five other states – Orissa, Andhra Pradesh, Mysore, Tamil-nadu and Gujarat led Utsa Patnaik to conclude:

A new class of capitalist farmers *is* emerging: this is a phenom-enon common to every region, insofar as every area has been subject to the same forces – albeit operating with varying inten-sity – of an expanding market and enhanced profitability of agri-cultural production. The rate at which capitalist development is occurring varies widely in different regions depending on many historical and current circumstances; it may be near zero in some, but the reality of the process cannot be denied. (Utsa Pat-naik, 'Capitalist Development in Agriculture', A Note in *Econ-omic and Political Weekly*, 25 September 1971.)

Unemployment has grown steadily over the last 20 years. Open unemployment was estimated at 2·5 million at the end of the First Five Year Plan in 1956. It rose to about 17 to 20 million by 1966. By official admission, successive Plans have failed to create enough jobs to absorb even the new entrants to the labour force, much less reduce the backlog of unemployed. In many rural areas, men can find work only about 200 days of the year, and very often only at peak planting and harvesting times.

Given its colonial heritage, India has always been tied into the metropolitan capitalist economies. The Indian bourgeoisie is not however purely a comprador class such as characterized

China as well as many colonial countries. A part of the bourgeoisie is a merchant capitalist group with firm roots in the Indian caste system. These are the Marwari, Gujerati, and South Indian Chettis, who were the moneylenders and merchants before the British came. The British did create in their image a commercial capitalist group recruited from agents of government and private English trading houses, mainly in the ports of Calcutta, Bombay and Madras. The textile industry was started in the 1860s mainly for exporting yarn to China, but moved to manufacturing cloth for the home market in the early 1900s. It was the cotton textile industry and other industry started during and after the First World War by native commercial capitalists which came into conflict with British capitalism during the 1920s and 1930s. This section of the bourgeoisie actively supported the nationalist movement from the late 1920s. By comparison the jute industry, enjoying a monopoly, did not come into similar conflict with British capitalism. The comprador group formed at that time the anti-nationalist Liberal Party, a rump of which reappeared in the Swatantra party in 1960.

A comparatively large and nationalist bourgeoisie with native industrial capitalism (which, though weak, is of at least a hundred years' standing), a native bourgeoisie with a large home market which makes it relatively independent of foreign markets but also attractive as a potential source of collaboration partners for foreign capital – this is the Indian bourgeoisie. The Indian government aided the native bourgeoisie immediately after Independence by financing the takeover of British capital (using India's sterling balances accumulated during the Second World War to pay compensation) and shielding it against encroachment by other foreign capital. Now that the Indian bourgeoisie is less xenophobic about foreign capital and actively seeks foreign collaboration, it finds some of these government policies restrictive. In 1948 foreign investments (mainly British) were valued at Rs. 2,876 million, being mainly in plantations, foreign trade and manufacturing. Even this volume of foreign capital is necessarily small in relation to total capital since the entire traditional sector has no foreign investment in it whatever. Bettelheim estimated that foreign capital and Indian capital share control of the modern sector on a 50–50 basis. In the period 1948–61, gross investment in cash and goods was Rs. 2,471 million. In the same period, the new outflow of foreign exchange due to repatriation of profits was Rs. 7,184 million. Collaboration agreements have been on the increase recently.

In the three Five Year Plans since Independence, foreign capital's share of total private investment has been successively 13 per cent, 23 per cent and 24 per cent. There has also been a large flow on public account – up to Rs. 58 billion by the end of the Third Five Year Plan and a further Rs. 30 billion between April 1966 and March 1969. Total external debt, both public and private, rose from Rs. 5 billion in 1948 to Rs. 27 billion by 1963. A large proportion of new aid is now granted for repayment of interest charges on old debts. This aid has come mainly from the USA (20 per cent), the UK, West Germany, France, Italy, Japan, Canada (16 per cent), and USSR (8 per cent). This diversity of sources has given the Government a certain ability to take advantage of rivalry between capitalist countries and also of the rivalry between the two blocs. India, however, remains very much in the nexus of international capital.

Let us now sum up. The Indian economy is by no means fully capitalist. Nearly 75 per cent of the population is engaged in agriculture, which remains predominantly pre-capitalist in character, stamped by feudal and customary relations. However, capitalist relations of exchange and exploitation have now achieved a significant penetration of the rural sector, especially in the more advanced regions. There is little division of labour on a truly national scale. Except for engineering and heavy industrial goods, most commodities are traded only locally. There is as yet no national market in food-grains. In this general context, it is clear that India is currently in the throes of a slow bourgeois–democratic revolution. It has by no means seen the clear end of this process and doubtless will never do so. A socialist revolution may well overtake it before it can come to fruition, and then accomplish its tasks in an uninterrupted transition to socialism, within the framework of mass proletarian power. But it is important, nevertheless, to be aware of the historical thrust of the present Indian state, however sluggard it may be.

How far do the recent trends in agriculture offer a way out of the record of slow economic growth, mounting unemployment and international indebtedness? As we said above, the fall in food imports from the US during the early seventies afforded the government a breathing space in its balance of payments situation; we need to examine, therefore, the origins of this 'Green Revolution'. In fact, the Green Revolution is made up of two phases. One is an Intensive Agricultural Development Programme started after 1960–61, which is concentrated in some districts and provides a package of improved seeds, fertilizer, water, pesticide, etc. A second more important phase is the introduction of high-yield-variety seeds (HYV), started in 1964–5 but interrupted by the famine years. Since 1967–8 output of food-grains has gone up from 95 million tons to 107 million tons in 1970–71. The Green Revolution has sometimes been discounted by the Indian Left as a spurious phenomenon mainly due to good rainfall, and/or denounced as helping only big farmers and aggravating the inequalities in the countryside. It is necessary to look at the record carefully.

As far as overall growth of food-grains production is concerned, critics of the Green Revolution have alleged that there is no miracle in the higher output. This, they say, is only the trend that existed before the famines and which is now resumed. From 1950–51 to 1964–5 (itself a high-yield year), the compound growth-rate of food-grains output was 2·98 per cent per annum, of which 1·34 per cent was due to expansion of area and 1·64 per cent due to higher productivity. We do not have the area data for more recent years, but the compound growth-rates of output between 1964–5 and 1968–9, during 1970–71 and (the forecast level of) 1971–2 were 1·3 per cent, 3·1 per cent and 3·4 per cent respectively. These were computed for three separate years to show that the answer depends on the year one chooses as the last year. The compound growth-rate of food-grains shows some increase over the years but we cannot firmly say that the growth-rate has speeded up. If the 1971–2 figure is confirmed then the growth-rate will have been raised. Comparing with the first post-famine year of 1967–8, we get for the three years compound growth-rates of 1 per cent, 4 per cent and 4·2 per cent for the same three years.

The Green Revolution as a matter of high-yield-variety seeds has been confined mainly to wheat and rice. Hybrid strains suitable to Indian conditions are being developed. The progress has been clearly spectacular in wheat, but not so much in rice. Once again there is a lack of data. The only state-wide data available for rice and wheat are for 1968–9 (which was a stagnating year) with some data for wheat for 1969–70, but none for rice. These show first an uneven growth-rate of rice and wheat; second an uneven regional growth in different parts of India. These rates are listed in Table 5 below. We see that for wheat, the compound growth-rate for yield (output per acre) goes up to 31 per cent in the case of West Bengal, and is as high for Bihar, Gujarat, Mysore, Orissa and Punjab. The growth-rate of total wheat output is given by adding together the growth-rates of yield and area, and is 9·4 per cent for 1968–9 and 10·2 per cent for 1969–70. By contrast, the growth-rates for rice are very low or even negative. A modest underlying rate of increase was interrupted by bad harvests such as that of 1965–6 and probably that of 1972–3. For the time being only the evidence for wheat is fairly convincing.

There is no doubt that at the present the package-deal of high-yield-variety seeds, fertilizers, water and credit are benefiting the larger capitalist farmer. In the future, this may mean a demand for these inputs from smaller farmers which the government may find difficult to meet. Much more likely, the larger successful farmers will buy out the smaller farmers or lease land from them. If the latter occurs, the tenancy legislation designed to alleviate rent exploitation will work *for* the larger farmers with a vengeance. At the same time, a section of the urban bourgeoisie will begin to specialize in the provision of rural inputs.

TABLE 5

Compound Growth-rates of Rice and Wheat (% per annum)

	Rice 1968–9 over 1964–5 *Yield*	*Wheat* 1968–9 over 1964–5 *Yield*	*Rice* 1968–9 over 1964–5 *Area*	*Wheat* 1968–9 over 1964–5 *Area*	*Wheat* 1969–70 over 1964–5 *Yield*	*Wheat* 1969–70 over 1964–5 *Area*
Andhra Pradesh	0·2	—	−1·7	—	—	—
Assam	0·5	—	3·8	—	—	—
Bihar	−0·5	17·7	0·7	13·5	11·8	11·7
Gujarat	−11·9	6·6	−1·5	3·2	7·4	−0·5
Jammu/ Kashmir	12·2	18·1	1·3	3·9	17·0	4·1
Kerala	3·6	—	3·6	—	—	—
Madhya Pradesh	4·2	1·6	0·5	0·2	2·4	−0·2
Maharashtra	−2·0	2·2	0·2	−0·8	0·0	−0·8
Mysore	2·0	8·9	3·3	−0·5	4·4	0·7
Nagaland	−2·0	—	−0·6	—	—	—
Orissa	1·6	25·2	−0·2	0·0	20·4	1·3
Punjab/ Haryana	1·2	18·0	1·8	5·2	16·8	5·4
Rajasthan	−20·5	2·1	5·1	−0·2	1·8	1·3
Tamilnadu	0·0	—	−0·7	—	—	2·0
Uttar Pradesh	−3·5	3·0	0·5	7·9	2·7	6·8
West Bengal	1·2	30·9	0·9	38·3	19·6	42·4
All India	0·0	5·0	0·2	4·4	5·8	4·4

India: Contradictions of Slow Capitalist Development

Instead of underestimating the incidence of the Green Revolution, we should look at the inherent contradictions which will attend upon its success. The Green Revolution will spur the accumulation process in the countryside and strengthen capitalist relations. The distribution of cultivated land (owned and leased) may become even more unequal than before. But its most important effect will be to replace the pre-capitalist economic relationships, such as sharecropping, by wage-earning. The encouragement to multiple cropping that the Green Revolution gives will generate a more even flow of labour-demand on the larger farms and lead to the gradual formation of a wage-earning rural proletariat finally divested of all control over means of production such as land. The rural proletariat has been neglected in Indian politics for a long time, since the emphasis was on programmes to alleviate rent exploitation of tenant cultivators. Radical movements have promised landless labourers small bits of land. Without the aid of ancillary inputs, granting of land to the landless will only aid the takeover of this land (by purchase or lease) by the larger farmers who can survive the competition better. A trend may develop towards organized struggle by the rural proletariat against the larger farmers in areas where the Green Revolution is successful.

Higher output of wheat has also meant a fear of falling prices. In the last two years, the federal government has been forced to reject the recommendations of the Agricultural Price Commission that the procurement price paid by the government for wheat should be lowered. The powerful agricultural interests of Punjab and Haryana, especially, have been able to prevail upon the government not to implement these recommendations. Lower prices are in the interests of the urban petty bourgeoisie and the mass of rural and urban poor who have to purchase food. A conflict of interests is clearly arising here between the rural bourgeoisie and urban petty bourgeoisie. A subsidy to the farmers in the shape of high procurement prices will be a burden on the federal budget which will be borne by the poor.

Meghnad Desai

If prices are allowed to fall then the farmers' support of the ruling party may be eroded.

The Green Revolution is therefore no panacea for Indian capitalism, though it will alter production relationships rapidly in the countryside. Even more radically than the land reform legislation, it is altering the status of landless labourers and sharecroppers. At this point it is necessary to look at the relative numerical positions of the various classes in India.

The Social Structure

What is the class structure in India? Bettelheim has attempted a comprehensive analysis in his book *India Independent*. His results can be combined with more recent data to give a picture of the rural and urban class system. Bettelheim classifies the population engaged in agriculture into three classes – *maliks*, *kisans* and *mazdoors*. Maliks are the rural bourgeois and rich peasants. Kisans are in the category generally called middle peasant. A proportion of them are tenants and sharecroppers. Mazdoors are landless labourers and the poorest peasants. The worse-off kisans have much in common with the mazdoor population; together they form the vast rural under-class.

The proportion of each category in the rural population in 1954 was as follows:

TABLE 6

	% population	% area	farm size (acres)	% holdings
maliks	17	52	11·4	35
kisans	45	36	7·7	35
mazdoors	38	8	2·9	20

In the cities, the bourgeoisie is defined by Bettelheim as that class which has an income of Rs. 10,000 ($2,000) or more. He reckons that the large maliks of the countryside and the urban bourgeoisie together comprise 1·5 per cent of the total population of India. Of these, what we have called the Big Bourgeoisie or national capital would be the core of 75 to 100 largest business houses, which own 50 per cent of all private company assets in India. The non-agricultural bourgeoisie is estimated to be a mere 0·5 per cent of the population, yet it receives 28 per cent of non-agricultural national income. The petty bourgeoisie includes such 'non-industrial wage-earners' as teachers, civil servants, bank and insurance employees and office workers, as well as the self-employed. They earn more than industrial workers and constitute what is known as the 'middle class' in India. According to the 1951 census, there were 4·6 million industrial wage-earners and 7 million non-industrial wage-earners in India. To the latter should be added 2·1 million self-employed. It is immediately apparent that the urban petty bourgeoisie is more numerous than the industrial working class itself. This urban petty bourgeoisie is a highly vocal group in Indian politics. It tends to form the bulk of the membership of all parties and a large proportion of their leadership. The apparent radicalism of some factions of the Congress Party, the PSP, and even CPI, derives largely from this group. It is not, however, revolutionary and traditionally has no links with the rural proletariat.

The most important points which emerge from any analysis of the Indian class structure are thus:

1. The small size of the classical proletariat, due to the low level of development of the forces of production. Urban workers of all types and their families now number perhaps 40 million out of a population of 550 million.

2. The preponderance in the towns of the non-industrial wage-earners and self-employed – in other words, the petty bourgeoisie. This is not a politically homogeneous group; sections of it have in the past aligned themselves with industrial workers.

3. The overwhelming weight of the rural proletariat and middle peasants. They constitute 80 per cent of the agricultural population and nearly 60 per cent of the total population.

All these figures are subject to one crucial qualification. Uneven regional development in India makes national computations difficult to translate without mediation into political correlations of forces.

The Problem of Regionalism

British imperialism everywhere sought to introduce a market in land in India, but the tenure system differed from region to region. In Bengal, for instance, it was a *zamindari* system in which the *zamindar* lord owned many villages at a time. Feudal services such as the *corvée* abounded in these parts, and the ownership pattern was extremely concentrated. In other parts of India, notably much of the south, the *ryotwari* system involved a considerable number of owner-cultivators; land distribution was naturally unequal, but it was not heavily concentrated in the hands of a few landlords. These variations in land tenure led to different systems of surplus creation and absorption, and the size of the surplus also differed. In present-day India, such regional disparities have greatly aggravated the inherent problem for the revolutionary Left of organizing the rural poor on a national scale. Thus in *zamindari* regions, landless labourers and middle peasants are nearly synonymous, while in *ryotwari* regions many middle peasants have taken to capitalist farming and are unlikely to combine with landless labourers. Since class composition varies from one region to another, the possibility of alliances of different categories of the oppressed classes necessarily varies with it. Historically, Andhra and West Bengal had serious peasant revolts in the late 1940s; Kerala and Tamilnadu also have traditions of rural unrest. By contrast Gujarat, Maharashtra and Mysore have no history of peasant resistance in the twentieth century. Different regions are also unevenly industrialized. West Bengal, with proximity to minerals and coal, has been heavily developed, and a substantial portion of its working class was imported from Bihar, Orissa and other states. Maharashtra and Gujarat, especially Bombay city, also possess an important industrial base and a cosmopolitan work-force. Elsewhere in India, industry is feebly developed and in large parts non-existent.

On the other side of the basic class-divide, there are critical antagonisms between regional and national capital. Growth of trade and commerce in colonial India meant the creation of jobs and educational opportunities at coastal centres like Bombay, Calcutta and Madras. This led to the emergence of some consumer industries in these enclaves and hence to the development of a merchant capitalist class which started to invest in industry. This gave these regions a head start over other regions before Independence was achieved. Today, these disparities have been accentuated and exacerbated by the later uneven development of India. For there are a large number of bourgeois entrepreneurs whose activities are confined to small regions. These businessmen rely for their labour and market on the local population. Their interests thus frequently conflict with the Big Bourgeoisie, which relies on a national market. For its part, national capital in India derives mainly from early merchant capitalists from Bombay and Calcutta who today control a major part of the industry, trade and finance not only in these cities but throughout the subcontinent. Naturally, the regional bourgeoisies of the different states, who arrived later on the scene, have resisted monopolistic control by the Big Bourgeoisie. In the fifties and sixties this produced violent struggles for the creation of 'linguistic' states, which mobilized both regional capital and the non-bourgeois opposition parties in such states as Maharashtra, Orissa and Mysore, often under the influence of Communists. Here the fight was allegedly

waged against Gujarati or Marwari capital, but in fact the unleashing of regional chauvinism often hindered the creation of
national class consciousness by the oppressed, and merely
helped regional capital in its competition with national
capital.

It should, however, be emphasized that despite the recent
conflicts at the political level, the growth of regional capital has
in no way hindered the complementary expansion of national
capital. Vigorous temporary clashes of interest between regional and national capital do not exclude an underlying harmony between the two. It can thus be seen that while they
intervene in every aspect of political life in India, on balance
regional divisions weaken the oppressed classes and the political organizations which seek to lead them much more than they
do the ruling class.

Another factor in the uneven regional development was the
growth of the education system. British imperialism linked
India to the metropolis via trade relations and the coastal areas,
especially round the ports of Bombay, Calcutta and Madras,
became the intermediate link acting as an agent of the metropolis to the Indian hinterland, and of the hinterland to London.
The first universities were established in coastal areas and an
educated professional class, mainly lower-paid government and
commercial clerks, grew up in these areas. These regions also
threw up an élite bourgeois group of lawyers who were involved
on both sides of the independence movement. The educated
petty bourgeois are politically conscious, and take the best
government jobs all over India. Their class interests make them
side with the national government, but they are coming into
conflict with the educated petty bourgeois of the backward
regions who see their own state governments as guarantors of a
share in the economic surplus.

Lack of a national economy in industrial products and the
predominance of small peasant agriculture leads to a further
tendency towards fragmentation of the class struggle into

regions, with inter-regional antagonisms added to class antagonism. A revolutionary movement in a single region thus gets isolated since the objective conditions of alliance with other regions are lacking. Having inherited the administrative superstructure of a nation state without an underlying base of national economy and national division of labour, the federal government can use this fragmentation and isolation of regional struggles to defeat them. The agrarian unrest in Telengana and the recent sporadic Naxalite activities are examples of such isolated struggles. The Naxalite movement has attracted a lot of attention since its beginning in 1969. Its localization in certain parts of India, especially West Bengal, Andhra and Kerala, meant that the federal government was able to counter it with the Central Reserve Police and the Army in each state separately. Attempts to link up these separate movements via a 'Great March' or formation of liberated zones met with little success.

Uneven regional development has meant, therefore, uneven and often isolated development of the class struggle in different parts of India. Inter-regional differences in the intensity of class struggle, and the inter-regional rivalry between the politically articulate petty bourgeoisie of different regions have extended to regional factions of political parties: while parties have national labels they have diverse regional existences. The ruling party has for a long time been a coalition of regional forces; when it is in power it can dispense jobs and patronage, which keeps this coalition together. For the purpose of perpetuating the coalition it has at its service the administrative superstructure and the ideology of nationalism first developed in the anti-colonial struggle, but kept on since then by an appeal to the 'Unity of India' against 'foreign enemies'. The Leftist opposition parties partake of this nationalist consciousness though they differ about the particular foreign enemy the country has to fight. Being out of power they find it hard to perpetuate the coalition of regional interests. Their best chance of coming to power is at a regional level. This makes them victims of all the contradictions of Indian political life simultaneously. The temptation is then to define the class struggle at the regional level alone, but that means recognition of impotence. The peculiar problems faced by the CPI(M) during their tenure of office in West Bengal afford a very good example of the contradictory pressures faced by a regional party. To understand them we need to look also at the history of the Communist movement in India.

Indian Communism

There are today two major factions of Indian Communism – the Communist Party of India and the Communist Party of India (Marxist) generally known respectively as the CPI and the CPI(M). The original Party split in 1963–4, when a large number of militants became dissatisfied with its policy of collaboration with the 'progressive bourgeoisie' represented by Nehru, and its subservience to the USSR.

Up to that date, the frequent zig-zags of the CPI could be traced mainly to ideological weakness, the class influences on its leadership, its obedience to political (mis)guidance from Moscow, and its failure to come to grips with the problem of Indian nationalism.

There were isolated workers in India sympathetic with the Comintern from 1920 onwards, and the British Government swiftly exercised repression against them (Cawnpore Conspiracy case of 1926 and Meerut Conspiracy case of 1929). A Communist Party was not fully established until 1933. It was to suffer much from Comintern and/or CPGB tutelage in ideological matters. The main stumbling-block for it was its assessment of the political character of Gandhi and the Indian National Congress. The Comintern, CPGB and CPI vacillated between claims that Congress's fight for Independence embodied a progressive inter-class alliance (although its leadership was bourgeois), and denunciation of the Indian bourgeoisie and the Congress Party as a wholly collaborationist and reactionary force. Throughout its early period, the CPI was a peripheral presence in Indian politics.

The Popular Front policies of the mid thirties brought the CPI into coalition with the more radical forces inside Congress such as the Congress Socialist Party. Once the Popular Front tactics had been decided by the Comintern, the CPI outdid even the CSP in its moderation and desire to stay within Congress. At the outbreak of the Second World War it briefly took a position to the left of Congress in denouncing the War as an inter-imperialist conflict. After Hitler's attack on the Soviet Union, however, it explained that this was now an antifascist 'people's war' and openly collaborated with the British Government, while Congress continued to fight against it for Indian Independence. This policy more than any other mistake alienated the CPI from nationalist feeling, and has had the grave consequence of impelling it to take an ultra-nationalist line since then to avert a repetition of 1941. Thus, on the question of India's relationship to Pakistan and the Kashmir issue, the CPI has always been chauvinist and, as we shall see below, it was its response to the Sino-Indian border clashes that ignited the final crisis within the Party.

From 1946 to 1948, the CPI leadership generally took a rightist line, in accordance with the post-war diplomacy of the USSR. It praised the Congress Party as a progressive alliance of many classes and was content to radicalize it by criticism from the outside. When the Indian naval ratings mutinied in 1946, the CPI promptly played down the revolutionary implications of the event. In 1948, however, the CPSU abruptly shifted international course at the inspiration of Zhdanov, and the CPI was launched on a left course of urban unrest, strikes and direct attacks on government property. This was in line with the Malayan and Philippino rebellions in Asia, and the French strike-waves in Europe. The CPI announced that

India was ripe for a revolutionary seizure of power, whereas in fact it did not have any evident mass support for its new strategy.

The only successful militant action during this period was the peasant uprising in Telengana, a region within the present state of Andhra Pradesh which was then partly in Madras and partly in Hyderabad. The Telengana peasant struggle had started autonomously in 1946, while similar rural upheavals were also going on in Bengal, Kerala and Tanjore. It lasted from 1946 to about 1950, and at one time peasant soviets ran many villages in two districts. Land was forcibly occupied, the landlords were driven off and many were killed. The CPI nationally had not encouraged the Telengana (or any other) struggles in the 1946–8 period, since it was then pursuing a right course. Local Communist cadres in Telengana did, however, lead the peasant struggles there. Yet even after the left swerve of 1948, Party emphasis was still officially on urban uprisings, and the Maoist inclinations of the Telengana Communists were not wholly approved by the veteran Stalinist Ranadive, then in charge of the CPI nationally. It was only in late 1948 that the CPSU and the Indian specialists in the USSR decided that a rural path might be permissible in India, and Ranadive was replaced by the Telengana group. From 1948 to 1950, the Telengana peasants fought the Indian Army itself, and they had not been defeated by 1950. In that year, however, the CPI suddenly abandoned the struggle, and adopted a parliamentary strategy, supporting Nehru's foreign policy and the 'progressive' aspects of his economic policy.

Thereafter, from 1951 till 1964, the CPI followed an orthodox electoralist path. It formed a 'United Front' with other left parties in several states in the 1952 elections, when it emerged as the second largest party in the Lok Sabha (Lower Parliament) in Delhi, and repeated this performance in 1957 when it also succeeded in forming the first Communist state administration in Kerala, with the marginal help of some Independents. The major success of this period, outside Kerala, was the CPI's role in the movement for linguistic states. A Telugu-speaking state of Andhra was created in 1954, after massive campaigns by a broad movement of big landlords, local bourgeois, peasants and educated petty bourgeois. The Andhra Communists were active in this campaign and they were thus able to show some strength in the first Andhra election.

After this, local units of the CPI everywhere joined in the movement for the creation of linguistic states. In most states, opposition to the Big Bourgeoisie (identified as an alien Marwari–Gujarat clique), cultural revivalism of the regional heritage and the self-interest of the local bourgeoisie and the educated white-collar groups who wanted jobs in a new regional bureaucracy all fused to form a large mass movement. In many states, the CPI tried to lead this coalition. But it did not try to radicalize it or to broaden the struggle against the Big Bourgeoisie to include the whole bourgeoisie. Its objectives were merely parliamentary gains. In Andhra, then in Maharashtra and Gujarat, success on the parliamentary front proved short-lived. As an anti-Congress strategy, these movements had very little hope of long-range success. Once in power locally, the regional bourgeoisies soon settled down to comfortable co-existence with the Congress centre (the recent example of the regionalist DMK in Tamilnadu is striking in this respect). CPI tactics did not seek to educate the masses or to raise the issue of class struggle in non-provincial terms.

Throughout this period, the CPI never had a clear position on the class nature of the Indian Government. It vacillated between denunciations of it as a big-landlord–big-bourgeois apparatus that was reactionary *en bloc*, and protestations that there were serious divisions within the bourgeoisie between progressive and conservative currents. Sometimes only the Big Bourgeoisie was denounced as an enemy force, while the progressive bourgeoisie (the 'national' bourgeoisie for the CPI) was praised for its doughty struggle against foreign domi-

37

nation. At other times, the entire Congress Party and the national revolution was regarded as progressive. A related problem for the CPI was its fluctuating assessment of the importance of foreign (British or American) capital in India. In practice, the leadership of the party assumed that this was overwhelming, and therefore the Indian bourgeoisie would necessarily resist it and in so doing be a progressive force. The opposition within the party, on the other hand, saw the Big Bourgeoisie as autonomous partners and not mere pawns of foreign capital, and therefore logically viewed it as the straightforward number-one class enemy of the Indian masses (undoubtedly the correct estimate).

There was also a virtually total neglect of any rural base by the CPI. Except in Andhra and Kerala, its peasant cadre was non-existent. At the same time, its leadership was petty bourgeois by its own admission, and a substantial portion of its rank and file was also white-collar workers and professionals. Membership of the Communist-controlled trade-union federation, AITUC, was less than a quarter the total number of unionized workers in India. Its industrial base was thus small. Regionally, the CPI had a following only in West Bengal, Andhra, Kerala, Madras (now Tamilnadu) and Punjab. It also had a certain union membership in Bombay City. In other parts of the country it was a negligible presence.

The long period of extreme rightism from 1951 onwards hid many ideological differences within the Party. In 1962 the trauma of the CPI's isolation during 1941–5 led the party leadership to slide even further to the Right during the Sino-Indian Border War. Many of the opposition faction-leaders within the Party were jailed by the Indian Government. In the middle of the crisis, the remaining CPI leadership published an ultrachauvinist resolution entitled 'Unite to Defend the Motherland against China's Open Aggression', whose sentiments were identical to those of any other petty-bourgeois nationalist party.

When the oppositional faction-leaders came out of prison in 1963 they were naturally resentful of the pro-bourgeois positions of the CPI and its complicity with anti-Chinese hysteria. They nevertheless took care not to be labelled a Peking faction, and have always maintained their distance from any orthodox Maoist line. In April 1964, the CPI finally and formally split. Since then a CPI (Right) and a CPI (Marxist) have disputed the heritage of Indian Communism. In 1964 the CPI(R) claimed a membership of 108,000 and the CPI(M) a membership of 119,000. The CPI(R) increased its membership to 173,000 by 1966, while left defections reduced CPI(M) membership to 83,000 in 1967 and 76,000 in 1968. No later figures are available for either party. CPI(M) membership is relatively more concentrated in the three states of Andhra Pradesh, West Bengal and Kerala (70 per cent of the total) than is the CPI(R) membership (only 40 per cent). Both parties are thus modest in size and have members concentrated in a few areas only.

On the electoral front the CPI(M) did somewhat better than the CPI(R) in 1967, gaining more seats in the Lok Sabha. It also played a leading part in the formation of the United Front governments which emerged in Kerala and West Bengal.

The United Front Experience in West Bengal

A Government with Communist participation in West Bengal represented a wholly new phenomenon in Indian politics, qualitatively far more important than earlier experiences in Kerala. For West Bengal is the most industrialized state in the country. Its capital, Calcutta, is the largest city in India, with a massive population of 9 million. Its proximity to the area of iron and coal mines has made it a major producer of engineering goods. It also includes large jute mills and tea plantations. Much of West Bengal's industry is dependent on the national market, while its tea and jute are exported into the international market. There is still large-scale British investment in West

Bengal industry, and domestic owners are part of the All-Indian bourgeoisie. The phenomenon of the small regional entrepreneur that abounds in Orissa or Maharashtra does not exist in West Bengal. This area saw the emergence of industry comparatively early, for Calcutta was already a major trading centre by the middle of the nineteenth century. The tenure system in the rural hinterland was *zamindari*, making for an idle élite class who developed a rich cultural life. Under British rule, a Western school system was soon implanted and there is today a large mass of educated middle elements in the province. Since the beginning of the century this class has had a tradition of terrorist activity and a belief in the efficacy of armed struggle. The peasantry is extremely poor: *zamindari* relations have created a vast rural underclass of small peasants and landless labourers. The urban proletariat is made up of migrants from the rural areas of Bihar and Uttar Pradesh, as well as of West Bengal. It is highly unionized and has a long tradition of militancy.

In the 1967 elections there were two United Fronts formed by the two factions of Indian Communism. The CPI along with the Bangla Congress (a splinter from the Congress Party) formed one, and the CPI(M) along with the Socialist Workers' party, the Socialist Unity Centre and other groupings formed another. For the first time, the Congress party failed to get an absolute majority (gaining only 127 out of 280 seats) and the possibility of the two Fronts forming a government together emerged. This they did in February 1967; Ajoy Mukherjee, leader of the Bangla Congress, became Chief Minister and Minister for Home Affairs.

The presence of the CPI(M) and the CPI(R) secured undoubted changes in the *modus operandi* of the state governments. While neither party tried in any way to implement measures of a revolutionary nature (which would have got them into conflict with their coalition partners and with the Central Government), they did materially assist the struggles of the working class in the cities and those of the landless labourers in the country. The bad harvests of 1965–6 and 1966–7 had resulted in a recession in 1966–7. The engineering industries centred in West Bengal were hard hit: employment fell by 300,000 between March 1966 and June 1967. This led to a heightening of strike activity and a novel form of industrial struggle which came to be known as the *gherao*. A *gherao* is the barricading by the workers of the management in their factory offices, until the workers' demands are met. The UF government did not actively initiate this form of combat, but it did assist it by preventing the use of police on behalf of the employers.

Between March and August 1967, there were 1,018 cases of *gheraos* affecting 583 industrial establishments. At one extreme some of them (15 per cent) lasted between half an hour and four hours; at the other extreme a few (8 per cent) lasted longer than twenty-four hours. Only 12 per cent of these *gheraos* were 'terminated' by police intervention and 16 per cent by search warrants. 31 per cent were ended by setting up bipartite conciliation machinery. Police power was restrained from being deployed against all strikers. The Ministry of Labour, which had always hitherto been an employers' mouthpiece, this time leaned towards the workers. There was a consistent demand by the Bengal bourgeoisie for Central intervention by Delhi to restore law and order.

In the countryside, the United Front connived at (or probably actively encouraged) the occupation of *benami* land by landless labourers. This is land left surplus after government imposition of legal ceilings on land holdings. In fact, these lands are usually occupied by the landlords to whom they formerly belonged. From then on their seizure by poor peasants and landless labourers was not prevented by the government, where a Congress régime would have mobilized the police to stop them. The United Front also exempted poor peasants from grain procurement policies, took over the Calcutta tramways

41

(refusing to raise fares), and supported the fight of Central Government employees for higher pay.

The Naxalbari revolt, led by the CPI(M-L), a pro-Chinese faction, caused the United Front grave problems, however. The Delhi government sent in the Central Reserve Police and the Army to quell this revolt. Both CPI(R) and CPI(M) condemned Naxalite activity as left adventurism; the CPI(M) was in exchange denounced by the Naxalites as a neo-revisionist sell-out group. In the closing days of the first United Front government there were rumours of a flight of capital from West Bengal and many ministers started to conciliate local business. The Government fell by a no-confidence motion in November 1967, but the successor Congress government could not survive for long and Presidential rule was imposed in West Bengal.

In 1969 the United Front coalition was triumphantly re-elected, winning 214 out of 280 seats. This time the CPI(M) emerged as the largest single party in the state, with 80 seats, though no majority. The intensity of industrial struggle was now, however, somewhat reduced since the Indian recession had come to an end in 1968. The CPI(M) obtained the Home Ministry and with it control of the police. Henceforward Jyoti Basu, the most popular mass leader of the party, was Deputy Chief Minister and Home Minister. The Government once again supported major strikes in the jute industry and tea plantations and checked the traditional use of police against the workers. But it did not change the system of urban property taxation or undertake any other economic measures to relieve the desperate situation of the Bengali poor.

The CPI(M)'s Political-Organizational Report for 1968 provides the following theoretical justification of the Coalition governments in which it had participated:

The UF Governments that we have now are to be treated and understood as instruments of struggle in the hands of our people, more than as Governments that actually possess adequate power that can materially and substantially give relief to the people ...

In class terms, our Party's participation in such Governments is one specific form of struggle to win more and more people and more and more allies for the proletariat and its allies in the struggle for the cause of People's Democracy and at a later stage for Socialism.

The document goes on to warn of the 'fake character of the power invested in the state Governments' and against the 'reformist delusion' that these governments can give any relief to the people. 'There is an ocean of difference between declaring them [state governments] straightaway as "instruments of struggle" and the direction to strive to utilize them as "instruments of struggle" [sic].' Having thus guarded against 'reformism' and 'adventurism', the CPI(M) saw its achievements in two ways.

1. Our Party's firm stand against the use of police against the popular struggles strengthened the democratic forces. The widespread working-class *gheraos* to redress some of their longstanding grievances and demands, peasant struggles in several districts against the evictions and for taking possession of Government's 'surplus' and wasteland from the illegal occupation of big landlords, the relief secured by the middle-class employees of the state Government and the civil liberties ensured for their legitimate trade-union activity, etc., were examples of how different oppressed sections of the people were utilizing the presence of the UF State Government for carrying on their just struggles and how our Party and others cooperating with it were assisting them in this struggle.

2. The important fact that should not be lost sight of is the extremely limited and curtailed powers and resources of the state Governments as they are at present constituted under the present Indian constitution. The devastating effects of the deepening economic crisis on the working class, toiling peasantry and the middle classes today are such that they cannot be removed by the meagre ameliorative relief measures that a state Government can provide, they can only be redressed by a radical and revolutionary change in the entire social set-up. It is the increasing aware-

ness of the people and their political consciousness of this truth that constitutes the acid test of whether the UF state Governments have been utilized as instruments of struggle or not in the people's revolutionary struggles for a revolutionary change.

The CPI(M) claims to be a revolutionary party. It is against any immediate armed struggle, as its condemnation of the Naxalite revolt clearly showed. On the other hand, the CPI(M) asserts that United Front governments have been utilized by the oppressed classes in their struggles for elementary demands. There is a certain truth in this. But by declining any economic reforms or relief measures, as well as confrontations (armed or otherwise) with the Central Government, the CPI(M) had chosen not to initiate any radical – let alone revolutionary – changes from its position within the United Front administrations. While state power is formally limited by the Constitution and factually by Delhi's control of the Army and Federal Budget, there are a number of transitional measures a state Government could take which would both provide material relief to the masses and help to unleash revolutionary struggles by them. The Congress land-reform programme, mild as it is, has never been fully implemented. Ruthless enforcement by a state Government of the law on *zamindari* abolition and tenants' rights, wholesale elimination of intermediaries and minimum wage legislation for agricultural labour would radically alter the situation in the countryside. A swingeing tax on residential property to finance slum clearance and improvement of Calcutta's public amenities would be another effective measure.

By ostentatiously denying that state Governments have any power, the CPI(M) had chosen the luxury of relying on the unaided initiative of the masses for social change. The United Front governments have never tested the limits to which a state Government can go in pursuing its policy before the inevitable confrontation with the Delhi Government comes. Yet defiance of Delhi in pursuit of local programmes is regularly practised by provincial Congress governments themselves: in this respect even the first Communist government in Kerala in 1957 was more activist. The verbal Leftism of the CPI(M) – profuse denials that state administrations have any power whatever – in fact concealed a policy of practical rightism and passivity, just as the apparent radicalism of Blum's famous declaration 'We are in office, not in power' served to justify the capitulations of the Popular Front in France in the thirties.

At bottom, the CPI(M) is pessimistic about the immediate possibility of any revolutionary upsurge in India. Thus it is against armed struggles, which it fears would be quickly isolated and defeated by the Army. It is acutely aware that both the CPI(R) and the CPI(M) are significant movements only in three or four states (Andhra, West Bengal, Kerala and, to some extent, Tamilnadu). A serious challenge to Delhi by any one of these states would not have any easy chance of success, and the states are not a geographically contiguous area either. Large parts of India, meanwhile, are dominated by mass Rightist movements such as the Jan Sangh. In this situation, the CPI(M) basically pursues an inter-class coalition against the Big Bourgeoisie, the large landlords and imperialist capital. It is ready to use state Governments as instruments in the task of building up such a coalition, but it is committed to a legal path of 'changing the Constitution from within' in its quest for a 'People's Democracy' in India (not socialism, which is relegated to a separate, more remote future).

Typologically, the CPI(M) might be compared within the world Communist movement to the PKI in Indonesia – a Left-centrist party preoccupied above all with building up its mass organizations, and masking an opportunist practice with a veil of revolutionary phrases. But popular support in one region, no matter how great, without a correct political strategy, will not ultimately benefit the CPI(M) any more than it did the PKI: West Bengal could well be its Java. Revolutionary vigilance and initiative are the only sure weapons of a Marxist party in the long run. It is to be hoped that the electoral reverse inflicted on the CPI(M) in March 1972, accompanied as it was by a vicious Congress terror campaign, will lead to a fundamental questioning of the Party's inherited ideology and strategy.

Conclusion

After coming to power in 1969 the CPI(M) faced a new faction, the CPI(M-L), on its Left. The intensity of inter-party conflict between the CPI(M) and the Naxalites increased after the removal of the United Front government in March 1970. Political violence and murders were frequent occurrences. The Federal Government was able to take advantage of this conflict and, through the Central Reserve Police, mounted a systematic campaign of arrest, torture and shooting in Calcutta and its immediate vicinities. The uncertainties of the inter-party clash among the Leftist groups meant that no united opposition to police terrorism could be mounted. The 'liberal' forces such as Congress (R) and CPI(R) could connive at police intervention in the interests of law and order, and the CPI(M) was not wholeheartedly against it as long as the police made an indiscriminate practice of arresting or shooting the Naxalites.

After starting in a rural base in West Bengal, the Naxalites faced a systematic campaign by the Central Reserve Police, local police and the Army in parts of India where they gathered support. Through 1970 and 1971 there was a shift towards urban terrorism, especially in Calcutta and in the towns of West Bengal. Naxalites appear as a decentralized phenomenon of autonomous groups of urban educated youth who are unemployed and are mostly between 16 and 25. Their shift of tactics to urban areas and concentration of their attack on the CPI(M) led to further fragmentation of their movement into several groups. Charu Mazumdar led one of these groups, but many other leading Naxalites such as Kanu Sanyal and many of the Srikakulam leaders were soon imprisoned.

During the course of the Bangladesh struggle, many of the problems and contradictions of the Indian Left became evident. The results of the mid-term elections of March 1971 reaffirmed the national status of Congress (R) and the regional nature of every other party. CPI(M) survived at the national level due to its strength in West Bengal, and for all practical purposes it may be regarded as a West Bengal party (whereas CPI(R), for example, is mainly a Kerala party). The emergence of the Bangladesh movement almost immediately after the elections caught everyone unawares. To begin with, it combined all the parties in West Bengal (and India) around an anti-Pakistan platform. The attitude of CPI(M) and CPI(M-L) was, however, confused. CPI(M) saw an opportunity of creating a United Red Bengal out of the Bangladesh situation and therefore accused Mrs Gandhi's government of doing nothing to aid Bangladesh refugees out of fear of such an eventuality. CPI(M)'s analysis also predicted that the imperialist pressures would prove strong and prevent the ruling party from aiding Bangladesh guerrillas. (This was only after a first month of euphoric forecasts from all Indian parties of imminent triumph of the Bangladesh movement against the West Pakistan Army – forecasts which were quickly belied.) CPI(M-L) was also actively involved at the outset in aiding the guerrillas, hoping to start a Bengali peasant revolution. Chinese support of Yahya Khan caused grave ideological problems, however, and some factions were caught defending Yahya Khan on the grounds that Mujib and the Awami League were bourgeois stooges and that Yahya Khan by his pro-Chinese foreign policy had taken an anti-imperialist stand. The Chinese support of Yahya Khan may prove to have had the same impact on the fragmented Naxalite movement as the Nazi–Soviet pact had on Western European parties, or as the Soviet Union joining the allies had on the CPI in 1941. (At that time the CPI took an anti-nationalist and pro-British stand on the ground that the threat to the Soviet Union was the paramount problem. In this sense the

Naxalites have proved as dependent on the Chinese for their ideological stand as the old CPI were on the CPGB and the Comintern.)

In the event, the decision to send the Indian Army into Bangladesh and the short and successful war took everyone, especially the CPI(M), by surprise. In West Bengal, Congress (R) could now pose as the liberator of Bangladesh and make inroads into CPI(M)'s regional support. The crucial mistake in CPI(M) analysis was regarding the degree of autonomy of the Indian ruling class from imperialist pressures. As we have shown above, while India is very much a part of the international capitalist nexus, the Indian ruling classes are not a comprador bourgeoisie. This relative autonomy will mean that, even *vis-à-vis* the Soviet Union, there is no prospect of India becoming a client state; not at any rate unless the bourgeoisie suffers some massive setback.

One such setback that is often forecast is the emergence of a United Red Bengal. During the course of the Bangladesh struggle it was hoped that a long-drawn-out guerrilla war in Bangladesh and the presence of ten million refugees could be transformed into a revolutionary war against India and Pakistan. Is there however an objective basis for such an alliance? Common language and culture do form a basis for Bengali nationalism, especially among the petty bourgeois, as they do in any other linguistic region of India. But the economic interests of the two petty bourgeois groups are in conflict, since a separate Bangladesh will guarantee jobs for the Bangladesh petty bourgeoisie which they may lose in a United Bengal. The dependent status of East Pakistan in the Pakistan economy was, after all, only a continuation of the dependent hinterland status of East Bengal in pre-Independence Bengal. West Bengal had all the manufacturing investment, better universities, a better port, while East Bengal was rural and agricultural. The dominant feudal *zamindar* class in East Bengal was Hindu, while the exploited group was Bengali Muslim peasantry. Bangladesh nationalism, while it shares Bengali culture with West Bengal, stands at present in a hinterland status as far as its economic life is concerned. In a United Bengal, it could easily stay in that position. In fact, the present friendly relations between India and Bangladesh may be short-lived once the competing interests of the two countries in exporting jute and tea become clear. The manufacturing industry and the trading interests of West Bengal may easily feel tempted to push Bangladesh back into its old dependent status. It is not enough to assert that the exploited masses of Bangladesh and of West Bengal will rise. An objective basis of alliance has to be defined.

The greatest setback to the Indian ruling class is likely to arise from its two main contradictions. The first is the alliance between the bourgeoisie and the petty bourgeoisie in a pro-gramme of capitalist economic growth with a state bureaucratic 'socialist' façade. In creating jobs for the middle classes and industrial profits for the bourgeoisie, an enormous wastage is incurred. The wastage due to government inefficiency, jobbery and corruption is added to the wastage due to conspicuous con-sumption and unplanned and wasteful industrial growth lead-ing to excess capacity and recessions. The inability of the ruling classes to pursue accumulation and growth has been seen in the continuously rising unemployment in the urban and rural areas. The cost of government waste and private wastage is reflected in inflation and rising commodity taxation which have a regressive bias. The bourgeoisie cannot, because of its weakness, pursue unbridled capitalist accumulation. The petty-bourgeois view of socialism and public-sector expansion means a creation of unproductive government jobs and the policing of the Big Bourgeoisie with a paraphernalia of state agencies. In this curious alliance lies the contradiction of the Indian ruling class. Its mass support is in conflict with its class interest. The deadlock results in slow and uneven growth insufficient to al-leviate unemployment and poverty.

This slow and uneven growth also strengthens the other main

contradictions: uneven regional development and inter-regional antagonism. Slow growth postpones the emergence of a national economy with division of labour on a national scale. In doing this, it also, however, frustrates the possibility of an alliance of the poor across regions. It keeps the class struggle fragmented regionally and diverts the energies of a regional struggle into chauvinistic channels. The example of Bangladesh will be remembered by those engaged in regional struggles, in case sometime in the future the failure of the ruling classes to alleviate working-class problems becomes so extreme that a regional movement can be organized successfully.

If the Green Revolution is successful in permanently increasing the output of food-grains, a national market in food-grains will emerge for the first time. Already surplus food-grain output at harvest time depresses the price and the government procurement programme has to step in to keep prices up each year. Sooner or later this situation will mean a national price for all food-grains. The Green Revolution will also lead to the creation of a rural proletariat. In the more advanced agricultural region of Punjab, rural labour is already being imported from neighbouring states at harvest time. From the creation of a rural proletariat in a sector with a national market, the inter-dependence of proletarian interests in different rural areas may emerge as an objective fact rather than a slogan.

Imperialism and the Growth of
Indian Capitalism
Prabhat Patnaik

A fundamental proposition underlying much Marxist thinking
on the Third World countries is that capitalist development is
not possible for them today – that their productive forces
cannot be adequately developed under capitalist relations.[1]
The proposition must be interpreted carefully. First it is not an
abstract economic proposition. Since spontaneous breakdowns
of the economic system do not occur some sort of growth will
continue to take place, and given time the productive forces can
always develop sufficiently. To believe, as many left-wing
groups do, that any serious challenge to capitalism must wait
till some form of automatic breakdown has proved that the
system has exhausted its potential is to court passivity. Such a
failure to expose the contradictions of capitalism allows it to
become relatively stronger and therefore renders the passivity
self-justifying and self-perpetuating. What needs to be looked
at is the totality of the situation, that is, the interaction between
all the elements, including the element of conscious action.

Secondly, there is no simple criterion for assessing whether
capitalist relations are a 'fetter' on development or not. Lenin
states: 'It would be a mistake to believe that . . . a tendency to
decay precludes the rapid growth of capitalism.'[2] Equally
wrong is the Narodnik-type argument that unevenness of
growth as such is equivalent to no growth at all. In reality, to

1. P. A. Baran, *The Political Economy of Growth*, New York,
1957.
2. V. I. Lenin, *Imperialism, the Highest Stage of Capitalism*, in
Collected Works (*Moscow* 1964), vol. 22, p. 300.

assess the achievements and prospects of capitalism we have to go behind the growth process to look at its nature – its structural implications, its ability to generate its own momentum, and of course its ability to meet people's aspirations, themselves changing through greater consciousness. By and large, studies on this theme have focused their attention on the role of imperialist penetration in Third World countries. An aspect of the question that has not received much attention, however, is the interrelation between the domestic bourgeoisie of the Third World countries and international capital. Even perceptive writers have tended to treat the domestic bourgeoisie either as a hindrance to development, as is foreign capital,[3] or as a genuinely progressive force thwarted by foreign capital.[4] In either case the domestic and the metropolitan bourgeoisie are looked at separately and their interconnection is lost. I shall in this essay sketch some aspects of this interconnection in the specific case of India.

Colonialism and the Evolution of the Indian Bourgeoisie

India is a specially interesting case, because the bourgeoisie there was more developed and mature compared to many other Third World countries, and there was only a small strictly comprador element (i.e. those involved only in foreign trade or in serving foreign capital in other ways, for example as local agents). Of course, like other national bourgeoisies, it developed in a colonial environment and therefore shared certain common characteristics, but there was a difference of degree partly reflecting the significant economic development which had taken place in pre-British India. The pre-British structure

3. P. M. Sweezy, 'Obstacles to Economic Development', in C. H. Feinstein, ed., *Socialism, Capitalism and Economic Growth*, Cambridge, 1967.

4. The latter view in particular characterizes much ECLA thinking on the subject.

was extremely complex with a hierarchy of land rights and also, at least to some extent, identifiable class relationships. There was considerable monetization and commodity production, with the consequent tendency towards differentiation among the peasantry and the emergence of trade as a two-way process between country and town.[5] Manufacturing was quite developed – non-mechanized but catering for an international market.[6] The system, whether or not we choose to characterize it as a feudal one,[7] was in a state of decomposition, and the possibility of a Japan-type development could not have been ruled out.[8] Merchant capital was significant and, though the later bourgeoisie was not the lineal descendant of the earlier one, there was some continuity. Domestic capital persisted in internal trade and a large section of the modern industrial bourgeoisie has a mercantile background.

Colonial rule destroyed this pre-capitalist economy in two phases. First was the so-called 'drain of wealth' which, one can argue, continued throughout the colonial period but which was particularly important in the late eighteenth century. Private loot and the East India Company's treatment of the administration as a profitable business resulted in a shortage of specie, leading to recession in agriculture and dislocation of trade and industry.[9] The second phase, starting after the Napoleonic

5. For a brief discussion see Irfan Habib, 'Distribution of Landed Property in Pre-British India', *Enquiry*, Delhi, Winter, 1965; see also B. N. Ganguli, ed., *Readings in Indian Economic History*, Asia Publishing House, London, 1964, pp. 80–81.

6. H. R. Ghoshal, 'Industrial Production in Bengal in Early Nineteenth Century', in Ganguli, op. cit.

7. D. D. Kosambi, in *An Introduction to the Study of Indian History* (Bombay, 1956), calls the structure a 'feudal' one. For a contrary view see D. Thorner, 'Feudalism in India', in R. Coulburn, ed., *Feudalism in History*, Princeton, 1956.

8. T. Raychaudhury, 'A Reinterpretation of Nineteenth-century Indian Economic History?', in *Indian Economic and Social History Review*, Delhi, 5, no. 1, March 1968.

9. For a summary of recent research on the subject, see T. Ray-

wars, involved the decline of handicrafts through factory competition. Urban handloom industry was more or less totally destroyed. The destruction spread to rural weavers as well, but many lingered on – partly through market imperfections and partly by cutting into subsistence – only to fall victim to the famines. The exhaustion of land, the increase in rents, and the fall in the wages of rural labourers suggest a large population being thrown out of employment, but how long and with what severity this process continued is still a matter for debate.[10]

It is hardly surprising in these conditions that Indian industrial capital did not grow. Being pre-empted from its potential markets, facing a state which followed a policy of 'discriminatory interventionism'[11] in the interests of British capital, and being excluded from the British-dominated old-boy network which controlled much of the banking and external trade,[12] it hardly had a chance. The Parsi businessmen with an entry to the exclusive club naturally did somewhat better. It is more difficult to explain the reluctance of foreign capital to start manufacturing on any large scale. Even Marx's prediction that the railways would herald the growth of metal and engineering industries remained largely unfulfilled.[13] Climate is a

chaudhury, 'Recent Writings in British Indian Economic History', in *Contributions to Indian Economic History*, vol. 1, Calcutta, 1960, edited by the same writer.

10. See Bipan Chandra's controversy with M. D. Morris on 'Reinterpretation of Nineteenth-century Indian Economic History', in *Indian Economic and Social History Review*, March 1968.

11. The phrase was coined by S. Bhattacharya, 'Laissez-faire in India', *Indian Economic and Social History Review*, 2, no. 1, January 1965.

12. A. K. Bagchi, 'European and Indian Entrepreneurship in India 1900–30', in E. Leach and S. N. Mukherji, ed., *Elites in South Asia*, Cambridge, 1970.

13. A. K. Bagchi, *Private Investment in India 1900–1939*, Cambridge 1972. Chapter 10 discusses the development of the engineering industry.

possible explanation.[14] It ruled out immigration from Britain, restricting the flow of skills and giving British capital only a transitory interest in India.[15] A more powerful factor perhaps was the very fact of British political control. Capital tends to be regionally concentrated. It creates an environment which draws other capital to it and this process is cumulative. The restriction of Indian capital broke this process. As the linkage effects were not spread through the economy, each act of investment became an isolated episode, no more than a shift of some processes in the manufacturing chain from England to India, and this further restricted capital inflow. Besides, since the market was carefully preserved, there was little need for industry to be established on the spot. Moreover political pressures sabotaged the growth of the potentially important locomotive industry.[16] For a long time, of course, no other industrial power was anywhere near providing effective competition to Britain.

The situation began to change around the turn of the century. Germany and America challenged Britain's lead and started penetrating the Indian market. In India a political movement led by the bourgeoisie took shape.

Periods of crisis for British imperialism, like the two World Wars, were of benefit to both major challengers – Indian industrialists and the Americans.[17] Fighting to keep its international rivals out, Britain made concessions to Indian capital. The

14. Baran, *The Political Economy of Growth*, chapter 5.

15. Complementarity between capital and skills-inflow is emphasized in R. Nurkse, 'The Problem of International Investment Today in the Light of Nineteenth-century Experience', *Economic Journal*, 1954.

16. F. Lehman, 'Great Britain and the Supply of Railway Locomotives to India', *Indian Economic and Social History Review*, 2, no. 4, 1965.

17. The nature of Indian gains is clear. Disruption of imports meant larger markets and profits. For American gains of markets, see L. Natarajan, *American Shadow Over India*, Delhi, 1954, chapter 2.

government's contract to buy steel helped the Tatas to set up India's first steel plant.[18] The introduction of protection on the 'infant'-industry criterion led to notable industrial expansion. At the same time, the system of imperial preferences, the dollar pool and the attempted freezing of dollar reserves were attempts to bind India closer to Britain. Despite all this, at Independence the United States had emerged as India's major trading partner. This trade reached a peak during the Korean War when, apart from jute goods, India exported large amounts of strategic materials such as monazite, mica and manganese ore, among others, in which American interest had been aroused for some time.[19]

But if the Americans had hoped to take over Britain's hegemonic role in India, the Indian bourgeoisie was not going to concede it. It sought to strengthen its own position with the help of the Indian state. This period of economic nationalism was characterized by the fight against foreign capital and the growth of state capitalism. Much of the old foreign capital had been closely connected with the Empire. It was in the form of branch investment and was in such areas as trading, insurance, banking, tea, jute and mines. With the passing of the Empire, its decline was inevitable. The nationalization of the Imperial Bank removed British capital from a commanding position. Indian big business took over a number of foreign enterprises, for example in jute, tea and trading. Some leading agency houses changed hands, for example Forbes & Campbell;[20] in others substantial minority holdings were offered to Indian houses, for example in Macneil and Barry. Where no changes in ownership were effected, there has been relative stagnation, as

18. S. K. Sen, *Economic Policy and Development of India*, Calcutta, 1966, chapter 4.

19. Natarajan, chapter 2.

20. Between 1947 and 1952, 66 concerns, of which 64 were British, were taken over by Indians. See K. M. Kurian, *Impact of Foreign Capital on the Indian Economy*, Delhi, 1966, p. 71.

in the case of Andrew Yule and Bird Heilger.[21] Little new foreign capital came in during this period. The increase in foreign assets in the early 1950s was largely due to the plough-back of profits or to asset revaluation.[22] It is true that India's industrialization had not begun and foreign capital was not yet interested, but mutual hostility was undeniable. With Russian backing, the government had denied the Germans substantial equity participation in the Rourkela Steel Plant. Government policy was at least partly the reason why America's imports of strategic materials from India declined, and why she turned elsewhere to develop captive sources of supply. Manganese mines in Gabon and Brazil were developed by US Steel, and in Ghana and Guyana by Union Carbide.[23] Finally this hostility took the form of open war between the government and the oil companies.[24]

The Nature of State Capitalism in India

The need for state capitalism was recognized early by the bour-geoisie,[25] but its precise form was a result of the class nature of the state. The colonial structure having left no single strong class, state power continues to be based on a coalition between the bourgeoisie and large landowners. More specifically, the coalition has three elements: the monopoly bourgeoisie whose members control business empires spread across a number of

21. R. K. Hazari, *The Structure of the Corporate Private Sector*, London 1966, chapter 7.

22. Kurian, chapter 3.

23. See G. R. Sheshadri's report on India in *Mining Annual Review*, June, 1969, p. 369.

24. M. Kidron, *Foreign Investments in India*, London, Oxford University Press, 1965, pp. 166–75; M. Tanzer, *The Political Econ-omy of International Oil and the Underdeveloped Countries*, Boston, 1969, part 2.

25. P. Chattopadhyaya, 'State Capitalism in India', *Monthly Review*, March, 1970.

spheres and a number of states; the small urban bourgeoisie consisting of businessmen confined to single industries or states and professional groups who are not direct exploiters but integrated into the system of exploitation, like lawyers, managers and upper bureaucracy; and finally the class of landlords and rich peasants, who live mainly by exploitation, either through rent or through wage labour or both. This last may appear too heterogeneous, but post-Independence land reforms have caused its constituents to coalesce into a more or less single category, so it is better treated as such. Bourgeois democracy and a federal political structure create the environment for this coalition to work. If state capitalism was considered a permanent phenomenon and the state did not contemplate handing over factories to private entrepreneurs as in Pakistan or Japan, it was because such a step would damage the alliance. It would necessarily benefit the monopoly houses; and the smaller bourgeoisie supported by the petty bourgeois class would oppose it.

The weakness of state capitalism lay in the fact that the nature of the state, while apparently giving it enormous strength, made it fundamentally weak. While on the one hand it had to maintain the balance of the class coalition (by effectively curbing any constituent group that became too strong) and to make periodic concessions to the exploited, on the other it could not challenge the position of any constituent group too strongly, for that would affect the collective strength of the coalition. Thus, although the state appeared independent, placed high above all classes, in reality it had to conform closely to the rules of the game. The limits to state action were sharply drawn, and any radical structural reform was ruled out. The precise location of this weakness we shall discuss later.

During the First Plan, state activity was largely confined to the construction of overhead capital. Serious industrialization only began with the Second Plan, which provided for a large outlay by the state sector, much of it for building up heavy industries.[26]

But this was the period of John Foster Dulles, and if the policy of non-alignment met with American hostility, so too did the economic policy, which was after all a similar move in the direction of relative independence. The industrialization programme was attacked – implicitly by a Ford Foundation team[27] and explicitly by a World Bank mission – as being 'over-ambitious'. A simultaneous attack was made against the state sector. The World Bank demonstrated it's willingness to finance private sector expansion by providing aid for the two private steel plants.

Of course, India's independence must not be exaggerated. In August 1956 the government agreed to buy surplus American wheat – which India did not need at that stage – at inflated prices, against rupee payments which gave the Americans potentially extensive powers over the Indian economy.[28] Again, although the Americans did provide large amounts of aid, most of it was either for food imports or for infrastructural investment. Aid for developing the industrial base was limited. American private capital was as yet hardly interested in India. Britain and West Germany by contrast showed greater willingness to come to terms with Indian policy and make the most of it. Suggestions of collaboration between the government and private German capital began as early as 1953 over the Rourkela Steel Plant. After the deal was completed in 1956, Britain followed up with a similar arrangement at Durgapur. Great eagerness was also shown to collaborate with Indian private

26. For a summary of India's planning experience see Charles Bettelheim, *India Independent*, London, 1968, chapter 7.

27. A critique of the team's report, 'Ploughing the Plan Under' is contained in D. Thorner and A. Thorner, *Land and Labour in India*, London, 1964.

28. V. I. Pavlov, *India: Economic Freedom Versus Imperialism*, Delhi, 1963, p. 120.

capital. The Soviet Union and the Eastern European countries provided more enthusiastic support for state capitalism. Beginning with cooperation in oil exploration and the setting up of refineries in the state sector, the Eastern Bloc gave strategic aid for building a heavy industrial base. The actual viability of state capitalism was thus closely linked with aid from the Soviet Union.

American attitudes changed noticeably in the late 1950s. Politically, Soviet influence could be counteracted only by greater participation in the development effort, while the economic benefits of such participation did not go unnoticed. With state capitalism expanding the Indian market, exports, especially of machinery and sophisticated manufactures, could be pushed up through development assistance (and here by her earlier reticence America had lost out even to Britain and Germany). Not only did America increase her aid, but she also insisted on tying it to prevent its being spent on cheaper European goods. This was an important change: as late as mid 1958, of the 5,000 million rupees India owed to the USA, 3,079·5 million was on account of food; only at the end of 1957 was $225 million promised to India for buying equipment. This change did not mean a letting-up of political pressures, and constant threats to postpone aid hung over India; rather, India flaunted Soviet aid to keep political strings to the minimum.[29] Thus Indian state capitalism survived without making too many compromises, partly because of the specific nature of the international situation.

The 'New' Foreign Invesment

Meanwhile, a new kind of private foreign capital was flowing into the country. The foreign exchange crisis of 1957–8 had led to drastic import controls, including quantitative restrictions. The resulting protection, combined with large government ex-

29. Pavlov, pp. 120, 126.

penditure, created extremely profitable markets in India for a whole range of commodities. To exploit this market Indian capital had necessarily to turn abroad for technology. Foreign capital was attracted both by the expanding market and by the need to jump tariff (and later quota) barriers. In the new circumstances it was necessary and useful to have an Indian ally, and the 'joint venture' emerged as a marriage of convenience.

This new foreign capital differed from the old in three main respects. First, it was interested in the modern, technologically advanced sectors of industry which were the most dynamic areas of the economy. Between 1948 and 1955 only 284 collaboration agreements were approved by the government, but there were 82 in 1956, 81 in 1957, 103 in 1958, 150 in 1959 and 380 in 1960. Since then there have been around 300 to 400 a year. Of a total of 1,051 such agreements studied by the Reserve Bank, manufacturing accounted for 1,006: 115 were for transport equipment, 250 for machinery and machine tools, 107 for metals, 162 for electrical goods and 177 for chemicals.

Secondly, foreign capital began to rely more on the participation of Indian capital. The form of investment was no longer in branches of a European company, but in local subsidiaries or more frequently in ventures involving a minority participation. Even in subsidiaries there was a fall in the parent company's share.[30] At the other end of the scale, pure technical collaboration agreements, though more numerous, either were of no financial importance (involving transfers of trade marks etc.) or more recently involved payment being made in shares. Out of 2,000 approvals before 1963, 1,750 were purely technical agreements. But in 1967, out of 341 of these agreements, 211 involved financial participation.[31] This suited the govern-

30. Reserve Bank of India, *Foreign Collaboration in Indian Industry*, Survey Report, Bombay, 1968, pp. 4, 102, 114.

31. R. K. Hazari, ed., *Foreign Collaboration*, Bombay, 1968, p. 140.

ment as well as the foreign partner, which got a foothold in the Indian market.

Lastly, the foreign partner, significantly, was normally a large international corporation interested exclusively in the Indian market. This was in direct contrast to the old foreign capital. In its total operations, the Indian partner was extremely small by comparison, particularly since it was the smaller monopoly houses which displayed the greatest enthusiasm for teaming up. Their gains were obvious. The Mafatlal group increased its total assets by 176 per cent between 1963–4 and 1966–7, largely by expanding its interests in chemicals with foreign collaboration.[32] If Indian capital was not to be swamped it needed state backing, and, in the first phase of development, the state retained a certain autonomy in relation to foreign capital and foreign states.

The Contradictions of Indian State Capitalism in the First Phase of Development

The situation, however, contained a number of contradictions. The weakness inherent in the nature of Indian state capitalism was expressed in its inability to mobilize adequate resources for economic growth. Given the level of productivity the possible rate of accumulation is determined by two factors – first, the growth-rate of agriculture, which provides the bulk of the necessities and second, the strength of the various classes, which determines the extent to which mass consumption or luxury consumption can be restricted. In essence, therefore, the resource problem is how to increase accumulation by acting on these factors.

The chief barrier to agricultural growth has been the structure of agrarian relations. Extreme inequality of ownership and operation generally leaves the bulk of the farmers with neither

32. Government of India, Department of Company Affairs, *Company News and Notes*, Delhi, 1 January 1969.

the means nor the incentive to invest. Meanwhile, for those who get the surplus, conspicuous consumption and gold-hoarding, moneylending, and the purchase of land for leasing out or cultivating with labourers all compete with productive investment in land. With production largely dependent on rainfall, the risks of productive investment are large, so the amount invested is relatively small. The coexistence of capitalist and pre-capitalist modes (i.e. petty tenancy and small-scale farming) implies a choice for the landowner between expansion of rent or wage exploitation by obtaining more land, and an intensification of wage exploitation by increasing the productivity of his existing land. The relative attractiveness of the former constricts the latter. Reform of this structure has been a minimum requirement for rapid agricultural growth.[33] And yet agrarian reforms, while eliminating some excesses like the very large absentee landlords who often controlled dozens of villages, left the old structure essentially intact.[34] Thus although a relatively more homogeneous landowning class was created, strengthening the ruling class-coalition, the barriers to growth remained. Agricultural output, virtually stagnant over the half-century before independence, increased in the 1950s at a rate of 3·5 per cent a year, the increase being almost equally attributable to increases in area and yield (45 per cent each)[35]

33. This remains true even now, despite the fact that under the stimulus of high agricultural prices and technological progress involving high-yielding seed varieties productive investment in agriculture has increased; see K. N. Raj, 'Some Questions Concerning Growth Transformation and Planning in Agriculture in "Developing Countries" ', United Nations, *Journal of Development Planning*, no. 1, 1969.

34. D. Thorner and A. Thorner, 'Agrarian problems in India Today', in *Land and Labour in India*, London, 1964.

35. B. S. Minhas and A. Vaidyanathan, 'Growth of Crop Output in India – 1951–4 to 1958–61: Analysis by Component Elements', *Journal of the Indian Society of Agricultural Statistics*, December 1965.

resulting largely from the extension of irrigation. There were limits to this process, however.[36] Poor rainfall disastrously affected output in the early 1960s, accentuating the resource problem.

The barriers to restrictions on consumption were equally strong. Mass consumption was squeezed through inflation, real wages in 1964 being not much higher than the 1951 level.[37] But despite its weak organization the working class was able to impose limits to this process. On the other hand, with savings and investment decisions still in private hands, and the state so closely associated with many vested interests, luxury consumption was not adequately restricted. After an initial increase the savings rate remained steady at around 10 per cent for over a decade.[38] Hence any attempt to raise the investment rate meant an exchange deficit which could be financed only through aid. Moreover, construction of an industrial base by means of import substitution requires, as its financial counterpart, an increase in the marginal savings ratio. The available resources are then concentrated on strategic sectors and not frittered away through unplanned shifts to other parts of the economy. Though statistical evidence suggests a high realized marginal savings-rate, this could be due to lags in consumption,[39] and it is doubtful if the ex-ante rate increased very much. In this situation a policy of import substitution merely shifted a range of manufacturing processes to India from abroad while maintaining Indian dependence on imports required for previous stages of production, such as machinery and maintenance. Other factors like a more liberal machinery-

36. Raj, op. cit. p. 34.

37. Government of India, *Pocket Book of Economic Information, 1969.*Compare tables 2.5 and 11.1 therein.

38. *Reserve Bank of India Bulletin,* March 1965; and P. D. Ojha, 'Mobilization of Savings', *Economic and Political Weekly,* Bombay, Annual Number, 1969.

39. K. N. Raj, 'The Marginal Rate of Saving in the Indian Economy', *Oxford Economic Papers,* 14, no. 1, February 1962.

import policy and the difficulties of finding Western collaborators for plant-making also played a role, but 'import-
dependent import substitution', with its continuous dependence
on aid to finance an exchange deficit, underlined state capitalism's failure to mobilize enough resources for the required
growth.

The possibility of import substitution in know-how was
equally limited. As most of the information based on research
within giant corporations was of a private character, India's
technological dependence could be reduced only if research was
undertaken within the country itself. Yet virtually no Indian
enterprise has any research department. Foreign collaborators,
far from stimulating research, tended to hinder it. Control over
technology was an effective tool in the hands of foreign firms,
while for many the sale of know-how was a lucrative business.
Thus some agreements explicitly put limits on the research and
development of new products by the Indian partner.[40] Foreign
collaborators possessed both a valid economic argument for
centralized research and a superior bargaining power which
enabled them even to withold vital technical information and to
keep strict control over the activities of their top technological
personnel. In addition, the free import of know-how reduced
the need for import substitution in it. Thus for large sectors of
industry technological parasitism was inherent in the situation.[41]

Finally, economic nationalism was possible because of the
specific nature of the internal political situation. There was no
serious revolutionary challenge to the hegemony of the ruling
classes. They had emerged strong from the independence
movement and the early challenge of the Telengana peasant
revolt had been dealt with successfully. As a result, the political
situation in the 1950s was tranquil. The bourgeoisie had felt

40. Kidron, *Foreign Investments*, pp. 287–96.
41. A. V. Desai, 'Potentialities of Collaboration and Their Utilization', in Hazari, ed., *Foreign Collaboration*.

secure enough at home to stake its claim *vis-à-vis* foreign capital. If the circumstances had been different, it might have had to turn abroad for help.

A New Phase of Development

The heightening of some of these contradictions coincided with a shift in the international situation. After the 1962 clash with China, India became militarily and politically more dependent on America. The large defence budget put an additional strain on resources, making the state even more vulnerable. Meanwhile, the Soviet Union began looking for a thaw in the Cold War. Its aid, never large, became less reliable. A new phase of development had begun in India.

If in the earlier phase state policy had been relatively autonomous, now there was greater subordination to imperialism. The net external liability of the official sector increased from Rs. 10,734 million in December 1961 to Rs. 23,416 million in March 1965.[42] Amortization of debt alone absorbed about 11 per cent of exports in 1966 – and 27 per cent if payments on investment income account are included.[43] Whereas in March 1967 total money-supply with the public was Rs. 50,030 million, United States government-owned deposits (the result of American Public Law 480 food-sales) were Rs. 20,700 million, giving America extensive powers over the Indian economy.[44] Foreign and local pressures on state policy led to a shift away from controls towards greater freedom for capital. Three specific aspects of this change deserve attention.

First, at donor countries' insistence, the attitude towards

42. 'India's International Investment Position in 1963–4 and 1964–5', *Reserve Bank of India Bulletin*, January 1967.

43. H. Magdoff, *The Age of Imperialism*, New York, 1969, p. 155.

44. 'Satyakam', 'P. L. 480 and India's Freedom', *Liberation*, 2, no. 5, Calcutta, March 1969.

foreign capital softened. If in 1948–9 the government, while promising 'fair' treatment had talked of 'carefully regulating' foreign capital and ensuring effective Indian control, in 1963 the Finance Minister thought 'we would be justified in opening the doors even wider to private foreign investment'.[45] Again, before 1962, the issue of shares to non-residents for considerations other than cash was disapproved of, but now share issues in return for plant and machinery or technical assistance were common. The trend was clear and foreign capital considerably expanded its operations in India. Some indication of its importance even as early as 1963–4 is given by a comparison of the total capital employed in all public limited companies with foreign financial collaboration (that is, subsidiaries and minority ventures) with total capital employed in a selected group of 1,333 public limited companies for which figures are available (Table 1). This latter group includes some, though not all, companies belonging to the former group. It is not too inappropriate for comparison because it represents a very large segment of the Indian corporate sector: the companies which are included account for about 70 per cent of paid-up capital of all non-financial and non-government public limited companies, and roughly the same proportion of paid-up capital in most individual industries.

Of course, we have included minority ventures, but 92 per cent of capital employed in this group was in companies employing Rs. 10 million or more, and the foreign share in such large companies is often substantial. Between 1956 and 1963, for example, of all the initial issues with foreign participation which were approved, forty-eight were minority ventures with an equity of above Rs. 10 million; and of these, twenty-eight involved foreign participation of above 25 per cent, often more than enough to ensure control. We can safely say, therefore, that foreign capital has a significant position in petroleum, en-

45. Quoted in Hazari, ed., *Foreign Collaboration*, p. 6.

gineering, chemicals and rubber.[46] Moreover, the Reserve Bank's study of what it calls 'foreign-controlled rupee companies', both public and private (limited), shows these to be growing much faster than Indian companies. For example in 1965–6 the gross capital stock of 320 foreign companies increased by 13·9 per cent, as against the 9·6 per cent increase of 1,944 Indian private and public companies.[47] Whatever the criterion, foreign companies are more profitable than the Indian companies in the corporate sector. All available studies show that they are also more profitable than their parent companies. Thus foreign capital, collaborating with and often dominating Indian capital, seems to have acquired a strategic hold over the most profitable and dynamic sector of the economy.

Though British investment continued to lead that of other countries, American capital had also begun to play an important role. To take agreements involving financial collaboration, the distribution in the period 1956 to 1960 was: UK 94, West Germany 36, and USA 18. During the following four years, 1961–5, on the other hand, the figures had changed to 120, 38 and 77 respectively.[48] This growth did not mean that capital had been flowing into India in large quantities. Even giant companies in India account for a very small share of the parent companies' operations. Besides, this growth itself had taken place while there had actually been a substantial outflow of surplus from India. For example, between 1956 and 1961 the net outflow (i.e. the excess of investment income and royalty

46. For global estimates of the share of foreign capital in the entire private corporate sector, see N. K. Chandra, 'Western Imperialism and India Today', *Economic and Political Weekly*, Annual Number 1973, and the author's 'Private Corporate Industrial Investment in India 1947–1967' (unpublished).

47. 'Finances of Branches of Foreign Companies and Foreign-controlled Rupee Companies', *Reserve Bank of Indian Bulletin*, June 1968.

48. Reserve Bank Survey tables on p. 25 and p. 53.

TABLE I
Ratio between (1) total capital employed in public limited
companies with foreign financial collaboration in an industry
and (2) total capital employed in companies belonging to
the same industry in the sample of 1,333 companies
(percentages).

| Industry | Capital employed in: | | |
	Subsidiaries	Minority Ventures	Total
Plantations and mining	0·3	28·3	28·6
Petroleum	48·0	51·3	99·3
Food, beverages, tobacco	19·7	10·0	29·7
Textile products	—	7·1	7·1
Transport equipment	14·5	56·1	70·6
Machinery and machine tools	8·1	33·0	41·1
Metals and metal products (excluding iron and steel)	13·3 / 29·43	13·9 / 30·96	27·2 / 60·39
Electrical goods and machinery	27·9	52·9	80·8
Chemicals and allied products (of which medicines and pharmaceuticals)	49·3 / 58·4	46·7 / 45·1	96·0 / 103·5
Rubber goods	82·5	—	82·5
Miscellaneous	3·4	23·6	27·0
Services	5·7	25·3	31·0
Total	13·1	24·1	37·2

Source: Compiled from Reserve Bank Survey tables pp. 22, 51,
and 'Finances of Indian Joint-stock companies, 1965–66',
Reserve Bank of India Bulletin, December 1967.

transfers over net capital inflow) on account of foreign private
enterprise was Rs. 672 million.[49]

A second aspect of the move away from controls on capital
was the tendency towards the removal of trade restrictions.
Caught in the contradictions of half-hearted import sub-

49. S. Kumarasundaram, 'Foreign Collaborations and Indian Balance of Payments', in Hazari, ed., *Foreign Collaboration*, p. 207.

stitution, the government, on World Bank advice, decided to
devalue in 1966 as well as to liberalize imports of some essential commodities. This was to be financed by aid organized by
the World Bank. Freer trade is not always in the interests of
metropolitan capital: if one metropolitan capital dominates an
economy, protection is after all protection of that capital; however, in India the control by foreign capital, let alone a single
country's capital, was far from complete. Freer trade thus enhanced the freedom enjoyed by metropolitan capital and was
particularly to the advantage of American capital so long as it
remained in second place.

Finally, the state's role as the controller of private capital
was being directly undermined, while its role as an investor was
being undermined indirectly. Even though state initiative is
necessary for private capital, state ownership implies so much
area of activity out of bounds to private investors. For this
reason sporadic attempts had been made to use aid as a means
of restricting the state sector. More important, the persistent
demand that aid be replaced where possible by foreign private
capital represented a systematic attempt in the same direction.
In any case 'where [foreign equity participation] does not
exceed 50 per cent of total equity, approval of such foreign
investment seldom encounters any difficulty'.[50] Furthermore,
with the liberalization of licensing procedure through the
sixties[51] private, including foreign, capital was being allowed
to operate freely over a large segment of the economy.

The Implications of Economic 'Liberalism'

These changes, constituting a move towards economic 'liberalism', were welcomed by many economists on grounds of
efficiency. To look at the matter in terms of efficiency, however,

50. Hazari, ibid., p. 7.

51. A very brief report on the position on licensing at the end of the
sixties can be found in the *Financial Times*, 29 September 1970.

is highly misleading; 'liberalization' of the economic régimes in underdeveloped countries has far-reaching implications which must be examined in their totality. 'Liberalization' *per se* does not improve domestic resource availability. No doubt a liberal import policy makes a fuller utilization of existing equipment possible, but given the large pent-up domestic demand which exists in most underdeveloped countries characterized by a network of controls, the additional output from fuller utilization is largely absorbed into domestic consumption. Indeed countries which have liberalized trade have usually become even more dependent on foreign aid and foreign capital than before. While their exports have undoubtedly increased, their imports have increased even faster – the gap being met by larger aid and foreign capital inflows.[52] (It is for this reason that trade liberalization has usually been a part of an overall move towards economic liberalism, which permits a freer play of private, especially foreign, capital.)

Economic 'liberalism' therefore further weakens the domestic state *vis-à-vis* foreign states and capitals. Moreover this weakening becomes a cumulative process for two reasons.

First, because of its greater foresight and preference for safety monopoly capital constantly needs external stimuli to sustain a rapid expansion;[53] the large state outlays which have enormously expanded the domestic market in many underdeveloped countries have played this role. Allowing greater free play for capital does not obviate this role of state expenditure.[54] On the other hand since state and private capital

52. Pakistan is a classic example; see K. N. Raj, *India, Pakistan and China*, Bombay, 1967, pp. 13–16. If trade liberalization in India's case was not accompanied by such a widening of the exchange gap, this was mainly because of the simultaneous existence of an industrial recession which began in the mid sixties and from which the economy has yet to recover fully.

53. P. A. Baran and P. M. Sweezy, *Monopoly Capital*, New York, 1966.

54. This argument would be weakened if foreign capital was eager

compete for the same resources, the greater the freedom of the latter the more restricted is the state. Reliance on aid enables it to maintain the momentum but only at the expense of further limiting its ability to encroach upon private capital, particularly foreign capital which enjoys the protection of the more powerful donor state. There are three formal possibilities here. First, the maldistribution of resources may not show itself in any immediate way through a large surplus outflow, for instance, if the state sector continues growing; but this needs a continuous increase in aid. Second, state investment may actually shrink, markets grow less fast and foreign capital look elsewhere. As a result the actual outflow of surplus increases, and long-run industrial expansion slows down. Third, the same rate of growth may be maintained for some time by means not of state investment but of providing large incentives to private capital, including concessions to foreign capital. Thus the maintenance of growth requires greater aid and/or more concessions, both leading to the progressive weakening of the state and the strengthening of foreign capital. But a weaker state means a weaker domestic capital as well, so that the latter tends to get swallowed by foreign capital and, as in Brazil, sections of the bourgeoisie are reduced to rentier status.[55]

The second reason for the cumulative nature of the domestic state's weakening by economic 'liberalism' is as follows: as the hegemony of the state is undermined, *internal* contradictions also help foreign capital. In India, the nationalization of domestically owned banks (a move forced by the smaller bour-

---

to enter underdeveloped countries to set up export-oriented industries; then the size of the domestic market would not be the primary consideration. Even though export-oriented foreign capital has entered some underdeveloped countries in recent years there is little evidence of such eagerness. The protectionist policies of developed countries are an important consideration here.

55. E. Galeano, 'Denationalization of Brazilian Industry', *Monthly Review*, November 1969.

geoisie against the growing strength of the monopoly houses), if it succeeds in restricting credit to big business and diffusing it wider, will indirectly strengthen foreign capital.

This is a point which is often overlooked. For example, some have argued that the Indian monopoly bourgeoisie, or a section of it, joins forces with foreign capital, at the risk of being dominated, to weaken the state. Thus a distinction is drawn between two groups among the bourgeoisie: one, consisting of the Big Bourgeoisie, is an ally of imperialism while the other is 'progressive' and anti-imperialist. The distinction is unreal and misleading: it is unreal because, with the American-backed Green Revolution, the landowner class (which is becoming a rural bourgeoisie) has emerged as a potential political ally of imperialism and one at least as important as the Big Bourgeoisie; it is misleading because it approaches the problem in an over-simplified manner. Where state power is based on a class coalition, contradictions exist among the ruling classes and between each class and the state. Therefore, each class or group manoeuvres to promote its own interest; for example, the smaller bourgeoisie demands bank nationalization, while the monopoly bourgeoisie demands the restriction of the state sector. As long as the state preserves a certain relative autonomy *vis-à-vis* foreign capital, the latter is kept at bay and cannot profit from these manoeuvres; but when this autonomy is undermined, foreign capital can profit, as it has, for instance, from the bank-nationalization move. Therefore it is not the manoeuvres themselves which are pro- or anti-imperialist; their effect on the interests of metropolitan capital depends on the objective conditions, that is, on how strong the state is against foreign pressures. The strength of the state, which must not be confused with the extent of the state sector, depends ultimately on its ability to raise resources domestically. It was argued above that, short of drastic changes which would hit at the ruling classes, including the bourgeoisie as a whole, the Indian state cannot raise sufficient resources internally.

Thus the position of the bourgeoisie is paradoxical – it wishes to introduce independent national development, yet it cannot do so without relying on metropolitan countries. It is nationalist, yet it must collaborate with imperialism. The failure to appreciate this paradox leads to the identification of one group of the bourgeoisie as nationalist, the other as collaborators. A contradiction which underlies the position of the bourgeoisie as a whole is identified as existing between sections of the bourgeoisie. Clearly, however, it is not the anti-nationalism of any particular group, but the nature of the situation which favours foreign capital. The weakening of the state and the bourgeoisie proceed apace, and the movement away from economic nationalism leads cumulatively to the imperialist camp. There is no half-way equilibrium.

An additional factor strengthens this tendency. So far we have concentrated on the resource question as a whole, taking the exchange deficit as a mere reflection of it. This need not always be the case, and an exchange deficit may arise from independent structural reasons when, for example, foreign capital which is exclusively interested in the host country's market imposes export restrictions. Of 1,051 agreements surveyed for India, 455 involved export-restrictive clauses; 52 per cent of these set out the countries (often India's neighbours) to which exports were permissible, 33 per cent required the foreign collaborator's permission and 8 per cent imposed a total ban. Agreements with restrictions made up 44 per cent of the total for subsidiaries, 57 per cent for minority companies and 40 per cent for companies with technical collaboration only. Since restrictions need not be explicit in the first group, nor important in the last group, the effective degree of restriction is probably greater. Moreover, restrictions were high in transport equipment (62 per cent of the total in this sector), machinery and tools (50 per cent), electricals (50 per cent) and medicines and pharmaceuticals (50 per cent), while relatively low in metals and metal products (39 per cent) and basic industrial chemicals, and very minor in food and textiles.[56] This means that as imports grow and the economy is at the same time deprived of potential exports from its most dynamic sectors, the resulting deficit requires further reliance on aid and foreign capital.

Thus there exists a constant tendency for capitalist underdeveloped countries today to be re-absorbed into the imperialist orbit; the so-called 'liberalization' results from and in turn strengthens this tendency. No doubt reversals to economic nationalism are always possible given favourable internal and international circumstances; even then, however, the tendency towards subordination would assert itself once again.[57]

Recent Developments

The Indian government has recently attempted to arrest the unambiguous drift towards economic 'liberalism' which had begun from the early sixties. Yet a closer look at this attempt, far from contradicting our analysis, only confirms its validity. Of course economic policy remains highly eclectic.[58] While de-licensing continues (with the object of encouraging higher production in important industries), the government in its 'anti-monopoly drive' is apparently discriminating against requests for expansion coming from large industrial houses and

56. Reserve Bank, *Survey*, pp. 106–8.

57. Of course, absorption into the imperialist orbit would not preclude growth. Such growth would however be jerky and uneven – dependent upon the whim of foreign capital. It would leave the bulk of social labour at a low level of productivity (after all, between 1951 and 1961 the proportion of the working force employed in manufacturing remained relatively unchanged in India) and exacerbate inequalities in income distribution, since conscious redistributive policies are likely precisely to put foreign capital off and hence eliminate the major remaining source of growth.

58. For a description of recent economic policy, see the *Economic Survey 1972–3*. Government of India, New Delhi.

foreign majority companies. While imports of several important commodities have been liberalized, a mandatory expansion of the role of public sector agencies in import-export business is visualized; also compulsory export obligations are being extended to a number of 'non-priority' industries. More significantly, since the Indo-Pak war over Bangladesh and the ensuing hostility towards the US, self-reliance as an objective has been emphasized.[59] Thus a groping towards economic nationalism, and hence a partial reversal of the trend which had set in from the early sixties, is discernible.

Not surprisingly, this reversal comes only after the Indian bourgeoisie has successfully resisted a new wave of internal political challenge to its hegemony – the second since Independence. Also, as one would expect, the contradictions inherent in such a reversal are already being felt. In response to Indian approaches the American government has recently agreed to release $87 million credits which were 'frozen' in 1971, and to participate as a full member of the Aid India Consortium.[60] Further, owing to the fall in reserves in the subsequent two years, India asked for $40 million of this released amount to be made available in free foreign exchange. The pressure on India arose partly, of course, from the precarious food situation. Even despite the low crop, however, if energetic food procurement measures had been taken by the government the need for food imports would not have arisen.[61] The crop failure of 1972–3 moreover came after a series of

59. The document, 'Towards an Approach to the Fifth Plan', envisaged the reduction of net aid to zero in the terminal year (1978–9) of the Fifth Plan.

60. While the World Bank had recommended in 1972 that India should be given debt relief of $200m. for each of the last two years of the Fourth Plan, the actual relief fell short by $70m., owing to the absence of any US contribution. See 'India wants $40m. in Free Foreign Exchange', *The Statesman Weekly*, 26 May 1973.

61. See 'Cost of Food Muddle', *Economic and Political Weekly*, Bombay, 20 January 1973, pp. 96–7.

good harvests. Had stocks been built up through adequate procurement in the past the crisis could have been tided over, but political pressure from the landowner class prevented this.[62] The food crisis and the reliance on imports and aid was therefore a result not so much of natural factors as the failure of the bourgeois landowner state. The extent of this failure was underlined by the fact that ever since the mid sixties industry had experienced a prolonged recession. *Ceteris paribus* its recovery would in any case have put considerable strains on the economy, undermining the viability of economic nationalism. Now that the retreat has begun even without there being any signs of such a recovery, when a recovery does take place attempts to maintain a nationalist posture would be even more hopeless.

Total freedom from imperialism demands, as a necessary condition, the removal of internal obstacles to growth, i.e. a transformation of the social structure. In the classical era of capitalism the bourgeoisie, having established its own state, demolished feudalism and went on to defeat the challenge of the embryonic proletariat in a process which Gramsci calls the 'permanent revolution'.[63] In France the aristocracy was destroyed, while in England it was absorbed into the bourgeoisie. In a later period in Japan the bourgeois revolution was carried through, without first demolishing feudalism altogether, by a

---

62. In 1968 itself the Chairman of the Agricultural Prices Commission had considered a 10 million tonnes buffer stock necessary for price stability. (See A. Mitra, 'Bumper Harvest Has Created Some Dangerous Illusions', the *Statesman Weekly*, 19 October, 1968.) The government's target and achievement, however, fell consistently and considerably short of this. Even at the end of June 1972, when procurement from the new *rabi* crop had pushed stocks higher than ever before, total stocks – buffer *and* operational (for the public distribution system) – amounted to 8·8 million tonnes. See Reserve Bank of India, *Bulletin*, October 1972, pp. 1716–17.

63. A. Gramsci, *The Modern Prince and Other Writings* (paperback edition), New York, 1968, p. 167.

fascist state which had its own colonies. Today, in India or other Third World countries, the bourgeoisie, arriving too late on the scene, is forced to ally itself with remnants of feudalism; and, having no colonies and being threatened by the increasing political consciousness of the people, it is re-integrated into the imperial structure. Compromising with feudalism, it is forced to compromise with imperialism. The fact that the Indian bourgeoisie seeks repeatedly to assert its independence testifies to its relative strength: the fact that it fails testifies to the objective limits to bourgeois revolution today.

Politics and Society in Bengal
Premen Addy and Ibne Azad

Bengal was the microcosm of British rule in India, the original seat of Imperial power, the base from which the East India Company set out on its career of aggrandizement, ending in the complete subjugation of the subcontinent from the Khyber to Cape Comorin. Private loot, the organized spoliation of commerce, industry and agriculture, far-reaching administrative innovations, educational reforms, the acceptance of new and liberating ideas from the West by a rising and articulate bourgeoisie, the intensification of certain archaic social relations by the colonial power – these were all part of the complex and contradictory fabric of colonized Bengal. It was against this background that initial indications emerged of an Indian national consciousness and of the rival forms such consciousness could assume. Through the prism of Bengal's historical experience were to be refracted significant themes of the later development of India as a whole.

The Delta and Bengal Society

The environment of Bengal is formed by the confluence of the Ganges and the Brahmaputra which drain the upper Gangetic basic and Tibetan Plateau. The vortex of these rivers has created one of the world's largest, most fertile and dynamic deltic expanses. And much of the specificity of Bengal's social and historical experience in South Asia derives from the social formation arising in this unique delta. The aboriginal migrants who progressively settled the delta – and whose descendants constitute the mass of Bengal's population today – developed techniques of deep-water cultivation and fishing intimately suited to the fertile but inundated and shifting alluvium of the delta. A relatively low division of labour and exceedingly unstable communications produced a decentralized and un-differentiated society.[1] As a result it proved particularly difficult to raise or impose the types of socio-religious order characteristic of the more centralized and stratified Aryan civilizations emerging in the upper Gangetic plain to the north-west. Moreover, situated in the extreme Eastern portion of the South Asian subcontinent, Bengal always remained peripheral to the processes of imperial consolidation of the earlier Hindu and Moghul periods. There tended to be a sharp division between the indigenous population of Bengal and those alien élites who conquered and reared a state apparatus above them. Moreover the Bengalis were often able to exploit the favours of geography – the inaccessibility and fertility of their land – to adapt to their conquerors on their own terms.

Brahmanism spread to Bengal during the consolidation of the Gupta Empire in the fifth century, while Islam followed in the wake of the Turko-Afghan conquest in the thirteenth century.[2] Both these invasions and their associated religions had similar effects on the indigenous population in Bengal. Both Hindu and Muslim conquerors promoted local conversion during their respective periods of rule. Blt the popular forms of Brahmanism and Islam differed radically from the orthodoxy of these

1. Ralph W. Nicholas, 'Ecology and Village Structure in Deltic West Bengal', *Economic and Political Weekly* 15, 1185–96; also 'Villages of the Bengal Delta: a Study of Ecology and Peasant Society', unpublished Ph.D. dissertation University of Chicago, 1962. For many helpful suggestions in the preparation of this article we would like to thank Richard Nations, Rokeya Rahman Kabir, P. N. Chaudhuri and Robin Blackburn.

2. Ramkrishna Mukherjee, 'Social Background of Bangladesh', *Economic and Political Weekly*, vol. 7, Annual Number, February 1972, pp. 265–74.

rulers.[3] The conquering castes of Brahman, Baidya and Kay-astha branded the local population ritually inferior and low caste, while the latter responded with mass support for every major anti-Brahminical movement throughout Bengali history – Buddhism, Vaishnavism and Islam. And when approximately half of Bengal's low-caste local population converted to Islam after it became associated with state power, the converts found themselves little better off in the professedly egalitarian eyes of the Turko-Afghan élites of Islam. These claimed themselves to be *Asharif* – Noble Born, descended from the line of the Prophet – while condescending to label their Bengali brethren *Ajlaf* – ignoble – an Islamic equivalent of 'low caste'.[4] More-over, the Islamic conquest incorporated the upper class of learned and landed Hindu castes as the privileged functionaries necessary to mediate Islamic rule with the local population.[5] And just as wealthy Hindus served the Moghuls in admin-istration, so they did in commerce as well. For the state formed an alliance with the House of Jagath Seth, North Indian *banyans* (a Hindu commercial caste), in order to develop luxury craft industries and commerce.[6] Historically Bengal special-

3. A. Karim, *Social History of Muslims in Bengal* (*down to 1538*), Pakistan, 1959.

4. Ahmad Imtiaz, 'The Asharif–Ajlaf Categories in Indo-Muslim Society', *Economic and Political Weekly*, 2, 1967, pp. 887–90.

5. Phillip B. Calkins, 'The Formation of a Regionally Oriented Ruling Group in Bengal, 1700–1740', *Journal of Asian Studies* 29, pp. 807–21.

6. In the concluding years of the seventeenth century Bengal pre-sented a remarkable picture of prosperity. The Venetian, Manouchi, who became Chief Physician to the Moghul Emperor, Aurangzeb, has left us the following description: 'Bengal is of all kingdoms of the Mogul best known in France. The prodigious riches transported thence into Europe are proofs of its great fertility. We may venture to say that it is not inferior in anything to Egypt, and it even exceeds that kingdom in its products of silks, cottons, sugar and indigo. All things are in plenty here, fruits, pulse, grain, muslins, cloths of gold and silk.' Yet in that century Moghul rule in Bengal bore the stamp of a foreign

ized in the production of muslin and other high quality cloths.

The majority of the population of East Bengal were converted to the Muslim religion, while the population of the smaller western part remained Hindu. No adequate explanation of this differing pattern of conversion has been advanced, though it is clear that rejection of the Hindu religion by the low-caste Bengalis was a form of revolt against the oppression and stigma to which they were subject. For a variety of reasons it seems that the traditional mechanisms of social control were more resilient in the western part of Bengal and even the appearance of a Muslim ruling power was insufficient to break the hold of the Hindu religion. Historically West Bengal occupies the moribund region of the delta which is not subject to the massive annual floods which inundate the eastern region. In the West there have long been more stable communications as a consequence, and more sophisticated forms of cultivation and social differentiation. Better communications meant that West Bengal could be more securely integrated into the Hindu culture of the upper Gangetic basin. A more elaborate social division of labour multiplied the different categories of social and economic organization, allowing caste organization to establish a firmer grip in the West than in the East. However it should be remembered that a sizeable majority of the population of Bengal as a whole did become Muslim. It was the prodigious growth of Calcutta which was later somewhat to increase the social weight of the western part and hence of those Bengalis who remained Hindu.

---

conquest, with much of its wealth drained away to other parts of India, in order to finance the wars of the Delhi Court. However, from 1700, under the stewardship of Murshed Quli Khan, it reached new heights of prosperity; its administration was without doubt the strongest and most stable in the country; its finances much the soundest. While the beams and rafters of the Moghul Empire were collapsing from inner decay, Bengal was about the only province to stand firm amid the confused ruins.

Thus on the eve of the British conquest Bengali society displayed a complexity of social division reflecting caste, communal and status differences. But underlying all these was the basic class division between the bulk of the cultivating and artisan population in the villages,[7] and the élites who lived off their surplus in the forms of state taxes, feudal exactions and commercial profits. These élites formed a class alliance of the dominant higher-caste Hindus and the Muslim aristocrats who controlled the administrative and military state machine, in conjunction with North Indian traders who controlled commercial capital. The British disturbed this order, introducing a new structure of collaboration,[8] geared to the evolution of capitalism in Europe. As we have seen, the Bengali élite had been able to accommodate to previous invaders on their own terms. But this new conquest brought in its train all the fateful and potent forces of ascendant capitalism and imperialism. The future was to show that the traditional mechanisms of accommodation and absorption were no match for these implacable furies. In a bid to adjust to the colonial system the order of

7. Most observers and historians of rural Bengal have commented on the common matrix of social and cultural forms which integrates Muslims and Hindus at the village level (cf. Uma Guha, 'Caste Among Rural Bengali Muslims', *Man in India*, vol. 45, pp. 167–69; Robert Glasse, 'La société musalmane dans le Pakistan rural de l'est', *Études Rurales*, 1966, nos. 22, 23, 24, 188–205) while popular forms of both Islam and Hinduism reflect a common pan-Bengali background (cf. A. R. Mallick, *British policy and the Muslims of Bengal, 1757–1856*, Asiatic Society of Pakistan, 1961; and Ralph W. Nicholas, 'Islam and Vaishvanism in Rural Bengal', in David Kopf, ed., *Bengal Regional Identity*, Michigan State University Asian Studies Centre. Occasional Paper, 1969, pp. 33–47).

8. The use of the word collaboration denotes a structural rather than a pejorative concept here. For a discussion of the relation between different structures of collaboration and imperial history, cf. Ronald Robinson, 'Non-European Foundations of European Imperialism: Sketch for a Theory of Collaboration', in *Studies in the Theory of Imperialism*, ed. Roger Owen and Bob Sutcliff, London, 1972.

dominance among the élites was to invert, while the mass of Bengal's cultivating population was to experience a severe intensification of social oppression.

The East India Company

Attracted by the commercial profits to be gained from trade in the luxury commodities produced in Bengal, the East India Company quickly stepped in to exploit the political and social contradictions in this rich Moghul province and bring it under control. Colluding with a section of the landed Hindus as well as with the Seths, whose profit margins were hampered by Moghul impositions on commerce, the East India Company arranged their victory at Plassey in a manner which, in the words of K. M. Panikkar, was 'a transaction not a battle, a transaction by which the compradors of Bengal led by Jagath Seth sold the Nawab to the East India Company'.

Once in control the Company rapidly opened Bengal to speculators and profiteers from Europe, and through vicious commercial exploitation directed the wealth of the province into the private fortunes and capital accumulation of the British.[9] In 1770, within two decades of British conquest, famine carried off 10 million people, or one third of the population of the province. This holocaust made it apparent even to the freebooters of the East India Company that only a pro-

9. Specific were the grievances voiced by some of the country's notables in a petition sent to the Calcutta Council: 'The factories of the English gentlemen are many and many of their gomastas are in all places and in every village, almost throughout the province of Bengal. They trade ... in all kinds of grain, linen, and whatever other commodities are provided in the country. In order to purchase these articles they force their money on the ryots and having by these oppressive methods bought the goods at low rate, they oblige their inhabitants and shopkeepers to take them at a high price, exceeding what is paid in the markets', quoted in R. C. Majumdar, et al., *An Advanced History of India*, London, 1965, p. 675.

ductive society is worth dominating. Attention was turned to stabilizing the internal order of Bengal, and thus the British shifted from commercial plunder to more orderly and permanent forms of exploitation and government.[10] In 1772 the fiction of the Nawab's authority was finally removed, and Warren Hastings, with an advisory council of four, was entrusted with the task of administration.

Private loot was now brought under stricter control, but there was no let-up in organized exploitation, of which the leading victim was the cotton weaving industry, the pride of Bengal, whose muslins and calicos sold in Asiatic and European markets. The weavers felt the full weight of the Company's newly acquired authority; and artisans were obliged to work for the Company's administered prices.

The Company, having acquired a virtual monopoly over the industry, squeezed and bullied the weavers into submission. The famine of 1770 had been a severe blow, for apart from carrying off thousands of village craftsmen, it caused irreparable damage to the domestic market. Nevertheless, even after this disaster the industry had its minor booms. The growing influx of cheap Manchester textiles however – the first fruits of the Industrial Revolution – signalled its end. And with it

10. 'The link between the forms of exploitation, the violent form by way of direct seizure and the "peaceful" form by way of exchange on an unequal footing, is particularly clear in the case of India. In the provinces of Bengal, Bihar and Orissa, the East India Company had acquired exemption from all transit tolls or export dues for its own international trade. But its employees soon began to apply this exemption, illegally, to internal trade, within these provinces where the Indian merchants were subjected to heavy taxation. "The company's agents whose goods were transported quite free of duty, whereas other merchants' goods were heavily burdened, quickly concentrated in their hands the whole of the country's trade, thereby drying up one of the sources of the public revenue"' [a contemporary observation] (Ernest Mandel, *Marxist Economic Theory*, London, 1968, p. 446). See also Paul Baran, *The Political Economy of Growth*, London, 1973, pp. 277–85.

went the dream of economic recovery, for the prosperity of Bengal had rested more on its domestic handicrafts than on its agriculture. The weaver-cum-agriculturist had now to depend entirely on agriculture, and this further weakened the position of the tenant *vis-à-vis* the landlord.

The Company's Land Tenure System, introduced in 1793, proved little short of a disaster, and its effects may be seen in Bengal even to this day.

The decline of the great towns of Bengal, and the rise of Calcutta, was a barometer of economic and social change. Dacca, the centre of a thriving textile industry, fell into a state of obvious decay. In 1765 it still had a population of 450,000; by 1800, this had dwindled to a mere 20,000. Murshidabad, the old capital, was fast fading into the greenery of the encroaching jungle; only Calcutta seemed to prosper and gain new life. The reasons were clear to see, for while the artisan-cum-agriculturist was yoked to a new tyranny, and the ruling Muslim aristocrat deprived of his power fell back on the memories of past glory, the nascent bourgeoisie, typified by the *banyan*, gained most from the changing economic situation.

The Permanent Settlement

The opening decades of the nineteenth century placed Bengal on the threshold of momentous social and economic changes which were to wrench it into the 'modern' world of global imperialism and dependent capitalist development. At the heart of the new social and economic order introduced by the British was the Permanent Settlement. Drawn from the enlightenment theories of the French Physiocrats and the later English Utilitarians, the colonial administration introduced private property relations in Bengal in conjunction with fixing *in perpetuity* the revenue demanded by the state. Guaranteed rights to the agricultural surplus and protected from the fluctuations of state tax, the landlord would presumably reorganize production along more profitable lines. The state however blundered in the implementation of the scheme. Since they were settling permanently with the Bengali landlords, the British established a taxation schedule which was much higher and more efficiently collected than the levies it replaced.[11] The excessively high revenue demands of the state were backed up by market auctions for arrears in payment. This drove the old Moghul estate owners to parcel, sell, and subinfeudate their patrimony. A revolution in land holdings followed which reversed the relations between the landed élites of the old Moghul system. For, well insured in the service of an alien power, it was the three upper Hindu castes who first rushed into the service of the European commercial houses and attracted the profits available to those who purveyed the credit and knowledge necessary for foreign traders to do business. These *banyans* – by the time of Plassey composed almost exclusively of Brahmans, Vaidyas, and Kayasthas[12] – gained the cash incomes and legal knowledge

11. In imposing the Permanent Settlement on the people of Bengal, Bihar and Orissa, the British government's aim was clearly stated by William Bentinck, the Governor-General, in 1828: 'If security was wanting against popular tumult or revolution, I should say that the Permanent Settlement, though a failure in many other respects and in most essentials, has this great advantage at least of having created a vast body of rich landed proprietors deeply interested in the continuance of the British Dominion and having complete command over the mass of the people.' (*Speeches and Documents on Indian Policy 1750 to 1921*, edited by A. B. Keith, vol. 1, p. 125.)

12. Before 1757, the majority of *banyans* belonged to the Vaisya caste whose traditional occupation within the Hindu system had been business and commerce. The dramatic increase in the private trade of the Company's servants in the period after Plassey saw a corresponding rise in the number of *banyans*, whose ranks were now swelled by high-caste Bengali Hindus migrating to Calcutta in fairly large numbers. Considerable fortunes were amassed. For example Hidaram Banerjee and Montur Mukherjee became millionaires, while Ramdulal Dey, with his profitable commercial and shipping interests frequently lent money even to American traders. The Bengali *banyan* was 'interpreter, head book-keeper, head secretary, head broker, the

necessary to capture the frantic land-market when the Moghul aristocracy were brought to book for arrears in revenue. Immediately after the Permanent Settlement the big estates were broken up and passed from Muslim to almost exclusively Hindu élites, who were already entrenched in the administrative service of the British and now consolidated their hold on the land as well.

Not only did the Permanent Settlement invert the hierarchy of the propertied classes of Bengali society, it also radically transformed the relations between the cultivating peasantry and those classes living off their surplus. Bengal agriculture traditionally and to this day has been organized by present families occupying small holdings which they cultivate with low technology and their own labour, supplemented marginally by the labour of the community and hired help. Under the Moghul system these families held the right to permanent occupation of their holdings against the obligation to cultivate the land and pay state tax, which although roughly equivalent to the peasant's surplus, remained reasonably fixed over the generations. The Permanent Settlement, by concentrating proprietary rights in the hands of the former state revenue collector (the *zamindar*), wiped out at a stroke the peasant's hold on his land at the same time as transforming payments from a constant form of tax to *rent* which could be legally set at any level pleasing the landlord. Against the peasant's appeal to custom and tradition the British land-laws placed the courts at the disposal of the *zamindar* to evict and distrain the property of the resistant peasant. Thus were knocked away the traditional barriers to the predatory exactions of the non-cultivating classes, and far from stimulating capitalist

---

supplier of cash and cash keeper'. He 'knew all the ways, all the little frauds, all the defensive armour, all the artifices and the contrivances by which abject slavery secures itself against the violence of power'. (Quoted in N. K. Sinha, Economic History of Bengal, Calcutta, 1956, vol. 1, p. 91.)

investment, British concepts of private property opened the way for urban-based rentiers to drain the capital from the countryside, disinvest agriculture, and impoverish the peasantry. By transforming the relations of tenure, the Permanent Settlement entirely blocked a similar transformation of the relations of production, instead it introduced rack-rents which intensified pre-capitalist exploitation.

The New Class Balance

The Permanent Settlement created a new alignment of class forces on the land. While the Moghul aristocracy dwindled into a noble penury, the traditionally landed Hindu élite extended their hold across the entire rural structure of Bengal through urban and comprador connections. Relations between the bulk of Bengal's peasant mass and their non-labouring landlords were stratified along class lines defined by unrestricted rent and increasingly subject to the forces of the global capitalist market. The British also contrived the destruction of a large part of Bengal's traditional textile industry by encouraging British firms to take over the Indian market while prohibiting the export of Indian textiles to Britain. Those who survived, prospered and seized the advantages of Bengal's new land system formed the nucleus of a new social élite and collaborationist class – the *bhadralok*.[13]

13. The *bhadralok* (literally 'respectable people' or 'gentlemen') was distinguishable by both class and caste, and became in the course of the next two centuries, an élite unique to Bengal. 'The great majority of these classes belong to the three great Hindu literacy castes, the Brahman, the Vaidyas (doctors), and the Kayasthas (writers), who are relatively more numerous in Bengal than are the corresponding castes in any other part of India. For untold centuries they have been the administrators, the priests, the teachers, the lawyers, the doctors, the writers, the clerks of the community. Every successive Government in Bengal has drawn its core of minor officials from among them, the British equally with their Muslim predecessors. They have therefore always formed an educated class, and it may safely be

The Bhadralok in Calcutta

The *bhadralok* was drawn from the dominant Hindu castes who had served in the military and administrative offices of the Moghuls. Collaboration with foreign rule, secured mainly through their mastery of alien languages, formed part of their social and cultural heritage. Thus if one foot of the *bhadralok* was deeply implanted in the Permanent Settlement land-system, the other stepped into the offices, judiciary, schools and professions opened up by the new colonial administration in Calcutta – the commercial and political centre of British rule in South Asia. Mastery of English and a fastidious concern over education became their hallmark. Thus garnished with the cul-

---

said that there is no class of corresponding magnitude and importance in any other country which has so continuous a tradition of literacy, extending over so many centuries. It has always been the first duty of every father in these castes, however poor he might be, to see that his sons obtain the kind of education dictated by the tradition of their caste.' (*Calcutta University Commission*, 1917–19, Report Cd. Papers 386, vol. 14, 1919, chapter 2, p. 28). Contemporary sociologists and historians stress the Weberian status group aspect of *bhadralok* culture. They are 'distinguished by many aspects of their behaviour – their deportment, their speech, their dress, their style of housing, their occupations and their associations – and quite as fundamentally by their cultural values and their sense of propriety.' (J. H. Broomfield, *Élite Conflict in a Plural Society: Twentieth-Century Bengal*, Berkeley, 1968, pp. 5–6.) It was possible to join *bhadralok* ranks through education as well as birth, but control of education networks was rigidly class-based. There was considerable social differentiation within the ranks of the *bhadralok*: the *abhjiat bhadralok* consisted of large property owners and senior Government officers and the *grihasta bhadralok* consisted of shopkeepers, small *zamindars* and white-collar workers. This element of social mobility through education and wealth is epitomized by the careers of Motilal Seal, a *subarnavanik* (unclean *Sudra*) and Gaurchand Basak, whose name denotes his origins as a weaver of low ritual status, both of whom were leading *bhadralok* of Calcutta.

ture of their new rulers, the *bhadralok* performed bureaucratic and professional functions necessary to mediate British rule to the native population.[14]

As in the past, the upper caste *bhadralok* remained aloof from the demeaning occupations of commerce. Hence the enormous wealth that was being accumulated by Bengal's integration in the world market fell into the hands of non-Bengali trading castes – principally Marwaris, Gujaratis, and Armenians. But if the *bhadralok* did not tap the wealth gained in commerce, neither did they descend into the dishonour of physical labour: and the metropolitan demand for menials, porters, domestic servants and the like was answered by the non-Bengalis from the famine districts of Bihar and Uttar Pradesh. Thus the *bhadralok* occupied in their own metropolis the position of a middle class, in the sense that the hands of non-Bengali classes were – in their eyes – soiled by trades or labour.[15]

14. The extent to which the high castes dominated official and administrative appointments is spelled out in the 1901 *Census of India,* Vol. 6, pp. 486 and 506:

	Appointments in covenanted and statutory civil services	High government appointments		% of total population
		Number	% of total	
Brahman Vaidya Kayastha	22	1104	80·2	5·2
Lower caste Hindus	0	131	9·5	41·8
Muslims	3	141	10·3	51·2

Source: J. H. Broomfield, *Élite Conflict in a Plural Society: Twentieth-Century Bengal,* Berkeley, 1968, pp. 5–12

15. According to the 1881 Census the population of Calcutta was 790,286, of which less than two thirds were Hindu and less than two thirds spoke Bengali as their mother tongue, while only 26·5 per cent of the inhabitants were born in the city; as many as 47·6 per cent came from Bihar, Orissa and Bhota Nagpur (all non-Bengali-speaking

And while the former grew richer and the latter toiled in poverty, the *bhadralok* secured fees in the middle ground of bureaucracy and education. This ethnic class stratification emerged in the pre-industrial period. But later in the twentieth century, when industrial capital and a proletariat were to accumulate in a concentrated belt of jute and cotton mills around Calcutta, the ethnic composition of the new classes was to remain the same. The *bhadralok* neither formed part of the new industrial bourgeoisie – composed mainly of Marwaris, Gujaratis and Sindhis – nor participated in the labour which generated their capital. Throughout the enormous social transformations which industry stimulated in Bengal the *bhadralok* were sustained by state employment and incomes from the land. Their 'middle class' position was to limit their social vision and so impede their political development. For the colonial land market and the bureaucracy of the raj secured the *bhadralok* all the advantages of the new order and placed them

---

areas). The pyramid of power had something of the following composition according to the 1901 Census. At the pinnacle stood 13,000 British who, secure in the control of government and the agency houses, formed one of the most exclusive and caste-conscious colonial élites in the imperial world. Beneath them were 16,000 Anglo-Indians whose reliable sycophancy earned them guild-like control of positions in communications, transport and customs. The industry developing along Hooghley-side in the processing of cotton and jute remained secure in European hands, while the burgeoning profits from inland trade in indigo, opium, jute, tea and sugar, etc., fell into the hands of a small community of Jews, Armenians, Bengali Hindu banking and trading castes, Gujerati Hindus and Muslims as well as Marwari Jain migrants from Rajputana. And as mentioned above the labour for services, transport, industry, etc., came from the rural immigrants from Bihar, UP and other non-Bengali provinces. The remainder were Bengali, and while a considerable proportion of these were *abhadra* (non-*bhadralok*) operating the marginal trades and markets, the majority were the white-collar, middle-class *bhadralok* who filled the offices, banks, courts, consulting-rooms, schools and colleges of the metropolis (op. cit., p. 3. Figures from the *Census of India* 1901, vol. 1, pt 1, p. 13).

at the centre of the economic, social and political contradictions of British Indian Bengal. The *bhadralok* were, first, the rent-receivers in a predominantly agrarian economy of insecure tenants, sharecroppers and casual labourers. Second, this Hindu élite had become landlords in a predominantly Muslim population. Third, the *bhadralok* were literate, English-speaking and prosperous in a society overwhelmingly illiterate, parochial and poor. Through their education, their professions and their cosmopolitan experience the *bhadralok* displayed to the mass of society the culture of their colonial overlords. Calcutta was capital of British India: as functionaries of alien rule, the *bhadralok* experienced intimate proximity to, but ultimate exclusion from, power.

The *bhadralok* reflected the essential ambiguity of all collaborating classes within Asian societies. Their vital role within the system of British rule stimulated the *bhadralok* appetite for political influence and power. But their lack of an *independence* grounded economically in control of capital, or socially in links with the proletarian and peasant masses, strictly compromised their politics and distorted their ideology: despite initiating the anti-colonial movement, the *bhadralok* ultimately failed to mount a radical challenge and transform Bengali society.

The Bengal Renaissance

The first four decades of British dominance brought a swift upheaval to the vegetative tranquillity of society in Moghul Bengal. The rapid social change, as well as the cosmopolitan and colonial experience of the *bhadralok* began to register itself from about 1813 in a new intellectual awareness which grew until the turn of the twentieth century. This period, called the Bengali Renaissance, is distinguished by the prodigious intellectual achievement of the *bhadralok* intelligentsia. Confronted with the overwhelming power of European domination, they learnt English, French, Hebrew, Greek and Latin in search of the essence of the culture of the West.

Science, philosophy, social reform and Western education were subjects of intense interest to the variously divergent social and intellectual currents of the Renaissance. But, beyond agreement on the importance of European culture, the question of its relation to indigenous Hindu and Bengali society provoked deep and antagonistic splits. The dominant school – the 'self-strengtheners'[16] – sought to incorporate western intellectual traditions in order both to adapt the *bhadralok* politically to the new colonial structure, as well as confirm their social hegemony over Bengali society within the overall framework of a renewed Hinduism. The 'radicals' on the other hand deployed the newly discovered intellectual tools not to reconstruct the inequalities and mystifications of a crumbling society, but to challenge them.

The outstanding figure of the period and the one who stamped the dominant themes for the 'self-strengtheners', was Ram Mohan Roy, born in 1773 of a prominent landed family and himself long an employee of the East India Company, where he learned excellent English. Ram Mohan forged an ideological anchor for his class in the swift social currents of the earlier colonial period. Confronted with the threat of Christian missionaries on the one hand and the decomposition of his own religious and social heritage on the other, Ram Mohan's ambition was to borrow from the former in order to revitalize the latter. He learnt Hebrew and Greek and was in addition a considerable scholar of Persian and Sanskrit. He sought to unravel the philosophy and monotheism underlying Christianity, and with these he set out to reform the ideological and social

16. The 'self-strengtheners' included two broad trends: the Westernized liberals on the one hand, represented for example by the *Brahmo Samaj*, and on the other hand the 'traditionalists', who tended to isolate themselves from Western rationality. Both groups helped to establish the Landowners Association in 1838.

practice of Hinduism. He translated the monotheistic Up-anishads into Bengali, and founded the *Brahmo Samaj*, a society based on reason and tolerance which attempted reform of a number of Hinduism's archaic social practices – child marriage, *sati* (burning of widows on their husbands' funeral pyres), etc. Right into the twentieth century the *Brahmo Samaj* was to form some of the greatest leaders of Bengali cultural and political life.

Politically, Ram Mohan attempted to resolve the contradictions of his class – on the one hand leaders of a colonized population, on the other, agents of the colonial power – by affirming a Whiggish ideal of progress: for Ram Mohan, a free India would emerge after a period of British tutelage, since English rule 'was creating a middle class in India which would lead to a popular movement of emancipation'.[17] Within this context Ram Mohan agitated for an extension of civil and bourgeois freedoms: principal among these was the cause of the 'free press' which was burgeoning rapidly in Calcutta; abolition of discrimination against Indians in the judicial system, of which the most notorious example was the Jury Act; and a programme of administrative reforms including such items as the Indianization of the civil service.[18] Consistent with this programme was his prescription for political action – the reasoned petition couched in the language of universal rights – based on faith in an inevitable progress in parliamentary representation. These remained the dominant themes and tactics

17. Amit Sen, *Notes on the Bengal Renaissance*, Calcutta, 1957.

18. Neither was he insensitive to great events in the world outside. 'Freedom movements in the West sustained and intensified his love of liberty. If the suppression of liberty in Naples hurt him, the success of the cause of liberty in the Spanish Colonies in America and in France (the July Revolution of 1830) threw him into ecstasies of delight. No less was his jubilation when the Reform Bill was passed in 1832.' (Nirmal Sinha, *Freedom Movement in Bengal, 1888–1904*, Calcutta, 1968.)

of middle-class Bengali politics throughout the remainder of the century.[19]

The Derozians

The second generation of Bengali intellectuals was marked by the appearance of a group called 'Young Bengal', in the opinion of whose leader, Vivian Henry Derozio, an Eurasian from Calcutta, Ram Mohan and his movement went only 'half the way in religion and politics'. Within the short space of his twenty-three years, Derozio himself absorbed the works of such major figures as Adam Smith, Bentham, Berkeley, Locke, Mill, Hume and Kant, as well as being deeply influenced by the ideas of the French Revolution, principally those of Rousseau.[20] Derozio gathered around him a constellation of young intellectuals who

19. In one important respect, Ram Mohan transcended his class background. His criticism of the Permanent Settlement included the following programme of peasants' rights: (1) a permanent settlement for the cultivator, (2) public rent rolls, and (3) a peasant militia. But however genuinely enlightened such a programme, it remained generally extraneous to Ram Mohan's own political thought, and certainly alien to the political behaviour of his class, which as we shall see was motivated by a concrete fear of the peasant masses. (See Sinha, ibid., p. 70 and *passim*.)

20. Tom Paine's *Age of Reason* considerably influenced the Derozians. The danger of this Alexander Duff, the well-known Christian missionary, pointed out in no uncertain terms. It was, he observed, 'some wretched bookseller of the United States of America, who – basely taking advantage of the reported infidel of a new race of men in the East (meaning the Derozians), and apparently regarding no one but his silver dollars – dispatched to Calcutta cargo of that most malignant and pestiferous of all anti-Christian publications. From one ship a thousand copies were landed, and at first sold at the cheap rate of one rupee per copy; but such was the demand, that the price soon rose and after a few months, it was actually quintupled. Besides the separate copies of the *Age of Reason* there was also a cheap American edition, in one thick Volume of eight of Paine's works, including the *Rights of Man*, and other minor pieces, political and theological.' (Quoted by Benoy Ghosh, 'Calcutta, City of Renaissance', *Frontier*, 3 March 1973.)

quickly rejected the intellectual pabulum of Ram Mohan's *Brahmo Samaj*. Rather than strengthen an atavistic culture, their critique struck at the roots of Hinduism's élitist priestcraft and mystification.[21] On social issues the Derozians went beyond reform of abuses to expose the hideous inequality and repression of Bengali society. Derozians argued for the emancipation of women,[22] the abolition of the caste system, and the liberation of the low and untouchable castes.[23] And whereas the *bhadralok* universally supported western education for their wealthy or poor brethren, Derozians promoted schemes for mass compulsory, state-supported education among the peasantry,[24] and female education, as well as a simplified style of the Bengali language which had become florid and incomprehensibly sanskritized in the hands of the *literati*.[25]

21. As a lecturer at Hindu College he gathered around him Bengal's young talent, whose great passion was to discuss the leading issues of the day in the light of reason, and who took delight in escaping the totems and taboos of popular Hindu beliefs and practices. They 'cut their way through ham and beef and waded to liberalism through tumblers of beer'. Derozio was accused of being a corrupter of youth and was eventually dismissed from his job.

22. Dakshinaranjan Mukerji donated the site for Bethune College for Women, and was later forced out of Calcutta society. K. M. Banerjea published a paper, 'Native Female Education', in which he supported mass education as the only means to emancipate women from male, and Hindu, tyranny. Also, Peary Chand Mitra and Radhanath Sikdar supported women's rights in their monthly, *Masik Patrika*.

23. Again K. M. Banerjea wrote a blistering denunciation of Brahmanical priestcraft, supporting the emancipation of Untouchables and the low-caste. R. Sikdar, a diarist and mathematician, wrote drawing attention to the oppression of coolies.

24. Lal Behari Day, although not considered a Derozian, reflected many of their ideas. In a vivid and relentless social novel, *Govinda Samanta*, he revealed the class structure of the *zamindari* system, and proposed a system of mass, compulsory education supported by a land tax.

25. The Derozian *Masik Patrika*, founded in 1857, crusaded for a simplified style of Bengali to promote mass literacy.

In the field of ideas the Derozians broke through the cramping limitations of both their conquerors and their class. In the work of the 'self-strengtheners' it is not difficult to detect a retarding influence of British bourgeois culture. The British ruling class transmitted to the new Bengali élite a measure of its own high-minded hypocrisy and religiosity, its hide-bound traditionalism and blinkered empiricism, its narrow and mean utilitarianism in practical affairs. That is why too many of the *bhadralok* intelligentsia spent their time poring over the Bible and Jeremy Bentham. But the Derozians were more successful in penetrating the thick fog of British mystagogy and making themselves familiar with the achievements of the Enlightenment and of the French Revolution. The tragedy of the Derozians was that their Enlightenment aspirations carried them far beyond the preoccupations of their own class without allowing them to establish an organic link with the mass of the exploited and the oppressed. Almost every leading Derozian was to be disinherited or run out of respectable Hindu society. However, the wider horizons they opened up were to be a permanent acquisition of Bengali culture, and their tradition was perpetuated through the newspapers and associations they founded.[26] Although isolation and harassment were eventually to drive some of the leading Derozians to embrace Christianity, it remains the case that their movement sowed a seed of secular and radical nationalism that was to be in sharp contrast to the reactionary obscurantism that was to play such a large part in the subsequent history of the subcontinent.

Derozio's own hopes are best summed up in a poem he addressed to his pupils at the Hindu College:

> Expanding like the petals of young flowers
> I watch the gentle opening of your minds,
> And the sweet loosening of the spell that binds

26. Derozian papers included: the *Athenium*, organ of Derozio's own Academic Association, *Mukherji's Magazine*, K. M. Banerjea's *Enquirer*, and the *Bengal Spectator*.

Your intellectual energies and powers
That stretch (like young birds in soft summer hours)
Their wings to try their strength. O how the winds
Of circumstances and freshening April showers
Of early knowledge and outnumbered kinds
Of new perceptions shed their influence,
And how you worship truth's omnipotence:
What joyance rains upon me when I see
Fame in the mirror of futurity,
Weaving the chaplets you have yet to gain
Ah then I feel I have not lived in vain.

The 'spell' that bound the intellectual energies and powers of Young Bengal was, regretfully, to prove most difficult to exorcise, since it was intimately associated with the peculiar social formation that colonialism had created in the province. Confronted with the oppression of British rule, even some of the latter-day Derozians were to search for consolations in India's past. The following poem by Madhusudan Dutt suggests the polished literary form which the Bengal Renaissance was to give to *bhadralok* aspiration : the King Porus it invokes is, of course, the monarch defeated by Alexander – like the British, Indians find the celebration of their defeats morally more stimulating than the celebration of victories:

But where, Oh! where is Porus now?
And where the noble hearts that bled
For freedom – with the heroic glow
In patient bosoms nourished –
Hearts, eagle-like that recked not death,
And shrank before foul Thraldom's breath?
And where art thou – Fair Freedom! – thou
Once goddess of Ind's sunny clime!
When glory's halo round her brow
Shone radiant, and she rose sublime,
Like her own towering Himalaye
To kiss the blue clouds thron'd on high!
Clime of the Sun! – How like a Dream –

> How like bright sunbeams on a stream
> That melt beneath gray twilight's eye –
> That glory hath now flitted by!

These yearnings for the glory that had 'flitted by' were to prove particularly insubstantial during the Mutiny: this attempt to chase away the colonizers and restore the past by force of arms met the uncompromising hostility of every *bhadralok*. 'How like a Dream', indeed. However regressive the social and political character of the 1857 uprising, it was nevertheless a remarkable display of Hindu-Muslim solidarity. More the pity that the *bhadralok* were unable to consolidate and develop this aspect of the Mutiny, within, of course, a different political perspective, during the course of the next fifty or a hundred years.

Thus the different strands of the Renaissance included those who imbibed the liberal ethos of British culture, and others who wished to modernize Indian traditions, as well as the more radical Derozians who attacked class and privilege but remained politically unorganized and alienated from a wider social base in Bengali society. The focus of *bhadralok* politics throughout the middle and later decades of the nineteenth century remained essentially that of enlightened collaborators: acceptance of the colonial order while agitating for reforms allowing a wider middle-class participation in the power it created. The British were to nourish constitutionalism by setting up elective bodies with limited power and on the basis of a narrow franchise.

The Bhadralok and the Peasantry

The peasantry did not meanwhile remain entirely passive under the arrangement imposed upon them by the colonial system. We noted above how the Permanent Settlement clarified the class stratification of agrarian society and placed the question of rent at the heart of rural social relations. Two major developments of the century, a rapid growth of population and the introduction of commercial crops, aggravated these relations, provoked a harsher oppression of the peasantry, and stimulated the emergence of organizations uniting Bengal's Muslim and Hindu cultivators.

The economic changes introduced by the British stimulated both the internal and international market demand for Bengal's agrarian produce from the beginning of the nineteenth century. The pace rapidly accelerated following 1870, when the revolution in industrial production and world communications – the growth of railways in Europe and North America as well as in India and Bengal, the opening of the Suez Canal – drew Bengal into a much more tightly integrated world economy.[27] Agrarian produce diversified and by the late nineteenth century involved a variety of commercial crops such as tea, indigo, rice, opium, jute and sugar-cane distributed throughout the hinterland of the Bengal Presidency. Yet the powerful market stimulus these crops exerted on agriculture failed fundamentally to transform Bengal's production along capitalist lines.[28] The

27. Binay Bhushan Chaudhuri, 'Growth of Commercial Agriculture in Bengal – 1859–1885', part 1, *The Indian Economic and Social History Review*, vol. 7, no. 1, March 1970, pp. 25–60; also A. Knowles, *The Industrial and Commercial Revolutions in Great Britain during the Nineteenth Century*, London, 1930, p. 182.

28. The reasons for this are: (1) capital remained largely in the hands of Europeans who found it more expedient to make advances to the peasants on contract, obliging them to sell the harvest often at a pre-determined and non-market price; (2) commercial crop production thus remained in the hands of the peasantry who organized it along traditional lines within the context of subsistence rice cultivation; and (3) what increased income market prices promised the cultivator was skimmed off by non-cultivating classes through rent, interests, and suppressed market prices. (Cf. Chaudhuri, ibid., part 2, op. cit, vol. 7, no. 2, June 1970, *passim*.) The exception is tea, which from the beginning was cultivated along modern capitalist lines on huge estates served by wage labour; but although stimulating the surrounding peasant economy, the tea plantation remained entirely outside the context of peasant agriculture.

growth of commercial crops raised land values and agricultural prices, but these were met in step by increases in both rent and interest, and a lowering of buying price, which together directed the increased surplus into the hands of rentiers and moneylenders. At the same time the demographic balance shifted against the peasantry, as the growth of population transformed Bengal from a land- to a labour-abundant economy. A plethora of labour and prospective tenants increased the landlord's leverage over the peasants.[29] Thus rather than bringing increasing prosperity to Bengal's peasants, commercial cropping simply touched off intensified exploitation, while exposing all the more clearly the parasitic nature of Bengal's dominant rural classes.

The peasantry did not however accept the continual deterioration of their social and economic condition without protest. And while the *bhadralok* were captivated to distraction by the liberal spirit, the peasantry organized throughout the hinterland on economic and social issues affecting most of them more specifically. The three major peasant movements of the nineteenth century – *Fara'idi* or *Faraji* (1810–30), the Indigo Riots (1859–60), and the Pabna Rent Revolt (1873) – were manifestations of the ground swell of popular reaction to the colonial structure. Moreover, the politics surrounding these events expose clearly how relations between the various communal, social, and political blocs composing Bengali society centred upon the class issue of rents. The first of these movements, the *Faraji*, began as a form of Muslim revivalism to 'purify' the

29. The basic fact of Bengali rural life in the nineteenth century and down to the present is that the majority of the landholdings are not sufficiently large to support the families who cultivate and live off them. The index of this fact is the overwhelming indebtedness of the Bengali peasantry, which is recorded throughout the reports of official commissions and district officers. (Cf., Binay Bhushan Chaudhuri, 'Rural Credit Relations in Bengal, 1859–1885', *The Indian Economic and Social History Review*, vol. 6, no. 3, September 1969, pp. 203–58.)

religious practices of Muslim Bengalis.[30] In Bengal the move-ment reflected the declining position of the Muslim aristocracy and the subordination of the majority of Muslim peasantry to Hindu landlords. By propagating strict Islamic observances, the movement first tended to rend the syncretic cultural fabric which tied Hindu and Muslim cultivators in a common social life. By 1810, however, although maintaining its religious cover, it had broadened along class lines, beginning most significantly in the areas where a system of commercial indigo plantations was being organized by European capital. A promi-nent *Faraji* leader, Didu Mian, organized cultivators, whether Hindu or Muslim, against European planters as well as indig-enous landlords and moneylenders, again regardless of re-ligion. By 1830, Titu Mian, the former leader's nephew, came into violent conflict with the English planters and native land-lords, and after a number of successes declared an entire area a free zone and assumed the title of Khalif. The British dis-patched the movement within a year and imprisoned or hanged its leaders. Discontent, however, smouldered, laying the ground for the much wider Indigo Riots of 1859.[31]

Indigo plantations were initially set up in Bengal in 1779 by the East India Company in order to meet American and Span-ish competition. West Indian planters with an intimate know-ledge of slavery first organized production along the conventional system of advances, but, once indigo had a hold in the community, relied increasingly on physical coercion and legal manipulation to force the peasant to grow the plant at a loss. By 1859 thousands of peasants had withdrawn their labour

30. The *Faraji* was merely the Bengali variant of the wider *Wahabi* movement throughout the Islamic world, by which the Muslim forces retreating under the advances of European colonialism attempted to retrieve their lost social and political stature through ritual purification. In many communities such as Bengal, once the movement took deep roots it was transformed along class lines.

31. Muin-ud Din Ahmad Khan, *The Fara'idi Movement*, Karachi, 1965.

and peasant organizations throughout the indigo districts resisted the repression of the planters and their armed retainers.
The breadth of agitation compelled the government to initiate
an official inquiry in 1860. And the combination of these
factors broke the plantation system in lower Bengal, forcing the
planters to move up-country to Bihar, where they re-established their operations on fresh ground.[32]

The response of the middle-class *bhadralok* to these peasant
movements revealed their own specific class interests and correspondingly underlined their political limitations. They
greeted the *Faraji* agitation with indifference, in contrast to
their unstinting support for the Indigo Rioters. Although the
latter event, with its anti-colonial and national character, was a
watershed in the awakening of Bengal's political consciousness,
the alliance between the middle and rural classes concealed a
fundamental ambiguity for whereas the *Faraji* movement was
directed against the *zamindari* system to which *bhadralok*
interests were intimately tied, the Indigo Riots focused much
more on European planters. Moreover, although indigo planting failed to interfere in production itself, it did advance new
credit agencies which uprooted local *mahajans* – moneylenders –
who were the central pillars of *zamindari* exploitation.[33]
Thus the *bhadralok* aligned with the peasantry in specific political opposition to the Europeans, while opposing generally
those interests of the peasantry which were at variance with
their own. The exceedingly tenuous basis of these alliances

32. B. Blair Kling, *The Blue Mutiny*, Pennsylvania, 1966; and
Dinabandhu Mitra, *Nil Darpan*. Girish Chandra Ghosh in his paper,
The Bengalee (August 1860), bore eloquent witness to the success of
the movement: 'not a spade was thrust into the soil in the cause of the
dye. Not a bucket was dipped into the stream to water an indigo plant.
The strike was universal and complete. For once Bengalees had united,
and not even cannon-balls could break the cohesion ... They went
into prisons by thousands and by tens of thousands ... It was at all
events a refuge from the godowns ...'

33. Chaudhuri, ibid., part 2, p. 229.

became much clearer during the Pabna Rent Revolt when no Europeans were involved.

The principal *parganas* (administrative units) of Pabna, which comprised the Raja of Notore's estate, were partitioned and bought up by the new squirearchy – the Tagores of Calcutta, the Banerjees of Dacca, the Sanyals of Sallop, the Parrasis of Sathal and the Bhaduris of Porjona.[34] As elsewhere, these pillars sank increasingly deep into the peasant's land through rack-rents and a myriad of extra-legal exactions. The predominantly Muslim peasantry organized against the landlords in the Pabna Agrarian League a peasants' union whose programme was clearly defined in terms of rent and similar issues and which, significantly, was under the leadership of two Hindus, Ishan Chandra Roy and Shambhunath Pal. A movement of general protest against absentee landlordism in the cash crop producing districts of East and Central Bengal, it brought to official attention the inadequacies of the existing law which regulated these agrarian relations. The landed *bhadralok* were quick to respond to the government-instituted inquiry, threatening legislation which might benefit the peasants. Under

34. The family tree of Rabindranath Tagore, Bengal's world-renowned poet, illustrates how the blossoms of *bhadralok* literary genius were firmly rooted in the collaboration, graft and landlordism which brought the Hindu élites to the top in the wake of British conquest. Jaya Ram, ancestor of the Tagore family of Bengal, took active part in the settlement of the 24 *Parganas* belonging to the East India Company. His second son, Darpa Narayan, learned English and French and through serving the French in Chittagong earned a huge fortune with which he bought a large *zamindari* in Rajshahi. Dwarkanath Tagore, *bhadralok* notable of Ram Mohan's generation and founder of the Landowners Association in 1838, descended from a junior branch of the family. Born in 1794 he learned English and Persian and became a law agent through which he acquired the landed property in Pabna. 'But it seems that his fortunes arose from his service as *serishta dar* (head clerk) to the Salt Agent and Collector of the 24 *Parganas* where he became a Diwan to the Agency.' B. Misra, *The Indian Middle Classes*, London, 1961, p. 127.)

the leadership of the Tagores, whose own estates were in question, the British Indian Association vigorously opposed any government intervention in tenant relations as a violation of the covenant between government and the landlords established by the Permanent Settlement. Moreover, organs of landlord opinion, the *Hindoo Patriot*, *Amrita Bazar Patrika*, and the *Halishahar Patrika*, indulged in the most odious obscurantism by claiming the League represented nothing more than the rabid communalism of Muslims bent on the plunder and arson of their Hindu neighbours. Despite these reactionary pressures the government instituted the Bengal Tenancy Act of 1885, partially relieving the landlords' grip on the cultivators by regulating questions of rent and conditions of property distraint.[35]

It is significant that while the mass action of the peasantry forced the British to make major changes in the agrarian structure such as the displacement of indigo plantations from lower Bengal, and the Tenancy Act of 1885, the constitutionalism of the Bengali liberals failed to achieve anything but minor concessions on issues that were of specific interest to them and hence of limited value to the great majority, such as the legislative and administrative reform, the Vernacular Press Act, etc. It is against this agrarian background of unrest and middle-class response that the political character of the Bengal Renaissance attains a clearer focus.

As the father of the Bengali Renaissance, Ram Mohan appears to be a classically bourgeois figure: rational in intellect, liberal in social matters, naïve in his optimism concerning political progress. There were however two crucial differences between him and other members of his generation, and the typical Enlightenment figure of the West. First, far from standing at the head of commerce, finance and industry, which were

35. Gupta, Kalyan Kumar Sen, 'The Agrarian League of Pabna, 1873', *The Indian Economic and Social History Review*, vol. 7, no. 2, June 1970, pp. 253–70.

carrying the European bourgeoisie to world hegemony, Ram Mohan represented a class based on land in a pre-capitalist society subordinated to colonial power. And second, for all his rationality, Ram Mohan and the 'self-strengtheners' clothed their intellect in the imagery of a Hinduism retrieved from decadent priestcraft and brought back to respectability.

And as the Whiggish optimism of his generation wore away under frustration at failure to achieve any significant political progress under British rule, constitutional reform was rapidly replaced after the turn of the century by mass anti-colonial militancy. But the *bhadralok*, unlike the Enlightenment bourgeoisie in Europe, could not give leadership to the mass movement on the basis of progressive economic and social issues.[36] They were themselves the product of the most retrograde social forces – rural rents and metropolitan collaboration; the only social base of anti-colonial power, their own tenants, presented a greater threat to their position than the British themselves. Renaissance politics stabilized the conflicting position of the *bhadralok* between the masses and the British into a Janus-like posture which looked to the colonial masters for enlightened reform, while turning the dark face of repression to the countryside. But under the pressures of mass unrest this posture became increasingly difficult to maintain. Against British repression, *bhadralok* enlightenment lost ground, while the threat of mass politicization persuaded significant sections of their class to seek in religion a bond with the peasant masses which material interest could not provide. And the continuing potency of religion must be seen as the ideological deposit of pre-capitalist social relations which imperialism had failed to transform. Over the next forty years the contradictions of the

36. There were instances where the *bhadralok* were able to generate forward-looking ideas. But it was their weakness that they failed to develop or incorporate them into a meaningful programme of social and economic change. The *Swadeshi* movement, which will be considered below, is a case in point.

bhadralok were to play themselves out in the concrete politics of the period.

The Indian Association

From 1880 the general crisis of Bengali society was beginning to be felt among the ranks of the *bhadralok* themselves. The growth of population along with an increased subinfeudation of landed estates combined to raise *bhadralok* numbers while simultaneously reducing the sources of landed income. Second, the Muslims responded to the colonial order – delayed by a generation – by placing their young on the competitive market for middle-class urban employment. And third, the up-country administrative and professional jobs which were formerly a *bhadralok* monopoly were increasingly reserved by the government for the growing numbers of the educated in the local community. As a net result the *bhadralok* were becoming more numerous as sources of employment and income declined. Increasing numbers of them were losing intimate touch with the village, becoming more Calcutta-based and dependent exclusively on urban employment. Thus the quarter of a century preceding the Partition of Bengal in 1905 is marked by the gradual emergence of class divisions within the *bhadralok*, between the older and landed families of the Renaissance generation and the concentrated Calcutta petty bourgeoisie which was increasingly to become the gravitational centre of *bhadralok* politics.

The social changes were responsible for mounting alienation from British rule, as well as the growth of more politicized and effective forms of organization which characterized the period between 1880 and 1905.

These developments led to the formation of the Indian Association. Among its founding members were a Derozian – Krishan Mohan Banerjea – and an energetic politician, Surendranath Banerjee, who returned from Europe influenced strongly by the Italian nationalist, Mazzini.[37] Banerjee had been dismissed from the Indian Civil Service for a minor misdemeanour which would have earned no more than a reprimand for an Englishman. He declared, 'I felt that I had suffered because I was an Indian, a member of a community that lay disorganized, had no public opinion and no voice in the counsels of government.'

Banerjee's association formed around the events of the Pabna Rent Revolt. Supporting the peasantry, the Indian Association split with the British Indian Association of the Tagores and the *bhadralok* gentry. Moreover, with the success of the peasantry consolidated in the Bengal Tenancy Act of 1885, Surendranath turned increasingly to the rural areas of Bengal as the social base for anti-British political activity. But although attracting mass audiences as he travelled throughout the hinterland, Surendranath addressed the peasants on classically urban and *bhadralok* concerns of the freedom of the press, native representation on the Legislative Council and civil service reform. Although not ignoring the question of rents, Surendranath's strategy was to stimulate peasant support for middle-class interests. And although mass meetings on civil liberties represented considerable progress on the pettyfogging constitutionalism of the British Indian Association, it failed to transcend the basic contradiction of *bhadralok* politics: any radical challenge – that is, questioning forms of property – to colonial authority threatened the social authority of its col-

37. Banerjee was soon campaigning all over India against one of Lord Lytton's many reactionary measures and Sir Henry Cotton, a distinguished civil servant, testified to his success: 'The idea of any Bengalee influence in the Punjab would have been a conception incredible to Lord Lawrence ... yet it is the case that during the last year the tour of a Bengalee lecturer lecturing in English in Upper India, assumed the character of a triumphal progress; and at the present moment the name of Surendranath Banerjee excites as much enthusiasm among the rising generation of Hultan as in Dacca.' (R. C. Majumdar, et al., *An Advanced History of India,* p. 890.)

laborators, the *bhadralok* themselves. Thus by exposing the abuses of the British, the new forms of agitation introduced by the Indian Association accelerated the cycle of alienation, colonial repression and mass militancy without providing the forms of class organization necessary if social unrest were to be politically effective.

It is at this point that the conflicting currents of the Renaissance movement separated, for the secular and nationalist tendencies of the Indian Association threatened to unearth popular forces the *bhadralok* could not control. It was left to the 'self-strengtheners' to produce a form of religious nationalism allowing the *bhadralok* to contain and lead a mass movement which might otherwise sweep them away. The turn of the twentieth century was marked by the emergence of a radical anti-British feeling cloaked in the symbols of Hindu revivalism.

Militant Revivalism

The cultural heritage of the Renaissance was pressed into political service shortly after the turn of the century. The 'self-strengtheners' had restored Bengal's ideological armoury with newly burnished Hindu cult figures, while poems, songs, novels and other recently turned genres became instruments to engrave the mass consciousness with vivid and militant religious images. Poets, *literati* and religious leaders such as Bakim Chandra Chatterjee proved skilful craftsmen in fusing political purpose with an evocative symbolism. The popular cult of *Sakti*, the traditional Brahmanical goddess of Divine Destruction and Cosmic Renewal provides an example.[38] For worship of *Sakti* offered a supernatural ally in, and justification for, the anti-colonial struggle, while simultaneously ratifying the existing social order: at a stroke the secular and religious contradictions underlying the Western-inspired Bengali Re-

38. Broomfield, ibid., p. 16.

naissance dissolved in atavistic indulgence. Under the inspiration of the Hindu pantheon and the leadership of the ritually superior castes, Bengal would regenerate, purge itself of the defeatism and passivity, and return to the Golden Age of independence and purity of classical Brahmanism. The Hindu reformer and revivalist Swami Vivikananda popularized such prayers as, 'Oh, Mother of Strength, take away my weakness, take away my unmanliness and make me a man', while later 'spiritual' leaders such as Aurobindo Ghosh and Brahmobandhav Upadhyaya blended political terrorism, Hindu ascendancy and Indian nationalism in a mystagogic vision comparable to that of Mother Russia and the Orthodox Church in the eyes of the Pan Slavs. As the confrontation between the Bengalis and the British escalated, religion was tossed in to fuel the national consciousness.[39] This revivalism tended, however, to be even more pronounced outside Bengal and it was Tilak, a Bombay Congressman, who was to be most influential in importing it into the national movement. Bengali revivalism could never entirely escape adulteration by the rationalist themes of the Renaissance.

The British Strategy and Partition

The British response to the pressures of mass politics was the classic tactic of 'divide and rule'. H. H. Risley, Home Secretary to the Government of India, put it succinctly: 'Bengal united is a power. Bengal divided will pull in different ways. That is what the Congress leaders feel; their apprehensions are perfectly correct and they form one of the great merits of the scheme ... It is not altogether easy to reply in a despatch which is sure to be published without disclosing the fact that ... one of our main objects is to split up and thereby to weaken a solid body of opponents to our rule.'[40]

39. A. Tripathi, The *Extremist Challenge*, Calcutta, 1969.
40. Op. cit., p. 95.

The *bhadralok* themselves had prepared the ground. For to the extent Hindu revivalism threatened the British, it divided Bengali society internally, generating opponents to itself and potential allies for the British. The colonial policy was merely to switch patronage to the Muslims with the same intention and effect as over a century ago when supreme favour was directed to the *bhadralok*: 'A separate administration, a separate High Court, and a separate University at Dacca would give extra opportunities to the Muslim middle class to emerge from their backward state and weaken the economic base of the Hindu middle classes. The Hindu *zamindari* patrons to the Congress would find the Muslim peasantry ranged against them, secure in support of the Dacca Secretariat. It would divide the nationalist ranks once and for all.'[41] The structure of collaboration which had brought the *bhadralok* to prominence was used against them immediately middle-class politics proved obstreperous. Curzon visited Dacca, the centre of Muslim Bengal, and made clear to the Nawab and other Muslim dignitaries how advantageous a partition of Bengal would be to the Muslims. In July 1905 the scheme for Partition was announced, and it was to take effect from October of that year. The response from Hindu Bengal was electrifying. One of the leading papers of the day, which carried as its motto the slogan 'Liberty, Equality, Fraternity', issued a call for the boycott of foreign goods. There were mammoth meetings and demonstrations where foreign cloth was ceremonially burnt. The slogan now was to buy *swadeshi* (domestically produced goods). The rich dispensed with their British-made luxuries; women came out of the seclusion of their homes to demonstrate; school and college students emerged from their institutions in procession; landlords, businessmen and professional people – all merged with the popular tide. It was the first mass

41. Op. cit., p. 157.

movement of modern India; its bard was Rabindranath Tagore and its tribune the fiery Bepin Chandra Pal.[42]

The Swadeshi Movement

Even though the idea of *swadeshi* had its roots in the Hindu *mela* (fair) there was every reason to believe that this agitation was ideally suited to the ambitions of a secular, bourgeois nationalist movement. Among the first to benefit from the boycott and burning of British cloth would be the large number of Muslim weavers. Moreover only stooges of the British, such as the Nawab of Dacca, had declared themselves in favour of Partition. Other leading Muslims declared against it, for instance, Abdul Rasul, Abdul Halim Ghaznavi of Mymensingh, Abdul Kasem of Burdwan and Liakat Hossain. Moreover the secretary of the Muslim College at Aligarh, Mohsin-ul-Mulk, reported that he and his colleagues were finding it increasingly difficult to keep the younger students away from the Congress. Rabindranath Tagore appeared to encourage such developments when he declared on Rakhibandan Day that all Bengalis, 'Hindus and Muslims, living in the separated parts of Bengal, were blood brothers'. Unfortunately these sentiments were only likely to reach the ears of the tiny minority of educated Muslims. It was essential for the leaders of the anti-Partition movement to communicate with the great mass of Muslims who constituted the majority of the population of Bengal. Instead these leaders chose to employ every device of Hindu revivalism from the very first day of the struggle.

On the day of Partition, 16 October, there took place memorable symbols of mass protest, charged with religious overtones. The *rakhi* thread was tied to the wrist of every friend, masses of Hindus ritually bathed themselves in the

42. Nirmal Sinha, *The Freedom Movement in Bengal, 1818–1904*. Calcutta, 1953.

Ganges, emerging to dedicate themselves to the anti-Partition struggle in front of the image of the goddess *Sakti*. B. C. Pal had vigorously defended such symbolism as the best way of popularizing nationalism. In his book *The Spirit of Indian Nationalism* he wrote of the goddess *Sakti*: 'It is impossible to conceive a better or more inspiring symbol of the Race-Spirit than this, and it is not at all strange that thousands of Bengali Hindus should stand before it and cry *Bande Mataram*.'[43] A nationalist paper, the *Hindu Patriot*, had declared on 22 September that 'the induction of a religious element into the movement will serve as a powerful stimulus, securing its perpetuity, for nothing catches so easily in this country as religious fervour'. Indeed the religious appeal must have seemed particularly convenient. It would provide a common bond with the large non-Bengali population of Calcutta and would help to insure against any inconvenient intrusion of class consciousness amongst oppressed or exploited Hindus. What it left out of account was only the mass of Muslims who could not conceivably join in devotion to *Sakti* or shout '*Bande Mataram*'. For too many Hindu *bhadralok* the Muslims did not really exist except as objects of occasional high-minded concern. Even Rabindranath Tagore, who was certainly no communalist, somehow never managed to write a single verse celebrating a Muslim hero. Like other great Bengali poets he always looked to Sikhs, Rajputs or Marathas for the glorious personages in his poetry. Thus some of the most generous aspirations expressed in the poetry written by Bengali Hindus of this time can have had little appeal to the Muslim. Rangalal's 'Ode to Liberty' is a case in point. It starts with the famous line 'Breathes there the man who would like to live, shorn of liberty'. Muslim appreciation of this splendid sentiment could scarcely be enhanced by the fact that it is put in the mouth of a Rajput fighting for his country against the Muslims. No doubt the historical back-

43. B. C. Pal, *The Spirit of Indian Nationalism*, London, 1906, pp. 36–7.

ground of Muslim domination of India was a greatly complicating factor, but any politically aware *bhadralok* leader should have been able to separate this background from the fact that the majority of his fellow Bengalis, including some of the most oppressed and downtrodden, were Muslim and that their support would be essential to a successful national movement. One of the few to grasp this was Surendranath Banerjee who warned of the dangers of playing exclusively on Hindu themes. In fact there is some sign that there was an attempt to make a religious appeal to the Muslim masses too and to combine it with the impressive Hindu mobilizations.[44] However, to imagine that the spirit of communal pride could be encouraged among both Hindu and Muslim without unleashing communal antagonism at the same time was a dangerous miscalculation. Naturally the British authorities did not hesitate to take full advantage of any communal division.[45] Indeed, as we have seen, the British had all along conceived the Partition plan with the aim of undermining the national movement.

The Muslim League

The fruit of British manoeuvres was the formation of the Muslim League on 30 December 1906, under the leadership of the late Agha Khan and the Nawab of Dacca, Salimullah

44. A number of Muslims attended *Swadeshi* meetings. In certain areas, 'particularly Barisal, the Muslim masses joined the Swadeshi movement and were inspired by folk songs composed for the purpose ... The mingled shouts of "Alla-ho-Akbar" and "Bande-Mataram" by Hindus and Mussalmans formed a characteristic feature of these meetings, and processions' (R. C. Majumdar, 'History of the Freedom Movement in India', vol. 2, p. 112). This historian is generally uncritical of Hindu revivalism. For an analysis of the relations between the two communities see Sumit Sarkar, 'Hindu-Muslim Relations in Swadeshi Bengal, 1903–1908', *The Indian Economic and Social History Review*, vol. 9, no. 2.

45. A. Tripathi, *The Extremist Challenge*, p. 161.

Khan. The League's programme contained the following objectives: 'to promote loyalty to the British Government, to protect and advance the political rights and interests of Mussalmans of India and respectfully represent their needs and aspirations to Government and to prevent the rise among Mussalmans of any feelings of prejudice to the other objects of the League'. Tripathi makes the apt comment that, 'the League started by declaring the partition as beneficial to the Moslem interests and condemned all methods of agitation like boycotting. Hence it would never really have to fulfil the third pious wish. Sir Syed's legacy was safe in the hands of the Aligarh and Bengal Nawabs. It would be pro-landlord and pro-British and anti-Bourgeois and anti-Hindu'.[46]

Muslim groups in East Bengal soon clashed with *Swadeshi* demonstrators, and two communal riots in Comilla and Jamalpur proved particularly vicious. Lord Minto, the Viceroy, noted with some relish that, 'they will be a useful reminder to the people in England that the Bengali is not everybody in India, in fact the Mohammedan community, when roused, would be a much stronger and more dangerous factor to deal with than the Bengalis'.[47]

The Partition provoked an upheaval of protest and agitation which registered opposition to colonial policy not only from Bengal, but from the whole of India.[48] Between 1905 and 1911 mass demonstrations, *Swadeshi* campaigns (Buy-Indian boy-

46. A. Tripathi, *The Extremist Challenge*, pp. 165–66.

47. Quoted in A. Tripathi, *The Extremist Challenge*, pp. 164–65. See also Hiren Chakrabarti, 'Government and Bengal Terrorism, 1912–1918', in *Bengal Past and Present*, July–December 1971. For a broad account of a later period see R. C. Majumdar, *History of the Freedom Movement in India*, vols. 2 and 3, Calcutta, 1963.

48. In his presidential address to the Benares session of the Congress in 1905, G. K. Gokhale remarked: 'The most outstanding fact of the situation is that the public life of this country has received an accession of strength of great importance and for this India owes a deep debt of gratitude to Bengal . . .'

cott of British goods) and political terrorism shook British confidence and undermined the overall effectiveness of their rule. The British were forced to give way, and in 1911 Partition was annulled and Bengal reunited. The moment was greeted with an avalanche of popular enthusiasm. The reversal of Partition was taken as a triumph of anti-colonialism and evidence of a rapidly growing national consciousness. But the fanfare concealed the persistence of *bhadralok* contradictions which this time had left their politics all the more contradictory, and Bengali society divided and weak.

In a society united in oppression, but riddled with religious, ethnic, linguistic, caste and cultural divisions, Hindu revivalism left large blocs of the Bengali population completely inert, if not, as among the Muslims, actively resistant. The *Swadeshi* movement and mass demonstrations were mostly urban and middle-class phenomena, exposing the extent to which the *bhadralok* were isolated from the *namasudras* (low-caste cultivators), Assamese, Biharis, Marwaris, Oriyas, etc., as well as from the nascent working class. 1911 therefore marked the defeat of the British and the first success of Indian nationalism, but at the high price of distorting the national consciousness through religion, implanting communalism as a virulent factor in Bengali politics and isolating the *bhadralok* leadership from the breadth of Bengali society. As a 'crowning blow' the British moved their capital from Calcutta to the formerly Moghul seat at Delhi. And thus the *bhadralok*, bred in colonial corridors, found the much-coveted state apparatus wrenched from their grasp and planted in the distant territory of North India. After a century on the threshold of power they rediscovered themselves in their traditional position on the periphery of South Asian politics. 1911 thus marked a watershed in Bengali politics: it signalled a triumph in the national movement, but also divulged the weaknesses of a class caught in a thoroughly contradictory position half-way between the colonial power above and the popular masses below, half-way between the archaic practices of the *zamindars* and traditional religion on the one hand and a bourgeois-democratic revolution on the other.[49]

Developments following the anti-Partition struggle had a radical impact on Bengali politics, leading to an even more profound split than that between the 'self-strengtheners' and the Derozians. Firstly there was a purely collaborationist upper stratum of *bhadralok* who were determined to serve the raj more faithfully than ever before; despite the movement of the capital to Delhi there continued to be openings for servile and highly educated Bengalis in the upper reaches of the judiciary and administration, loyally aspiring to a knighthood or an OBE. Advancement of this sort could not offer any solution to the bulk of the *bhadralok* however. The experience of the struggle against Partition had encouraged a radicalization of Bengali politics of a highly specific sort. On the one hand the fierce clash with the imperial power had shaken the old belief in constitutional progress; on the other the explosive popular response, with its communalist overtones and Muslim backlash, had provoked alarm among the *bhadralok* élite. Up to this time Bengalis had been very prominent in the affairs of Congress.

49. Tagore sought solace in the dream of Eastern spirituality to which M. N. Roy, perhaps the last spiritual heir of the Derozians, made a sharp rejoinder: 'The belief in India's spiritual message to the materialist West is heady wine. It is time to realize that the pleasant inebriation [it produced] offered a solace to proud intellectuals with inferiority complexes. The legacy of that psychological aggressiveness is not an asset but a liability.' Elsewhere he was more directly critical of Tagore's idealization of India's past: 'His solution to the present social problem is to replace the existing form of property-relations by an earlier form, already left behind in the evolution of modern civilization. He would replace capitalism by patriarcho-feudal aristocracy. He begrudges the working-class that relatively higher standard of living which incidentally follows an improvement in social production. He is against modern industrialism because it disrupts the class of landed aristocracy to which he belongs.' (Quoted in Hay, *Asian Ideas of East and West,* pp. 263 and 261–62, Cambridge, Mass. 1970.)

Between 1885 and 1909 there were just under 20,000 delegates to sessions of Congress of whom nearly 4,000 were Bengalis (the other leading areas were Bombay and Madras). After the beginning of the struggle against Partition Bengalis were prominent in the so-called 'Extremist' wing of the Congress and it was at this time that a number of younger militants formed a terrorist association to combat the British. Very frequently those who were most 'extremist' were also most enthusiastic about Hindu revivalism and, conversely, some of the more prominent opponents of communalism reconciled themselves with the colonial power, perhaps out of a feeling that they did not have the mass basis to challenge it. The two main terrorist associations, *Anusilan Samity* and the *Jugantar Party*, were exclusively Hindu; among the initiation rites for a new member would be bathing in the Ganges and dedication to *Sakti*. In theory the aim of the terrorists was to annihilate the top ranks of the British raj through the bomb and the bullet. Unsuccessful attempts were made on the lives of the Governor of Bengal and the Viceroy, though the terrorists were more successful in killing supposed renegades and traitors within their own ranks. Although these movements did signal a break with the traditional *bhadralok* politics of constitutional petition, they did not break with their equally pernicious revivalism and élitism.

The Role of the 'big Babus'

The emergence of terrorism, communalism and the beginnings of popular militancy were calculated to alarm the old-style Bengali leaders. On the death of Edward VII Surendranath Banerjee went so far as to express his sorrow at the departure of the King-Emperor on bended knee at a public meeting. And in the subsequent period even the so-called 'extremist' Congress leaders drew back from really involving the masses in the national movement. The caution of the Bengali Congress leaders when it came to methods of mass agitation became very clear after Gandhi sought to introduce a new style into Congress politics at the time of the First World War and afterwards. Gandhi was by no means more hostile to the colonial power than the traditional leaders of Congress: he even engaged in a recruiting campaign for the British Army during the latter stages of the war. Yet Gandhi was prepared to take up on a mass scale the very themes and tactics of agitation which the Bengali Congress leaders had pioneered but not pursued. It was not just that Gandhi widened the basis of the national movement; there was also a marked hesitation among many Bengali Congress politicians to repeat agitational tactics which had yielded such ambiguous results during the anti-Partition struggle. On the other hand younger Bengalis, who had broken with Congress conservatism and timidity, were distinctly unimpressed by the Mahatma's blend of moderation and moralism. They were to be drawn to terrorist conspiracies rather than *satyagraha* and passive resistance. Thus in the summer of 1917 Gandhi urged a mass passive resistance campaign in protest at the internment of Annie Besant, a Theosophist who had helped to found the Indian Home Rule Movement. In the subsequent agitation non-Bengali Congress politicians were to complain 'only Bengal is giving us half-hearted support. The fact is that in Bengal the old leaders can't bring themselves into line with new developments and the younger men don't believe in constitutional agitation. Besides, it is characteristic of Bengal, that unless it is directly touched by anything it does not move.'[50]

Gandhi's subsequent moves were to evoke a particularly ambiguous response from the Bengali Congress leaders. On the one hand it was men like C. R. Das who pressed Gandhi to develop Congress as a secular and modern political organ-

50. T. B. Sapru to Sita Ram, 30 June 1917; quoted by Judith Brown, *Gandhi's Rise to Power*, London, 1970, p. 143. This book is a valuable addition to the literature on the Indian national movement.

ization; on the other hand many Bengali Congress politicians were to be found in the ranks of those who resisted the mass non-cooperation movements launched by Gandhi. Thus at the time of the 1920 non-cooperation movement the Bengal Government reported, 'Non-cooperation in practice may be said to be dead in Bengal, Gandhi is regarded with veneration and any abuse of him would not be allowed, but his non-cooperation programme is regarded almost with the tolerance extended to children's games.'[51] Of course the tactics of non-cooperation with the colonial power threatened the livelihood of the many *bhadralok* who remained its servants. However a recent history of this period points out:

Non-cooperation was taking root among groups who had been untouched by *bhadralok* pioneers of nationalist politics, and were unlikely to produce statistics for non-cooperation in terms of withdrawal of lawyers, title holders or council members. Among them were the poorer Hindus for whom *Nayak* spoke when it denounced *bhadralok* nationalism as 'a diplomatic manoeuvre to deceive the ruling class and to earn celebrity' by the 'Babus of Calcutta and the mossafil, including the Moderates and the Extremists, the democrats and the aristocrats'. The same paper commented after [the Conference at] Calcutta, 'Congress has at last become the property of businessmen, shopkeepers, agriculturalists and the people at large. It is they who constitute the present Congress and they are the guardians and protectors of non-cooperation which will be spread and circulated by them.' It was no use, explained *Nayak*, to expect the *bhadralok*, 'the big Babus', to counteract non-cooperation: they could not converse with lesser folk who could not understand their English or anglicized Bengali even had they been willing to go into the villages to explain their politics. The Muslims of Bengal, similarly outside the range of the 'big Babus', were also deeply stirred by Gandhian non-cooperation, because the Mahatma had Muslim preachers as an intermediary layer of mobilizers for his cause.[52]

51. Brown, op. cit., p. 280.   52. Brown, op. cit., p. 280.

Those stimulated into political activity by the non-cooperation movement of 1920–22 were to discover that Gandhi would develop reservations about the struggle not so different from those of the 'big Babus'. A brief recapitulation of Gandhi's entry into the national movement will illuminate the reasons for this.

Gandhi's Début

We noted earlier how in the late 1860s the Bengali peasantry forced European indigo planters out of Bengal to settle in upper Bihar. It was in the district of Champaran where the indigo system established deep roots and provoked the same class antagonism, that Gandhi made his début in Indian mass politics. In a tactic evocative of Bengali middle-class response to the Indigo movement, Gandhi focused on exploitation by the *European* indigo planters while leaving the structure of the *zamindari* system completely unquestioned. Class feeling among the peasantry was politically exploited, but the peasants' concrete socio-economic interests were barely met. N. G. Ranga, at the time a critic from the Left, was later to remark,

'Just as the earlier Congress agitation led by Romesh Chandra Dutt against temporary settlements did not embrace the exploitation of the *zamindars*, so also this agitation led by the Mahatma in Champaran did not lead up to any fight against the main causes for the terrible poverty and sufferings of Champaran peasants, namely the excessive rents and exorbitant incidence of debts ... It does strike us as rather significant that both he [Gandhi] and Rajen Prasad should have remained scrupulously silent upon the ravages of *zamindari* system.

Another onlooker was to comment: 'I am told that Mr Gandhi was at one time anxious to extend his investigations to the whole field of relations between the *zamindars* and their tenants. It is well known that the disabilities of the tenants are by no means confined to the indigo plantations owned by

Europeans. But the local politicians cannot afford to set the *zamindar* party against themselves and that is the reason why Mr Gandhi's investigations are so much restricted.'[53] And even against the Europeans Gandhi employed peaceful and re- strained agitation designed to bring about a favourable inter- vention from the authorities. Indeed Gandhi argued that campaigns of this sort were aimed to strengthen the true pur- poses of the raj. During his subsequent agitation for a remission of the land tax in view of the bad harvest in Kaira he declared: 'I venture to suggest that the Commissioner's attitude con- stitutes a peril far greater than the German peril, and I am serving the Empire in trying to deliver it from the peril within.'[54] As much of Gandhi's subsequent activity was to show, he greatly valued the British connection and looked for- ward to its survival even after the achievement of *Swaraj* (his deliberately vague term for self-government). Further limi- tations of the Gandhian approach were to be revealed in his intervention in the dispute at the Ahmedabad mills in 1918. Given the complete inexperience of Indian workers in trade- union agitation Gandhi's intervention no doubt assisted the Ah- medabad workers' movement. However, his own predilection for solving labour disputes with moralistic appeals to the owners led him in the end to threaten them that he would fast until they conceded the workers' demands. The local District Magistrate wrote that this decision had been prompted by Gandhi's desire to allay the workers' suspicions about his re- lations with the mill-owners. 'The weavers assailed him bitterly for being a friend of the mill-owners, riding in their motor-cars and eating sumptuously with them, while the weavers were starving. It was at this point and when stung by these taunts that Gandhi took his vow that he would eat no food until the weavers' terms were granted by the mill-owners.'[55] On their

53. Brown, op. cit., p. 76.
54. Brown, op. cit., p. 75.
55. Brown, op. cit., p. 118.

own terms all these preliminary skirmishes were successful. It was not until Gandhi was in a position to launch an all-India non-cooperation and *swadeshi* campaign in 1920–21 that he ran into precisely the sort of problems that had erupted during the anti-Partition movement.

Although Gandhi's conception of the Indian national struggle was deeply religious, he was also most concerned to develop a Hindu-Muslim alliance. His recipe for this alliance was to be a combination of Hindu revivalism and Muslim revivalism. During the latter stages of the war the Indian Muslim community was greatly concerned at the fate of the Caliphate in the event of Turkey being on the losing side. Gandhi was able to garner considerable support among leaders of the Muslim community by espousing this cause. It was mainly for this reason that Gandhi was able to draw on Muslim support when he came to challenge the old leaders of Congress. At the Calcutta and Nagpur conferences of Congress in 1920 his plan for national non-cooperation triumphed. The subsequent agitations led to massive popular involvement in the national movement which it had generally lacked up to this point. However by the latter half of 1922 the movement had gone far beyond the bounds laid down by Gandhi concerning the proper methods of pursuing *Swaraj*. Neither Gandhi nor Congress had a well-organized political machine in most parts of the subcontinent. Consequently they were quite unable to control the pent-up social forces released by their campaign of opposition to the Government. In Malabar, for example, impoverished Muslim peasants broke out in open rebellion, slaughtering and pillaging their Hindu landlords and neighbours. The Viceroy was to report: 'The lower classes in the towns have been seriously affected by the non-cooperation movement. In certain areas the peasantry have been affected, particularly in parts of the Assam valley, United Provinces, Bihar and Orissa and Bengal. As regards the Punjab, the Akali agitation has penetrated to the rural Sikhs. A large proportion of the Mahomedan population throughout the country are embittered and sullen.'[56] In Bengal itself several thousand 'Volunteers' were organized to prosecute the non-cooperation movement. The Bengal Government complained that its police were 'terrorized' by the Volunteers. It declared: 'Reference has already been made to the change in status of the men enlisted in this way. They are now distinctly of a lower class than at first, and are backed by the riff-raff of the town, recruited on payment of a daily wage to do whatever work is demanded of them.'[57]

The British fear of the Volunteers came from an acute awareness that their rule rested on an extremely slender base of material force. However, Gandhi was as concerned as the British at the course the movement was taking. In February 1922 twenty-two policemen in Chauri Chaura, UP, were killed in the course of a peasant disturbance. Horrified by 'the inhuman conduct of the mob at Chauri Chaura' Gandhi took it on himself to call off the whole non-cooperation movement. The Resolution ending non-cooperation also stated: 'The Working Committee advises Congress workers and organizations to inform the peasants that witholding of rent payment to *zamindars* is contrary to the Congress resolutions and injurious to the best interests of the country.' In fact rural notables were to become the backbone of Congress organization in the countryside; not the large feudal landowners so much as smaller landowners, rich peasants and the rural middle class. Thus the same resolution went on to assure 'the *zamindars* that the Congress movement is in no way intended to attack their legal rights, and that even where the ryots have grievances, the Committee declares that redress be sought by mutual consultation and arbitration'.[58]

56. A. R. Desai, *The Social Background of Indian Nationalism*, Bombay, 1966, p. 189. This book furnishes an excellent introduction to the study of the Indian national movement.

57. Brown, op. cit., p. 282.

58. Desai, op. cit., p. 352.

Premen Addy and Ibne Azad

Hindu-Muslim Tensions

Although Gandhi was able to protect the class character of Congress, he had much more difficulty preserving its inter-communal character. After all, neither the workers nor the peasants yet possessed independent organizations or an independent leadership of their own. When Gandhi called off the movement they had no means of continuing it. The Muslims, however, did have organizations of their own and a leadership of their own. These had been prepared to support Gandhi so long as he seemed to be offering some sort of challenge against the British, but they were soon to discover the severe limits that he was to place on this challenge. Thus during the height of the non-cooperation movement there was a fierce battle between Gandhi and Hasrat Mohani and other militant Muslim leaders who were insisting that Congress should clearly state that *Swaraj* meant 'full Independence free from all foreign control' and that all means necessary should be used to obtain it.[59] Although the Muslim movement was in a sense more backward than the older Congress movement it was, partly for this very reason, less integrated into the structures whereby the British governed India and less mesmerized by the British connection. The Hindu politicians of Congress had been loyally petitioning the British Government for decades, had long participated in British supervised elections, and had been drawn into every level of the British administration. Once they were aroused the Muslims saw no reason to stop short of complete Independence and they tended to be greatly frustrated by the tactics Gandhi sought to impose on them. The Bombay Commissioner of Police remarked: 'It is clear that there is a party to whom the policy of non-violence is repugnant; it is I understand regarded as degrading that a race that has hitherto taken pride in its martial valour and has been respected for it should now ally itself with an unbelieving leader whose religion forbids him to

59. Desai, op. cit., p. 284.

take any sort of life and should moreover accept its policy from him; and there are many who argue that nothing has ever yet been achieved by non-violence.'[60]

Such strains in the Hindu-Muslim alliance were compounded by the communalist undertones which surfaced in the wake of the non-cooperation movement. A Bengali Muslim paper commented in 1921: 'The manner in which Mr Gandhi is being worshipped in the country makes it impossible for the Moslem community to pull on with him. We are ready to work with the Hindus as their brethren; we can even forego *korbani* (cow sacrifice) for their satisfaction, but we will never allow the holy crescent to lie low at the feet of Sri Krishna.'[61]

So long as the nationalist leaders made no attempt to combat the influence of religion, communal reactions were inescapable. They were encouraged not just by the machinations of the British and the backwardness of the nationalist leadership but by the whole structure of the Indian social formation after more than a century of British imperialism. Throughout India the social relations of production combined a capitalist market on the one hand with pre-capitalist forms of exploitation on the other. Outside the towns capitalism had scarcely penetrated the underlying process of production, yet at the same time it had introduced a qualitatively stronger market framework than had existed hitherto.[62] Communal and caste organization acquired

60. Brown, op. cit., p. 336.

61. Brown, op. cit., p. 329.

62. See Utsa Patnaik, 'The Development of Capitalism in Agriculture', *Social Scientist*, New Delhi, vol. 1, no. 2, September 1972. The expression 'colonial social formation' refers to a specific combination of capitalist and pre-capitalist modes of production and has nothing to do with the factitious notion of a 'colonial mode of production'. That a social formation can combine more than one mode of production is, of course, an elementary principle of historical materialism and renders quite redundant attempts to invent new modes of production to explain such combinations. Cf. Ernesto Laclau, 'Feudalism and Capitalism in Latin America', *New Left Review* 67, May–June 1971.

a new significance in these conditions since corporate competition on the market was mediated through it. There is in fact reason to believe that just as the market intensified forms of pre-capitalist exploitation so also it lent a new virulence to communal and caste antagonisms. By bringing into question the nature of the central political power, without being able to offer a clear solution, the national movement further aggravated the situation. Of course a clear solution would have had to be a class solution, but the Indian bourgeoisie was too weak to be able to sustain one at this point, while the exploited and oppressed classes lacked even the most rudimentary organization or leadership. Seen in this light the restrictions which Gandhi sought to place on the national movement had a certain logic. The Indian bourgeoisie was in no position to launch an uncompromising liberation struggle since this would threaten to engulf it in communal and class conflict which it would be quite incapable of controlling. It was therefore driven back on the tactic of making a moral-political appeal to the British to recognize that their best interests lay in a peaceful decolonization that would leave the underlying structure of imperialism intact.

Aftermath of Non-cooperation

All these tendencies were, of course, only embryonically apparent after the first non-cooperation movement. It is however significant that Congress waited nearly a decade before launching another campaign of this sort. When they did so the results were very similiar, with uncontrolled outbreaks which scandalized the Gandhian leadership, and a growing rift between Muslims and Hindus. Moreover on this occasion Gandhi sought to secure the support of the Untouchables in a very similar way to his earlier approaches to the Muslims. On the one hand he baptized the Untouchables with the odiously patronizing name *Harijan* (children of god), on the other he continued to proclaim the sanctity of the Hindu social categories. Not surprisingly the more militant Untouchable leaders, such as B. R. Ambedkar, developed a fierce hatred of Gandhi's self-delusions and hypocrisy on this question.

Gandhi's action in calling off the 1920–22 non-cooperation movement disconcerted or angered many Congress leaders. An important section of the Bengali Congress, led by C. R. Das, reverted to the more traditional tactics of pressing for *Swaraj* through participation in the electoral bodies set up by the British. At the same time there was considerable pressure in Bengal, Bombay and other places for the development of more adequate organizational forms which would enable Congress to promote a subsequent agitation more successfully. In 1920 an All-India Trade Union Congress had been founded but it had been too weak to coordinate the strikes which had erupted in every part of India during the non-cooperation movement. The working class was generally most militant in Bombay, where there had been a general strike in support of Tilak, the Congress 'Extremist', as early as 1907. The war had led to a considerable development of industrial employment and created the conditions for the rise of an organized trade-union movement. In Bengal there were unorganized strikes during the non-cooperation movement, and afterwards Das and other Congress politicians had encouraged the development of trade unions. However it was not until the late twenties and early thirties, with a general deterioration of economic conditions for the working masses as a consequence of the depression, that really strong strike movements developed in Bengal. When this did occur it helped to push Congress to the Left and led to the most blatant class-collaborators being ejected from the AITU Congress. This helped to reinforce a certain Left trend within Congress itself which wished to base the national movement on a more secular and modern philosophy than Gandhi's abysmally reactionary, obscurantist nostalgia for the authoritarian simplicity of a mythical Hindu past in *Hind Swaraj*.

Premen Addy and Ibne Azad

Congress 'Socialism'

It was at this time that men such as Nehru began confecting Congress 'socialism'. However, instead of challenging Gandhi's mystifications head-on, Nehru and others sought to supplement them with an economic doctrine that would be more relevant to the problems of the Indian bourgeoisie and petty bourgeoisie. As so often happened in the history of relations between India and Britain, the dismal backwardness of the political traditions in the two countries helped to reinforce and confirm one another. Nehru and other Congress socialists were able to draw on the doctrines of Fabianism, just as the Fabians had been able to point to Gandhi as the alibi for their own deep complicity in imperialism. Tom Nairn has well described the core of Fabian ideology:

They [the Fabians] adapted and transformed third-rate bourgeois traditions into fourth-rate socialist traditions, imposing upon the working class all the righteous mediocrity and worthless philistinism of the pious Victorian petty bourgeoisie. Fabianism was derived from Utilitarianism, the timid and dreary species of bourgeois rationalism embraced by the British industrial middle class during the Industrial Revolution. In it bourgeois rationalism became socialist rationalism chiefly through the substitution of the state for the magic forces of the *laissez faire* capitalist market: the former was seen as bringing about the 'greatest happiness of the greatest number' almost as automatically as the latter had been. According to this ideology of minor functionaries, although the working class made socialism *possible* (with their votes), the new society would actually be created by an eternal 'élite of unassuming experts ... exercising the power inherent in superior knowledge and longer administrative experience'. [These latter phrases are taken from Beatrice Webb.][63]

63. Tom Nairn, 'Anatomy of the Labour Party', *New Left Review* 27, September–October 1964, pp. 44–5.

It may be imagined that the not inconsiderable number of minor functionaries in and around Congress were extremely receptive to this brand of socialism. However the mere fact that Nehru and the Congress socialists, unlike Gandhi, at least inhabited the modern world was not sufficient to establish their hegemony over Congress. Just as the British Labour Party needed the immense upheaval of the First World War to bring it to accept even Fabian 'socialism', so Congress was only led to adopt its variety of 'socialism' by the long travail of the national movement between 1922 and 1939. During this time the defects of Gandhian ideology were to be thrown into harsh relief by the ravages of the depression, the repressive and cynical manoeuvres of the British, the evident perils of communal division and, last but not least, the stirrings of a genuine national and class consciousness among the mass of Indian peasants, workers and students. The hegemony that Nehru was able to exercise at the end of this long-drawn-out process did signal a major advance for the Indian national movement and for the Indian bourgeoisie in at least one vital area. It meant that a brand of secular politics had relegated the Mahatma's religious obscurantism to a subordinate position. Although a heavy price still had to be paid for Indian nationalism's prolonged flirtation with Hindu revivalism, and millions were to perish in Partition and the subsequent Indo-Pak wars, at least the Indian state was established on a secular basis.

Jawaharlal Nehru was a fake socialist, but he had a genuine antipathy to communalism and religious politics. Specifically with reference to the religious element in the anti-Partition movement he insisted: 'Socially speaking, the revival of Indian nationalism in 1907 was definitely reactionary.'[64] However, had the struggle for secular nationalism been left entirely to Jawaharlal Nehru and his circle we may doubt whether this decisive transformation would ever have been achieved. Nehru never clashed openly with Gandhi. Although he did not share

64. Desai, op. cit., p. 332.

the Mahatma's religious obsessions, he always treated them most indulgently. Nehru's attitude to Gandhi sprang from an awareness that Gandhi enjoyed a rapport with the Indian masses which his own aristocratic and intellectual outlook denied him. Nehru was only able to grasp the reins of power in Congress as a consequence of battles against Gandhian ideology and leadership in which radical and secular nationalism was to find doughtier champions than himself. In the first of these battles Nehru assumed the Presidency of Congress at the Lahore Conference of 1930 in alliance with a dynamic and popular young nationalist from Bengal, Subhas Chandra Bose. Although Nehru and Bose were able to push Congress to adopt a more radical programme and to resume nationalist agitation, Gandhi was still entrusted with the implementation of the subsequent Civil Disobedience Movement. A second battle against Gandhian ideology was to arise out of the débâcle of the Civil Disobedience Movement, and Subhas Bose was again to play a prominent role. But although Bose triumphed in 1939 he lacked the ideological and organizational resources to consolidate his victory. Nehru and Congress 'socialism' were able to step into the vacuum with Gandhi's benediction. Although Gandhi continued to play a major role in Congress, especially during the Second World War, the successful challenge to Gandhian ideology in the late thirties undoubtedly strengthened Nehru's position *vis-à-vis* the Mahatma.

The Radicalization of Congress

Ideologically Subhas Chandra Bose was a militant nationalist, who eschewed religious themes and sought to replace them with a belief in the historical destiny of the East. The victory of Japan over Tsarist Russia in 1905 had already stimulated a current of political feeling in Bengal that might be termed premature Third Worldism. Surendranath Banerjee greeted the Japanese victory as a vindication of the potentialities of the eastern nations. In some cases, as with Aurobindo Ghosh, similar sentiments were accompanied by an attachment to Hindu revivalism and a belief in Asia as the moral regenerator of the world. More frequently pan-Asianism was seen as a way of transcending any purely Hindu communal ideology and thus providing a base for Hindu-Moslem unity. Tagore sought to spread the message of a universal brotherhood created by the spirituality of Eastern Man and was to remain an admirer of Japan until its imperialist depredations became too blatant for him to ignore. C. R. Das devoted a part of his Presidential address to Congress in 1922 to the theme of pan-Asianism in the hope of providing ideological cement for the already threatened alliance with the Muslims. Subhas Chandra Bose sought to blend pan-Asianism with the radical social and political themes which came to the fore in Bengal in the twenties and thirties following the non-cooperation movements. The agitation of students and workers in the late twenties, combined with acute frustration at Gandhian methods to produce a growing interest in radical politics and a recrudescence of terrorist tactics. The writings of Marx and Lenin were eagerly read even by many who by no means considered themselves Marxists. *Forward*, a paper run first by C. R. Das and then by Bose, often serialized writings of this sort on the grounds that Indian nationalists should be aware of the ideas and tactics put forward by those engaged in struggle elsewhere.

Meanwhile terrorist activities were resumed, and with greater success than before. In the course of 1930–31 the Inspector General of Police in Bengal, the Superintendent of Police, a District Magistrate and a Sessions Judge were all assassinated. In June 1931 the Chittagong Armoury was raided and 64 police killed. The radicalization in Bengal during these years acquired mass proportions which had a considerable impact on Congress. In 1928 there was a general strike in the Calcutta jute mills involving hundreds of thousands of workers. When Subhas Chandra Bose pressed Congress to adopt Complete Independence as its goal at the Calcutta Conference of 1928 he was supported by a demonstration of 50,000 mill workers. Although Nehru and Bose were to succeed in changing the objectives of Congress at the subsequent Conferences, Gandhi was still placed in charge of the Civil Disobedience Campaign. But while Gandhi attempted to restrict this movement to a narrow circle of those he had personally trained in the tactics of passive resistance, the movement developed an even deeper mass character than the campaigns of 1920–22 and, as we have seen, was far from peaceful in Bengal. Peasants in a number of areas went over from non-payment of taxes to non-payment of rents, predictably incurring the anger of Gandhiji. After vigorous peasant disturbances in UP Gandhi issued the following statement to the UP landlords:

I shall be no party to dispossessing the propertied classes of their property without just cause. My objective is to reach your hearts and convert you so that you may hold all your private property in trust for your tenants and use it primarily for their welfare ... The Ram Rajya of my dream ensures the rights alike of prince and pauper. You may be sure that I shall throw the whole weight of my influence in preventing a class war ... Our socialism or communism should be based on non-violence, and on the harmonious cooperation of labour and capital, the landlord and tenant.[65]

As the rural and urban middle class were the backbone of Congress after Gandhi's rise within it, he had every reason to maintain these amazing mystifications. It should be remembered that trade unions were still very weak and peasant associations practically non-existent. In Bengal the Congress attitude towards peasant agitation allowed a Muslim organization, the Krishak Praja Party, to win influence among the Muslim peasants by promising an end to the *zamindari* system. In general the Congress only survived in Bengal during these years because Bose was able to give Congress policy in the Province a

65. *Maratha*, 12 August 1934.

Politics and Society in Bengal

more dynamic and radical twist. After the breakdown of attempts to negotiate with the British, Gandhi first sought to divert the mass upsurge by announcing that he was embarking on an indefinite fast, and then advised the suspension of the entire Civil Disobedience Campaign. Subhas Bose issued a manifesto jointly with Vithalbhai Patel, who had led peasant agitation in Gujerat, denouncing Gandhi: 'The latest action of Mr Gandhi in suspending Civil Disobedience is a confession of failure ... We are clearly of the opinion that Mr Gandhi as a political leader has failed. The time has come for a radical reorganization of Congress on a new principle, with a new method, for which a new leader is essential.'[66]

This was the beginning of a campaign which led to Bose's election as President of Congress in 1939. However, although Congress temporarily acquired a new leader in this way and was impelled to proclaim a radical nationalist programme, the change was to prove illusory. Bose employed a rhetoric of national and social liberation that was often couched in the language of revolutionary socialism. But Bose's apparently clear and rational commitment to socialism and anti-imperialism was in its own way as much a mystification as the maunderings of the Mahatma. Although Gandhi was often dismissed as a saintly but impractical dreamer, in fact his every action corresponded to the real interests of the Indian bourgeois–landlord classes. He successfully welded together a class bloc that stretched from big industrial magnates such as Birla, Ambarlal, Sarabhai, Kasturbhai, Lalbhai and others, to petty rural notables throughout the Indian countryside. Even his blatantly patronizing approach to *Harijans* and industrial workers ('Capitalists are fathers and workers are children') was somehow rendered palatable even to some of those it abused, since it was accompanied by the Mahatma's apparent willingness to sacrifice himself in their cause. Moreover Gandhi's supposedly saintly unconcern with practical matters was a myth

66. Desai, op. cit., p. 367.

which concealed great skill at political manoeuvring and manipulation.

The triumph of Bose in 1939 was to reveal that he was in a much weaker position. Unlike Gandhi he had no secure class base and was dependent on the unstable moods of radicalism that swept the Bengali petty bourgeoisie. The Big Bourgeoisie of Calcutta naturally did not support him, and had indeed been ardent Gandhians since the days of the first non-cooperation movement. On the other hand the workers' and peasants' organizations in Bengal were still comparatively weak – weaker, for example, than the trade unions and peasant associations in and around Bombay. As a flamboyant popular leader Bose could mobilize large masses of people, but this did not correspond to any really effective forms of mass organization. The Communist Party did dedicate itself to trying to develop these forms of organization and gave support to Bose at this time. But although Communism was able to build up considerable popular prestige in Bengal in the thirties it had no more than a thousand actual Party members by 1940. In general it had more success in organizing cultural associations such as the Progressive Writers' Workshop and the Indian People's Theatre Association than in establishing really strong trade unions. In the event Bose lacked the hard organizational and social base he would have needed to consolidate his success in securing election as President of Congress. Although Bose succeeded in getting Congress to accept militant and radical resolution, Gandhi made sure that he did not gain real power through a series of organizational arrangements that would have done credit to a British trade-union bureaucrat or a Tammany Hall political boss. The Congress machine was entrusted to Vallabhai Patel, who enjoyed good relations with Indian big business. Bose confirmed his own political weakness by resigning his post without a struggle. Gandhi and Nehru re-established control – though, as we have argued, the former's ideological hold on the national movement had been broken.

However the resulting dominance of secular politics came much too late to avert the communal bloodbath of Partition.

'Netaji'

Bose attempted to create a political organization of his own, the Forward Block, and was soon placed under house-arrest by the Government. He escaped and left India for Nazi Germany, by way of Afghanistan and the Soviet Union. Having failed to mobilize a sufficiently strong internal movement he now sought an external deliverance from British domination. He eventually threw in his lot with the Japanese and formed the Indian National Army from among prisoners of war at Singapore. The fact that a large number of the prisoners of war were prepared to participate in Bose's venture showed that he could still attract significant support for his ideas. Moreover Bose's following was genuinely inter-communal in character. After the tide of battle turned decisively against the Japanese, Bose attempted to leave Japan for the Soviet Union, but died in an air-crash. Had he lived he would have played an important role in post-war developments. As it was, British attempts to put on trial those who had taken part in the Indian National Army helped to provoke the unrest and mutiny which preceded Independence. Certainly Bose was one of the very few Indian leaders who appealed to both Hindus and Muslims: among his close associates were two leading Muslims, Shah Nawaz Khan, who later rose to prominence in the Indian Government, and Captain Habibur Rahman, who opted for the new state of Pakistan.

Since Bose's death Calcutta has been subject to frequent convulsions following rumours that *Netaji* (the Great Leader) Subhas Bose was alive and in hiding, and that he would return at the time of his people's greatest need – which for the urban petty bourgeoisie and middle class has been every moment of their lives these past twenty-five years. At enormous open-air meetings, amid the stirring echoes of devotional speeches and songs, his memory has been kept alive in the public mind. The *bhadralok* find in such occasions a welcome distraction from the trials and tribulations of their fallen state; hope mingling with despair, they re-affirm their faith in his Second Coming and look forward to it as their hour of deliverance. However, although an entity known as the Forward Block still survives, it is not a major political factor in West Bengal politics. The passing of Subhas Bose left a vacuum which has largely been filled by local Communism. At a by-election in mid 1949 an important defeat was inflicted on Congress when the Communist Party joined forces with Subhas Bose's elder brother, Sarat Bose. Whatever the limitations of this party – and they are many – its success in the forties, fifties and sixties marked a profound development and advance in Bengali politics. The ability of Communism to establish a powerful position in the Province must certainly be traced back to the intellectual and political traditions of the nineteenth and early twentieth century. Although it will not be possible to present a systematic account of the rise of Communism in Bengal in this article, a brief indication of the nature of this development will furnish an appropriate conclusion.

Marxism and Bengal

The October Revolution met with a quick response from the most advanced nationalist circles in Bengal. Tarkanath Das sent a letter from the Tagore Castle in Calcutta on 12 December 1917 addressed: 'To the Honourable Working Men's and Soldiers' Council of Russia through Leon Trotsky, Petrograd, Russia'. It read: 'A revolutionary India rejoices at the idea of a free Russia, with the true idea of government of the people, by the people, and for the people.'

Throughout the twenties enthusiasm of this sort was to be

expressed by radical and militant nationalists in Bengal. Other Bengalis – mostly based in Berlin where they had gone in the hope of winning support from Germany – who were attracted to Marxism included such men as Bhupendranath Dutta (brother of Swami Vivekananda), Abani Mukherji, Nalini Gupta and Virendra Chattopadhaya. Of these the most outstanding was Chattopadhaya, a fine scholar and linguist, who was later to vanish without trace in Russia during Stalin's purges.

At the same time, Communism was able to attract some of the most brilliant figures of the nationalist movement, notably M. N. Roy. However, as an organized force Communism remained extremely weak in Bengal, as in the rest of India. Militant nationalists did not see the necessity for a strong Communist Party; moreover their admiration for Russia by no means implied an understanding of Marxism or Leninism. M. N. Roy had been drawn into politics by the agitation against Partition and had been a member of a terrorist group. Sent on a mission abroad at the time of the First World War, he met Borodin, under whose influence he became a Marxist. At the Third International's second congress Roy was able to contribute major clarifications to the Theses adopted on colonial questions. He insisted that the formulations initially proposed by Lenin incorrectly attributed a revolutionary role to the bourgeoisie of the colonial lands and ignored the complicity between the imperialist and the colonial bourgeoisie which was frequently to be encountered, especially in countries such as India. Roy also stressed the importance of establishing revolutionary workers' parties in the colonial land, which would alone be able to give resolute leadership to the national revolutionary struggle, and which should aim to develop this struggle towards the establishment of peasant and worker soviets which would challenge the colonial and semi-colonial state structures. After a prolonged discussion Lenin and the other leaders of the International accepted Roy's theses and amendments.[67] Roy was to make a notable contribution to Indian Marxism through a host of books and pamphlets, on politics, history and philosophy. During the twenties he travelled widely as an emissary of the Comintern but played little direct part in Bengali politics. In the early thirties Roy broke with Stalin and returned to India but was soon imprisoned by the British. Although Roy was later to abandon Marxism, his attacks on religious mystification and on Gandhi continued to influence the radical and secular current in Indian nationalism.

M. N. Roy's absence from Bengal during the twenties meant that the task of organizing Communism there fell to others. Significantly, many of these were to be former Muslims, such as Muzaffar Ahmad, Abdul Razzak Khan and Abdul Halim. It was also able to recruit former terrorists, including those responsible for the most remarkable action of this type, the raid on the Chittagong Armoury. However by 1934 the Party still had less than forty members. Communism was weakened in Bengal and India as a whole by a sectarian policy towards Congress during the Comintern's Third Period. This meant that radicalization of Congress in the late twenties and early thirties was led by Nehru and Subhas Bose with negligible Communist intervention. But it remains the case that Communism evoked infinitely less response in India than in many other countries, especially China. This demonstrates the remarkable strength of the pact between British imperialism and India's indigenous possessing classes – a strength that was both ideological and material and grew out of the special character of the colonial social formation.

In the thirties Communism was able to make somewhat

67. See V. I. Lenin, 'Report of the Commission on the National and Colonial Questions', *Collected Works*, vol. 31, pp. 240–50 Moscow, 1966. Also Leon Trotsky, *The First Five Years of the Communist International*, vol. 1, p. 236, New York, 1945.

greater headway. The attention that Communists paid to organizing workers and peasants allowed them to win some important positions in Bombay, Bengal and some other areas. With the advent of Popular Front policies the Party also made a turn to Congress which enabled it to benefit from the radicalization of the late thirties – notably in Kerala but also in Bengal. However the turn to Congress was accompanied by a virtual abandonment of its class approach to the national struggle. Education within the Party on the need to smash the colonial state apparatus, on the nature of imperialism and on the role of the working class and peasantry was to become extremely vague and equivocal. Often Communism was presented as simply a more radical and consistent species of Congress socialism.[68] Too often being a Communist meant simply having a positive attitude towards the Soviet Union and a belief that, after Independence, the state should control the economy. The overlap between this sort of 'Communism' and the 'socialism' of petty functionaries is evident enough. Stalin's insistence on the anti-imperialist role of the so-called national bourgeoisie was further to weaken the Party's already inade-

68. Colletti has argued that there is similarity between the confusion of German Social Democracy on the question of the capitalist state and developments in the Communist Parties in the Stalin and post-Stalin periods: cf. Lucio Colletti, *From Rousseau to Lenin*, London, 1972, pp. 45–111 and 219–229. In India Comintern pressure on the Communist Party to abandon the Leninist conception of the state was supplemented by strong internal pressures from sections of the Indian bourgeoisie who were attracted to a neo-Menshevik Marxism which accepted the inevitability of a bourgeois democratic stage in the Indian revolution. An opposition Communist, Saumyendranath Tagore, was to comment in the late thirties: 'At the present time, we are passing through a phase which can well bear comparison with that period in Russia known as legal Marxism. Marxism shorn of its revolutionary content has become the fashion of the day ... The Indian bourgeoisie through its sympathetic consideration of Marxism, tries to vulgarize Marxism and turn it into a respectable evolutionary theory.' (*The Bourgeois Democratic Revolution and India*, Calcutta, 1939.)

quate grasp of the class dynamic of the national struggle. The incantatory formulas of Stalinism, the incense burning before the image of the Great Leader and the belief that blind obedience would lead to providential deliverance, fitted into well-established indigenous traditions only too easily. The ideology of Indian Communism was further debauched during the war when the Party gave vociferous support to British imperialism after the Soviet Union was invaded. This meant that the Party actively opposed the great nationalist upsurge at the time of the Quit India Movement. The opposite but complementary aberrations of the Communist Party and of Subhas Bose thus allowed Congress to re-establish its hegemony over the national movement after the serious radical challenge of the 1930s. However, the Party retained enough support to become a significant factor in the pre-Independence upsurge. In Bengal it began to challenge Congress at this time and Communists were prominent in the great Tebhaga peasant uprising in 1946.[69] An ill-prepared and premature attempt to stage an insurrection in the late forties was followed by an accommodation with Congress and the Indian bourgeois state in the fifties.

69. The Tebhaga movement of 1946–7 was led and organized by the Bengal provincial branch of the Kisan Sabha, whose membership had swelled from 11,080 in 1937 to 250,000 by 1945. In areas where the movement was most successful, communal harmony between Hindus and Muslims remained firm and unshakeable in spite of the best efforts of the Muslim League to whip up sectarian passions. The Calcutta *Statesman* carried an eye-witness account testifying to the reawakened militancy of the peasant: 'Dumb through past centuries, he is today transformed by the shout of a slogan. It is inspiring to see him marching across a field with his fellows, each man shouldering a *lathi* like a rifle, with a red flag at the head of the procession. It is sinister to hear them greet each other in the silence of bamboo groves with clenched left fists raised to foreheads and a whispered "Inquilab, Comrade!".' (Quoted in Sunil Kumar Sen, *Agrarian Struggle in Bengal*, Delhi, 1972, p. 38. The author was a prominent leader in the Tebhaga movement and his book is full of fascinating detail.)

A Break with the Past

The rise of the Communist Party in West Bengal signified a break with much of the élitist tradition of *bhadralok* politics. Under its leadership the trade unions became a powerful and militant force in the Calcutta factories, integrating many non-Bengali workers. In the countryside the Party also developed its organization and established strong peasant associations. At the same time the Indian variety of Stalinism allowed some of the most negative *bhadralok* habits to linger and even acquire new forms. When the Communist Party split in the early 1960s the bulk of the Bengal Party joined the Left grouping, the CPI (Marxist). Neither the remnants of the CPI nor the new CPI(M) undertook any re-examination of the Party's history or ideology.[70] Although the CPI(M) was subsequently to

70. The CPI is beginning to take the first halting steps towards a documentation of the Party's early history (see *Documents of the History of the Communist Party of India*, vol. 1, 1917–22, edited by G. Adhikari, Delhi, 1971), due weight at last being given to the achievements of its early militants, notably M. N. Roy. Moreover, there is far greater discussion in the party on the role of Stalin and the regressive consequences of his rule. When the Soviet Union invaded Czechoslovakia, the issue was debated at considerable length, and it was only with difficulty that the leadership was able to carry the day in favour of Moscow's action. On the debit side one has to record the great domestic concessions the CPI have made to Indira Gandhi's régime. Haunted, as it were, by the ghost of 1942, when it cooperated with the British in opposition to the 'Quit India' call of the Congress, disturbed by the memory of its indulgent attitude towards the Muslim League and its considerable though indirect contribution to the partition of the subcontinent, with all its baleful and tragic consequence, the CPI has swum with the tide of every chauvinistic current, whether against Pakistan or China, as if in expiation of its past record.

The CPI(M) is neutral, as between Moscow and Peking, but less one suspects by choice than by compulsion. Its internal structure is far more authoritarian than that of the CPI, its outlook more in the Stalinist mould. When it rails at 'revisionism', it is merely expressing its profound dissatisfaction at attempts to tamper with old and hallowed catechisms. On the occasion of Stalin's ninetieth birth anniversary, B.

break from the tutelage of both Moscow and Peking, its subsequent performance has proved that in itself this was by no means sufficient to free it of the sorry traditions of Indian Communism. The Party has twice dominated governments formed in West Bengal without discovering any strategy that would enable it to use its position decisively to advance the revolutionary cause. Most of its activity had been concentrated on electoral concerns and on the illusory hope of 'neutralizing' the bourgeois state machine by government manipulation. While in office its governments failed to develop a dynamic anti-capitalist and anti-imperialist programme. In place of genuine extra-parliamentary mass mobilization, the Party leaders contented themselves with impressive but transitory public demonstrations.

The real problem to which the Party should have devoted itself was that of using its government position to assist a mobilization of Bengali peasants and workers against the bourgeois state machine, leading to the creation of a revolutionary power and an armed popular force. No one can pretend that the problems to be solved were easy ones, but the CPI(M) completely failed even to identify the problems. It was as if Lenin's *State and Revolution* had never been written; which from the

---

T. Ranadive remarked in a panegyric that the dead dictator would have been saddened by the sight of the personality cult of Chairman Mao in China. Here, truly, was a touch of the absurd. Not surprisingly the CPI(M) leaders sent a telegram of congratulation to the Kremlin within forty-eight hours of the Russian invasion of Czechoslovakia. The party rank and file were not called upon to lend weight to this decision. Nevertheless, in matters relating to India, the CPI(M) is much the more militant of the two parties particularly in its opposition to the ruling Congress. On the other hand it lacks a consistent political strategy, which its record in office in the states of Kerala and West Bengal showed only too clearly. All things considered, the appellation of Right or Left, if applied in the truest sense to either of the Communist Parties, would amount to something of a misnomer.

point of view of Indian Communism is just about the case. Moreover, if Lenin was a distant, half-remembered figure, Trotsky's theses on the nature of a transitional revolutionary programme and on the class dynamic of permanent revolution were totally obscured for Indian Communists by Stalinist mythology. The political tactics of the CPI(M) not only failed to confront the question of class power but actively mystified Indian politics by a series of improbable alliances. In Kerala and Bengal it was prepared to ally with any group that opposed Congress, while in Delhi it even voted for Mrs Indira Gandhi in 1969. Mrs Gandhi, however, displayed a surer grasp of the class interests she represents: CPI(M) support for her was repaid in a murderous campaign waged against the Party by Congress thugs in West Bengal.[71]

Survivals

The persistent but unavailing electoralism of the CPI(M) inevitably bred a Left revolt by some of the Party's best militants. This contributed to the so-called Naxalite rebellion. But if the CPI(M)'s politics are disturbingly reminiscent of the constitutionalism of Surendranath Banerjee or C. R. Das, so the revolt of the Naxalites was to echo the obsessional religious exaltation of the early terrorists. The obsolete patterns of *bhadralok* politics had been perfectly preserved in the embalming fluid of Stalinist ideology. The great advance that the rise of a mass Communist Party could have signalled for Bengal had been heavily compromised. Lenin said of the Russian terrorists that they encouraged passivity in the masses by resorting to the individual elimination of members of the ruling

71. Even hostile accounts of the Party concede the scale of its mass work; e.g. M. F. Franda, *Radical Politics in West Bengal*, London, 1972. For an account of the Congress campaign against the Party see Biplap Dasgupta, 'West Bengal Today', *Social Scientist*, vol. 1, no. 8, March 1973.

class. The Naxalites were only more advanced in that they involuntarily failed to eliminate any important ruling-class figure. Unfortunately they displayed the same taste for dubious alliances as the CPI(M) and entered into association with the gangster element in Calcutta who were to play a part in the Congress campaign against the CPI(M). The following account evokes this sad chapter in the history of the revolutionary movement in Bengal:

A Fearsome Catharsis

This quinquennium has been one of the goriest in the history of revolution-mongering in this country ... from urban guerrilla ventures to merciless internecine war much blood has been spilt, umpteen dogmas have been aired and practised, talents have been recruited and laid to waste, enormous courage has been displayed by several thousand young men and women ... Even in West Bengal, the cradle of the Naxalbari movement, the outcome has been a fantastic backlash and the Congress Party is now entrenched in a manner without any precedent; elsewhere in the country, Naxalbari has become a synonyn for a joke; across the border in Bangladesh the adherents of the movement, a mere handful, are on the run: however hard they try now, it will be most difficult for them to get out of the stigma or allegation that they opted out of the war of national liberation ... Misinterpreting the symptoms of discontent in the wake of spiralling food crisis, all agog over reading Lin Piao's thesis about how the country surrounds and encircles the city, they concluded that the revolution was for the taking. No need to organize the masses before the event, they will join the revolution once the sparks start flying; no need to be excessively mulish about imparting political education to fresh recruits – even the so-called antisocial elements, wagon breakers and professional murderers included, would be pressed into service; let violence be afoot for fire turns everything pure and once the revolution is abroad in India, in the afterglow nobody will be sorry if the person who slashed the throat of the class enemy was a genuine ideologue or a ruffian from the market place. Revolution by the short cut was Charu Mazumdar's obsession. The Chinese strung him along for a while, and dropped him quietly after it became obvious what a dead-end he was reaching towards. The pragmatist *goondas* with whom he had struck an alliance soon deserted him; the police, they soon discovered, had a better percentage to offer. Amble down the streets and bylanes of Calcutta, it will be a revelation of a sort: the same young men who, two seasons ago, steeped in the teachings of Mazumdar, were scribbling invocations to Mao Tse-tung are now engaged, on a full time basis in deification of Indira Gandhi ...

A chapter is now ended: Lin Piao disappeared from the scene, the leaders of the great Chinese Party in a faint echo of the Soviet revisions, have started entertaining the unspeakably savage ones who are the perpetrators of the crime of Vietnam, the Naxalbari movement has been puffed out practically everywhere, the CPM is on the run, the revolutionary slogans are all gone from the West Bengal walls, and Charu Mazumdar is safely in prison. Meanwhile so many bright and fearless ones got themselves killed ... and so much is lost for the traditional leftist movement in the country. Who knows what historical process has been served by this fearsome catharsis?'[72]

The Fate of East Bengal

Caught in the maelstrom of religious nationalism, Bengal had been sundered by the Partition of 1947. As the leaders of the Congress and the Muslim League negotiated the details of India's Partition, two Bengali leaders, H. S. Suhrawardy and Sarat Chandra Bose, the elder brother of Subhas, proposed the creation of a united, sovereign, independent Bengal, a plan which ultimately foundered on the opposition of the two major political parties. So against a background of pestilence, famines and communal rioting, Bengal, like the rest of India,

72. 'Naxalites: End of a Chapter', by a correspondent, *Economic and Political Weekly*, 22 July 1972.

was severed in two. In the crucial period before Independence the Communist Party in the East went to extraordinary lengths to submerge itself in the Muslim League. Thus a Communist militant, Shamsuddin, was secretary of the Muslim League in Dacca, the president being the Nawab of Dacca.

In the new province of East Pakistan public euphoria was to give way to disenchantment. Barely seven years after Independence, on 8 March 1954, in the first provincial elections, held under restricted franchise, an opposition United Front led by Fazlul Huq, H. S. Suhrawardy and Maulana Abdul Hamid Khan Bhashani won a crushing victory. Of the 309 seats contested, the ruling Muslim League won only 10. The Chief Minister, Nural Amin (later Vice-President of Pakistan) was conclusively beaten by a young law student, and his ministerial colleagues were similarly routed.

The Muslim League was never to recover its old authority; its pretence to representing any but the most reactionary and microscopic sections of East Bengali society was destroyed. From now on only Mammon from Karachi, Sialkot and Rawalpindi could give it strength, and only the bayonets of a Punjabi-dominated army could give it courage. The League had become, for the vast majority of Bengalis, the symbol of a new servitude.

When the Bengali members of Pakistan's Constituent Assembly wanted their language to be accepted as one of the two national languages of the new state, a not unreasonable request since the population of Bengal exceeded that of the combined numbers of the rest of Pakistan, their request was rejected by the Prime Minister, Liaquat Ali Khan, in the following terms: 'Pakistan is a Muslim state and it must have as its *lingua franca* the language of the Muslim nation ... It is necessary for a nation to have one language and that language can only be Urdu ...' The innuendo that Bengali was alien or hostile to Islamic tradition was in later years to become a battle cry of Yahya's soldiery. It was this unsuccessful attempt to secure national equality within Pakistan which sparked off the struggle of the Bengali people[73].

Meanwhile, the economic exploitation by West Pakistani landlord and business interests assumed a scale and dimension which bore comparison with the East India Company at its worst. Popular resistance deepened and, while increasing numbers of peasants and workers were involving themselves in the struggle, the main thrust nevertheless came from the bourgeois and petty bourgeois, whose principle voice was the Awami League. The smaller size of the Communist forces in East Bengal has failed to save them from a débâcle almost as momentous as that in West Bengal. They permitted the question of East Bengal's oppression by West Pakistan to be virtually monopolized by a bourgeois Party, the Awami League. Having lost the leadership of the national movement, the divergent wings of Communism in Bangladesh proceeded to compound their error in the post-Independence period. The pro-Moscow wing supported Mujib as he consolidated his rule through corruption and demagogy. The other wing allied with the most backward communalist forces in an unsuccessful attempt to make electoral gains. Mujib, who so disastrously adopted the tactics of constitutional petition with the brutalized military machine of General Yahya, has now belatedly discovered the uses of fire-power as he encourages his thugs to gun down dissident students and workers. Only the impotence of his compromised opponents enables him to trample on all the hopes which liberation inspired.

In a summary and impressionistic fashion this study has sought to focus on the dialectic of continuity and discontinuity in Bengal's history. Of all the regions of the subcontinent, Bengal has perhaps been most subject to influences from other countries. The access to world culture and to new and liber-

73. Tariq Ali, *Pakistan: Military Rule or People's Power*, London, 1970, pp. 46–51. The position of the Communist Party in the pre-Independence period is documented in an appendix to this book.

ating ideas that this has entailed has frequently allowed Bengalis to make a notable contribution to the liberation struggles of the subcontinent. But, as we have seen, the impact of external forces has also served to preserve and consolidate some of the most backward and reactionary characteristics of Bengali society. British colonialism sought to base itself on an intensification of the most archaic forms of exploitation; British policy nourished a belief in constitutional progress while seeking to provoke the most virulent communal forces as soon as Bengalis started to produce a politics of their own. Invocation of the shrivelled ideology of the British Fabians led a generation of Congress 'socialists' to drown in the stagnant and fetid waters of Indian capitalism. The cynical formulas of Stalinism wrecked the best hopes of the Bengali popular movement and allowed it to become the expendable pawn of the Russian and Chinese leaders. In the end all these influences helped to produce a certain secularization of Bengali politics, but at the heavy price of many disguised survivals of the past. Only a revolutionary internationalism based on the best energies of the worker and peasant masses can exorcize these ghostly revenants and sweep away the archaic and oppressive conditions that give them a semblance of life.

The Ceylonese Insurrection
Fred Halliday

In April 1971 a revolutionary insurrection exploded in Ceylon.*
Unanticipated by imperialism, and unexpected by revolutionaries elsewhere thousands of poorly armed peasants rose in
organized rebellion against the very government they had voted
into power in the previous May. This upsurge marked a totally
new phase in the hitherto relatively tranquil history of the Ceylonese state. But the insurrection also had an importance far
beyond the coasts of Ceylon itself. A brief résumé of the political situation in which it exploded will indicate its as-
tounding and unique character. The government against which
the people rose had come to power on a verbally 'anti-imperialist' and 'socialist' platform, and included representatives of
the pro-Moscow Communist Party and the ex-Trotskyist
Lanka Sama Samaj Party. It was generally regarded in imperialist circles as a dangerous and dogmatically left-wing régime.
Secondly, the resistance to this government did not take the
form of fragmented and spontaneous resistance, nor of organized strikes, nor even of initial low-level guerrilla actions: it
assumed the form of a widespread armed insurrection, the most
advanced and most complex form of all revolutionary combat.
Moreover, the organization which led this insurrection, the
Janata Vimukhti Peramuna (People's Liberation Front), had
an extremely unusual political origin and formation: it had
developed as a split on the left from a pro-Chinese Communist
Party. After working in clandestinity for five years before

* Sri Lanka since April 1972, but for clarity referred to throughout as
Ceylon – Ed.

emerging in the election campaign of 1970, and after a further year of public work subject to constant harassment, it was able to marshal thousands of insurgents against the Bandaranaike régime. Finally, the international line-up of support for the Ceylonese Government represented a wider and more advanced degree of international counter-revolutionary intervention than has been seen anywhere else to date. Within a few weeks of the outbreak of the insurrection, the Ceylonese bourgeois state had received military aid from the US, Britain, Australia, Russia, Yugoslavia, Egypt, India and Pakistan; and economic aid and political approval from China.

The Ceylonese insurrection was also strategically of great significance for the revolutionary movement in Asia as a whole. In the preceding twelve months, Great Power rivalry in the Indian Ocean had been on the increase, while popular wars in the Gulf (Oman) and Eritrea had consolidated and advanced. The Ceylonese insurrection came a month after the defeat of the US invasion of Laos, and coincided with the popular resistance to Yahya Khan in Bengal. It thus formed part of creeping social conflagration throughout the Asian continent and represented the opening of a new social revolutionary front, in between East Asia and West Asia, at a nodal point where the economic and strategic interests of imperialism had previously appeared to be secure. In the twelve months after the uprising, analogous upsurges in the other Indian Ocean islands of Mauritius and Madagascar further underscored the instability of imperialist control of the whole region. What follows is an attempt to grasp the specificity of recent Ceylonese history, and the nature of the present economic and social crisis in the island, which gave birth to the JVP and the astonishing insurrection of April 1971.

The Advent of Colonialism

Ceylon is a small tropical island, of some 25,000 square miles, separated by a narrow defile of water from the Indian sub-continent. It is divided into different regions by both topography and climate. The whole coastal rim, and the northern and eastern interior, form a flat lowland; in the south-centre, however, a high massif rises sheer above the plains to dense, forested peaks of over 7,000 feet. Overlapping this division is an extremely sharp climatic contrast between a triangular wet zone in the south-west corner of the island, with heavy rainfall, fertile land and irrigated cultivation, and a dry zone haunted by drought and scrub, which occupies the whole of the north and east of the island. In the early pre-colonial epoch, much of this was watered by extensive hydraulic systems, and formed the homeland of the Ancient Sinhalese kingdoms which vied with the Tamil states in the far north of the island. The network of tanks, dams and canals had, however, fallen into disuse and decay by the thirteenth century, well before the arrival of European conquerors; and, as a consequence, the centre of Sinhalese culture and society had shifted southwards to the highlands of Kandy in the south-west. It was in the latter zone that cinnamon was collected wild in the jungles: this spice became the first object of Portuguese plunder in the sixteenth century.

Ceylon underwent a longer historical experience of colonization than any other country in Asia. It bears the marks of this past – some 450 years of European domination – to this day. The Portuguese invaded the island in 1505, and rapidly conquered the coastal lowlands, isolating but not subjecting the Kandyan kingdom in the fastnesses of the south-central highlands. They established a rudimentary but effective trading control over the island, exploiting it for the collection of wild cinnamon, of which Ceylon then had a world monopoly. In the succeeding 150 years they also succeeded in converting a relatively high proportion of the Sinhalese population in the south-western coastal strip, centred on Colombo, to Catholicism, thereby dissociating them both culturally and economically

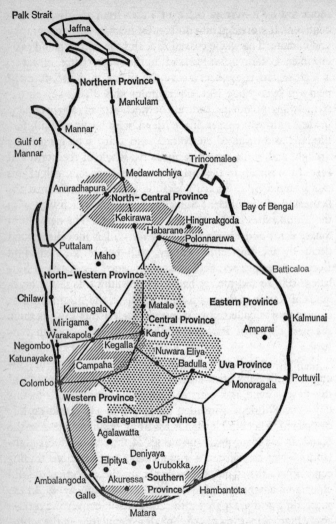

Palk Strait

Jaffna

Northern Province

Mankulam

Mannar

Gulf of
Mannar

Trincomalee

Medawchchiya

Anuradhapura

North-Central Province

Kekirawa

Hingurakgoda

Habarane

Polonnaruwa

Bay of Bengal

Puttalam

Maho

North-Western Province

Batticaloa

Chilaw

Kurunegala

Matale

Eastern Province

Mirigama

Central Province

Kalmunai

Warakapola

Kandy

Amparai

Negombo

Kegalla

Nuwara Eliya

Katunayake

Campaha

Badulla

Uva Province

Colombo

Monoragala

Pottuvil

Western Province

Sabaragamuwa Province

Agalawatta

Deniyaya

Elpitya

Urubokka

Ambalangoda

Akuressa

**Southern
Province**

Hambantota

Galle

Matara

On this map of Ceylon the diagonal shading indicates areas of insurgent activity. The central massif is represented by dots and the main roads by straight lines.

from the Sinhalese in the beleaguered Kandyan uplands. A singular mark of the Portuguese impact on the low-country Sinhalese was their mass adoption of Lusitanian names. To this day, De Souza, Perera, and Gomes proliferate in the southwest: a phenomenon whose only parallel in Asia is to be found in the Philippines, where the Spanish monastic *frailocracia* achieved an even more spectacular success in formally converting and hispanizing the indigenous population. Portuguese rule, however, came to an end in 1658, when the Dutch seized their territories in the island in collusion with the Kandyan nobility, during the long Ibero-Dutch wars of the seventeenth century. The new rulers developed and modernized the economic system bequeathed to them by their predecessors. The Dutch cinnamon economy was now based on organized plantations, in which production was rationalized and yields increased. The blockade of the unsubdued highlands was tightened, and the social and political system of late Kandyan feudalism gradually disintegrated within the ring of Dutch forts and settlements which surrounded it. Holland was not interested in mass conversion of the local population, given the more pronouncedly particularist and racist character of Protestantism: but it did introduce the peculiar system of Roman-Dutch law which has survived in the island down to the present.

The Plantation Economy

Another 150 years later, Ceylon underwent its third European conquest. Once again, it fell to a new colonial master as a byblow of international conflicts within Europe itself. The formation of the Batavian Republic in Holland in 1795, ally and client of the Directory in Paris, led to a British attack on Ceylon as part of England's worldwide counter-revolutionary and imperialist offensive against the French Revolution and its sequels. Kandyan feudalism collaborated with the British expeditionary forces as eagerly and short-sightedly against the Dutch, as it had with the Dutch against the Portuguese. Once the Dutch had been evicted, London proceeded to complete the unfinished work left by Amsterdam. In 1815, the British fomented a revolt by the Kandyan aristocracy against the last Kandyan monarch and marched into the uplands to depose him at their request. Three years later, when the same nobility rose against British rule in a fierce rebellion in which their villagers participated heroically, they were crushed by the occupiers they had themselves invited into their remote redoubts. A subsequent rising in 1848 was soon stamped out; a communications network was constructed to end the old inaccessibility of the uplands; and for the first time, colonial rule now covered the whole length and breadth of the island. The military and political preconditions had now been laid for a massive economic transmutation of the island. In the 1830s, coffee was introduced into Ceylon, a crop which flourishes in high altitudes. The principal impetus to this development of capitalist production in Asian Ceylon was the decline in coffee production in the West Indies, following the abolition of slavery there; similarly, the development of mass cotton production in Egypt for the Manchester mills came in 1861 when the US civil war cut off the supply of US cotton to Britain. Speculators and entrepreneurs from England swarmed to the new conquered uplands, and expropriated vast tracts of forest on the higher slopes of the Kandyan valleys from the villagers who had traditionally used them as common lands for fuel and fruit-gathering. The right to seize this land was 'purchased' from the British state at nominal prices: it was then cleared and converted into enormously profitable coffee plantations. The Kandyan villagers refused to abandon their traditional subsistence holdings and become wage-workers on these new capitalist estates. Despite all the pressure exerted by the colonial state, they could not be broken into the mould of a plantation proletariat in the nineteenth century. British imperialism thus had to draw on its limitless reserve army of labour in India itself, to man its lucrative new outpost to the south. An infamous system of contract labour was established, which transported hundreds of thousands of Tamil 'coolies' from Southern India into Ceylon for the coffee estates. These Tamil labourers died in tens of thousands both on the journey itself, and in the nightmarish conditions of the early plantations.[1] Nearly a million were imported in the 1840s and 1850s alone: the death rate was 250 per 1,000. The decimation and super-exploitation of this class founded the fortunes of British imperialism in Ceylon. The creation of this vast immiserized mass not only generated the surplus-value pumped regularly home to London: it divided the oppressed population of the island as well, allowing the colonial state to manipulate and exacerbate ethnic antagonisms between Tamil and Sinhalese in a classic strategy of divide and rule. The coffee economy collapsed in the 1870s, when a leaf disease ravaged the plantations. But the economic system it had created survived intact into the epoch of its successor crop. In the 1880s, tea was introduced on a wide scale and soon had ousted coffee completely. The main social alteration to which this led was not in the structure of the labour force, which remained as before composed of contracted Tamil coolies, but in the nature of the entrepreneurial units. Tea was more capital-intensive and needed a higher volume of initial investment to be processed. The result was that individual estate-owners were now supplanted by large English consolidated companies based either in London ('sterling firms') or Colombo ('rupee firms'). Monoculture was thus increasingly capped by monopoly within the plantation economy. The pattern thus created in the nineteenth century has remained essentially identical ever since: Liptons and Brooke Bonds rule the Ceylonese massif down to this day. The only significant modifications to the colonial economy were the addition of a

1. E. F. C. Ludowyk, *The Story of Ceylon*, London, 1967, pp. 195–9.

rubber sector in the foothills below, and the enlargement of coconut cultivation in the coastal region near Colombo. These three crops, in descending order of importance, henceforward dominated the island's commercial agriculture.

Ceylon's Ethnic Divisions

The importing of Tamil labour levelled off in the twentieth century, leaving a social and ethnic configuration in Ceylon which has fundamentally determined the subsequent character and course of class struggle there. It can now be summed up as follows. 70 per cent of the population are Sinhalese.[2] They are concentrated in the south and centre of the island, and are themselves divided into 'low-country' and 'Kandyan' Sinhalese, according to their region of residence and date of conquest by European colonialism; the latter were naturally much less deeply affected than the former, and have preserved traditionalist superstructures (religion and kinship) more jealously. The bulk of the Kandyan Sinhalese are subsistence peasants, cultivating rice in small plots in the upland valleys. Colonial rule, however, by no means wiped out the traditional ruling class which had squeezed this peasantry with its oppressive exactions before conquest. A grasping neo-feudal stratum of aristocratic and clerical landowners, chieftains and monks, retained sizeable holdings and dominated village life, which was steeped in reactionary Buddhist superstitions. This stratum was recruited in the upper Goyigama caste and wielded immemorial local power. Keeping to its paddy estates, it did not participate much in the cash-crop agriculture established by the British. The low-country Sinhalese, by contrast, who outnumbered the Kandyan Sinhalese by some 3 to 2, had been exposed to three centuries' more European rule: their social structure was consequently far more hybrid. While many subsistence villages remained relatively untouched, large numbers

2. B. H. Farmer, *Ceylon – A Divided Nation*, London, 1963.

of low-country Sinhalese were inducted into the coconut and rubber plantations, while others formed the nucleus of the urban working class that developed in Colombo and other ports in the island. At the same time, the commercialization of coastal agriculture by the British created new opportunities for the privileged, who had long acquired some of the basic skills for profiting from colonial rule, under the Portuguese and Dutch. Thus low-country landowners participated on a significant scale in the development of the rubber sector, and rapidly dominated the coconut zone. A business élite based on local commerce burgeoned in Colombo. Many of these wealthy and powerful low-country Sinhalese were recruited from the Karawa caste (originally linked to fishing, and hence well below the Goyigama in the caste scale), and were Roman Catholics with Portuguese cognomens. They sedulously imitated and parodied the culture and customs of their British overlords. They were flanked by the small community of descendants from the Portuguese and Dutch themselves, the 'Burghers', who formed an arrogant Eurasian minority in the towns.

The Tamil population of Ceylon, for its part, is even more divided than the Sinhalese. Numerically, it is equally distributed between the so-called 'Ceylon Tamils', who are overwhelmingly the majority community in the Northern Province of the island, and extend in strength down the east coast, and the so-called 'Indian Tamils', who are clustered on the plantations of the central massif. The 'Ceylon Tamils' are those who have resided in the island from its earliest history – indeed, since before the Christian epoch. They form a compact rural society in the north, concentrated mainly in the Jaffna peninsula; this society is organized along rigid caste-class lines. The peasantry was not affected by plantation encroachments, and ekes out a living from arid soil under the pressure of the exploitative higher caste groups. A trading stratum benefiting from proximity to southern India has long been entrenched in

Jaffna. The Hindu landowners and businessmen maintain a tight social control of the population by a network of communal influences and organizations. Together with the richer peasants, they provided many of the recruits to the island civil service created by the British, who deliberately promoted a Tamil influx into the colonial bureaucracy and police in order to batten down the danger of rebellion by the Sinhalese, who constituted the majority of Ceylon's inhabitants. The 'Indian' Tamils, on the other hand, existed in another geographical and social world altogether from the 'Ceylon' Tamils. They formed, as has been seen, a solid mass of captive wage-workers in the central massif, the rural proletariat which produced the bulk of the country's wealth. Given the superimposition of a tea and a rice economy in the Kandyan uplands, these Tamil workers (by the mid twentieth century permanent inhabitants of Ceylon, of course) co-populated the massif with the Kandyan Sinhalese peasantry; on its eastern flank, however, where plantations were created out of dense jungles without previous Sinhalese settlement, in some districts they constituted a very large majority. The Tamil rural proletariat does not share village residence with the Kandyan peasantry: it is located in barrack-like 'coolie lines' of its own, usually on hills above the level of the Sinhalese hamlets below.

In the early decades of this century, Ceylon – 'Jewel of the Indian Ocean' – had become indeed a polished gem in the treasure-trove of British imperialism. It was not only a highly prosperous plantation economy. It was also, largely because of this, one of the most smoothly and easily governed colonies in the Empire. The British were able to use the ethnic divisions of the island, crystallized in the pattern of the labour force, to defuse any threat of serious struggle for independence. A basically bipolar system of the Ceylonese type was much more malleable for this purpose than the polyethnic mosaic of India proper, where the sheer multiplicity of regional and linguistic groups cancelled their diversity out to some extent, and created the space for a genuinely nationalist movement against British rule (eventually, of course, itself split by Gandhi's reactionary confessionalism, but even so preserving a trans-ethnic character). Tamil-Sinhalese antagonisms were much easier for English Governors to manipulate. Moreover, the British had at their disposal a uniquely subservient and pliable local élite from both groups, formed by three centuries of European colonialism before they themselves had even arrived in Ceylon. The landowners and traders of Colombo and Jaffna were not only already inured to obeying white overlords. They had no independent sources of capital accumulation such as the much more powerful merchants of Bombay and Calcutta had in India, with its far more developed pre-colonial industries and its much larger post-colonial domestic markets. The result was that no equivalent to the Indian Congress Party ever appeared in Ceylon. The indigenous bourgeoisie simply basked in the sunshine of Edwardian imperialism and complacently mimicked its masters. It did not even produce a *single political party* before Independence – surely a record even in the annals of the Commonwealth.[3] The British themselves paid the best tribute to the matchless obsequiousness of the bourgeoisie – Sinhalese and Tamil – when they voluntarily granted Ceylon universal suffrage in 1931, before any other colony in the Empire, and without a single group in local political life having asked for it! Such was the docility of the fawning parliamentarians of the Legislative Council and the seeming passivity of the masses. (The Conservative MP co-responsible for this happy stroke unabashedly evoked the example of Disraeli's coup in granting the Second Reform Bill of 1867 in Britain.[4]) Even after the establishment of universal suffrage, no party system emerged: rich notables and dignitaries were elected to the Legislative Council as individuals, and there acquired the

3. Ludowyk, p. 246, and S. A. Pakeman, *Ceylon*, London, 1964, p. 155.

4. Pakeman, p. 126.

'training' necessary for eventual transfer of administrative responsibility to them.

A Socialist Party

In the last years before the Second World War, however, a small group of Marxist intellectuals appeared on the paralysed political scene in Colombo. In 1935, they formed the LSSP, which campaigned against the imperialist oppression and exploitation of Britain, and attacked the grovelling complicity of the Ceylonese bourgeoisie with it. It elected two members to the state Council in 1936; more significantly, its agitation gradually started to arouse sections of the plantation workers and peasantry. A sudden upswing of class struggle in the rural regions coincided with the onset of the Second World War. The LSSP, which had hitherto been a loose organization grouping all tendencies on the Left, now split: a minority which supported Stalin was expelled and the Third International was denounced from positions similar to those of Trotsky in early 1940. In consequence, the LSSP did not follow the path of class-collaboration with the British pursued by the Indian and other Communist Parties once Germany had attacked the Soviet Union. It denounced the British military build-up in Ceylon during the war, and intensified its efforts to mobilize the exploited classes in the towns and countryside against the colonial power. The result was a mounting series of strikes and riots on the plantations, which created panic among the estate-owners and tea companies. Threatened both by the LSSP's uncompromising hostility to its war effort in Asia, and by its political awakening of the Ceylonese masses, British imperialism acted swiftly to cut off the possibility of a national liberation movement under the party's leadership. The LSSP was dissolved in June 1940, and its leaders jailed. Ruthless suppression of underground resistance followed. Many of the LSSP leaders subsequently succeeded in escaping to India during a Japanese air-raid, where they transferred the centre of gravity of their activities during the rest of the war. Incipient mass radicalization was thus repressed before it achieved a durable political form in Ceylon.[5]

Thus, after the war, Britain was able to arrange a leisurely 'transfer of power' to a Ceylonese oligarchy that had scarcely even feigned an independence movement against it. The prospect seemed an extremely fair one for neo-colonial stability. Ceylon was not plagued by over-population of the Indo-Pakistani type. It had less than 8 million inhabitants, whose per capita standard of living was by now well above that of the subcontinental mainland. During the war, its traditional rice imports from Burma had been cut off; to prevent the danger of social unrest in time of war, the British were obliged to establish an official rationing system and to fix the price of imported rice at state cost somewhat below its market levels, while simultaneously guaranteeing prices for domestic paddy producers. The practical result was a welfare system of subsidized rice, which was continued after the war when world prices rose considerably. A complementary characteristic of the British legacy was the exceptionally high level of education in Ceylon – again rendered possible because of the small size of the island and therefore the comparatively modest cost of a school system to imperialism. Literacy was thus some 65 per cent in 1945 – an extremely high figure for Asia at that time. The social and political significance of both these mechanisms – very atypical for any colonial or ex-colonial country – are evident: they reflect an unusual capacity of the state to control the population by peaceful mystification rather than physical repression. Budget allocations expressed this Ceylonese peculiarity dramatically: as late as a decade after independence, state expenditure on food subsidies and social services, including education, was no less than ten times that on the armed forces.

5. G. J. Lerski, *Origins of Trotskyism in Ceylon*, Stanford, 1968, pp. 222–5 and 233–5.

The latter were to remain miniscule by comparison with the norm in the so-called Third World, some 4,500 men in 1962.

Family-Bandyism

It was this apparently tranquil land which the British handed over to the Ceylonese oligarchy in 1948, after the latter had hastily formed the United National Party. The UNP was duly installed in office, after elections under a special British-made Constitution, replete with a 'Defence Agreement' which gave Britain a naval base at Trincomalee, an airfield at Katunayake, and training control of the embryonic Ceylonese Army, which was liberally stocked with British officers. The provincial bourgeoisie of Jaffna had created its own ethnic party, the Ceylon Tamil Congress, which collaborated with the UNP government. The opposition was provided by the re-emergent LSSP (itself temporarily split into two wings), which affiliated to the Fourth International but now found itself sealed off from the plantation workers by a separate 'Indo-Tamil' communal organization sponsored by the British: its base was henceforward mainly in the urban working class of Colombo and the island's small trade-union movement. The UNP régime which now presided over the first eight years of independence was one of unbridled, old-world reaction. The Prime Minister and symbol of the 'best of the British tradition' was Don Stephen Senanayake, a plutocratic landowner whose fortunes were derived from the graphite mines on his inherited estates, and whose political style was a comico-repulsive replica of the English ruling class. Senanayake's régime was run by a family clique whose corrupt nepotism had few parallels anywhere else in the world, outside perhaps the monarchies of Saudi Arabia or Ethiopia. Thus D. S. Senanayake himself was not only Prime Minister, but Minister of Defence and Minister of Foreign Affairs; his son Dudley Senanayake was Minister of Agriculture; his nephew John Kotelawala was Minister of Commerce;

his cousin J. R. Jayawardene was Minister of Finance; while another nephew, R. G. Senanayake, subsequently became Minister of Trade. The only prominent member of the UNP Cabinet not integrated into the nexus of 'family-bandyism' by kinship to Senanayake Senior was S. W. Bandaranaike, who held the important portfolio of Local Administration. The government's first and most fundamental act was to rush through the infamous Ceylon (Parliamentary Elections) Amendment Act No. 48 of 1949, which at one stroke disenfranchised the totality of the 500,000-strong Tamil plantation proletariat of Indian origin. Bandaranaike was later to be fond of calling Ceylon the 'Asian Switzerland', because of his allegedly neutral foreign policy. In fact, no soubriquet could have been more appropriate. For the Ceylonese bourgeoisie, like the Swiss, had now succeeded in excluding the central core of the working class which produced the bulk of its surplus-value from the political framework of the nation altogether: Ceylonese capitalism, like Swiss, was to be built on the backs of 'foreign' workers with not even the most elementary formal rights of citizenship within the country. The UNP régime thus in advance rendered totally impotent any parliamentary perspective for the Ceylonese Left, and set rolling the avalanche of rabid Sinhalese chauvinism which was to crash over the country in the next decade. After this basic achievement, the Senanayake government did very little: virtually no new economic development was promoted, although the Korean War boom temporarily hiked Ceylonese export prices to record heights.

In 1952, Senanayake died – appropriately enough, from a riding accident during a mock-English equestrian outing. A violent tussle between his son Dudley Senanayake and his nephew John Kotelawala ensued for his succession. Lord Soulbury, the English Governor-General, arbitrated in favour of the son, much to the chagrin of the nephew. Dudley Senanayake's premiership, however, was cut short by the first major social crisis after independence. World rice prices had rocketed because of the Korean War, to a point where the traditional rice subsidy alone took 20 per cent of the total budget. Faced with sudden economic difficulties, the younger Senanayake slashed the rice subsidy, stopped school meals and hoisted rail and postal charges. The Left, led by the LSSP, promptly mobilized the masses to resist this direct attack on their standard of living. A day of civil disobedience or *Hartal* was called, backed by a general strike launched by the main non-communal trade unions. The popular response was overwhelming. The government thereupon panicked and deployed the Army to suppress the movement. The result was to radicalize a peaceful protest into armed clashes in which there were numerous casualties. In the absence of serious planning or leadership, the *Hartal* was crushed. But the younger Senanayake was badly damaged by the crisis, and had to resign. His swashbuckling cousin Kotelawala took over the premiership. The rice subsidy was partially restored, and various foreign policy initiatives were undertaken to brighten Ceylon's image abroad (entry into the UN in 1955); but by now the political isolation of the UNP – widely dubbed the 'Uncle–Nephew Party' – and the hatred of the masses for its super-anglicized landowner and comprador oligarchy was manifest.

In 1956 Kotelawala called a general election. The UNP was now for the first time confronted by a major bourgeois rival, led by Solomon Bandaranaike – the Sri Lanka Freedom Party. Bandaranaike, an original pillar of the UNP, had hoped to succeed the elder Senanayake before the full extent of the latter's 'family-bandyism' became apparent. Disgruntled by the preferment of the younger Sananayake and Kotelawala over his head, he had seceded from the UNP in the early fifties. Bandaranaike was of virtually identical social background to the Senanayake clique. He was the son of a low-country owner of vast lands in the Western Province, who had been the Maha Mudaliya or 'Chief Native Interpreter' to the British

Governors in the previous century – the top ceremonial position of the tame local aristocracy in the nineteenth century. He was married to the daughter of one of the highest Kandyan chiefs. Bandaranaike's aim was to propel himself into power by building a political machine that could defeat the UNP. He saw his chance with the growing unpopularity of the Kotelawala government. The increasing social radicalism of the rural masses could be used as a battering-ram for his own ambitions. Naturally, Bandaranaike could not mobilize this discontent for anti-capitalist goals: to do so would have been to contradict the very reason for existence of this big bourgeois. At most, he offered the masses the watery palliatives of a few municipal nationalizations (port and bus companies) of the sort that any self-respecting advanced capitalist country had accomplished long ago, and the termination of the defence agreement with Britain. But into this otherwise feeble potion he mixed one searing toxic, to make the heads of the masses swim until they could no longer see their real class enemies: religious and racial chauvinism.

Posturing as the champion of Sinhala Buddhism against 'alien' and 'privileged' elements in Ceylonese society, Bandaranaike feinted an attack on the low-country Christian élite behind the UNP while in fact delivering rabid demagogic thrusts against the Tamil working class and peasantry. He himself was a turn-coat Anglican who had adopted Buddhism, so furthering his political career: he now whipped up religious frenzy against the non-Sinhala population in Ceylon by denouncing their sinister 'usurpations' of the central role that Buddhism should play in national life. The very name of his party was a confessional programme in itself. Sri Lanka means 'Holy Ceylon' and designates precisely the messianic chauvinism that is inseparable from Buddhism in the island. For religiosity and racism cannot be dissociated in Ceylon: the local brand of Therevada Buddhism claims, much like Judaism, that the Sinhalese are a 'chosen people' and that Ceylon is their sacred island, divinely elected to its unique historical and spiritual destiny by Buddha himself. This wretched mystification naturally excludes the Tamils and other minorities from any equal role in national life. Bandaranaike thus campaigned raucously for 'the exclusive use of Sinhala as an official language' in Ceylon – again ostensibly attacking English while in fact suppressing Tamil. The banner of 'Sinhala Only' rapidly mobilized the rural notables in the Kandyan uplands, in particular. Bandaranaike was able to rally the landowners, monks, teachers and ayurvedic physicians in the villages of the massif against corrupt 'cosmopolitan' and 'foreign' influences. This stratum had been comparatively by-passed by the UNP, and now struck out vigorously for an increased share of power. Much the most important component of this group was the Buddhist *sangha* or monastic orders. These Buddhist orders were everywhere large landowners in their own right, and exercised great ideological sway over the Sinhalese villages. It so happened that the year 1956 was the 'Buddha Jayanti', or 2,500th anniversary of Buddha's decease and death-bed consecration of 'Sri Lanka': the UNP government had already allocated massive state funds to celebrate this mythical event. In a climate of frenzied clerical fervour, a formidable phalanx of Buddhist monks or *bhikkus* was formed into *Eksath Bhikku Peramuna* or United Monks Front, at the behest of the ambitious and unscrupulous Venerable Mapitigama Buddharakkhita Thero.[6] Buddharakkhita controlled the key Kelaniya temple and had been a founder member and patron of Bandaranaike's SLFP since its inception in 1951. Swarms of his acolytes now criss-crossed the island urging the population to 'be ready to sacrifice your life for the Restoration of Buddhist Ceylon'; innumerable bonzes virulently anathematized the 'westernized' Kotelawala and his UNP. Buddharakkhita himself lavishly dispensed the ample funds of the Kelaniya temple, in a personal tour by chauffeured

6. D. E. Smith (ed), *South Asian Politics and Religion,* Princeton, 1966, pp. 490–99.

limousine, for this holy cause. He was later to state that his own contribution to Bandaranaike's campaign was of the order of 100,000 rupees.

Swept along on a tide of foaming clericalism and racism, laced with 'anti-imperialist' cant, the SLFP won a massive triumph in the general elections of 1956. In no sense whatever was the victorious party more 'progressive' than the UNP; nor did it represent the 'petty bourgeoisie', as was often alleged abroad, although it had a strong petty-bourgeois following. Bandaranaike and his entourage were big bourgeois like the Senanayake clan. The SLFP organization did rest on a more traditionalist and Kandyan-oriented sector of the propertied classes than the UNP: paddy-owners, for example, predominated over plantation-owners in its parliamentary ranks – in other words, the rural interests behind it were at this date more linked to rice than to rubber, coconuts or tea, and were here less directly tied to imperialism.[7] But these were no less malignant or reactionary in their exploitation of the poor peasantry and landless labourers. The Buddhist *sangha* gained enhanced corporate power. The urban Karawa businessmen and merchants who had previously backed the UNP financially without participating in its political leadership now simply switched their funds to the new régime in exchange for similar pay-offs. From this point of view, the SLFP was simply the alternative party of the Ceylonese bourgeoisie. However, there is no doubt whatever that Bandaranaike had succeeded in capturing, canalizing and *confiscating* the deep frustration and wrath of the impoverished rural masses, both Low-Country and Kandyan Sinhalese, which had been accumulating against the old order represented by the UNP. The function of his rabid clerico-chauvinist demagogy was precisely to *divert* the pent-up anger of the poor against their class brothers of another ethnic group: the Tamils. Moreover, it was precisely the prior

7. Marshall Singer, *The Emerging Elite: A Study of Political Leadership in Ceylon*, Cambridge, Mass., 1964, pp. 85–7.

historical absence of a genuine nationalist movement against the *British* which permitted a belated intoxication of the masses in a pseudo-nationalist movement against the Tamils. Bandaranaike's party thus appropriated and perverted both the gathering social crisis in the countryside and national sentiments bottled up under the English and never released against them. This is what gave it its false dynamism and mass energy, and made the SLFP potentially a more dangerous enemy of the workers and peasants than the discredited Uncle–Nephew Party itself. Events were to show this conclusively within a short space of time. Even if the SLFP represented a different faction of the bourgeoisie, it was equally incapable of fighting imperialism or of freeing the masses at home.

Once in office, Bandaranaike promptly rammed through a 'Sinhala Only' Bill. He also terminated the Defence Pact with Britain and nationalized the Colombo Port Authority and Omnibus Company. But these measures were strictly a sideshow. No agrarian reform, needless to say, was implemented, despite pre-electoral promises to this effect. Meanwhile, the reactionary ideological concoction of 'Buddhist socialism' served to distract the masses and stoke up chauvinist hostility against the Tamil communities. The logical and predictable result of this propaganda was a wild anti-Tamil pogrom in May 1958, which wreaked a terrific toll on the minority throughout the island. After this achievement, the government moved on to muzzle the urban working class by passing the Public Security Act in 1959, the most savagely repressive law in the whole arsenal of Ceylonese bourgeois legislation, specifically designed to crush strikes and demonstrations by the oppressed wherever necessary; it was liberally used by both the UNP and the SLFP in the years to come. This, however, was to be the culmination of Bandaranaike's career. For the very forces of clerical chauvinism which he had unleashed and manoeuvred with such calculation now had no further use for him. Buddharakkhita had come to be known as 'Buddy Racketeer' as he in his turn honeycombed the SLFP organization and built up a private financial empire from his luxurious air-conditioned flat behind the Kelaniya temple. Thwarted in one of his crooked deals over a government rice contract and impatient with the slow-down in the anti-Tamil drive after the riots of 1958, Buddharakkhita ordered the execution of the politician he had helped so decisively to loft into power. Like a South Asian Dollfuss, Bandaranaike was gunned down by a hired monk on his own verandah in September 1959 – victim of the clerico-chauvinism he had himself promoted and symbolized.

A brief period of parliamentary confusion followed. Then in June fresh elections were held. Leadership of the SLFP, in the best traditions of the UNP, now devolved on to Solomon Bandaranaike's closest relative – his wife Sirimavo Bandaranaike. It was she who now presided over another electoral victory and a new five-year government. Scarcely any new policies were implemented, however. The immobilism of the Sirimavo Bandaranaike régime was accompanied by a second flowering of 'family-bandyism'. Her nephew Felix Bandaranaike became the key figure in the Cabinet, controlling the critical Ministry of Finance, and the Parliamentary Secretaryships of External Affairs and Defence; while her cousin William Gopallawa was made Governor-General two years later. Working-class unrest soon erupted in a sequence of demonstrations and strikes throughout 1962, by dock and transport workers and others. Then, in 1963, a broad trade-union front hammered out a common programme of 21 demands of an economic, but anti-capitalist, character and began mass struggles for it. Seriously threatened for the first time by an opposition to its left, the Sirimavo Bandaranaike régime reacted by offering to co-opt the LSSP into its government in exchange for a few token concessions. This manoeuvre was aimed at breaking working-class resistance by buying off and integrating the most important section of its traditional leadership. It was successful. The

LSSP accepted Sirimavo Bandaranaike's offer and was forth-with expelled from the Fourth International. The LSSP, in its origins a courageous vanguard in struggle against the British, had degenerated into a standard reformist organization. Its political principles and will had been submerged under the torrent of pseudo-radical chauvinism that marked the rise of the SLFP, and it had now become only the miserable ruins of its former self. Henceforward it abandoned any vestige of socialism and decorated a ferociously rightist and obscurantist bourgeois government, by doing so accepting the Sinhalese suprematism of the Bandaranaike clan to boot. It was promptly set to work strike-breaking for the régime in late 1964. A small minority of genuine revolutionary militants had broken away from it to form the LSSP(R), headed by the trade-union leader Bala Tampoe, secretary of the Ceylon Mercantile Union. The major achievement of the Cabinet was the notorious Sirimavo–Shastri Pact, which henceforward legalized the mass deportation of Tamil workers to India.

The coalition SLFP–LSSP government, however, lasted only eight months before defections from it led to its defeat. New elections were held in January 1965. They resulted in a come-back by the UNP, which reconquered enough of the rural vote to form a new government, and to underline the interchangeability of Ceylon's two main capitalist parties. Now under Dudley Senanayake's leadership once again, the UNP outdid even the SLFP in professions of Buddhist zeal and was not far behind in neutralist piety. The whole calendar was reorganized to make the Buddhist Polya holy days the (irregular) rest days of the week henceforward. Humble applications to the World Bank produced modest loans; the Italian ENI was induced to finance an oil refinery. Much more important, the UNP systematically suppressed the wage-demands and social protests of both the urban and rural masses, reducing the rice ration and cutting expenditure on education. Using the Public Security Act passed by the SLFP six years earlier, the UNP ruled for no less than three and a half years of its five years of tenure under emergency regulations. By the end of this time, the Ceylonese masses were in a mood of unprecedented and nation-wide dissatisfaction and militancy.

The Economy in Crisis

During the late 1960s Ceylon's neo-colonial political and economic structures were, silently, starting to come under critical pressure. There were three general indices of this situation: Ceylon's sinking export income, growing foreign debt, and escalating unemployment. As the most recent census (1963) indicated, Ceylon has a distinct urban working class, but the majority of the population are employed in the rural area, in agriculture and in rural handicrafts.

TABLE I
Occupations

Agriculture, forestry, hunting, fishing	1,682,000
Handicrafts	416,000
Power and Hydro-power	9,000
Mining	9,000
Manufacture	313,000
Construction	85,000
Trade, Banking and Insurance	289,000
Transport and Communication	138,000
Others	494,000
Occupations Inadequately Described	175,000
Total	3,610,000

Since 1963 there has been no significant alteration in the relative proportions shown by the census.

Throughout the 1960s the share of industry in GNP remained almost constant, rising from 12 per cent to 13 per cent (at constant 1959 factor cost prices); the major source of income continued to be services and agriculture.

173

TABLE 2
GNP at 1959 Factor Cost Prices[8]

Sectors	Amount (Millions of Rupees)		
	1967	1968	1969
Agriculture, forestry and fishing	3,040	3,248	3,321
Manufacturing, mining, quarrying, electricity, etc.	1,104	1,206	1,288
Construction	351	446	527
Trade, transport and other services	3,731	3,999	4,299
Gross Domestic Product	8,226	8,900	9,435
Net factor income from abroad	−44	−39	−65
Gross National Product	8,181	8,861	9,370

Yet this dependence on primary agricultural products was far greater for export earnings than for production as a whole. Nothing was done to lessen this dependence and the Ceylonese masses suffered increasingly from declining export prices and rising import costs. In 1967, a typical year, total exports were Rs. 1,690 millions: of these 63 per cent (Rs. 1,061 m.) came from the export of tea, 17 per cent (Rs. 282 m.) from the export of rubber and 10 per cent (Rs. 167 m.) from the export of coconut. In other words, 90 per cent of all Ceylon's export earnings came from the exports of three primary products. Throughout the 1960s the income generated by these exports steadily fell.

As import prices rose over the same period, Ceylon came to have a growing foreign exchange deficit. The deficit rose steadily, from Rs. 95 m. in 1957, to Rs. 349 m. in 1966, to Rs. 744 m. in 1969.

The political reasons for this degeneration were clear enough. Ceylon's economy was controlled by a coalition of imperialist firms and a local bourgeoisie parasitic on, and participant in, this exploitation. The precise workings of this

8. Central Bank of Ceylon, *Annual Report* for 1969.

TABLE 3

Loss of Import Capacity Due to Change in the Terms of Trade (in Millions of Rupees) (1959 Base)

	Tea	Rubber	Three Major Coconut Products	All Products
1960	−31·9	+37·3	−26·0	−10·6
1961	−36·9	−24·5	−90·3	−150·6
1962	+1·47	−13·3	−79·6	−81·9
1963	−133·7	−55·7	−63·1	−241·8
1964	−156·0	−93·7	−84·4	−315·8
1965	−211·8	−103·5	−12·0	−308·9
1966	−317·7	−145·3	−44·6	−505·3
1967	−419·2	−190·1	−54·7	−667·1
1968	−484·5	−261·7	−17·7	−783·8
1969	−545·7	−193·8	−49·7	−810·7

relation can be shown by an analysis of Ceylon's major export, tea.[9] 35 per cent of all tea estates (comprising 29 per cent of all tea-growing lands) were directly owned by British ('sterling') firms, such as Liptons and Brooke Bond, while British capital was also strongly represented in the Ceylon-registered 'rupee' firms that owned another 30 per cent of the estates. But these crude ownership statistics understated foreign control of Ceylonese tea since its marketing was almost entirely in the hands of foreign, mainly British, agency houses. British capital controlled the buying, pricing, marketing, shipping and insurance of Ceylonese tea. In 1967 69 million pounds of tea were sold by the agency houses at Colombo auctions, and another 110 million pounds were sold at the London Auctions in Mincing Lane. Only 8 million pounds, under 2 per cent, were sold directly by Ceylon to foreign purchasers. Ceylon's subjection to imperialism was also shown by the markets for its tea: the major buyer is the UK (35 per cent in 1968, 30 per cent in

9. *Ferguson's Ceylon Directory*, 1970–71.

1969), followed by the US (7 per cent in 1968, 10 per cent in 1969), Australia (8 per cent in both years) and South Africa (7 per cent in 1968, 6 per cent in 1969). The only major purchaser not an imperialist country is Iraq (9 per cent in 1968, 8 per cent in 1969).

Ceylon's continued dependence on its traditional primary exports and the vested interest of the ruling class in these commodities thus had an inevitable concomitant: growth in Ceylon's foreign debt and hence in external political control over the island. The surplus for investment, and for financing the foreign trade deficit, had to come from foreign loans and running down Ceylon's foreign exchange reserves.

TABLE 4
Ceylon's Foreign Debt 1955–69[10]

Year	Rs.m.
1955	205·0
1960	293·7
1965	489·3
1966	548·8
1967	739·3
1968	1074·3
1969	1375·5

Yet this foreign credit was used only to a very limited extent to check the deterioration of the economic situation as a whole. Industrial production did not rise as a percentage of total output, while imports of consumer goods, in particular food, continued to rise. For example, in 1970 Ceylon spent more just on importing chillies than she earned from tourism, and rice (a Ceylonese crop) formed 15 per cent of all her imports. Over two fifths of Ceylon remains tropical forest, and the potentiality exists for the island to become a net exporter of foodstuffs: in 1971 they made up 53 per cent of her imports. The

10. Central Bank of Ceylon, *Annual Report* for 1969.

existing relations of production had been such that Ceylon's foreign exchange position continued to decline, together with its internal economic situation, while direct foreign political control through the IMF and other imperialist agencies correspondingly increased.

This overall deterioration was reflected in the rise in domestic unemployment – itself highlighted by two additional factors that generated intensified popular reaction to it. These were the steep rise in population and the extremely high literacy level in Ceylon. In 1946 Ceylon had a population of 6·6 millions; by 1970 it had almost doubled to 12·5 millions, and population density had risen from 263 persons per square mile in 1946 to 536 in 1970. At the same time, the average age of the population had fallen steadily so that by 1971 8·5 millions out of a total of 12·5 were under the age of 35. This rise in population has reflected the high standard of public health, and a developed set of public services which is also, as has been seen, reflected in the education system. Ceylon, with free primary and secondary education, today has the highest literacy rate of any capitalist country in Asia after Japan – 80 per cent by official figures. There are 5,000 primary schools and 5,000 secondary schools, and nearly everyone under 35 has had both primary and secondary education. Every year 100,000 new school leavers come on to the job market. Yet, in contrast with this extremely advanced level of education and welfare services, average per capita income in 1971 was $132. Moreover, the ruling class was not only failing to develop the economy but was throwing increasing numbers of young Ceylonese out of work. Unemployment, even by official accounts which report only the *registered* unemployed, rose constantly.

Official estimates for 1970–71 suggest an accelerating rise. An estimate for early 1971 spoke of 585,000 out of work, out of a total available labour force of 4·4 millions.[11] In his October 1970 budget speech N. M. Perera had, more realistically,

11. *Le Monde*, 18 June 1971.

stated that: 'It is roughly being estimated that the number of unemployed people in Ceylon, at the moment, adds up to 700,000.'

TABLE 5
Unemployment[12]

1945	21,336
1950	65,122
1955	71,010
1960	151,092
1965	199,655
1966	238,901
1967	257,070
1968	276,339
1969	341,286

On top of this came another direct consequence of the decline in export earnings. The tea exports, produced by imported Tamil labour, had historically been the financial basis for the welfare programme used to placate the Sinhalese masses. Hence the system ensured that the masses were doubly disarmed – they were split by ethnic divisions, and drugged by welfare concessions. The collapse of the export system forced the government to cut back on the welfare service – successive budgets instituted charges for services that had previously been free – and cut back on the rice subsidy. At the same time the pauperization of the Sinhalese who had depended on the export earnings in other ways highlighted the common class character uniting Tamil and Sinhalese.

The Rural Sector

The economic crisis was felt most severely in the rural areas. Agricultural production is dominated by four crops – the three

12. Ibid.

export crops (tea, rubber, coconut) and rice grown for domestic consumption. In 1968 tea was grown on 597,490 acres, rubber on 674,539 acres and coconut on 1·2 million acres. Rice lands covered 1,742,469 acres. Productive relations within these different sectors are quite varied. In the tea sector the dominant form of landownership is the tea-estate, where over 80 per cent of the labour force are Tamils of Indian origin. In 1968 only 17·8 per cent of tea lands were owned as small-holdings by Ceylonese farmers; 29·14 per cent were owned by British companies, 25·93 per cent by Ceylonese companies and 24·15 per cent by Ceylonese entrepreneurs. Rubber and coconut lands, on the other hand, were held more by individual Ceylonese small-holders, and coconut in particular was known as the 'small man's crop' since over 70 per cent of all coconut-producing lands were held in units of 20 acres and under. Small-holding is even more predominant in the rice-growing areas.

The decline of the economy affected the two rural sectors in distinct ways. The Tamil workers on the plantations are not peasants but, as we have already noted, rural proletarians, and they have a special history and situation. They still remain isolated in communal and semi-company unions, set apart from the rest of the Ceylonese population. The potentiality and need for change within that sector have been increased in the past decade. With the spread of health facilities the population pressure has increased. At the same time the introduction of new agricultural methods, especially cloning,[13] has raised productivity and lowered the area of cultivated land. Hence on the one hand there has been a rise in the amount of land potentially usable for growing other crops to substitute for imports, while on the other unemployment has risen so that in 1971 54,000, i.e. 20 per cent of the men on the tea plantations, were unemployed, and of these 43,000 were aged between 15 and 19. The other 80 per cent worked on average 16–18 days a month.

13. The process by which plants are produced asexually and in multiples from a sexually produced ancestor.

Fred Halliday

The workers in the non-plantation sector are peasants, or the descendants of peasants, rendered landless by the gradual development of capitalism in the countryside and by demographic or economic pressures on the land. Pre-capitalist village relations had not been destroyed but had altered with the encroachment of capitalist relations and with the increasing pressure of population. The Ceylonese population tripled between 1911 and 1970 but, despite movement to the towns and some increase in the amount of land cultivated, the average cultivated area fell by 50 per cent from 27 to 13·5 acres. What this plainly meant was a rise in the number of totally landless peasants and in the number of those with too little land to subsist on, who had to work part of the time for other landowners. In the 1960s 30 per cent of the peasantry were landless peasants working as sharecroppers. As the non-plantation sector continued to dissolve, successful capitalist farmers were able to expand by buying land from indebted peasants and hiring those they had expropriated. The obvious measures to counter these trends would have been land reform and increases in productivity, but both were blocked by the hierarchized structures of village life.

In 1958 a minimal land reform act, the Paddy Lands Act, was passed. It purported to guarantee the rights of those who worked on lands or rented them, and it set up 'Cultivation Committees' to enforce this and carry out the agricultural development laid down in the law. The response of the landowners was to evict their tenants – there were 14,500 cases by the end of 1959 and over 40,000 cases by the end of 1971. Only 7,000 cases of restitution were recorded. The legalist and propertied ideologies of those who administered the law prevented it from being implemented. The Committees in general were powerless or in the hands of rich peasants. A similar fate befell the attempt to set up cooperatives: 14,400 were set up, of which 5,000 went bankrupt and the rest were controlled by rich peasants and bureaucrats.

Dumont analyses how the social structure prevented technical developments that would have increased productivity. He shows that sharecroppers had no incentive to use fertilizers to increase production, since they would benefit little from this. He shows how peasants wanted proper strong hoes, *mammoty*, to till the ground, but were provided only with Ceylonese-made ones that break easily. Poor peasants were prevented by the rich from forming unions and cooperatives, and the shortage of land gave the landlord a control over the peasants he might otherwise not have had to the same degree. MPs and civil servants used state funds for their own purposes in rural areas; initiatives from the top were not matched by spontaneous enthusiasm from below, and local initiatives were blocked by lack of support from above. Too much emphasis was laid on grandiose projects: Dumont points out that small hill-side dams can be built without using any foreign exchange and at a cost of Rs. 500–1,000 for every hectare irrigated. The Mahaveli project, trumpeted by the Colombo régime, will certainly bring electricity, but it has a 38 per cent foreign exchange component and the cost per hectare irrigated is Rs. 16,000. Because of the lack of mass enthusiasm labour was under-utilized, water was wasted, cropping was inefficient, import substitution was ignored. The result was the continued decline of the rural non-plantation sector.[14]

In the two and a half decades from independence to the 1971 insurrection there was no agrarian reform, while foreign loans were used to finance the import of consumer goods and the building of costly public works. The concatenation of rural crisis, unemployment and high literacy can be seen very clearly

14 René Dumont, *Paysanneries aux Abois: Ceylan – Tunisie – Sénégal*, Paris, 1972. Chapter 2 provides a detailed discussion of the rural economy based on first-hand observation, and has been drawn on heavily here. Dumont's analysis conforms to his usual pattern: ruthless honesty and a commanding knowledge of agronomic technique, combined with political vagueness and an uncertain humanitarianism.

in the official estimated figures for early 1971. The total
number of unemployed was estimated to be 585,000; of these
460,000 were in the rural areas, 230,000 were under 19 years of
age, and 250,000 were aged from 19 to 24; 167,000 of these
had been to secondary school or university. The contradiction
between the vital needs and aspirations of the unemployed educated youth of Ceylon and the structural limits of Ceylonese
capitalism had reached explosion point.

Little echo of this developing social crisis was to be heard in
the Colombo Parliament. Ceylon's parliamentarianism was regarded in bourgeois circles at home and abroad as an index of
its 'developed' political status: in fact, it represented its extreme backwardness, the failure of its ruling class to evolve an
even token anti-imperialism and the chasm that separated an
imported and imitated political system from the real life of the
Ceylonese people. During the 1960s both ruling parties were
forced to take superficial note of the economic dangers to this
system, and proclaim measures that pretended to check them.
Ambitious plans for industrialization and import substitution
were announced; foreign borrowing rose and selected businesses
were occasionally menaced with 'Ceylonization'. But the neo-
colonial character of both the UNP and SLFP naturally pre-
cluded any substantial moves to challenge Ceylon's dependence
on imperialism. A liberal Ceylonese economist, writing in
1968, described this situation in measured, if euphemistic,
tones:

All political parties affirm that among their principal objectives is that of economic development. But neither of the major
political parties who contend for power has put up a programme
which the electorate may either reject or approve. In consequence
elections have been fought on considerations other than the
overtly economic. One may conjecture here that this attempt to
belittle or even ignore the seriousness of the consequences that
follow from a slow rate of economic growth follows from a failure of leadership. This hypothesis is, on the face of it, denied by

the eagerness with which each government has taken to economic planning. In 1946, while Ceylon was still a Crown colony, the Board of Ministers published the *Post-War Development Proposals*. In 1954 the Government published a *Six Year Programme of Investment*. In 1958, the Government issued a *Ten Year Plan*. It may be said without prejudice to the authors of these publications that planning has consisted of little more than good intentions, providing employment opportunities for a few men who read economics at the university. Good intentions, however, are a dozen to the penny, and one looks hard for leaders who convert these good intentions into programmes of action.[15]

The United Front Government

Oblivious of the deepening crisis within the whole structure of Ceylonese rural society, the UNP campaigned for the general election in May 1970 on the platform of its 'economic achievements': it claimed that it had reduced rice imports from 600,000 tons per annum to 300,000, won Italian cooperation in constructing an oil refinery outside Colombo, and reached agreement with the World Bank on finance for the Mahaveli hydro-electric scheme. In fact, as has been seen, unemployment had been soaring and rice imports had been cut by reducing domestic consumption. Against the UNP, a so-called 'United Front' of the SLFP, LSSP and the pro-Russian CP had been formed, with a programme of vaguely reformist promises (restoration of the rice subsidy, control of the export–import trade, 'Ceylonization' of selected businesses, and so on) burnished with rhetorical references to socialism. Desperate for alleviation of their condition, the Ceylonese masses turned once more – for the last time – to the SLFP and its allies on the 'Left'. The illusions of the exploited and oppressed workers and peasants found a tumultuous, if temporary, expression in a landslide

15. G. Uswatte-Aratchi, 'Why Ceylon Needs Foreign Aid', *Asian Review*, Vol. 1, No. 2, January 1968.

electoral victory of the SLFP–LSSP–CP coalition, which won 125 out of 151 seats (the SLFP took 90 alone). Popular enthusiasm and expectations were at their height as the returns came in: crowds in Colombo marched on the Lake House combine, newspaper stronghold of the plutocracy, and attempted to sack it within hours of the announcement of the poll results. In the interior a spontaneous occupation of big estates followed the United Front victory.

Yet, within five months, the British *Daily Telegraph* was reporting that: 'Ceylon's popular mood has slumped drastically from euphoria and hope to dismay and discontent. Seldom can Ministers have had to disappoint their followers so unkindly, backtrack so rapidly and pigeon-hole promises so irreverently.' It went on, however, to comment on the 'heartening' fact that 'the new Ministers, though largely armchair Marxists or doctrinaire Socialists wedded to untried and antique economic dogmas, have shown an unexpected readiness to temper their ideals with reality.'[16]

The SLFP were the dominant force within the coalition: they held 19 of the 23 Cabinet posts, while the Communists held one and the LSSP held three economics posts; the 'socialists' were there to provide left cover. It is clear that the coalition programme, even if implemented, would not in itself have altered the crisis inside Ceylon. What is certain is that the new Bandaranaike government was unable to make even a pretence of carrying it out. They were prevented from so doing by both internal and external forces. At home the very contradiction between the enormity of the problems and the class interests of the government meant that there was no middle road: any policy that would have tackled the problems frontally would have involved a revolutionary restructuring of the Ceylonese economy and of class relations. Externally the régime quickly succumbed to the pressures of the international monetary agencies, especially the IMF. With its spiralling foreign

16. The *Daily Telegraph*, 27 October 1970.

debt the régime had either to break totally with these financial extensions of imperialism or capitulate and accept their 'advice'. The further capital needed for development, and for debt servicing, could in the eyes of the coalition only come from foreign capitalist donors. Hence they were 'forced' by their own perspective to put through the standard IMF package of anti-inflationary measures, austerity, and encouragement to foreign capital. What has aptly been called 'international debt slavery' proved too much for the reformist fantasies of the Ceylonese bourgeoisie, just as it had undermined the socialist rhetoric of the Indian bourgeoisie in the late 1950s and the Goulart régime in Brazil.[17]

Before the election, the SLFP–LSSP–CP had promised to reverse the rise in unemployment: its rate of increase *accelerated* after the election victory and, in his October budget, LSSP leader Perera announced that unemployment was now estimated at 700,000. They had sworn to restore the rice ration to the 1965 level – but they did so at a price nearly three times higher than they had promised. They were committed to 'Ceylonizing' some of the tea estates, but in October Perera announced: 'We have agitated for the nationalization of the tea estates for the past forty years. After assuming office, I realize that it is not advisable to do so now.' The Coalition had promised to nationalize foreign banks – this plan was also shelved. They had said they would curb the power of the reactionary Lake House press combine; but nothing was done.

In foreign policy, the Bandaranaike government took some easy measures that involved little material cost and won it left approval: it suspended links with Israel, and established diplomatic relations with North Korea, North Vietnam and the Provisional Government of South Vietnam. But although preaching anti-imperialism, it continued the Rs. 10 million

17. See Cheryl Payer, 'The Perpetuation of Dependence: the IMF and the Third World', *Monthly Review*, Vol. 23, No. 4, September 1971.

worth of tea exports to South Africa, and soft-pedalled even at the wretched Lusaka conference of 'non-aligned' countries. The coalition had promised to expel US Ambassador Strauss-Hupé, named by the US Senate Foreign Relations Committee as a CIA associate and vetoed as Ambassador to Morocco; he remained US Ambassador to Ceylon. The UF had attacked the UNP government for capitulating to imperialist financial agencies; yet Perera's first trip abroad as Minister was to the IMF meeting in Copenhagen, and in April 1971 he signed a letter of intent, the sixth since 1965, to arrange a stand-by credit. In his October 1970 budget speech Perera had promised to reveal the contents of future letters of intent: the terms of the April 1971 deal were kept secret. Moreover, the UF had committed itself to ending cooperation with the World Bank in the Mahaveli River scheme, because this gave the Bank a determining say in Ceylonese government expenditure and in the import of capital goods. This cooperation still continued.

The Emergence of the JVP

Such a blatant record of apostasy and complicity with imperialism was bound to have serious consequences on the workings of traditional political mystification in Ceylon. In their economic despair, the masses had turned to the established Left and to the SLFP; but the extreme seriousness of the crisis prevented either Sirimavo Bandaranaike's lachrymose hypocrisy or the fake Left of Perera and Keuneman from retaining control, or of meeting the real challenge that came from a force that had broken with the paralytic structures of Ceylonese parliamentarianism and was in direct contact with the exploited. This challenge came from the *Janatha Vimukhti Peramuna* (People's Liberation Front). The JVP originated in a split from the pro-Chinese Communist Party in 1965, when it criticized the Party for concentrating too exclusively on urban work and for ignoring the Ceylonese peasantry in the non-plantation sector. It had begun its political life on the basis of two theoretical premises, which had evolved out of its critique of the pro-Chinese Communist Party and of the other parties of the established Left. These were: (i) that there was no independent national bourgeoisie in Ceylon, and (ii) that the non-plantation peasantry were the 'main force' of the Ceylonese revolution. Both Communist Parties and the LSSP held that the Bandaranaike clan represented a progressive national bourgeoisie which was to be supported in its fight against imperialism. The JVP attacked and denounced this myth:

In order to understand the nature of the SLFP, it is necessary to analyse the nature of the national bourgeois class that it represents. This is a weak and vacillating class which has no independent social status. On the one hand it was created by the imperialists and as such has affiliations to them. On the other hand when they feel threatened economically and socially by the imperialists they become 'socialists' and raise their voices against imperialism. This empty cry of socialism is born out of pure opportunism. It began with Bandaranaike and is still continued by the SLFP ... In a neo-colonial system like Ceylon it is characteristic of the national bourgeois class to form, in the final analysis, a united front with the imperialists. In a neo-colony the capitalist system is maintained to cater for the needs of the imperialists. Therefore it follows that the national bourgeois class, by protecting capitalism in Ceylon, is in fact supporting imperialism. In the short run the national bourgeoisie leans on the oppressed classes in order to gain political power. But in the long run they get support and sustenance from the capitalists and imperialists ... It is not possible to fight imperialism through a parliament which was set up by the imperialists. But the national bourgeoisie of this country is not prepared to wage extra-parliamentary struggles against the imperialists. In this context anyone who thinks that he can achieve socialism through aligning with the national bourgeoisie is either a fool or an agent of the capitalists.[18]

18. 'The SLFP – The Agent of the National Bourgeoisie', *Vimukhti*, No. 7, 20 December 1970.

The JVP's second main thesis concerned the non-plantation rural sector. For it was there that the process of economic decline in the sixties was most clearly felt, and where there was the largest number of young unemployed. The JVP argued that there were three basic revolutionary forces in Ceylon: the urban proletariat, the plantation proletariat and the non-plantation peasantry. The urban proletariat were historically the most combative and best organized. However, 'the urban sector is controlled and organized under reformist leaders. These leaders have continuously fooled the masses with revolutionary rhetoric and have abandoned them at the moment of decisive struggle. As a result of its disenchantment with a reformist leadership, which has allied itself with the coalition government, the urban proletariat is now waging continuous struggle and is seeking an alternative revolutionary party.' The JVP considered the Tamil plantation proletariat to have fallen victims to the chauvinism of the SLFP and its allies, and hence to have become immured in a defensive communalism of its own: this fundamental revolutionary force was thus, they claimed, politically cut off from the other exploited classes within Ceylon, both in the town and in the country.

For the JVP the 'main force' of the Ceylonese Revolution, because it formed the overwhelming numerical majority of the population, was the peasantry in the non-plantation sector. Contrary to the theses of the reformist parties, the JVP argued that this sector was now effectively capitalist, although broken remnants of feudal relations of production undoubtedly remained.

Neo-colonialism prevails in the country today. According to existing social relations there is a capitalist system here. Ceylon is a capitalist society designed to fulfil the class needs of the foreign imperialists and their allies. There is no feudalism in our country today. Only a few remains of the old feudal system are to be found ... The capitalist economic system has swallowed up the fertile lands in the up-country and wet-zone areas, thus creating a great shortage of land for the Ceylonese people ... Liptons, Brooke Bonds and other white imperialist companies own thousands of acres; 90 local families share one acre ... The so-called left-wing leaders of our country have said that the peasantry is not revolutionary, and that they are against socialism. These leaders will never understand the problems of Ceylon. Due to a failure to analyse the problems of the peasantry scientifically and accurately, there has been no attempt to establish a worker–peasant alliance nor any move to unite the entire oppressed class and to work towards a socialist revolution ... It is only socialism that could permanently liberate the up-country landless peasant, the peasant in the wet zone whose crops are being constantly destroyed by the floods, the dry-zone peasant who is the victim of droughts, the agricultural labourers, chena (slash-and-burn) cultivators and sharecroppers.[19]

In its period of clandestine maturation the JVP also developed a third thesis that was fundamental to its politics, the thesis that in Ceylon armed insurrection and not guerrilla war was the appropriate form of revolutionary combat. This developed partly from an analysis of the geographical and demographic structure of the island, a small densely populated area with a relatively weak repressive machine. But it also expressed an instinctive rejection of the reformism of the established Left, and a straightforward enthusiasm for the most immediate militant alternative. It was this thesis, not very explicitly formulated but latent in the formation of the party, that guided its revolutionary strategy in the confrontation that began when the JVP emerged publicly in early 1970.

The JVP spent its first five years concentrated in the rural sector. JVP cadres gave elementary classes in political thought, divided into five categories, and these political lecturers often hid themselves behind curtains, while speaking, to avoid police detection. According to one account the five lectures were on the following subjects: the greatness of the Sinhalese past and

19. 'The Peasantry is the Main Force of the Ceylonese Revolution', *Vimukhti*, No. 4, 30 September 1970.

of the Buddhist kings; the economic crisis and the colonial formation of the tea economy; Indian expansionism through the tea plantations; the history of the Left in Ceylon and the failure of parliamentarism; the 'Sinhalese road' to revolution – attacks on the police stations, then popular insurrection.[20]

A leading militant later described the experience of breaking with the sclerotic practices of the orthodox reformist parties and discovering the life of rural Ceylon for the first time.

During this time groups of revolutionaries, disillusioned with all established political parties, met to discuss the future of Ceylon and how to establish a true socialist government. We discovered in the course of our discussions that there wasn't a true Marxist–Leninist party, or a revolutionary party, or a party for the poor masses in the country. We realized the urgent necessity to mobilize the people to establish socialism in Ceylon ... Our discussions lasted several months. We decided it was necessary to visit the villages with the intention of explaining to the people the causes of their oppression. We went to the villages and spoke with the people and convinced them of the correctness of Marxism-Leninism. In the villages we also studied thoroughly and deeply the difficulties and problems of peasants, workers, students, fishermen and even street-hawkers and unemployed young men and women. We went all over the island and met the poor masses ...'[21]

The JVP first emerged publicly during the election campaign of early 1970. The incumbent UNP government claimed there was a plot against it, and arrested about 12 young people suspected of connections with the JVP, including their public leader Rohan Wijeweera. They were accused of being 'Che Guevarists' – a term they have never applied to themselves – and also of being CIA agents. The JVP at this stage gave support to the SLFP–LSSP–CP programme; hence the opposition parties committed themselves to releasing the JVP inter-

20. Dumont, op. cit., p. 75.
21. Interview with the President of the Deshapremi Student Front of the JVP, in the *Ceylon Sunday Observer*, 23 August 1970.

nees if elected. Even at this stage, however, the coalition was very wary of the JVP and it took the new Bandaranaike government two months, till July, to release the JVP supporters arrested by the UNP. For a brief space of time the JVP now enjoyed relative political freedom, and was able to publish its paper *Vimukhti*, and hold public meetings unimpeded. At this stage, the JVP consistently reminded the government of its pre-election promises. In particular, the JVP pressed the following demands: the nationalization of the plantations and land reform; the expulsion of all imperialist political and cultural agencies; the nationalization of banks and agency houses; the implementation of all measures promised in the election campaign. They were demanding the implementation of a programme that was socialist in practice as well as in words – 'true socialism', as they called it.

The government in reply refurnished the old accusations first coined by the UNP régime. The JVP were 'CIA agents' – according to the SLFP, the LSSP and the pro-Moscow Communist Party, who spoke with one voice. The JVP retorted by presenting its own independent position. The first issue of *Vimukhti* (1 August 1970) carried an editorial stating that the JVP was 'pledged to liberate the people of Ceylon from oppression and exploitation' and 'to solve the problems of the unemployed youth of the country'. It added: 'We certainly wish to destroy British and US imperialism and Indian expansionism and capitalist anti-revolutionary plots. But we do not want to destroy any socialist programme that the government wishes to carry out.' On 10 August the JVP held its biggest public meeting to date, in Colombo, at which Wijeweera was the main speaker: 'We will continue to support the government if they progress towards socialism. They will receive all our support, but if they fail to reach the socialist goal, then we will do so,' he declared.[22]

22. 'We will support Govt. but want results, says PLF leader'. *Ceylon Daily News*, 11 August 1970.

But the political situation was already changing rapidly. During August the armed forces announced that they were taking special measures to prevent JVP supporters from staying in or entering the army. The size of the police force was raised by 55 per cent. Young people were being arrested in rural areas, while JVP meetings were everywhere harassed. The army and police further set up a special 'Counter-Insurgency Unit' to coordinate their work, of which a subsequent ornament was Peter Keuneman, leader of the pro-Moscow CP. In September government forces shot dead two workers on a plantation at Keenagelle, and a strike was ruthlessly broken and several trade-union militants sacked at the Velona textile plant, one of Ceylon's biggest factories. In October Perera announced his first budget, containing an all-round retreat from the coalition's original economic policy. After the September strikes, the JVP declared: 'The government's socialism is socialism as practised by big company owners. This is why the government has used the police force to break up the strikes.'[23] The October budget it denounced as 'the same medicine in a new bottle'.

From August 1970 onwards, the JVP faced a difficult strategic problem: how to attack the government, moving carefully enough not to outpace the disillusion of the masses yet fast enough to hit before the government struck at it. Ultimately, the JVP had to prepare for a violent seizure of power *after* the masses were prepared and *before* the bourgeois state could strike it down. As the government discredited itself, the JVP rapidly grew in popular strength. Vast crowds of many thousands were now regularly drawn to its public meetings of explanation and denunciation. Yet this process also alerted Ceylonese reaction to the danger which was building up for it, and impelled it ever faster towards general and outright repression. This posed problems of pace and of preparation of an ex-

23. 'If we are Proscribed . . .', *Vimukhti*, No. 4, 30 September 1970.

tremely difficult character for the JVP in late 1970 and early
1971.

Throughout these months the JVP was warning the masses
of a possible government attack, while it prepared its own organization and sought to build contacts with the plantation proletariat and the unionized urban workers. Hitherto, it had
confined its efforts to the Sinhalese peasantry of the centre and
south of the island. By doing so, it had won a firm base in the
very strongholds of rural traditionalism which had provided the
SLFP with its mass electorate: indeed it was soon to become
apparent that the JVP had its greatest support in precisely those
regions where the SLFP had scored its largest victories at the
polls in May 1970. Naturally, this conquest of its home terrain
alarmed the Bandaranaike clique intensely. However, this same
fact also underlined the great *limitation* of the JVP's organizational work hitherto. Its political success was so far mainly
confined to the Sinhalese peasantry, and among them especially
rural youth. It had therefore not yet overcome the structural
division of the exploited classes in Ceylon into two hostile
ethnic communities. Given the dark history of Sinhalese chauvinism from the late forties onwards, it was absolutely essential
for any vanguard aiming to achieve a socialist revolution in
Ceylon to break down this division decisively and create class
unity between the Tamil and Sinhalese masses. The very
success of JVP mobilization in the Sinhalese central and south-
western countryside thus also held a latent danger – that of the
particularism which had been fostered and manipulated by the
Bandaranaikes and the *sangha*. The deep rural radicalism of
the Sinhalese peasantry that had been distorted and confiscated
by 'Buddhist' demagogy was now for the first time finding an
authentic expression; but for it to consolidate into a socialist
consciousness, a class juncture with the Tamil rural proletariat
and the urban working class was indispensable.

The JVP leadership thus now became increasingly conscious
of the urgent need to extend its base to the urban and rural

proletariat proper. To this end, there were tentative contacts with the two revolutionary nuclei which already existed in the urban working class and among the Tamil plantation workers: the LSSP(R), a group of 50–100 cadres, led by Bala Tampoe, and the Young Socialist Front led by Ilanchelyan. Tampoe was secretary of the clerical-workers union, the Ceylon Mercantile Union, which has some 35,000 members and wields great economic power because of its strategic control of the port in Colombo. The YSF was a new group of Tamil revolutionaries which had emerged in struggle against the traditional communal unions of the plantation workers led by Thondaman and Aziz, whose extreme reactionary character had hitherto been an insuperable obstacle to radicalization of the tea-workers. Thondaman is actually a large plantation-owner himself who has been made a 'distinguished citizen' of Ceylon for his work on behalf of the ruling class. The birth of the YSF was thus one of the most vital and hopeful developments in Ceylon for many years: it cooperated with the LSSP(R) and was very close to it politically. A convergence of all three organizations could thus have laid the ground-work for achieving the central goal of class unity between all the exploited in Ceylon. In November 1970, the JVP, LSSP(R) and YSF organized a joint mass meeting at the Keenagelle estate, where two workers had been shot by the police in September. The speakers included Wijeweera for the JVP, Tampoe for the LSSP(R) and Ilanchelyan for the YSF. In February 1971, the JVP held another mass rally in Colombo itself, attacking the Government's policies and demonstrating an increasing audience among the urban proletariat. But these were preliminary moves, and did not reflect a concrete practical alliance between the different organizations, let alone a sense of solidarity among the masses among whom these organizations were working.

By March the economic situation was cascading towards disaster, and the JVP was winning more and more popular influence. Its success now posed an imminent threat to the

SLFP–LSSP–CP coalition government and the local and international interests it represented and protected. The government thus decided to strike first. On 6 March there was a demonstration outside the US Embassy by the Mao Youth Front, an ultra-left organization led by Dharmasekera. In the course of it a policeman was killed. *The JVP had nothing whatever to do with this demonstration outside the US Embassy,* which it promptly denounced: it was either a deliberate government-organized provocation, or a confused mêlée used by the government as a pretext to attack its opponents. At all events, the government now moved against the JVP. On 16 March, the cabinet announced that a JVP 'plot' to overthrow the government had been discovered, and declared a State of Emergency. A dusk-to-dawn curfew was imposed, and the police and army were given full powers of arbitrary arrest and disposal of bodies without having to carry out inquests or inform the relatives of those killed. Sirimavo Bandaranaike went on the radio to broadcast an 'appeal' to the Ceylonese people for 'vigilance against terrorist groups'. By 26 March the government had announced the arrest of 'about 300' people suspected of connection with the JVP, and reports of discoveries of arms caches were broadcast almost daily.

The objective of this all-out attack by the government was to destroy the JVP as a political organization, and eradicate its influence in Ceylon. It was intended to catch the JVP head-on, before it or its allies had yet built a coherent base among either the Tamil plantation workers or the urban proletariat. For it was the fusion of these three exploited classes into a single revolutionary front that would have inevitably spelt the end of capitalism in Ceylon. It was above all to pre-empt this menace that the Ceylonese bourgeoisie now struck out viciously at the newly created vanguard that was threatening to bring this about. The JVP was consequently put in a grave dilemma. It had put down strong roots among the low-country and Kandyan Sinhalese peasantry; and it had a nation-wide youth cadre. But it had not yet achieved any penetration of the Tamil proletariat, and had only embryonic contacts and links with a part of the urban working class. Organizational convergence with two revolutionary forces already working in these sectors was under way, but not yet consolidated. In principle, it was thus obviously premature to make a direct bid for state power at this stage. But on the other hand the government's offensive threatened to annihilate the JVP as an organization if it did not resist and hit back. It had been prepared by years of clandestine work, and had seen from the lessons of Iraq and Indonesia that a party is only revolutionary if it is prepared to defend itself when attacked.[24] There was a debate inside the JVP after the government's wave of arrests and imposition of the State of Emergency. Two main strategies were defended: armed insurrection or protracted guerrilla warfare. The protagonists of armed insurrection swung the decision within the JVP leadership, arguing that the longer the JVP waited the more time the government had to crush them. The party therefore gave instructions to its militants for a counter-attack.

The Armed Insurrection

On the night of 5–6 April, three weeks after the declaration of the State of Emergency, police stations in different parts of the

24. *Vimukhti*, No. 5, 1 November 1970, carried an article, 'Lessons from Indonesia', which contained the following assessment: 'The communists had not accepted the fact that the strongest weapon of the neo-colonialists was anti-revolutionary action. Thus they had not prepared or organized themselves to face such a situation. In short, their mistakes were: the lack of understanding of the nature of the enemy, mouthing parrot-like the sayings of Chairman Mao but neither understanding them nor applying them in practice, and failing to arm the oppressed classes to fight against the national bourgeoisie. Due to these mistakes, the communist party had no power to avert the right-wing coup. Those who sacrificed their lives in Indonesia have taught us a lesson which should never be forgotten.'

island were assaulted by JVP cadres in groups of 25 to 30. It appears that one group attacked prematurely the night before, since on 5 April the government announced that a police station at Wellawaya in Uva Province had been attacked on that night and imposed a curfew in five administrative districts (Badulla, Kandy, Moneragala, Amparai and Nuwara Eliya).[25] JVP's weaponry in these attacks was entirely home-made: they had to get their first modern equipment by seizing these government outposts. The aim of this first attack seems to have been to capture a stock of modern arms, and to consolidate in a liberated region of the interior, blocking communications across the island and providing a base for a second offensive. On this first night several police stations fell, and the government soon evacuated many more: at the height of the insurrection between 90 and 100 police stations had been abandoned or had fallen to the JVP. The government's first announcement spoke of attacks on 25 police stations, but this may have understated the number of attacks on *that* night and they certainly remained silent about subsequent attacks. Later in April a truer picture emerged: 'the government which had earlier said only about 25 posts were attacked, now says more than 30 were captured and held for several days by the insurgents. In at least nine areas of the countryside covering hundreds of square miles, the rebels maintained control uncontested by government forces.'[26]

The government's immediate response to the situation was to panic at the prospect of an insurrection in Colombo itself, and it temporarily withdrew its forces to hold the capital, trying to calm the situation by issuing confident announcements. On 6 April the curfew was actually reduced, and a day later the Minister of Defence and Internal Affairs announced that the armed forces had achieved 'complete control' and were mopping up a few areas of resistance. But on 8 April a clearer picture began to emerge from government announcements: it

25. *Financial Times*, April 1971.
26. *New York Times*, 25 April 1971.

was revealed that the insurrectionaries had set up road blocks at Warakapola and Kegalle on the main Colombo–Kandy road, and that the air force was attacking JVP positions on a strategic bridge at Alawwa. The next day the government imposed a 24-hour curfew throughout Ceylon and foreign newspaper reports spoke of 80,000 to 100,000 insurgents challenging the government. While these figures were almost certainly exaggerated they reflected the intense alarm that had seized ruling-class circles when the extent of the rebellion became apparent.

On 9 April Sirimavo Bandaranaike made another characteristic broadcast in which she informed the Ceylonese people that the JVP was the tool of 'big money, diabolical minds and criminal organizers'. A terrorist movement, 'hatched in secret', had launched a surprise attack on the Ceylonese way of life. There was no hint in this speech that the insurrection had any social or economic basis whatsoever. In fact, it immediately became clear that the JVP had both mass support and a far-reaching organization in the south-centre and south-west of the island, and the insurrection covered almost the whole of the Sinhalese countryside. It is clear that the overwhelming bulk of the fighting was performed by units of armed youth, often including many members in their teens. The core of the insurrection seems to have been formed by ten administrative districts where the army were given full control on 12 April:[27] these were Kegalle, Matale, Kurunegala, Anuradhapura, Matara, Polunnaruwa, Galle, Hambantota, Ambalangoda and Katunayake. On 10 April AP reported from Kegalle police station that it was 'the only one in a district of 700 miles not yet burnt down or abandoned in the face of a Cuban-style insurgency by an estimated 80,000 rebels'.[28] Later in the month it was revealed that the JVP had held and administered two sizeable towns in the Southern Province, Elpitya (50,000 popu-

27. The *Guardian*, 12 April 1971. Other reports spoke of only six such districts.
28. *Evening Standard*, 12 April 1971.

lation) and Deniyaya: liberated in the initial onslaught, they were only reoccupied by government forces on 23 April (Elpitya) and 25 April (Deniyaya).[29]

Western press reports, our only source so far, have stressed the villagers welcomed the JVP and gave them supplies and information. 'There is no doubt that the villagers are sympathetic to the young rebels. They were all received in a friendly manner by the local population.'[30] Even a British tea-planter, whose estate was occupied by the JVP for three weeks, stressed their political formation and precise intelligence.[31] The tea plantations in the highlands seem to have been relatively unaffected, but in Colombo there was definite, if limited, supporting action by a JVP underground network. On 11 April the government announced that all but one of the Governing Board of the Ceylon broadcasting corporation had been sacked: a JVP network had been uncovered, using the obituary and Listeners' Choice programmes to send out coded messages to the militants in the field. A day later there was an attack on the runway of Katunayake Airport, where military supplies were being flown in.

In the tempest of the April crisis, while JVP units were manoeuvring and fighting in the hills, the precarious hold of the government on the working class began to falter. Allegedly loyal trade unionists were sent to the provinces to guard police stations – but many had to be withdrawn rapidly because they developed sympathies for the JVP. Moreover, the government introduced new and unprecedentedly repressive labour laws on 21 April, banning the distribution of handbills and posters within employers' premises without the prior permission of the capitalists concerned, and imposing penalties for absenteeism

29. The *Guardian*, 2 April, reported the reoccupation of Elpitya; the *International Herald Tribune*, 26 April, reported the recapture of Deniyaya.

30. *Le Monde*, 30 April, 1971.

31. *The Times*, 4 May 1971.

and late attendance at work – a clear attempt to force JVP militants to return to work or to expose themselves by their absence.[32] The government also conducted a systematic purge of the educational system, by summoning all teachers to report on pain of dismissal if they failed to do so. 25 per cent of those who did show up were arrested. But the most striking index of the fear-stricken isolation of the Ceylonese bourgeois stratum was a government decree calling up reserves and recruiting new police and soldiers, which specifically excluded recruitment of *anyone under the age of 35*. A new regiment, the *National Service Regiment*, was recruited on this basis. There could be no more damning sign that it felt the whole of the country's youth to be in opposition to it. The very measures taken by Ceylonese capital to suppress the JVP only underlined the reality of its mass strength.

'We Have Learnt Too Many Lessons from Vietnam'

By the end of May, after extremely fierce fighting and continual redeployments by the JVP, the government had temporarily driven the insurgent groups back into the upland forests and re-established its control over the rural interior. There are two aspects of the government's counter-offensive that stand out: the extreme savagery of the repression, and the extraordinary line-up of international allies that rushed to Sirimavo Bandaranaike's aid. During the initial government counter-attack in Kegalle, around 17–20 April, the first reports began to appear of summary executions. Sandhurst-educated Lt.-Col. Cyril Ranatunga was quoted as justifying the execution of his prisoners: 'We have learnt too many lessons from Vietnam and Malaysia. We must destroy them completely.'[33] Another officer was quoted as saying: 'Once we are convinced prisoners are insurgents we take them to the cemetery and dispose of

32. *Financial Times*, 6 May 1971.
33. *International Herald Tribune*, 20 April 1971.

them.' The government subsequently denied this, but in later weeks hundred of bodies of young men and women were seen floating down the Kelaniya river near Colombo, where they were collected and burnt by soldiers: many were found to have been shot in the back.[34]

René Dumont, in Ceylon during the insurrection, estimated that 8,000 people had been killed. Dumont wrote: 'From the Victoria bridge on 13 April I saw corpses floating down the river which flows through the north of the capital, watched by hundreds of motionless people. The police, who had killed them, let them float downstream in order to terrorize the population.' Wijeweera, in a statement from prison in 1972, said that 15,000 revolutionaries had been killed, but twice that number of innocent people had also died. Other estimates range from the official figure of 12,000 to as high as 50,000.[35] What is clear is that the police and armed forces launched an indiscriminate attack on the peasant population as a whole. The *Washington Post* reported in early May that an army major had even welcomed the insurrection: 'We have never had the opportunity to fight a real war in this country,' he was quoted as saying. 'All these years we have been firing at dummies, now we are being put to use.'[36] In fact, the army panicked. 'Ceylon's outnumbered and unprepared police force and army have resorted to mass arrests, torture, executions and other terror tactics in attempting to put down young well-organized armed insurgents.'[37] *Le Monde* correspondent Decornoy gave the following picture:

At Galle, in the south, we saw three 'terrorists' who had just been arrested and whom the police were taking away. A local inhabitant remarked: 'They will be killed tonight, and their bodies will be thrown into the river.' The police, traditionally

34. *New York Times*, 25 April 1971.
35. *Nouvel Observateur*, 23 May 1971.
36. *Washington Post*, 9 May 1971.
37. *New York Times*, 25 April 1971.

hated and today used without reserve by the 'progressive' government, are openly compared to Duvalier's 'tontons macoutes' and their crimes have shocked the population. Here are some examples, which it would be wrong to see as isolated incidents. At Kataragama, a village in the south, a girl was stripped and killed on the spot. At Akuressa, two young people were shot in front of the inhabitants and left to die, but only did so later, when their bodies were burnt. At Kosgoda, corpses were left hanging in public for several days. At Kandy, a lecturer in geography was so savagely beaten that he died in hospital; a history student was tortured for two days. At Bandaragama a young man was beaten up and the sole of his foot was cut open and covered with pepper. Another young man, while on a road outside Colombo, was arrested, tortured and left to the red ants. What is the point of going on?[38]

The Theory and Practice of Neutrality

This government repression carried through in April and May received powerful support from an unprecedented bloc of international allies. The Sirimavo Bandaranaike government had shown that its domestic 'socialism' was a feeble fraud: its reaction to the April insurrection revealed that its foreign policy was equally bogus. When the State of Emergency was first declared in March, sections of the imperialist press expressed doubt as to whether it was really justified by the importance of the JVP and suggested that the real reason for it was that the coalition government wished to smother popular criticism of the deteriorating economic situation. Then, after the insurrection had begun, the same press adopted a tone of triumphant arrogance. While enthusiastically supporting the régime's requests for arms, the London *Daily Telegraph* told its readers that: 'It seems absurd in many respects that Britain

38. *Le Monde*, 16 June 1971. Decornoy's series of four articles on the insurrection, beginning in *Le Monde* of 16 June, give a forceful account of both the rising itself and the subsequent repression.

should be supplying arms for Mrs Bandaranaike's irresponsible and bankrupt government', and concluded by saying that 'if she has not learned her lesson it must be hoped that the people of Ceylon have done so.'[39] A week later, while warning of the danger of the Russian presence in Ceylon, the *Telegraph* did not miss the opportunity to belabour 'the egregious and self-righteously non-aligned Mrs Bandaranaike'.[40] *The Times* headlined its editorial 'Ceylon can learn from the shock',[41] while the *Sunday Times*'s Frank Giles was equally jubilant: 'For the present,' he wrote, 'one's thoughts turn to the extra-ordinary situation in Ceylon and Mrs Bandaranaike's spectacular demonstration of the theory and practice of neutrality. Of course we ought to wish her well, but I just hope she knows what she is about.'[42]

Sirimavo Bandaranaike, of course, knew very well what she was about. In January she had demurred from the British government's policy of selling arms to South Africa, during the Commonwealth Conference in Singapore, but she had always continued Ceylon's trade with South Africa and the first supplies of foreign arms she received in April were flown by Air Ceylon Trident from the British base in Singapore. These initial supplies consisted of small arms stored in Singapore, and the first consignment arrived on 10 April – four days after the start of the insurrection. On 11 April the British government announced that it had received a request for helicopters, and had agreed to supply Ceylon with six Bell Jet Rangers: as Britain had none of these herself she bought them from the US for Ceylon, at $100,000 a time.[43] The US also

39. *Daily Telegraph*, 14 April 1971.
40. *Daily Telegraph*, 21 April 1971.
41. *The Times*, 21 April 1971.
42. The *Sunday Times*, 25 April 1971.
43. The official British statement on these supplies was made in Parliament on 22 April in reply to a question of dubious spontaneity from a Conservative MP. This was the *third* occasion within six months when a British-armed and -trained army had attacked a popu-

flew in supplies of helicopter spare parts. Meanwhile both India and Pakistan were sending in arms and counter-insurgency experts to Ceylon. On 13 April 'at least four Indian warships' were reported patrolling off Colombo harbour, and on 14 April six Indian and two Pakistani helicopters arrived in Ceylon. India was alarmed at the prospect of revolution just off her shores,[44] and Pakistan sent aid in return for the landing facilities provided at Katunayake airport after India blocked direct flights between Pakistan and Bengal. On 21 April Australia announced that it too would send arms to Ceylon, following the lead of Britain and the US. The Soviet response was equally prompt and enthusiastic. On 17 April an Air Ceylon Trident was dispatched to Cairo, via Karachi and Bahrain, to collect a consignment of nine tons of Soviet weapons from stores in Egypt,[45] and on 20 April four Antonov transport planes arrived from Tashkent with sixty-three Soviet technicians and helicopters packed in crates.[46] On 21 April Antonovs

---

lar movement with intense savagery: in September 1970 the Bedouin army of King Hussein (the former 'Arab Legion') had launched a genocidal assault on the Palestinian resistance; in March 1971 the Pakistani Army had murderously attacked the whole people of Bengal. A few months afterwards, the Sandhurst-trained Sudanese Army launched a fourth such massacre in the Sudan. British imperialism, which prides itself on the tranquillity of its domestic politics, has nothing to concede to other imperialisms when it comes to neo-colonial brutality. The continuing killing in Ireland is a further reminder of the violence bequeathed by the British.

44. On 16 April the Indian paper, *The Hindu*, wrote: 'This is the first time since Independence that Indian personnel have been sent out to help a friendly neighbouring country in distress, barring India's participation in the international peace-keeping operations under the auspices of the United Nations in Korea, West Asia, the Congo, Cyprus and the Indo-China states. But India has given arms aid to countries like Burma, Indonesia and Malaysia in the past for their internal defence against insurgency and subversion.'

45. *Daily Telegraph* and *The Hindu*, 18 April 1971.

46. *Daily Telegraph*, 21 April 1971.

brought six Mig-17s for assembly in Ceylon.[47] The Soviet pilots refrained from flying combat missions against the JVP and agreed only to train Ceylonese pilots – for some future insurrection, perhaps. On 6 May the Soviet Union announced that it would also send twenty armoured cars.[48] Yugoslavia, loyal to a fellow 'non-aligned' country, supplied mountain artillery which was reported by *The Times* to have been particularly useful to Lt.-Col. Ranatunga in his counter-offensive in the Kegalle region.[49]

As if this consortium of suppliers was not enough, Ceylon also received emergency economic aid from China, in the form of a Rs. 150 million interest-free loan, announced on 26 April. This loan constituted a direct and express support for the Ceylonese counter-revolution: it was accompanied by a personal message from Chou En-lai to Sirimavo Bandaranaike giving a blanket blessing to her capitalist government in its suppression of the popular rebellion led by the JVP. This abject document faithfully repeated the language of Colombo officialdom about the JVP.[50] In fact, not even the most rabid imperialists were

47. *The Hindu*, 22 April 1971.
48. *Financial Times*, 6 May 1971.
49. *The Times*, 22 April 1971.
50. The text of the Chinese letter, published in the *Ceylon Daily News* of 26 May, is printed as Appendix 4 to this book. It was reported in June that Chou En-lai, in a conversation with the Ceylonese Ambassador to Peking, I. A. Karannagoda, had disavowed the 'Guevarists' and had criticized the political practice of Guevara himself. 'The Ambassador said the Chinese Premier was surprised that the left-wing Government was being attacked by "revolutionaries." Chou added: "Who can we support in Ceylon except Mrs Bandaranaike?"' (*Morning Star*, 21 June 1971, quoting a Reuter report from Colombo.) The Chinese provision of economic aid to Ceylon could in isolation have been seen as part of legitimate state policy, a continuation of China's earlier economic aid to Ceylon. But the letter to Bandaranaike giving explicit *political* support and the timing of the loan leave no doubt that Chinese policy is of another character altogether.

pretending that the JVP represented 'a handful of persons'. References in the letter to Mao Tse-tung merely figure as an ideological cover for the naked great-power opportunism of the Chinese intervention. One of the most basic principles of Marxism and of Leninism is that *when the masses rise, revolutionaries support them, even if their action is adventurist, as Marx did over the Paris Commune and Lenin did over the July Days.* In fact, far from solidarizing with the oppressed, the Chinese government went out of its way to congratulate and aid their oppressors – in company with the USA, USSR, Britain and India. Chou En-lai's letter was released in Colombo on the same day as the ceremony in which the Chinese Ambassador signed the new loan to the Bandaranaike government and publicly applauded the 'happy coincidence' of this occasion with the first anniversary of the coalition's tenure of power. Thus did Chinese diplomacy celebrate the grim date of a year of uninterrupted betrayal and repression of the Ceylonese masses by the United Front régime.

China's action constituted an outright violation of proletarian internationalism, in actively helping a capitalist government to suppress a mass rising. Defenders of the Chinese position have argued that this aid accorded with China's general line at the time, one of working on an international scale to form an 'international united front' of small nations to combat the US and the Soviet Union. Diplomatic alliances with capitalist governments form part of the foreign policy of any socialist state, so long as they are genuinely directed against the most dangerous imperialist powers. The Chinese claim that their present united front work on the international scale is a generalization of the united front work they did within China during the anti-Japanese struggle. But there are two crucial differences, highlighted by the Ceylonese events, and by China's actions in Pakistan and the Sudan. United front work must always include the ability to criticize the bourgeois partner – whereas China has remained uncritical in these instances.

And no revolutionary concept of a united front can be stretched to cover active support for bourgeois régimes in counter-revolutionary activity. It is no defence of China's actions in Ceylon to say that they flow from her general line, since it is this general line itself which is exposed by the specific applications of it. The pro-Peking Ceylon Communist Party has praised China's actions: 'It was only the correct diplomatic behaviour of the Chinese and their generous aid that prevented the government sliding completely into the imperialist camp', wrote party secretary Sanmagathasan after the events. What this assumes is that the task of revolutionaries is to inflect the policies of bourgeois régimes with aid and support – whereas what the JVP had shown was that the Bandaranaike régime should be overthrown. On the purely empirical level, the rightward drift of the régime ever since it came to power should dispel any illusions about keeping the Ceylonese bourgeoisie out of the imperialist camp.[51]

The cynicism of the Chinese collusion with Ceylonese capital may be judged from the fact that Chou En-lai's letter was carefully concealed from the Chinese people themselves. The Chinese press, indeed, censored all news about the mass upsurge in Ceylon, no word of which has been published in China. Symbolically, in a map of 'the excellent situation in the world', published in *Renmin Ribao* on 22 May 1971, there was an emblem for mass action in India, but nothing whatever for Ceylon.

After the Rising: Permanent Emergency

The insurrection raged until the end of May, by which time the government succeeded in restabilizing the situation. A few small groups continued to survive in the remoter jungles, but

51. For a more general assessment and critique of China's foreign policy, and of the relationship between her state relations and her professions of internationalism, see Fred Halliday, 'China's New Course', *7 days*, No. 18, 1–7 March 1972.

they constituted no threat to the régime, and subsequent alarms about a repeat of the insurrection did not prove accurate. In all, the government now held over 16,000 people in detention: some arrested under the State of Emergency regulations, some seized in the fighting, and some who had given themselves up under the various government amnesties and now found they were not being released. They were held in overcrowded prisons and in converted university buildings; within these centres there was a continued political discussion, and in several cases detainees were shot dead attempting to escape or in disputes with prison officials. Though opposition political activity outside was banned, a newly-formed Civil Rights Movement, founded by opposition intellectuals, was set up and proceeded to challenge the State of Emergency. They called for the restoration of democratic rights, and for the trial or release of those detained. They also insisted on government investigation of crimes committed by the army and police in April. One particular case, involving the multiple rape and sadistic murder of a local beauty queen in the town of Kataragama, received publicity outside Ceylon but was censored from the Ceylonese press itself. A British observer sent by Amnesty International in September was thrown out of the country.

Although the government promised to bring the detainees to trial, they did not begin to do so until more than a year after the revolt began. They could neither release nor try them. In a speech to parliament in July, reviewing the course of the revolt, Premier Bandaranaike said that trials would begin once the detainees had been investigated. But in November Interior Minister Felix Bandaranaike reported that the government could not start the trials as long as the legislation remained unchanged: the emergency laws now in operation would have to be made into permanent features of the statute book. But although this was announced in November it was only in April 1972 that the Criminal Justice Commissions Bill was put through parliament, and the first trials began only in July 1972.

The bill enabled the Governor-General, in consultation with the prime minister, to set up special courts outside the Common Law to hear specific types of case. There was no right of appeal against the decisions of these courts, except when death penalties were pronounced, and the Commissions set up under the law were free to decide what procedure they thought best for discovering the truth. Under a special new law on evidence, confessions 'given' to police officers were to be classed as valid evidence – with the result that hundreds of young people ended up maimed as a result of police attempts to extract these 'confessions' through torture. Under the new laws defendants were not entitled to know what charges were pending against them, or even whether they would appear as defendants or merely as witnesses in specific cases. The Commissions were entitled to hold proceedings *in camera* whenever they so wished, and those who had served their sentences or who had been acquitted were not entitled to automatic release. It is odd that the Ceylonese régime even bothered to put through the law making these Commissions operative: they might just as well have abolished law and the courts altogether.

While holding the detainees and repressing political activity, the government faced the continuation of the economic crisis that had contributed to the April insurrection. Perera's November 1971 budget was a prolonged lament: whereas Sirimavo Bandaranaike herself had put the total cost of the revolt at Rs. 100m. Perera now upped it to Rs. 400m. and blamed the JVP, together with foreign capitalists, for the economic situation. He pleaded for time to institute 'socialism', quoting from Isaac Deutscher's *Stalin* to compare the Ceylon of 1971 to the Russia of the NEP. He reminded those who invoked the models of Cuba or Yugoslavia that the Cuban prime minister had just offered to resign after the failure of the 10-million-ton sugar harvest, while Yugoslavia was crippled by inflation and had to export hundreds of thousands of its workers to the EEC.

Unemployment in Ceylon was now at 550,000 – 12 per cent

of the labour force – and the terms of trade had declined by another 4 per cent in the year 1970–71. Perera's response was a series of austerity measures: attempts to increase the price of flour and ration sugar met with backbench opposition and had to be dropped, but a levy was now imposed on the free hospital service for out-patients, and the price of rice was raised by 25 per cent. Perera, unable to conceal the bankruptcy of his policies, ended in tearful form. He said:

This has been a hard budget. It has not been a pleasant or easy task for me. Poignant memories of the past keep crowding round me. All my life I have fought to ease the burdens of the poor and the humble. I am now the instrument not of easing but of heaping additional burdens on them. Even with a heavy heart I have to act with a vision of the future. Even as we travel in the midst of the gloom and the darkness of the present, I can see a light of distant dawn. We have begun well. By our indefatigable energy and selfless devotion, let us usher in the dawn of prosperity for all.

Perera's hypocritical speech and his attacks on the 'striplings' of the JVP deceived no one. Far from ushering in prosperity, his government continued to avoid the necessary anti-imperialist measures and to protect the interests it represented. A key added expenditure was the new allocation to the armed forces. In the year 1972–3 the expenditure on the army went from Rs. 81m. to Rs. 152m. while that on the navy went from Rs. 24m. to Rs. 37m. The amount for the purchase of arms and ammunition rose from Rs. 1·5m. to Rs. 4·8m. The army and the police were to be expanded by 25 per cent.

The opportunists in the government realized, however, that they had to take certain token anti-imperialist measures in order to head off popular anger. The UF government instituted a faint attempt at import substitution, banning the import of chillies and of onions. In a series of nationalization measures some British tea estates were taken over, and the number of British tea-planters dropped from 100 to 30 by the spring of

1972. A land reform act set a maximum of 50 acres per family unit, and income was limited to Rs. 2,000 per month. Constitutional reforms were also brought in. The senate was abolished in September 1971, and in April 1972 a new constitution was instituted, breaking Ceylon's allegiance to the British Crown and declaring a republic under the name of Sri Lanka. But these feints were a substitute for concrete anti-imperialism. The country remained crippled by its dependence on imperialist markets: in February 1972 alone its import bills rose by £11 million with the rise in world prices for crude oil, milk foods and sugar. The real diversification that could have broken Ceylon's ties with the West was not undertaken, and the land reform, putting a ceiling on larger holdings, was no answer to the poverty and growing landlessness of the Sinhalese peasantry. The constitutional changes were standard demagogic moves. Ceylon's decision to break with the British monarch went together with her continued membership of the neo-colonial Commonwealth federation. As for her renaming herself – it is a traditional ploy of neo-colonial régimes to conceal the continuation of their ties with imperialism by a cultural flourish of this kind. An imperialism that had kept its grip on Eire, Zaïre and Malawi was unlikely to have any trouble in swallowing Sri Lanka.

Indian Expansionism

In foreign policy the régime strengthened its ties with both the United States and with China. Whereas before the insurrection relations with the US had been muted, and Ceylon had bleated about the need for 'non-alignment' in the Indian Ocean, the US now stepped in as a welcome ally to the Bandaranaike clique. In the first months of 1972 US ships of the Seventh Fleet paid a series of visits to Colombo. The first ship to arrive, the 18,000-ton supply ship USS *Mobile*, brought $3m. worth of military aid, and armoured cars, helicopters and transport planes were to follow. In March, Admiral John McCain, Commander of the US Pacific Fleet, paid a four-day visit to Ceylon. The commander of the murderous naval war against the Vietnamese people was greeted by Sirimavo Bandaranaike. At the same time, the strengthening of ties with People's China developed and went beyond the lines already established in previous Sino-Ceylonese relations. After the economic aid of April, China went on to provide military aid as well. In December she gave Ceylon five military speedboats, equipped with rockets, and in May 1972 she sent guns and ammunition to assist Ceylon's 'internal defence', according to Sirimavo Bandaranaike. Economic relations were also encouraged: a new joint shipping line was instituted, and the annual rice-for-rubber deal was signed on terms particularly favourable to Ceylon.

The major reason for these policies was the Ceylonese fear of Indian expansionism, and hence of that of the power backing India, the Soviet Union. The weight of India had always hung over Ceylon: it constituted a real threat, and was also mystified by Sinhalese chauvinists wishing to turn the masses against the Tamil plantation workers. Both India and Pakistan had used the April insurrection to insert a military presence for themselves in the island, but the defeat of Pakistan in the December Indo-Pakistani war put an end to this competition. From then onwards India became the dominant power in the subcontinent. With a strengthened and aggressive bourgeoisie, it was clearly able to dominate Ceylon; and the latter's overtures to China and the US reflected a fear of this.

Within Ceylon itself politics was still dominated by the April insurrection and its aftermath. The coalition party that experienced the greatest difficulties was the pro-Moscow Party, four of whose six MPs opposed the Criminal Justice Commissions Bill; it was frequently rumoured to be about to resign from the government, and its position must further have been weakened by the government's attempts to resist Soviet influence as manifested through India. Both the pro-Moscow Communist Party and the LSSP had difficulty in controlling their extra-parliamentary membership, in particular the youth; although these followers did not support the JVP they were provoked by the emergency laws and by the government's failure to meet the crisis of the country's economy. Another index of the government's drift was its growing closeness to the faction of the opposition UNP led by Jayawardene. Two years before, the United Front had been voted into power against the UNP, promising to make sweeping changes in Ceylon and to institute socialism. Now, in the spring of 1972, there was so little difference between the interests of the two formations that there was open talk of a coalition, without there being any compelling technical reason for it, such as a precarious parliamentary majority.

Outside the parliamentary lobbies, the political situation was less clear. By prolonging the life of parliament to six rather than five years, and by quelling all popular expression, the government ensured that it was as insulated as possible against popular angers. The small pro-Peking Communist Party had had its leadership arrested and its offices broken up during the insurrection, but it continued to deny any support for the JVP and in time was able to restart its activities. It began calling for an end to the State of Emergency and to the release or trial of those in detention. In an analysis of the insurrection written while he was imprisoned, Party Secretary Sanmagathasan recognized the courage and honesty of the JVP rank and file, but judged the movement as a whole to have been 'counter-revolutionary'. He also repeated, in a disguised form, the thesis that reactionary forces had contributed to the growth of the JVP, and he advanced the fantasy that 'this movement was called into being to oppose the growing influence of Mao Tse-tung thought in Ceylon'. In the summer of 1972 this party split, with a majority favouring closer ties to the régime. The small urban-based LSSP(R), led by Bala Tampoe, did not condemn the JVP, although it had criticisms of the insurrection. The LSSP(R) was not, on the other hand, affected by the kind of repression that fell on the pro-Peking Communist Party. It was able to continue some of its public activities, and it addressed a series of public appeals to the government, calling on them to rescind the State of Emergency and release the detainees.

The greatest question-mark hung over the JVP itself. In the year following its defeat, no clear position emerged from its leadership on the lessons of April, the state of the movement or the future path to be followed. Loosely coordinated in the first place, it was further fragmented by the defeat of the rising. Many cadres were dead, many others in hiding, and many in different prisons with no way of communicating with each other. Discussion continued within the prisons, and morale remained high. Outside, popular resentment against the government continued. But the JVP in its 1971 form appeared to have ceased to operate. The nucleus of a future revolutionary organization joining ex-factions of the JVP to other non-JVP elements existed. But in the immediate context it did not present a direct threat to the government, or a structure around which revolutionary individuals or groups could organize.

Conclusions

Any full assessment of the Ceylonese insurrection will have to await the long-term development of Ceylonese politics. But certain effects are already clear. The insurrection was an ambitious and highly organized attempt to seize state power: it failed to achieve *this* aim. After three weeks of widespread military activity, the courageous Ceylonese revolutionaries were driven on to the defensive. Thousands of militants were killed, wounded or arrested; an unknown number of Ceylonese youth not directly part of the JVP were also killed. The JVP organization was severely hit. It is possible that such a blow could set the revolutionary movement in Ceylon back for some years and demoralize or terrorize the masses who rose enthusiastically to support the JVP; although, as will be seen, there are good reasons for doubting whether this will in fact be its effect. The insurrection has also alerted and hardened the Ceylonese régime and its international allies: it has 'revolutionized the counter-revolution' in Debray's phrase. Quite apart from the direct military aid given in April, imperialism will now redouble its vigilance. This is no doubt that political and military organization will be more difficult in the future than hitherto.

Nevertheless, the Ceylonese insurrection was in no sense a putsch. Despite a superficially 'blanquist' character, owing to its apparent suddenness, the rising was a popular insurrection in which a vanguard organization led the impoverished rural masses against a capitalist state. Why did it not succeed? No revolution can be a hundred per cent sure of success, so the fact of its temporary defeat is not in itself proof that it should not have been attempted. But the insurrection was launched in conditions and in a form that limited its chances of success and validated the strict Leninist insistence on the necessary preconditions for a successful socialist insurrection. First of all, at the *political* level, the JVP seems to have had a loose and unsystematized internal structure. It was not a Leninist party; there were loosely coordinated factions within the leadership, reflecting different groups that had fused in the JVP at the beginning, and the relationship between these factions and the base was imprecise; so far as is known, the JVP had never held a national congress and had no elected officials. Moreover, there was an internal tendency towards adventurism as a spontaneous reaction at once against the predominance of parliamentarist reformism in Ceylon and out of the realization, blinding to a generation reared on the bromides of the Pereras and Keunemans, that the achievement of socialism ultimately demanded armed struggle. This tendency was strengthened by the sense of imminent government repression in the period after August 1970, when it seemed that the JVP militants might well be struck down 'in their beds'. The experiences of Indonesia and Greece seemed the relevant warnings. The result was that after a debate within the JVP, the decision was made to hit the government with an armed insurrection rather than a protracted guerrilla war, and to strike immediately after the State of Emergency.

On the *military* level, the JVP was also at a disadvantage. It could not have avoided the birth of the international consortium of arms suppliers that developed. But its work among the armed forces, an essential Leninist precondition of insurrection, had been hampered since August by careful government screening. Thus there was no significant weakening of the police or army during the rising. A case of 18 naval cadets going over to the JVP was reported,[52] but a counter-revolutionary army can always sustain a certain level of *individual* desertion – it is only decisively crippled by mass desertion, or by the mutiny and loss of whole units. In Ceylon, the army appears to have gone into battle unimpaired. The JVP was also weakened by its lack of independent arms supplies: the traditional revolutionary practice of acquiring arms by winning them from the enemy is adequate for protracted guerrilla war, but the rapid escalation involved in an armed insurrection puts a great premium on acquiring sophisticated weapons very rapidly, and this does not seem to have been achieved in the first few days of the JVP offensive.

The last, and much the most fundamental, of all its handicaps was that the JVP did not have the necessary *social* base for a truly nation-wide insurrection. It was solidly implanted among the low-country and Kandyan Sinhalese peasantry of the central massif and the south-west. But it was only just developing links with the Tamil rural proletariat and the urban working class. The communal and reformist leadership of these two classes had not yet been really undermined. Thus when the insurrection broke out, the JVP quickly found itself penned

52. *Daily Telegraph*, 6 May 1971.

within the south-central foothills and the north-central dry zone, where the bulk of the actual fighting seems to have been done by rural unemployed youth. Moreover, the lack of a revolt in Colombo was fatal to the chances of the rural rising, because it allowed the State to deploy the full panoply of its military apparatus in the countryside after the first few days. The seclusion of the plantation workers meant that the central productive branches of the economy of the island were not affected by the insurrection. These twin basic absences probably doomed the rising to short-term defeat independently of any other factors. The attitude of the urban working class to the insurrection was not clear: sections of it were confused and misled by their reformist trade-union leadership. The preventive government measures recounted above prove that the potential proletarian sympathy with it was nevertheless very great. But the JVP urban cadre was still too weak to be able to mobilize this into effective actions. This was in contrast to the Great Hartal of 1953, in which urban and rural movements coordinated spontaneously; it was also in contrast to JVP theory, which called for a three-way worker–rural-proletarian–peasant alliance, in which the peasantry would be the 'main force'. One source of this problem lay in the gap between the JVP leadership and the rank and file. The energy behind the movement came from the frustration of the Sinhala peasantry, and the JVP expressed the contradictory aspects of this frustration. There is no doubt that in their attacks on Indian expansionism and foreign domination the leadership were careless about the danger of this arousing anti-Tamil feeling among their less politically formed followers. And in their critique of monoculture and Ceylon's economic crisis, there was a mixture of a *prospective* call for a socialist economy combined with a *retrospective* invocation of a mythical Sinhala past. The spontaneous response of many peasant societies faced with an imposed economic crisis is to look backwards to a mythical communist golden age: ever since the German *Bauernkrieg* of 1525, pre-capitalist peasantries have reacted to the advance of market relations in this way. The task of a socialist leadership is to redirect and transform this movement ideologically, to provide a materialist and attainable policy instead of the fake historical dreams that the movement spontaneously throws up. But in Ceylon the JVP did not show whether it could have carried through this task and built the ideological and organizational structures to link the three oppressed sectors of that society.

Equally important in analysing the weaknesses of the JVP is the question of what they intended to do if they gained power. The confused semi-chauvinist view of the rural crisis evident at the base, and the failure to work within the urban working class, were paralleled by a vagueness about the concrete alternatives. This is not to say that revolutionaries must have a blueprint. But the JVP seem to have based their alternative on a mystical return to primitive pre-capitalist subsistence. More concrete evidence of their confusion is provided by accounts of what actually happened in the liberated areas which they held in April and early May. There is little evidence of their actively mobilizing the population and incorporating them into their work. So far as is known there was no land distribution and confiscation of landlord property. Their insurrectionist and militarist conception of the revolution appears to have connected here with their lack of perspective about the form that revolutionary economic and political power would take.

Nevertheless, despite their defeat, the JVP has shown that armed insurrection is a real and possible form of revolutionary struggle in colonial and ex-colonial countries today. Debate since 1945 about revolutionary strategy has tended to concentrate *either* on various forms of protracted guerrilla struggles (liberated areas *v.* mobile *focos*, urban *v.* rural groups) *or* on a critique of parliamentarist reformism on the one hand and élitist military putsches on the other. Despite and through its defeat, the Ceylonese insurrection has re-emphasized the possibility of armed insurrection, 'the highest form of political struggle',[53] under definite and carefully prepared conditions. The insurrection led by the JVP suffered from political, military and social limitations, which after a month of the utmost self-sacrifice and heroism led to its defeat. Unconditional solidarity with the rural poor and their vanguard, who fought with the most primitive weapons against the massed might of the Ceylonese bourgeois state and its array of international allies, is an absolute duty of all revolutionaries elsewhere. A critical Marxist balance-sheet of the insurrection does not contradict but reinforces this solidarity. The socialist revolution has no need of falsehoods and euphemisms: it has confidence in the truth. The history of the international working class is rich in cases of successful revolutionary movements living through defeats and learning from them. There can be no doubt that the *lessons* of the April insurrection are being studied and assimilated by the underground in Ceylon today. A long hard task of preparation and consolidation now confronts the JVP and its allies: but it has proved itself to be a genuine vanguard of the masses and has shattered the parliamentary veil that has hung over Ceylon for fifty years.

The Ceylonese insurrection of April 1971, like the French revolt of May 1968, was unexpected by revolutionaries and counter-revolutionaries alike. But Marxists can never accept the concept of 'surprise'. Mass explosions cannot occur without a long previous history of silent oppression: the very unexpectedness of such an event is itself a contribution to the violence of the subsequent outburst. The JVP was able to win deep popular support because it expressed the underlying crisis of the Ceylonese society itself – a crisis that was ignored by the political parties that dominated the island's life and concealed by the wide cultural and social gap that divided the palsied

53. A. Neuberg, *Armed Insurrection*, New Left Books, London, 1970, p. 25. Chapter 2, 'Bolshevism and Insurrection', presents the Leninist position on insurrection. Cf. also the review of this book by Ben Brewster (*New Left Review* 66).

philo-British oligarchy of Colombo from the urban and rural masses. This crisis has not disappeared since the insurrection: it has deepened. There is little prospect of halting the remorseless rise in unemployment, the growing pressure on the land, or the increasing disaffection of the younger generation. Systematic terror and demagogic appeals to the country's 'misguided' youth by the SLFP–LSSP–CP government will not win back the masses who followed the JVP into rebellion. It was the insurrection that gave authentic voice, for the first time since independence, to the real crisis of Ceylonese society.

It is for this reason that the JVP's rising will reverberate, again and again, throughout the island even after its suppression. For there are some spectacular defeats which from the very moment of their consummation are already secret victories, because the time in which they occur and the spirit with which they are fought lead to a sudden political awakening far beyond themselves. Their hidden effects can act like a depth-charge for wider and wider layers of the exploited masses, within a very short space of time. The Ceylonese insurrection of 1971 has every chance of being such a turning point. For its most important lesson of all is that, in Ceylon, the masses have a revolutionary character. Despised, exploited and manipulated by their traditional 'leaders', the rural poor of Ceylon surprised the world and their own domestic enemies by the ferocity of their revolt. They have written another heroic chapter in the history of the Asian and world revolution. All revolutionaries throughout the world must hope that the present lull will be followed by an even greater and successful storm.

Speech to the Ceylon Criminal Justice Commission

2 November 1973

Rohan Wijeweera

Chairman and Members of the Commission:

A representative of one social class is addressing the representatives of another social class. That is what is happening here. A representative of the exploited and oppressed proletariat is addressing the representatives of the exploiting and oppressing class. We should not forget that the living reality which transpires here is a struggle for the fulfilment and class interests of two opposed social classes. Although I have been designated the 'thirteenth suspect' by this Commission in the present inquiry, the Chairman himself has stated that I am the chief suspect. That being so it will be necessary right at the beginning to tell you who I, the thirteenth suspect, am. I am a Marxist–Leninist. I am a modern Bolshevik. I am a proletarian revolutionary. Marxism–Leninism is a clear doctrine. In no way is a Marxist–Leninist a conspirator. I, a Bolshevik, am in no way a terrorist. As a proletarian revolutionary, however, I must emphatically state that I am committed to the overthrow of the prevailing capitalist system and its replacement by a socialist system.

To disown capitalism which has turned grey, reactionary and obsolete in the course of human social development, to say that this system must be replaced with the new socialist system of production which has come to the fore as befitting the latest and noblest historical stage in the course of the development of human society, and to act accordingly, is in no way a conspiratorial act. I am not a conspirator in the context of the development of history. I am no conspirator in the context of the development of society and humanity.

Honourable Members of the Commission: May I make one request to begin with? I have been subjected to every possible indignity and harassment at the hands of the ruling class and have been for several years the target of numerous defamations, slurs and slanders, mudslinging and character assassination – and all this without any protection from the law. The only request that I make of you, is to respect my right to express my innocence freely and without any let or hindrance. The ruling clique of capitalists will gag me for a long period, if not for all time. In these circumstances I do not wish to blame myself for not saying all that I have to say before you now. I beseech that I be not gagged.

This suspect, who is making use of his right to state the facts that will prove his innocence, does not intend under any circumstances to refrain from saying what he has to say. This capitalist institution has been used against me in a somewhat heavy way. I am not surprised. I know that the ruling class sets up its institutions to serve the needs of capitalism. Pleading my case before this Commission could be considered a futile exercise if it simply provided a legal cover for the unscrupulous and arbitrary decisions, and the disgraceful course of action, on which you have embarked. But I intend to explain the historical process which led to the most furious, the most barbarous and the most widespread human slaughter that has taken place in the recent history of our country.

Honourable Members of the Commission: 'The noblest, the most valuable, the greatest and supreme treasure that a man has is his life. He lives only once. He should spend that life in such a way that his dying moment he will have no cause for regret, repentance, shock or sorrow; in such a way that he could really be happy in the thought of having sacrificed his life advancing the development, the liberation and the victory of mankind – the people of the whole world.' This is a Soviet writer's interpretation of life. I agree with this aspiration and do not wish to have any reason for sorrow should the capitalist ruling clique cut short my life in the prime of my youth.

The Charges against us

I have no regrets whatsoever about my life and the fate in store for me. I hope to tell you everything concerning the history of the April incidents, without any qualms about possible reprisals against my person. The charges made against us are grave. We have been charged with the breach of Sections 114 and 115 of the Penal Code. According to the writ issued to you by the then Governor-General, and also according to the indictment served on us, the period at issue is that between the beginning of 1968 and the end of 1971. It is said that during this period we 'conspired against the Queen's government'. It is said that during this period we conspired criminally to overthrow the Government of Ceylon. It is said that we have 'waged war against the Queen' or have abetted such acts. Similarly, the opening submissions of the State Prosecutor have attempted to show that the birth of the *Janatha Vimukhti Peramuna* was in itself tantamount to a conspiracy. What we actually said and did during this period is the crux of the matter; accordingly my own views and conceptions are as much the subject of inquiry as anything else.

Mr Chairman: There was a time when Ceylon was a direct colony of the British Empire on which, it used to be said, the sun will never set. When the second imperialist war was raging, these colonies were trampled under the yoke of Admiral Geoffrey Layton's war chariot; the colonial government engaged in a ruthless suppression of the leftist movement of this country after incarcerating the leaders and proscribing their parties (the Lanka Sama Samaja Party and the United Socialist Party); the masses were full of sorrow and racked by oppression; colonial troops were ransacking the Island and autocracy was in complete command, with capitalists raking in more and more profits and revolutionaries languishing in jail. It was in such a sad and dark time, similar to the present, that I was born in Tangalle, in July 1943. I grew up in Kottegoda, a small village in the Matara district. I was admitted to the Godanda Government Primary Boys' School in the middle of 1947, where I received primary education until 1953.

When a whole country's progress is obstructed, when the forward march of an entire nation has been halted, when a whole people find themselves poised on the brink of a dark abyss, it is not difficult to understand why just and honest men will show no signs of fear as they enter prisons and suffer untold hardships, face constant harassment and even sacrifice their lives for the purpose of saving their country and their people from that national calamity. After the second imperialist war the administration of this country was handed over to the local capitalist class, as part of a neo-colonialist stratagem, and the country continued along the same bankrupt path of capitalist development. In such an atmosphere my generation entered their youth. We inherited by this time a vast reservoir of experience from our parent society. It was this social experience that pushed us towards the path of revolution.

My Path to Marxism

In 1954 I was admitted to the Godanda Government Senior English School. That same year this school was transformed into a Sinhala language school. It was there that I obtained my secondary education. I found myself drawn towards the Communist Party as a result of the massive agitational campaign against imperialism and capitalism conducted throughout the South by my political mentor Comrade Dr S. A. Wickremasinghe, the present General Secretary of the Ceylon Communist Party, and also as a result of the experience I had gained from society. It was during these days that I first read the Sinhala edition of that historic document of Marx and Engels, *The Communist Manifesto,* and also Liu Shao-chi's *How To Be A Good Communist,* though I must admit that at that time I failed to understand them correctly. I learnt the ABC of politics at the propaganda rallies and Youth League seminars of the Communist Party. I am grateful to Comrade Dr Wickremasinghe for this.

As a member of the Communist Youth League I took part in political activity for the first time in my life with a sense of feeling and understanding. In July 1959 when I was studying science for the GCE (O Levels) I had to leave my school because of the shortage of science teachers and enter Dharmasoka College, Ambalangoda. In December of that year I passed the GCE (O Level) exam in science.

At the General Elections of 1960, the Ceylon CP entered the fray with 53 candidates – the highest number it had ever put forward at an election in its entire history. As it was a small party I had to focus all my endeavours on its election campaign. The experience I gained in this election campaign in remote areas like Aparakka, Dandeniya, Urugamuwa and Radampola was considerable. One day, after the elections, I read a news item in the magazine *Soviet Land* to the effect that the Soviet Premier, Khrushchev, who was on a tour of Indonesia in the middle of 1960, would shortly be opening an International University in Moscow for the benefit of youth from the colonial countries of Asia, Africa and Latin America. By this time I was finding it difficult to continue higher studies due to economic factors. During the 1947 General Election, my father, who was organizing the election activities of the Communist candidate for Hakmana, Comrade Premalal Kumarasiri, found his jeep forcibly stopped by reactionaries. He was abducted and beaten up, an experience that left him a permanent invalid. My family found it materially impossible to finance higher education for me. At my own wish I applied for entrance to the proposed new People's Friendship University of Moscow.

On winning a Medical Degree Scholarship, I left for Moscow on 25 September 1960. After the preliminary examination held there I was admitted to the Faculty of Philology on 1 October 1960, to learn the Russian language. At seventeen, I was then the youngest student at the university and I cannot forget the great assistance my Soviet teachers extended to me. I studied Russian till June 1961. In addition, I attended the lectures on World History and Historical Materialism held there in the English language. I refer here with gratitude to the well-known Soviet historian Professor Metropolski. Had I not been his pupil, it is possible that I would not be here before you today. It was this great man's ideas that helped me to understand how I could be of greater service to mankind in this present era, by giving up my love for medical science and becoming a revolutionary rather than a doctor.

In June 1961 I passed with distinction the final examination in the Russian language and was accordingly selected a member of the University delegation that was to visit Soviet Georgia in August. In the meantime I spent the first month of the summer holidays (July 1961) in Soviet Moldavia. During that month I worked as an agricultural worker in a village in the Torspol District of the Soviet Moldavian Republic and also on a nearby State farm. This was the first employment I ever had. During this month we had the opportunity, every evening after work, to see the other farms, factories and electric power stations in the area. It would be completely true to say that it was here that I was convinced of the evil of the private property system and the value of the collectivized property system. It was here that I received the magnificent opportunity to live and work and exchange views with the Soviet working class and to see and understand the victories of socialism.

Speech to the Ceylon Criminal Justice Commission

The Impact of Sino–Soviet Dispute

On 1 September 1961 I commenced my medical studies. In the same educational year I studied, as additional subjects, Political Science and Russian Literature at this university. In the same month I was elected Deputy General Secretary of the Union of Ceylonese Students in Russia and accordingly I had to engage myself in student welfare work too.

At the time of the 22nd Congress of the CPSU I witnessed the differences of opinion which were boiling and brewing within the international Communist movement burst their seams and spill out into the open. By this time we were feeling dissatisfied with the policy and programme of the Ceylon Communist Party of which we had become staunch followers due to our meagre knowledge of Marxism. We felt that rightist and social-democratic tendencies had become the predominant force inside the Ceylon CP. We thought that the Ceylon CP was degenerating into a social democratic party and that to save the Communist Party from this disaster we should launch an ideological rectification campaign within it. Together with the present National Organizer of the Communist Party, Comrade K. P. Silva, who was then on a visit to the Soviet Union, and the late Comrade Dharmakerthi, I took the initiative of setting up a 'Marxist Education Circle' for the benefit of Ceylonese students.

During the summer holidays of 1962 I came back to Ceylon, but returned to the Soviet Union with my confidence in the Communist Party shattered still further. In September 1962 during my second year in the Medical College, my interest in politics came to the fore, pushing my interest in medical science to a secondary place. I had the opportunity of discussing the Chinese Communist Party's position in the Sino–Soviet ideological conflict with comrades like Murad Aidit, a close friend of mine and brother of the then leader of the Indonesian CP, the late Comrade D. N. Aidit, and Comrade Che Ali who was an Indonesian students' union leader. As a result of these discussions I felt that I was in a position to agree with most of the views put forward by the Chinese CP and accordingly I found myself on the Chinese side in the Sino–Soviet dispute. This in no way means that I became anti-Soviet. This conflict appeared to us at the outset as a fraternal ideological struggle between the Chinese and Soviet parties with the common object of arriving at a correct programme. I did not then realize that it was to develop into a conflict between enemies. I thought it would remain a fraternal debate. I did not like the idea of having two conflicting and contradictory voices in the international communist movement. However I admitted the fairness of having two voices, one right and one wrong, rather than having only one voice and that one wrong. But what was most unfortunate here was that, though there were two voices, both these voices happened to be wrong.

At this moment I would like to raise a question which is of vital importance in relation to this trial, namely, the view of Marxists in regard to peace and violence. I do so because the question of violence is related to most of my evidence. The two most important issues of contention between the Soviet and Chinese Parties were the following problems: the question of transition from capitalism to socialism, and the question of relations between the capitalist and socialist systems in the present world. Members of the Commission, our view concerning the transformation from capitalism to socialism has become a subject of your inquiry. Therefore I will explain it in some detail.

The Question of Violence

Whether a peaceful transition from capitalism to socialism is possible has been the subject of keen and heated controversy within the world communist movement and the international working class for a fairly long time. It was suitably answered as far back as 1847 by the young Engels. In his treatise, *Principles of Communism*, he poses this question as follows: 'Can private property be peacefully abolished?' and gives the following reply:

It would be desirable if this could happen, and the communists would certainly be the last to oppose it. Communists know only too well that revolutions are not only useless but even harmful. They know all too well that revolutions are not made intentionally and arbitrarily, but that everywhere and always they have been the necessary consequence of conditions which were wholly independent of the will and direction of individual parties and entire classes. But they also see that the development of the proletariat in nearly all civilized countries has been violently suppressed, and that in this way the opponents of communism have been working towards a revolution with all their strength. If the oppressed proletariat is finally driven to revolution, then we communists will defend the interests of the proletarians with deeds as we now defend them with words.

Engels's answer is quite clear. We who are Marxists, we who are revolutionaries are most desirous of seeing state power peacefully transferred from the hands of the exploiter capitalist ruling class to the hands of the proletariat. We would be very glad to receive peacefully from the few owners of property the means of production and hand them over to the custody of the entire people. If a peaceful abolition of the system which is based on the exploitation of man by man could be easily and readily brought about we would have no objection. If class distinctions in society can be abolished without any conflict and in a friendly manner we would have no reason to object. In fact, we communists would most certainly prefer peaceful methods for the realization of our objects, for the fulfilment of our aspirations – for the establishment of communism on behalf of all mankind so that antagonistic class distinctions no longer exist, where the disgraceful process of man exploiting man no longer exists, where all the means of material production are vested in society as a whole and where the noble policy of 'from each according to his ability, to each according to his needs' is actually practised. However it must be emphatically stated that it is not proletarian revolutionaries who have to decide whether the proletarian socialist revolution will take place peacefully or will necessitate the use of violence.

Marx has shown clearly that the exploiting, property-owning class has never voluntarily abandoned its ruling power nor its privileges at any time in history. Not a single property-owning class can be picked out from the entire globe which has bowed its head peacefully when confronted with the verdict of history embodied in the needs and will of the majority and given up its privileges voluntarily. The class which holds state power in this society makes use of this state power to protect and consolidate its property system. In order to protect their property there will be no cruel or disgusting crimes against the oppressed masses which these capitalist ruling classes will not commit.

The capitalist classes make use of their unlimited power in this society to subordinate members of the oppressed classes to bourgeois ideology. If the threat of an independent ideological development is observed within the ranks of the proletariat, the ruling classes realize the danger and employ all their customary methods to destroy it. They will infiltrate their agents to mislead and entice it towards them and to win over degenerate and traitorous individuals within it. They will seek by every devious means ideologically to disarm this independent movement inside the proletariat. They will resort to disgraceful slanders in order to divide and humiliate it, its policies and its disciplined members. When all these efforts fail, they seek its destruction through capitalist laws, courts, prisons, repressive rules and regulations and, in the end, even resort to violent attacks and massacres. This is the truth, tested out in the annals of the class struggle.

The state machine is an institution brought into being as a

result of the emergence of class divisions based on the system of private property and the resulting class conflict. It arose and developed as a powerful weapon necessary for the ruling class in power to repress and govern the proletariat it exploits. Without the assistance of this institution – the state machine – which is the creature of the class struggle, the ruling class cannot secure or improve its class needs and interests. It has never been impartial. In any society where a class system exists the state machine safeguards the interests of one class. It serves one class. The state machine in a feudal society is the class weapon of the aristocracy. In a capitalist society it is the weapon of the capitalist class. In a socialist society, of course, the dictatorship of the proletariat is at the service of the proletariat. The entire history of present-day society bears witness to the fact that whenever the proletariat, together with other oppressed groups in society, tries to secure its rights or change the existing social system by peaceful means, the exploiter classes, which represent a tiny minority in society, always act to protect their property system by completely negating and annulling the peaceful struggle of the proletariat by the use of violence.

We Marxists are proletarian revolutionaries. We do not conceal this fact from anyone. We hope for a complete revolutionary change of the existing social system and act with that goal in view. Ours is not the role of sitting on the fence with folded arms waiting for the day when this capitalist system is taken for burial on the shoulders of others; this capitalist system has bequeathed suffering and oppression to the working class of this country, which is over three million strong. It has made poverty and want the sole inheritance of the middle and lower peasants who comprise more than half the population of this country, it has brought unemployment to the youth and malnutrition to the infant, it has become the fount and source of each and every contemporary social problem that the bulk of the nation suffers. The socialist revolution in a country can be hastened or delayed depending on the degree to which objective conditions are ripe and subjective conditions, i.e. consciousness, organization and leadership, have developed.

Counter-revolutionaries resort to violence. Therefore to ensure the safe delivery of the new social system, it becomes necessary for proletarian revolutionaries to resort to revolutionary violence against the violence employed by the capitalist class.

The fundamental issue is the question of state power. The main task in any social revolution is the destructon of the capitalist state and the creation of a proletarian state, in other words, the dictatorship of the proletariat. For us Marxist–Leninists the consolidation of the proletarian dictatorship is the essential precondition for the transition to a socialist system. No socialism can be built without the proletariat first capturing and later consolidating state power. To retain state power the capitalist class will use violence. We Marxists are not preachers of violence. We only predict the certainty of violent acts in the course of the revolution. We prophesy that the decaying ruling classes, to prevent the forward march of society through a socialist revolution, will resort to counter-revolutionary violence and the proletariat will answer with its own revolutionary acts of violence.

CHIEF JUSTICE FERNANDO: If a burglar comes to you for advice, you may tell him: 'Well it may be necessary for you to carry a revolver because the owner of the house might also have a revolver.' Under our law you cannot carry a revolver in those circumstances.

THIRTEENTH SUSPECT: You have a good knowledge of your law. The knowledge that I have is of the views I hold and of the things I have said and done. What we have said and done has been presented here in a completely distorted form. But when the entire truth is made known, you will be able to take any course of action the law allows.

Speech to the Ceylon Criminal Justice Commission

Departure from the Soviet Union

After I was cured of an illness in February 1964, the doctor advised me to take leave for one term. I decided to spend this leave in Ceylon and arrived back on 24 March 1964. During the latter half of 1963 the Ceylon Party split into Russian and Chinese wings. My political mentor Dr S. A. Wickremasinghe remained in the leadership of the Russian wing, but I took the side of the Chinese wing in accordance with the policies and views I held. I even sent my congratulations from Moscow to the Congress of the Chinese wing.

JUSTICE ALLES: Would it be correct to say that you were refused a visa to return to Russia?

THIRTEENTH SUSPECT: After my return to Ceylon I worked as a sympathizer of the Chinese wing. During this period I was invited by a number of student unions and other public associations from several districts to speak to them on socialism and about the Soviet Union. I was questioned by the audiences on the factors which led to the Sino–Soviet polemics and answered these questions from the Chinese point of view. For this reason the local leaders of the pro-Moscow Party became angry with me. In August 1964, when I applied for a visa to return to the Soviet Union, the Soviet Embassy refused my application without giving any reasons. At that time I was taking a greater interest in political work in Ceylon. That is the answer to the question posed by Justice Alles.

JUSTICE FERNANDO: Why did it surprise you? When they refused you a return visa they treated you correctly. You came back from Moscow and you attacked Soviet Communism.

THIRTEENTH SUSPECT: No. I am not anti-Soviet. Even today I admit that the Soviet Union is a workers' state. I will always defend it against the onslaughts of the capitalist class. But there are theoretical problems that divide the Soviet Union from us. They are family problems. If you attack the Soviet Union I shall defend it. But I reserve the right to criticize openly and state the differences between the Soviet Union and us.

Origins of the JVP

In the middle of 1967, according to a prior agreement, a comrade whose name I cannot disclose and comrade Sanath came to my mother's house in Hunnadeniya. We had a discussion there related to our future course of action. As a result of this, at the end of 1967 a discussion was held by several of our sympathizers and ourselves. The discussion was of historic importance since it paved the way for the emergence of a new political movement – the *Janatha Vimukhti Peramuna*. There was a special reason for conducting these discussions over this period. A new political trend had grown on an international level and was gaining ground even in this country.

After the killing of comrade Che Guevara in Bolivia, and through the Tricontinental Congress and OLAS, this trend received world-wide publicity and had an important repercussion. The Cuban Embassy in Ceylon had various speeches and texts by comrades Castro and Guevara printed in Sinhala and widely distributed throughout this country. Among these were Castro's *History Will Absolve Me* and *The Second Declaration of Havana, The Path the Latin American Revolution Should Take, Those Who are Not Militant Revolutionaries Are Not Communists* and *From Moncada to Victory*. As a result of this many of our sympathizers felt that Ceylon should take the same path and emulate the heroic example of Che. The essence of this view was that under present conditions the revolution can take place without a revolutionary party. This view rejected the Leninist conception of the necessity of a fully fledged revolutionary organization for the victory of the proletariat and the socialist revolution. According to this view the betrayal of the Old Left Movement in the face of capitalist repression had created a situation where a revolutionary party could not be formed; revolutionaries should commence the armed struggle so that the oppressed masses would be awakened by the sound of gun-fire, a process which would rally them behind the revolution. The same comrades maintained that political activities, political classes, discussions, agitational campaigns and ideological struggles to organize the proletariat as a class and fight for the revolution, were either impossible or unnecessary. Those who wanted to follow the Cuban road had not even properly understood it themselves. They held the mistaken view that the revolution was launched, fought and won by eleven men with guns. They did not realize that broad sections of the masses – the *Llano* organization and the 26 July Movement – had been mobilized against the cruel Batista dictatorship. This false concept was completely rejected at the Kallatawa discussion. We defeated the petty-bourgeois adventurism which had developed behind the cover of the Cuban model and discussed what to do next. The innumerable negative examples we gained within the Old Left Movement and the breakaway pro-Chinese grouping, which claimed to be revolutionary, and our considerable experience of the international communist movement became useful to us as the basis of our discussions.

Tasks of the Revolution in Ceylon

We held, first, that the views we had in regard to the development of the Ceylonese revolution, when we were in the Chinese wing, were incorrect. When we were in the Chinese wing, we held that the present stage of the revolution was that of struggle for a people's democracy. At the Kallatawa discussion we rejected that view. What was relevant for Ceylon was a socialist and not a people's democratic revolution. I must explain why we rejected the concept of the people's democratic revolution.

This concept was copied by the Ceylonese Party from the leadership of the former Third (Communist) International and from China. On an analysis of the present nature and stage of social development in Ceylon and the international nature of capitalism, we came to the view that the anti-imperialist and anti-feudal tasks of the revolution in colonial and semi-colonial societies can be carried out only by attending to the socialist tasks, since in the epoch of imperialism (the extension of capital internationally) no anti-imperialist task can ever be effectively completed without socialism. The uncompleted and neglected tasks of the bourgeois democratic revolution, such as national independence, agrarian revolution and democracy can only be accomplished through a socialist revolution. They can be carried out only by the proletariat.

To argue that a new democratic stage exists between the capitalist system and the socialist system is to ignore the principles of social development and mutual class relationships. World capitalism, taken in its entirety, has developed sufficiently to provide the objective conditions suitable for a socialist revolution on a global scale, and therefore socialist tasks are the order of the day even in the underdeveloped countries of the world.

At the same discussion we argued that a proletarian revolutionary party must be established. However, there cannot be a Marxist party without Marxists. What has the Old Left Movement done during the course of thirty years and more to develop Marxists? It was quite apparent that the Old Left leaders had succumbed to capitalist ideology and paid scant attention to the question of providing the working class with a basic Marxist understanding. These Old Left leaders did not have the cadres who could have propagated Marxist ideas in Sinhala. Although they conducted a political class or two on certain subjects in a haphazard and irregular fashion, they did not provide the working class vanguard with systematic political education. They took no serious steps to raise and maintain political consciousness within their own ranks. As a result, when they turned to the Right, there was no strong group of Marxists to fight back effectively, and most of their members followed suit.

Political Education

I say all this to try and show you the context in which our five education classes came into being. Considering the negative experiences we had gained through the Old Left, we realized that to provide the people with a knowledge of Marxism, a correct, simple, established method should be adopted so that they would be able to grasp the subject readily. I am not going to conduct these five lessons here. I will only give you a brief introduction.

The first class was on the subject: 'Economic Crisis'. As it is the mode of production or the economy of a social system on which other structures rest, we realized the importance of making a fundamental analysis of the economy. We analysed the economic situation, its crisis, its origin, its causes, its development, its future and its inevitable consequences. We explained that the economic crisis in colonial and semi-colonial societies is in the process of being transformed into a political crisis, that before long it would result in a great national calamity and how the only way of escaping this calamity was to take the forward path of class struggle, establish the dictatorship of the proletariat and hasten both socialist industrialization and the collectivization of agriculture.

The second class was entitled: 'Independence – a neo-colonial stratagem'. This provided a basic Marxist interpretation of the socio-economic–political meaning of the change of flags – the lowering of the Union Jack and the raising of the Lion – that took place on 4 February 1948. In this class we explained that what was received was neither full independence nor economic independence. We showed how the strategy of

British imperialism necessitated a neo-colonial device to protect its colonial investments and property from the rising tempest of anti-imperialist liberation struggles resulting from the change in the international relationship of forces at the conclusion of the Second Imperialist War. We maintained that political independence without economic independence was a sham.

The third class concerned the way in which Indian expansionism affected Ceylon. The idea of 'Indian expansionism' was first put forward by the Chinese Communist Party. The editorial board of this party's daily newspaper, *Renmin Rebao,* published two articles entitled 'The Chinese–Indian Border Struggle and the Nehru Doctrine'. These gave a lengthy *exposé* of the class needs of the Indian ruling class and its basic philosophy, and argued that the Indian capitalists aimed at spreading their economic and political dependence over their smaller neighbours. This process was named 'Indian expansionism'. In our class we discussed how this affected our country. We explained the class needs of the powerful Borah capitalists in this country; the way in which these compare with Indian expansionism; the racist politics they engage in for the purpose of keeping the estate workers of Indian origin separate from the rest of the working class and under their own heel. We stated that the capitalist class had misled the estate workers of Indian origin and trapped them, and we determined to rescue these workers from the ideological grip of the capitalists. However, we had no cadres to do this. The many efforts we made to build cadres among comrades of the national minorities were fruitless.

The fourth class was on 'The Left Movement in Ceylon'. The purpose of this class was to learn the lessons from the unhealthy experiences of the Old Left and understand the reasons for its failure. Here we criticized the policies and programme of the Old Left from the 1930s onwards. This was done primarily so that we could learn the lessons of previous defeats.

The fifth class was the most important class. As there have

been incorrect references to it, I expect to take some time to speak about it. It involved burning questions of the Ceylonese Revolution. The fifth class was originally referred to as 'The Path To Socialism in Ceylon'. Later on, after the text *The Path the Latin American Revolution Should Take* became well known, certain persons referred to this class as 'The Path the Ceylonese Revolution Should Take'.

After the publication of Che's *Guerrilla Warfare* certain of our sympathizers, as well as members of other groups, thought of seeking solutions to the prevailing economic crisis by similar methods. Two other books appeared in Sinhala at this time: Lin Piao's *Long Live the Victory of People's War* and Mao Tse-tung's *Selected Military Writings*. Some sought to apply the remedies prescribed in these volumes. The Chinese wing and their supporters thought that the Ceylonese revolution should be a repeat of the Chinese revolution, with protracted war moving from the countryside to the towns. There were others, especially those groups that broke away from the Lanka Sama Samaja Party, who advocated the example of the Russian Revolution. It was these factors which led us to prepare the fifth class.

Our purpose was to defeat mechanical materialist concepts and show how incorrect and unscientific they were, and also provide our supporters with correct ideological tools. Through this class we intended to make a fundamental analysis of the experience gained by the international working-class movement in the class struggle, starting from the Paris Commune of 1871, up till the present time. We explained the difference between social reform and social revolution and showed how reforms serve the capitalist class and revolutions the proletariat. We showed how the path a revolution had taken in one country in a certain period and under certain conditions had been different in another country in a different period and under different conditions and how, therefore, socialist revolutions do not follow a single uniform path, but vary in their paths depending on the time, the place and the conditions peculiar to each occasion. In this way we demonstrated that the Chinese Revolution was different from the model of the Russian Revolution, and the Cuban Revolution was different from them both, and that therefore it was possible to see the emergence of a model different from previously cited experiences.

This class, like the other four, was political, theoretical and philosophical. If you want me to conduct these classes in full, I am ready to do it. It has been stated that there was something secret about these classes. Therefore if you want me to conduct the fifth class on its own in full I am ready to comply. [*Justice Fernando declines the offer. His words are not clearly recorded in the Court record.*]

At the Kalattawa discussion we agreed that, after these classes were held, those who showed political interest or keenness and were ready to go ahead should be further educated, and that this should be done in educational camps where theoretical classes on Marxist economics and Marxist philosophy would be conducted. I want to make it clear that we did not expect anyone to become a Marxist by following these five basic classes. They were merely a bridge to draw people away from the influence of bourgeois ideology and closer to Marxism.

From 1968 onwards I began holding classes all over the country. They took place at the rate of two or three a day or night, depending on the times at which people could attend. During this period I began to visit the Land Development Department LDD-work-sites in various parts of the country and hold classes for the workers there. We managed to start political work in the Land Development Department Workers' Union. For this reason the first classes I held were mostly for worker comrades in that Department. We also began classes for other worker comrades, peasants and sections of youth.

During the year 1968 I held classes in eighty different worksites of the LDD. At the same time I conducted political classes for workers and clerks in the Colombo office of the LDD and in many private places. With the increasing demand for classes there was a corresponding need for more people to conduct them. Towards the end of 1968 other comrades began to conduct political classes. One question needs to be explained at this stage.

A large number of persons brought before this Commission have been young. Why did these youths seek connections with the JVP? I will attempt to explain this. The new situation created by the general crisis of capitalism; the lessons learnt via the Sino–Soviet ideological battle; the new echo of the Cuban revolution which resounded throughout the world after the death of comrade Guevara; the clamour of OLAS; the struggle of the Indo-Chinese people, in particular, of the Vietnamese, as well as other circumstances, generated a new wave which had repercussions not only in Asia, Africa and Latin America, but even in Europe and North America – the bastions of modern capitalism. This radicalism of youth was by no means limited to Ceylon.

The entire history of capitalism tells us that when the working class is passive and lethargic, other sections of society suffering under capitalism will find it necessary to protest against the existing social system. It is no secret that by 1968 the working-class movement had been misled internationally by a reformist leadership and left demoralized and dispirited before the capitalist system. It is no longer a matter of controversy that the working classes of France and Italy were thrust away from the path of class struggle into the backwaters of class collaboration. They were ideologically disarmed by the decadent, increasingly reformist leaderships of the Communist Parties in the face of a capitalist onslaught. What happened in colonial and neo-colonial countries like ours was no different.

The leaders of the Old Left in Ceylon were reformists who had their heads filled with Fabian ideology. These leaders, though they called themselves Marxists, were in reality guided by the writings of Laski and Keynes, and invariably betrayed the aspirations of the workers. They tied the trade-union movement to their brand of reformist, parliamentarist politics. The final betrayal was the abandonment of the 21 demands, which destroyed the United Workers' Trade Union and the United Left Front by open collaboration with the capitalists. This historic class betrayal left the working class discouraged and demoralized. Under the UNP government a generalized bitterness developed, and both students and young workers began to demonstrate their hostility. On several occasions during this period (1968–9) the Peradeniya University students clashed with the armed forces. Students from Colombo University crashed into the Parliament building and declared that it was nothing more than a den of thieves. In 1968 a number of youths who had attended our classes entered the universities, and by the end of that year we succeeded in winning over a large section of sympathizers of the Russian and Chinese wings inside the universities. At this point we started our classes inside universities and schools.

The Right to Rebel

As a Marxist I have held, and still hold, the view that a people has the right to rebel against an arbitrary government. This is not a view held only by Marxists. Throughout history, people believing in various ideologies and religions have accepted the right of a community to rebel against a cruel administration. We are charged, before you, of rebelling against the Queen's government, of attempting to rebel, of abetting a rebellion, and conspiring to rebel.

Honourable Chairman, some time ago I learnt that as far back as 1649 the people of Britain led by Oliver Cromwell rebelled against their monarch, Charles I, an ancestor of the present Queen of England. They wanted him off the throne and they succeeded. On that occasion the British people held the view that to rebel against an oppressive régime was fair and just.

Speech to the Ceylon Criminal Justice Commission

No doubt you are aware of how in 1778 the American rebellion under the leadership of George Washington succeeded against the British empire. You are also aware of the 1789 events in France known as the French Revolution. What this indicates is that even before the advent of Marxism people in various countries held the view that they had the right to rebel. In your capacity as judges you may have had occasion to read *Vindicia Contra Tyrannos*, written under the pseudonym of Stephanus Junius Brutus, in which it is stated not only that there should be insurrections against autocratic governments, but even that they should be led by judges! The fact that liberal thinkers have supported the right to rebel is illustrated vividly in the French *Declaration of the Rights of Man*. A passage in it reads: 'When a government violates the rights of the people, insurrection is for them the most sacred of rights, the most imperative of duties.' A glimpse into our own history will show how *Mahawansa*, *Chulawansa* and other works record innumerable popular insurrections against cruel rulers. We are not the first to be charged with rebellion against the Queen's government. Similar charges were brought against Keppetipola Adikarama and others in 1848. This demonstrates that the right to rebel was accepted by the people of our own country. In the same way I, too, accepted the view that people have the right to rebel against an oppressive régime. I still hold this view.

The next question before you is whether we did rebel during the month of April 1971. I will give you my answer in detail.

In this social system the privileged classes are the imperialists and their local lackeys. In this system there are a number of problems that have been growing for a long time. You know that a free education system began in this country when we were children. A large number of us from both rural and urban areas had an opportunity of receiving education. The degree of educational opportunity is almost on a par with developed countries. This is obvious when you compare Ceylon with India, Pakistan and Nepal. This has given a considerable impetus to the development of a proletarian consciousness and a proletarian political education. According to government statistics the number of children attending school was 3,500,000, and of these 270,000 leave school in search of employment every year. 50,000 have had an education up to senior level. To say that the remaining 220,000 had received a lesser education means that under this social system they have no prospects of employment above that of ordinary wage-earners and labourers. Every year about 220,000 semi-educated persons enter society as serfs and labourers. This process has continued since the end of the 1950s. Increasingly many university graduates also found it difficult to obtain jobs and there were instances where they, too, were compelled to become general labourers.

According to government statistics issued in 1969–70 there are 3,333,000 wage-earners in this country. 56 per cent of these were rural workers and 26 per cent were estate workers working on the tea, rubber and coconut plantations. The urban workers numbered 18 per cent. Over the last seven years the economic, social and political problems confronting these three groups of workers have been increasingly acute.

The condition of the peasantry within this social system requires special attention. In the rural areas the lower peasants suffer from the problem of landlessness. An official report of the Kandyan Peasantry Commission appointed by the Bandaranaike government stated that 180 Kandyan families live in each two-acre zone. Ninety families would thus live on one acre. This gives you an idea of the enormity of the problem of landlessness in certain areas. Within this social system utter misery and destitution have become the common lot of the villager. And we find that only 4,000 of the more than 2,000,000 families in this country have a monthly income of Rs. 1,000 and over. [£1 = Rs. 30.] Government figures confirm this fact. In brief, two million families have a low income and lead a miserable life. It is under these social conditions that the political unrest arose which led to the April incidents.

Origins of the April Incidents

It is necessary to bring to your attention certain specific incidents which occurred in 1971. The *Janatha Vimukhti Peramuna* was implanted in the rural proletariat, the lumpen proletariat and certain petty-bourgeois layers. In the urban working class and the estates the influence of the Old Left was still paramount. In the rural areas, before our intervention, the traditions of the Sri Lanka Freedom Party (SLFP) were strongest. The SLFP won most of its seats in the rural areas. The worst massacres during the April incidents took place in the areas held by the SLFP. The SLFP politicians had shamelessly sown the germs of communal discord against the Tamil minority. In the 1956 elections the CP and the LSSP stood for parity on the language issue. But what did they do a short time later? They were not only against equal status for Tamil and Sinhala, but opposed even the granting of any lesser rights. It was in these conditions that we became disillusioned with them. That is why we struggled. If anyone willingly risks his or her life, or is prepared to be shackled as a prisoner, this can only be because there is no alternative. Chairman, you are aware that after the Government came to power we started our political activities in the open and they were immensely successful. Look back and see the picture of our public meetings held in various parts of the country such as Kandy, Kegalle, Kurungala and Southern Province and Colombo – you will see the mass of humanity, thousands and thousands of people that flocked round us, to see us and listen to us. And these were not people we had forced or cajoled with the use of guns to attend our rallies, nor had we supplied them with free lorries and buses, but people who had come of their own accord because of their interest in our politics. With every passing day we were moving forward. This process continued while another parallel process was taking place: dissatisfaction with the UNP resulted, with our blessing, in the election of the United Front government, with over a two-thirds majority. The LSSP and CP had told the people that if they were brought into power with a two-thirds majority they would amend the constitution, change the system of internal administration and open the way to socialism. The ordinary people took them at their word. They expected the new government to perform miracles and that is why they put the cross against the star and key and not against the elephant.

I have already mentioned that in the early days we were not strong in the urban working class. But by 1971 we had begun to spread out from the villages to the towns and, through our political agitational campaigns, our impact was beginning to be felt in the cities, specifically in certain sections of the working class. Young workers in factories and work-sites were beginning to listen. It was then that the Old Left began to understand the threat we posed to them. They attempted to devise a course of action to deal with us. The first method was branding us as CIA agents, but you are aware that this attack failed. Then they resorted to the second method. This can be described in the words of Mr Sarath Muttattuwagama, a leader of the CP. In a speech made at a CP mass rally in Ratnapura during the latter half of 1970, he stated that the repression of the Che Guevarists should not be left to the police. It should be the responsibility of the CP! During the same period the LSSP leaders also discussed the threat we posed. A meeting of their Politbureau issued instructions to their locals to unleash physical attacks against us. They asked for police protection to carry out this task. I have already mentioned these facts at our public meetings. When the second method failed, they discussed the matter in the new Cabinet and considered ways and means of suppressing the *Janatha Vimukhti Peramuna* so that it could not become an effective political force. They decided, according to a recent statement by the Prime Minister, not to ban us as it would have made heroes out of us. The capitalist class is well aware of the futility of banning a Marxist party. So this government suspected that even if they banned us we would carry on political activities under another name. They devised an alternative scheme which was and continues to be implemented.

You are aware that the country is facing a severe economic crisis. It is something which everyone admits. But the crisis has not materialized out of thin air. It existed on 5 April 1971. It was there before that date. At that time the government was not in a position to add to the distress of the people, to place the economic and social burden they have now placed on the masses with impunity, because there existed a revolutionary force that would have roused the people and led them to protest against these measures. It was necessary to destroy our movement before stern measures could be taken. And accordingly they prepared their plans. After January 1971 things came to a head. Mr S. A. Dissanayake, a former Inspector-General of Police, was appointed Additional Permanent Secretary to the Ministry of Defence and External Affairs, with effect from 1 March 1971. Long before this, the CID had been using its full powers to investigate the activities of the JVP. A separate unit had been set up, which had gathered sufficient facts by April 1971 through raids and arrests of comrades from various parts of the country. They also planted agents inside the JVP rank and file.

By 1 March 1971 arrangements had been completed for the deployment of military units in various parts of the country to collect intelligence about our activities. Press reports in relation to these manoeuvres appeared between 1 and 5 March. In the same week police powers were vested in officers of the Army. On 5 March the police rehearsed a plan in order to find out how much time it would take them when the alarm was sounded. This rehearsal was to test their alertness in an emergency and it was conducted in Colombo as well as in other parts of the island. On the sixth there was an attack on the US Embassy which supplied them with the excuse needed to repress the revolutionary movement. On 13 March I was arrested and on 16 March a State of Emergency was declared. 4,098 people were arrested *before* 5 April 1971.

In April 1971 the revolutionary preconditions for the seizure of power by the proletariat and for an armed revolutionary struggle were absent. That is my view. In the absence of a revolutionary situation – i.e. both objective and subjective conditions – an armed uprising was not possible.

My view is that the conditions were not ripe for organizing an armed revolutionary uprising to seize state power. The objective conditions were maturing fast, but they were still unripe. It had not reached a stage where the masses saw no other solution but revolution. It is true, however, that then, as now, society was moving in that direction. The subjective conditions were also lacking: that is, the existence of a revolutionary party that has steeled itself, won the support of the masses and is fit to lead them in an armed struggle for power. The *Janatha Vimukhti Peramuna* was developing and moving towards that goal, but had not reached full maturity. We had failed at that time to establish the JVP in the Northern and Eastern provinces and in the Estate sector as a political force. And then there was the question of mass support. It is true that out of the millions who voted for the Coalition Government, tens of thousands had by this time washed their hands of it. It is also true that this section was the politically developed section. They were abandoning the Coalition Government and moving Leftwards towards the JVP. But there was a section which, although disgusted and frustrated, did not break away from the government during those eight months. In other words the JVP had not yet reached the stage where the masses could see it as a real alternative to the government, accept its leadership and join in the class struggle under its banner. In our Marxist conception, a revolution – an armed uprising – is not something done behind the backs of the masses.

JUSTICE FERNANDO: Have revolutionaries in any part of the world never made mistakes?

THIRTEENTH SUSPECT: Mistakes have been made. In fact they have learnt lessons from these mistakes. Mistakes can happen in the future as well.

JUSTICE FERNANDO: I said a mistake. I meant a miscalculation.

THIRTEENTH SUSPECT: There can be no revolution without the participation and active support of the people. That is our stand.

I told you earlier that I reject the position that it was a JVP decision to seize state power on 5 April 1971. I do not admit that. But as I discovered later and something I do not deny is that there have been instances when certain comrades of the JVP, in the face of intolerable repression, resorted to a struggle against such repression.

'More buds will bloom . . .'

In March 1971 a class need arose for the ruling class to suppress the revolutionary movements of this country, especially the JVP. They acted accordingly. The April incidents were the result. I interpret the process as one initiated by the counter-revolution. This does not mean that anyone who acted against capitalist repression on 5 April, or had mistaken a decision taken by others to be a JVP decision, or even decided on such a course on their own in the absence of another alternative, was thus a counter-revolutionary. A number of close comrades of mine are no longer living. The entire revolutionary leadership of the Matara district exists no more. Comrade Susil Wickrema, Comrade Jayatissa of Deniyaya, Comrades Piyatassa, Loku

Mahatmaya, Suraweera, Jayaweera, the two Bogahawatta brothers were all both personal friends and fellow comrades. No one can speak about their fate. On inquiring from their homes all I have learnt is that they are no longer among the living.

For me, Honourable Chairman, the April episode was an occasion when the capitalist class found its existence as a class increasingly threatened by the proletariat. It is a result of a counter-revolutionary course of action on which the capitalist class of the country embarked in order to save the capitalist system from the proletariat. It has been part of that course of action to ban the JVP today. A large number of persons connected with the JVP, but belonging to the Leftist parties, have been murdered. A large number of persons connected with the JVP have been put in prison, as have many who had no connection with us. It has become possible to continue the repression of the JVP in particular and the revolutionary movement in general.

In conclusion this is what I have to say: I admit that the capitalist class has been temporarily victorious. But I do not see it as a defeat for the proletariat. This is only a big retreat for the proletariat; yes, I call it a big retreat. A retreat is not a defeat, but a phase from which it is possible to recover and march again to certain victory. No revolutionary movement has raced non-stop to victory in a straight line from start to finish. Forward marches followed by retreats are quite common in revolutionary movements. That is the position with which we are confronted today and it is from this position that I have come to give evidence before you. I have not spoken here by stretching my principles for personal gain. I remain an unrepentant Marxist and what I am defending here are Marxist principles rather than my person. For as a revolutionary Marxist I have nothing else to defend.

Whatever the capitalist class may have expected to gain through the April incidents, their ultimate result has already been expressed by a revolutionary poet in the following stanza:

> See these blossoms strewn on earth and withered lie
> Their fragrance shall abide, shall never die.
> To raise its sweetness high to limits limitless,
> More buds will bloom and bloom and multiply.

The poet expresses himself in clear and plain terms. The flowers of revolution have blossomed, but now they lie withered and dead. But their perfume has not ceased. To enhance that perfume and with that aim in view other buds will continue to bloom. In fact, gentlemen, the capitalist cause has no real reason to celebrate its success. For in the class struggle victory is a see-saw until the proletariat finally emerges victorious. That is our belief. I have concluded my evidence.

The Economic Structure of
Pakistan and Bangladesh
Richard Nations

Only twenty-four years after its formation the 'Homeland of Islam in the subcontinent' – Pakistan – disintegrated under the pressures of military repression, national struggle and war of intervention. But, paradoxically, this violent finale stemmed directly from what has been described as 'a decade of development, prosperity and success' for the Pakistan economy. An autopsy of the old Pakistan must examine this Janus-like 'success' – one which generated both real economic advance and bitter social and political antagonisms.

Pakistan began as an anomaly. Theology was the only rationale for uniting into one sovereign state two territorial units separated not only by geographical distance but by linguistic, cultural, social and ethnic differences which had no mediation other than the reactionary bond of religion. Across this artificial structure, where the centre of 'national' power was separated from the majority of the population by over 1,000 miles of hostile Indian territory, the course of capitalist development wove an intricate fabric combining the features of both class and colonial exploitation. Within this complex, Bengal has suffered the compound contradictions of a system which simultaneously channels the production of the poor into the consumption of the wealthy, and the surplus of an agricultural dependency into the industry of the suzerain metropolis. The political economy of Pakistani capitalism, as it has evolved since 1947, is the fundamental explanation of the national and class upsurge which is giving agonized birth to Bangladesh today. The purpose of this essay will be to show the essential mechanisms of this economy, the reasons why it eventually led to the crisis in Bengal, and the reciprocal impact which this crisis is certain to have on West Pakistan.

Class Structure

A brief sketch of the class structure of Pakistan is a necessary precondition for understanding the pattern of economic development since Partition.[1] The vast rural expanse of West Pakistan is dominated by large landlords, who form a traditional aristocracy and gentry, owning over 30 per cent of the privately cultivated land. For although rapidly transforming the rural economy of large parts of Pakistan – particularly the intensively irrigated region of the Canal Colony in Punjab – capitalism has not developed through an antagonism between the class of *kulak* farmers and the old feudal orders. Capitalist and feudal modes of exploitation often *coexist* and *complement* one another on the same estate, and under the régime of the same landlord. These landlords extract both feudal rents and capitalist profits from their estates, which are tilled by combinations of dependent peasants and wage-labourers. The emergence of capitalism has thus fused into a social formation which reinforces rather than weakens the social power of the previously dominant classes. In its incipient stages, capitalism has thus placed in sharper relief the social antagonism between the land-surplus classes – those with 25 acres or more – and the vast underclasses of dwarf-holders, micro-tenants and sharecroppers, landless labourers and rural unemployed who vegetate in various gradations of misery and social impotence.

In the towns, a parvenu industrial bourgeoisie has burgeoned from virtually zero since the Second World War. It is important to underline the peculiar composition and character of this

1. Cf. Tariq Ali, *Pakistan People's Power or Military Rule*, London, 1970; Hamza Alavi, 'Élite Farmer Strategy and Regional Disparities in Agricultural Development in West Pakistan', mimeo, to be published.

class, since much of the configuration of political power in Pakistan has been determined by it. When Partition occurred, there was practically no industry in the provinces of Sind, Baluchistan, Punjab and the North-west Frontier. Throughout the subcontinent, the Muslim bourgeoisie, of whatever ethnic origin, had played a negligible role in the development of a manufacturing capitalism. Some minority communities of Muslims, however, had traditionally specialized in selected commercial and speculative functions (bullion-broking, for example), mainly in Bombay and Calcutta. The most important of these were the Halai Memon, the Dawoodi Bohra and the Ismali and Isnashari Khoja.[2] These groups migrated to West Pakistan after Partition with what capital and skills they possessed, and there formed the initial nucleus of the entrepreneurial class in the Western provinces. Later, they were joined by a similar Punjabi trading minority, the Chiniotis, but even today some half of the millionaire élite which dominates the urban sector of the Western economy is composed of Gujarati-speaking immigrants from communities who represent less than 0·3 per cent of the total population. In 1947, these were newcomers to Karachi, with very slender assets. They therefore became overwhelmingly dependent on the patronage of the state bureaucracy for the finance and import licences crucial to business enterprise in the early years.

In the absence of any native capitalist class, the nascent Pakistani government, for its part, had to fall back largely on these trading communities as agents of its industrialization programme. Thereafter, they grew steadily, together with their Punjabi counterparts, in a client relationship to the Pakistani Civil Service, which provided them with the privileges and

2. These Gujarati-speaking communities originate from either Gujarat or Kathiwar (between Karachi and Bombay). The Chiniotis were originally a quasi-caste group of traders in leather hides and skins; as the market for these commodities changed so did their fortunes.

protection necessary for accumulation in the inhospitable conditions of the North-western subcontinent. In exchange, of course, corruption seeped ever wider in the ranks of the Pakistani bureaucracy itself, as business repaid the debts to its patrons with bribes, amenities, donations and kick-backs. Thus however wealthy Pakistani businessmen became (enormously so, it will be seen), their direct political power was always truncated: for rather than an independent capitalist class, government patronage produced a bourgeoisie tied to the pre-existent structures of the military brass and bureaucracy. The key personnel of both these latter apparatuses were in their turn recruited from the landed gentry and aristocracy, which had always traditionally provided the indigenous staff of the upper echelons of the British colonial state in India. The top military officers and the élite functionaries who have wielded effective political power throughout the history of Pakistan formed an increasingly symbiotic union with the new tycoons in the sixties, during which all three groups rapidly enriched themselves. The comparative 'social' weakness of the West Pakistani business class has persisted; but today it is compensated by its enormous economic power within the country. In 1968, 22 families controlled 66 per cent of the country's total industrial capital, 70 per cent of insurance and 80 per cent of banking.[3] This concentration of wealth has been wrung out of an industrial working class in Karachi, Lyallpur, Lahore and Rawalpindi which suffers a degree of exploitation uncommon even in the underdeveloped capitalist world today: in 1954, the share of wages in value-added manufactures was 45 per cent (in England it is 75 per cent): in 1967 it had actually dropped to 25 per cent.[4]

3. *Business Recorder* (Karachi), 25 April 1968. These figures were first quoted at a management convention by one of the Government's chief planning economists, Dr M. Haq. Since then, however, further estimates put the control of insurance at 97 per cent.

4. Op. cit.

Richard Nations

Class in East Bengal

East Bengal has presented a very distinct class constellation. Before Independence, the feudal *zamindari* who wracked the countryside had been Hindus. With Partition, this class fled virtually *en bloc* to India, taking with it most of the exiguous industrial capital in the province as well. The land they left behind was redistributed among the sharecroppers and poor peasants in units with a 33-acre-ceiling. Hindu moneylenders departed with the landlords as well. Thus at one stroke the countryside was purged of two of the chief parasites that drain any rural economy. Partition therefore generated a rural social structure overwhelmingly dominated by a mass of peasant smallholders, the great majority of whom own less than 5 acres of land, producing cash crops for the market: jute[5] and cotton. However, market forces and state policy collaborated to erase this relative hiatus in class differentiation. Much in the tradition of their British predecessors, the Ayub régime cultivated the loyalty and complicity of the rural élite with legislative concessions. In 1961 the land ceiling was raised from 33 acres to 125 with retrospective effect. Whenever the original *zamindars* could be traced, they got back the difference. Furthermore, by confiscating the peasant's surplus through control of the market, state policy left the peasantry vulnerable to usury and again under the thumb of the rich peasant–merchant–moneylender. Moreover, Ayub's programme of 'Basic Democracies' institutionalized the political hegemony of the rich: '... the

5. Jute is a fibre crop which is manufactured into a variety of textiles used for sacking, rug-backs, or mats. At Partition jute was produced almost exclusively in East Bengal and exported throughout the world. Although the jute export market has grown considerably since that time, so have new competitors. East Bengal now competes with India, Russia, Brazil and China in raw jute production, while jute itself has to hold a shrinking cost line against a number of increasingly cheaper substitutes deriving from either other agricultural or synthetic fibres or from paper and plastics.

rural rich completely dominate the political scene in rural E. Bengal.'[6] As a result the old forms of exploitation were to return, and with them both a decline in absolute living standards and a notable increase in village stratification.

Meanwhile, in the urban areas the bulk of what modest industry developed fell into the hands of West Pakistani investors. During the sixties, a handful of local contractors and entrepreneurs emerged, feeble creatures of the state bureaucracy and its agencies, with little specific weight in East Bengali society. The local civil service gradually filled up with Bengali functionaries, but the Central segments of the bureaucracy in the West remained largely impervious to this process, despite some belated tokenism in the last days of Ayub's régime. The Army has throughout been a wholly West Pakistani preserve. Thus, the leading class in East Bengali society has been an amorphous petty bourgeoisie of traders, functionaries, professionals, intellectuals and rural notables, who float uneasily above the swelling peasant sea below them.

The Mechanisms of State Economic Policy

The power structure in Pakistan had thus always instrumentalized the subordination of the rural and urban masses of West Pakistan and the whole population of East Bengal to the landlord-bourgeois bloc of the West, and its military–bureaucratic apparatus, which had in practice governed the country without the mediation of a party system since the early fifties. It will

6. 'The "Basic Democrats" to whom was entrusted the power and responsibility to run local governments, to whom all civil servants, including the police, within the respective areas turned for guidance and, most important of all, who had an important say in the management of local finances, came almost exclusively from the upper sections. Successive surveys of the Basic Democrats in 1959, 1961, 1964 clearly showed this.' (N.K. Chandra, 'Agrarian Classes in East Pakistan', mimeo.) For effects of 1950 land reform, cf. Azizur Rahman Khan, *The Economy of Bangladesh*, London, 1972.

now be seen how these classes have manipulated State power at the Centre to direct the surplus of the whole economy, East and West, into their hands. At the time of Partition, Pakistan's economy had one obvious and main asset: a cash-crop agriculture, predominantly sited in the East, which exported both raw materials and food products. Bengali jute, in particular, enjoyed a world monopoly. The primary exports generated a significant quantum of foreign exchange. This was the economic base upon which the government determined to build import-substitution industries through the 'free enterprise' of a small group of immigrant trading communities. Its practical goal was therefore to redirect the wealth generated by agriculture to the benefit of its chosen candidates for entrepreneurship. This involved three tasks: expropriating the agrarian surplus to provide initial 'risk' capital for industry; centralizing the foreign exchange earned by agriculture to pay for the necessary imports; reorienting rural commodities to become raw materials for domestic manufactures.

Given these objectives, capitalist planning in Pakistan registered some spectacular successes in the late fifties and sixties. Let us see how it was done. The basic trick was turned in a comparatively simple fashion by manipulating two economic powers reserved to the Centre. The first was the power to determine the exchange rate of the domestic currency and the second to control imports into the country. The strategic weapons of accumulation therefore became the overvaluation of the currency and the strict control of imported products. These two work together; we shall, however, consider manipulation of the exchange rate first. Throughout its history the Pakistani government has artificially held the price of the Pak rupee about 50 per cent above its open market value *vis-à-vis* all other currencies. In other words, if, as in the late fifties, a pound sterling drew Rs. 20 on the open market in Hong Kong, the official price set the pound at about Rs. 13. There are two inevitable results when any currency is overvalued. Exports are discouraged, while conversely imports are boosted because the overvalued currency makes the price of domestic products relatively high and that of foreign products relatively low. The structural consequence of overvaluation is thus a rapid drain of foreign exchange as export earnings decline and import payments increase following price incentives. A second effect is that the differential between the official rate and the open market rate (around 50 per cent in Pakistan's case) is lost to whoever sells the currency at official prices and only gained by whoever buys abroad.

Overvaluation thus leads to value differential, stimulated imports and depressed exports. In other words, of itself, overvaluation would rapidly destroy any economy. However, by its manipulation of another set of controls the Pakistani state was able to direct the consequent forces to its advantage. The first of these devices was the state's monopoly of foreign currencies: all export earnings of foreign exchange had to be surrendered to the government at the official rate. Thus the value differential between the official and the open market rate was siphoned off the exporter's surplus by the state. Second, the government imposed an import licensing system to determine who was to import and how much of what products. These licences had a twofold function. First, bureaucratic intervention blocked the foreign exchange drain which market forces would otherwise have caused. Second, the control of import commodities effectively determined who was to gain and who was to lose the value differential between the official and the market price of foreign currency earnings.[7]

The Effect of Overvaluation and Import Control

A similar use of overvaluation and import control is of course a fairly common device in developing countries. But its impact

7. For a good description of this system, see Stephen R. Lewis, *Pakistan, Industrialization and Trade Policies*, London, 1970, chap. 2, pp. 20–37.

has probably nowhere been so extreme and dramatic as in Pakistan. Pakistan's exports were totally agricultural in the early fifties. The largest foreign exchange earner was the jute industry: yet this was not a heavily capitalized plantation sector. Bengali jute was grown by the small proprietor on an average holding of under 3 acres. The foreign exchange he earned from sales abroad was surrendered to the government in return for Pakistani rupees at the official rate. In the transaction the peasant lost approximately 50 per cent of the buying price to the government; an amount which remained as concealed value in the foreign currency itself. Thus at one stroke the state simultaneously confiscated a large proportion of the peasants' surplus and centralized the most vital economic resource in an underdeveloped country, foreign exchange. The import licensing system then allocated these resources at the government's discretion. The licences to import, as well as the foreign exchange necessary to pay abroad, were handed over to the business clientele of the bureaucracy, whether Gujarati or Punjabi. These licences were then used to bring in both commercial and industrial imports to meet current consumption needs and industrialize the country. The concealed value lost to the peasant when he surrendered his foreign exchange earnings was therefore recovered by the importing merchant or industrialist when he bought abroad. Thus the importer received a direct and uncompensated subsidy from agricultural producers. A good idea of the differential values received by the exporter and importer is provided by the relative rupee/dollar ratios which obtained for manufactures and agriculture respectively. These ratios fluctuated, but on average from 1951 to 1964, the agricultural exporter received approximately Rs. 4·25 while the manufacturer received over Rs. 8·61 for one dollar of foreign currency.[8]

Furthermore, these differentials reflected not only the absolute values for those dealing directly with foreign exchange,

8. Ibid., p. 65.

the exporter and importer, but also the relative values for the whole of the manufacturing and agricultural sectors of the economy respectively. For while most agricultural goods competed with exports for resources, the opposite was true of all manufactures, since they were either imports or competed with imports. As a result, the whole of the marketed sector of agriculture was affected by the exporter's adverse terms of trade. Therefore, the prices the peasant received for his products, whether sold abroad *or* in the home market, were driven well below their opportunity cost to the economy. This fact had a secondary benefit for the industrialist; since food was the major wage good, capital had a proportionately lower price to pay for the subsistence of its workers. Even when market fluctuations threatened to bring agricultural prices up, the state intervened directly to insulate capitalists from the ramifying effect of such price movements on wages. Compulsory procurement of agricultural products in the country and their sale beneath market prices in the city passed a further subsidy from the peasant surplus to urban incomes. Where government procurement was awkward, there was always a plethora of PL 480 food commodities from the USA to flood the market and bring rising agricultural prices down again. These three mechanisms: adverse terms or trade, forced procurement and pressure from Nebraskan hand-outs were orchestrated by the Centre to hold agricultural prices to a bare minimum. As a result, agricultural prices levelled at an average of about 52·9 per cent of what they would have received on the international market for the full period from Partition through the Second Plan Period.[9] The upper urban income groups, and particularly industrialists, gained the remainder through low food prices and rock-bottom

9. Ibid., p. 65. The fiscal year runs from July to June. The dates of Pakistan's Five Year Plan Periods are: Pre-Plan Period = 1950/1–1954/5; First Plan Period = 1955/6–1959/60; Second Plan Period = 1960/61–1964/5; Third Plan Period = 1965/6–1969/70.

wages, as well as through access to foreign exchange at two thirds of its value.

Protective Devices

Although this multiple pricing system for foreign exchange effected enormous concealed and uncompensated transfers from agriculture to industry, it alone hardly accounted for the full margin of capitalist profit, nor conversely, for the extensive costs to Pakistani society in inflated prices and sheer waste. For having mobilized an interest-free finance and the necessary foreign exchange, the state then offered its full administrative panoply to protect domestic production from the harsh winds of international competition or the exigencies of efficient production. The first of its protective devices was a system of tariff barriers and quantitative controls, whose function was to drive up the price and limit the numbers of competing imports coming into the country. The use of these policies worked grotesque distortions in the price structure by giving manufacturers precocious monopolies in the home market; where one firm, and family, did not control the whole market, price leadership was practised among the 'competitors'. As a result, the Pakistani consumer in the not unrepresentative year of 1964 paid an average of 2·5 times the world market prices for the full range of Pakistan's consumer manufactures! In return for outrageous prices he received notoriously shoddier quality as well. During this same year for example, Pakistani silks and silk textiles were 4·5 times the price of comparable and better quality goods on the world market; popular clothing for its part cost 3·25 times the world market price in Pakistan; sugar, 3 times; electrical appliances, 4 times, and so forth.[10] Virtually nothing manufactured in Pakistan could not be obtained abroad more cheaply from India, Japan or Britain.

The accumulated effects of government's assiduous pro-

10. Ibid., pp. 79–83.

tection of industry led both to windfall profits for the capitalists and bizarre wastes for society. 'In the extreme case ... nine industries had levels of protection that imply the processing industry was contributing nothing to the value of the inputs it used.' Which amounts to literally 'free' enterprise in that 'the value added in the industry was negative'![11] Indeed, the average industry was not far from the absurd extreme: in the median case in 1963-4, for example, 78 per cent of value-added in production was due to protection.[12] However, if this cornucopia of agricultural subsidies and barricade of protection were not enough to encourage 'entrepreneurship', the government undertook the job itself. Semi-autonomous agencies such as the Pakistan Industrial Development Corporation, financed and controlled by the state, would first initiate and establish enterprises, then turn them over to private ownership once they were off the ground. The early PIDC industries included sugar refineries, jute textile mills, fertilizer and cement plants; later more basic industries were undertaken, such as machine tools, heavy electrical equipment and petro-chemicals. Finally, having set up the economy to pump the surplus wealth of the countryside into capitalist profits, the government was loath to take them away. Both corporate and personal taxes were extremely low, when paid; more often they were eluded through a maze of loop-holes and concealments, tax holidays, depreciation allowances, concessions, and so on.

Papanek's plaudits

This rickety *dirigisme*, one which expropriated the immediate producers in order to distribute their surplus according to the vagaries of bureaucratic politics in windfalls, bonanzas or waste, was hailed by its advocates as a 'free market economy'. Professor Gustav Papanek, Director of Harvard's Develop-

11. Ibid., p. 84.
12. Ibid., p. 80.

ment Advisory Service exulted: 'The combination of incentives and obstacles produced an environment in which success was likely only for the ruthless individual, possessing some foresight and considerable energy ... This environment, in turn, produced a remarkably able group of entrepreneurs, whose economic behaviour was not too different from their robber-baron counterparts of the 19th-century Western industrialization.'[13] For such rhetoric, of course, it was irrelevant that English, French or German industrialists never enjoyed anything comparable to the fiscal and economic system which in Pakistan directs the flow of surplus through multifold subtle paths from the productive poor to the limited number of 'ruthless and energetic robber barons'. The exact magnitude of this transfer is difficult to ascertain; however, sophisticated estimates have been made of the percentage of output lost to agriculture by the prevailing system. Based on the alternative assumptions, the most comprehensive study concludes that during the Second Plan Period from 24 per cent to as much as 49 per cent of agriculture's annual income has slipped through subsidies into the manufacturing sector.[14] This drainage did not come from agriculture's exporting sectors alone; in one way or another the surplus of every peasant who had any connection whatsoever with the market was tapped.

Savings and Investment

It is patent that the productive wealth of the country was systematically redistributed to the benefit of the upper income groups and particularly the capitalist class. This pattern was openly proclaimed and rationalized by the US advisers to Pak-

13. Gustav F. Papanek, *Pakistan's Development, Social Goals and Private Incentives*, Cambridge, Mass., 1967, p. 36.

14. A. H. M. Nuruddin Chowdhury, 'Some Reflections on Income Redistribution and Intermediation in Pakistan', *Pakistan Development Review*, Summer 1969, p. 99.

istan. The bard and apologist of the new Pakistani bourgeoisie, Professor Papanek, expressed it thus: '*Great
inequalities* were necessary in order to create industry and industrialists ... [For] the concentration of income in industry
facilitates the savings which finance development.' Moreover,
in a new version of the Hidden Hand, 'Inequalities in income
contribute to the growth of the economy which makes possible
a real improvement for the lower income groups.'[15] Two questions are posed by these very representative statements. First,
to what extent did deliberate 'income disparities' in fact lead to
increased and productive savings: in other words, who has
financed investment? Second, did investment and subsequent
growth lead to a 'real improvement for the lower income
groups'?

Let us take the question of who finances investment first, by
turning to an analysis of savings recorded in the Second Five
Year Plan (1960/1–1964/6). During the first half of the
sixties, total development expenditure came to Rs. 26,330
million; of this amount, no more than Rs. 16,230, or 61·5 per
cent, was mobilized from domestic resources (the remainder
came from capital imports abroad). This comes to an annual
average of Rs. 3,264 millions. It has been calculated that of this
amount no more than Rs. 1,335 million and perhaps as little as
Rs. 554 million went into private, non-agricultural productive
investment. These are notably low figures; they indicate that
no more than 26 per cent and perhaps as little as 10·5 per cent
of domestic resources found their way into productive non-
agricultural investment.

However, it cannot be assumed that even this limited amount
of investment was financed from the savings of the upper urban
income groups. For in fact a greater amount of income was
transferred from agriculture into the industrial sector than was
invested in this latter sector in any one year. In considering a
balance sheet of commercial transactions between agricultural

15. Papanek, op. cit., pp. 242–3; emphasis mine.

and manufacturing sectors for the average year of 1964–5, the difference between rural sales and purchases comes to Rs. 3,662 million. Although an estimate, this figure may be taken as an approximation of the typical order of magnitude of resource transfers from agriculture to private urban incomes. A comparison of this amount with the figures representing productive investment by this latter sector suggests that between 63 per cent and 85 per cent of savings transferred from agriculture were dissipated in non-productive expense.[16] What has become of this? The Pakistani élites are renowned for the sumptuous tastes they cultivate. On this point there is no dearth of comment. In West Pakistan, 'the potential surplus of these savings units was used to consume more, to buy more ornaments, jewellery and consumer durables and to bid up the prices of real estate and farm lands, helping their owners to disinvest. Often such surplus was devoted to luxury house construction or to open up one more retail store in the already crowded streets and bazaars.'[17] In East Bengal, a study in Dacca revealed that 42.5 per cent of urban personal savings were spent on gold ornaments, consumer durables and housing.[18] This pattern in Pakistan is only surprising to those who cling to some of the more hoary savings-ratio dogmas in the liturgy of classical bourgeois economics. Echoing the Neanderthal School in this matter, Papanek comments: 'Concentration of income contributes to the growth of the economy and real improvement of

16. Keith B. Griffin, 'Financing Development Plans in Pakistan', *Pakistan Development Review*, Winter 1965, pp. 612–13. Griffin's figures probably represent a very conservative underestimate of the amounts transferred from the agricultural to the urban sector. Other estimates increase Griffin's figure between 59 per cent and 224 per cent. Cf. Chowdhury, op. cit., pp. 96–9.

17. Ibid., p. 100; see also Planning Commission, Government of Pakistan, *Third Five Year Plan 1965–70*, Karachi, 1965.

18. M. Habibullah, *Pattern of Urban Savings, A Case Study of Dacca City*, Dacca, 1964.

the lower income groups only because inequalities in income result substantially in increased savings and *not in consumption.*'[19] The opposite, of course, is more often the case; among other reasons, because commodities have symbolic dimensions as well as utility. They differentiate, clarify and order the social hierarchy: fountain pens and wrist watches serve vital prestige functions for those who never have to write and are indifferent to time.

'Hello Officer'

Rather than basic investment in rural infrastructure or producer technologies the Pakistani economy has relied on an increasing consumption spiral where the urban wealthy spend in a whirl of 'Pakola', cars, radios, silks, air conditioners, fountain pens and so on. A reporter for the *Pakistan Times* evokes this style in a passage reporting a fashion show held in the Intercontinental Hotel, Lahore, on 10 November 1968: 'The mannequins received a big hand from the elegant crowd as they moved up and down the brightly lit catwalk modelling the dresses. Some of the creations which the audience warmly applauded were "Romantica", "Raja's Ransom", "Sea Nymph" and "Hello Officer" ... The Eleganza '69 look was defined as a blend of the soft and the severe.'[20]

Lower down the social hierarchy import substitution has turned out a swarm of light consumer foods and soft drinks which bias the economy towards increasing levels of non-essential consumption rather than savings. In Karachi the consumer may choose among Bubble Up, Canada Dry, Citra Cola, Coca Cola, Double Cola, Kola Kola, Pepsi Cola, Perri Cola, Fanta,

19. Papanek, op cit., p. 234; emphasis mine.

20. *Pakistan Times* (Karachi), 11 November 1968; quoted in Tariq Ali, *Pakistan, Military Rule or People's power?*, London, 1970, p. 163.

Hoffman's Mission, and Seven Up: there are only three bottled-milk suppliers in the city.[21]

Hoarding

Simultaneously the high degree of monopoly in industry tends to divert the potential investment of the 'non-privileged' wealthy into sterile forms of hoarding such as gold, land and housing. With interest rates on savings often lower than inflation, much of the wealth of those groups with no direct access to industrial lucre slips out of the country into foreign accounts. Meanwhile foreign investors in Pakistan themselves frequently repatriate profits which exceed their contributions to real output and initial capital flow. 'Thus one witnesses the paradox of fighting the threat of capital outflow and inflow at the same time, both of which result in leakage in domestic savings.'[22] It is not surprising therefore that the most comprehensive study on savings in Pakistan concludes that 'the rural area would still appear to be contributing at least three quarters of total private savings.'[23] The state-created complex of subsidies and concentrated incomes has thus not led to increased savings and productive investment in Pakistan. In the light of past experience the Third Five Year Plan's proposal to 'continue the transfer of resources to the higher savings groups' more closely resembles parody than policy.

Such low productive investment among the 'high savings' sectors of the economy raises the question of who then actually

21. Herbert Feldman, 'AID as Imperialism', *International Affairs*, April 1967, p. 229.

22. Chowdhury, op. cit., p. 106.

23. Asbjorn Bergan, 'Personal Income Distribution and Personal Income Savings in Pakistan 1963–4', *Pakistan Development Review*, Summer 1967, p. 186; Bergan's is the only study of the whole savings and income pattern for Pakistan. Though comprehensive, it suffers from being limited to data for one year only. However, his main arguments are reinforced by other similar studies.

has financed development in Pakistan. The answer, of course, is that only 61·5 per cent of development expenditures in the Second Five Year Plan Period was mobilized from domestic resources. Of the remainder, 38 per cent came from foreign 'aid'. This figure represents 6·3 per cent of the Second Plan Period's GNP, a very high proportion. A Pakistani economist confesses that 'in proportion to GNP and on a per capita basis Pakistan receives more foreign aid than any of her neighbouring countries. Without it the accelerating growth of the sixties would not have been possible'.[24] During this same period Pakistan's receipts in *per capita* foreign aid more than doubled those of India. As a dynamic model of capitalism in South Asia and an imperialist client on China's borders, Pakistan received credits from all quarters in the West[25] (as well as from Russia and the Eastern European bloc). However, the majority of funds came from the US and could not be used without the consultation of such men as the Director of Harvard's Development Advisory Service, whom we have quoted a number of times. These quotes alone give some clue to the role of US aid in the nexus of political and economic relations which subordinate the Pakistani masses to the foreign policy interests of the West. Still others are suggested by the dramatic change in the structure and composition of aid finance between the First and Second Plan periods. For a while its absolute level doubled, the proportion of development expenditure financed by aid declined from 51 per cent to 38 per cent. The quality deteriorated as well: interest-free grants declined while loans (mostly 'tied') increased four-fold. 'It is perhaps unfair as well as indelicate to suggest that grants decreased once Paki-

24. Swadesh Bose, 'Public and Private Enterprise in Pakistan's Development', *Pakistan Development Review*, Winter 1969, p. 275.

25. Pakistan's eleven-nation AID Consortium includes, Belgium, Canada, France, Germany, Italy, Japan, Netherlands, UK, US, Sweden and Switzerland. Russia, Yugoslavia, Czechoslovakia and China are the main non-Consortium contributors.

stan's alignment with the West, its acceptance of US military aid, and its membership in SEATO and the Baghdad Pact (later CENTO) were assured.'[26] More indelicate than inaccurate no doubt. However, a former member of DAS naïvely remarks, 'it is ironical but true that the strongest prop of the planning enterprise in Pakistan is the nation's continued dependence on foreign aid.'[27] The irony here should be viewed against the background of the fact that 'tied loans' increased the dollar area imports into Pakistan from 26 per cent to 46 per cent within three years from 1961 to 1964. With almost one half of total investment expenditures coming from foreign aid imports one suspects more 'free enterprise' in Washington than in Karachi. Against this background, Papanek's bland confidence that 'high incomes are more acceptable, politically and morally, because they are used chiefly for investment rather than for conspicuous consumption'[28] reads like sheer satire. Income disparities have in fact led mainly to luxury consumption, while investment remains financed by the indigenous rural and urban masses, and the imperialist powers.

The *Decade of Progress*

Equally wide of the mark is the axiomatic assurance that 'growth of the economy makes possible real improvement of the lower income groups'. In fact, the growth of Pakistani capitalism has progressively impoverished the majority of the population since Partition. From the early fifties the real wage index has been steadily sinking: a temporary improvement in the early sixties proved to be illusory, for in the same period both working hours and family size had increased more than pro-

26. Griffin, op. cit., p. 614.

27. Wayne A. Wilcox, 'Pakistan', in E. E. Hagan (ed.), *Planning Economic Development*, Homewood, Illinois, 1963; quoted in Griffin, op cit., p. 615.

28. Papanek, op cit., p. 243.

portionally. Capital has ruthlessly kept wage costs down while increasing labour's factor share in production: a task rendered possible by the military dictatorship that has outlawed strikes as well as by the existence of a permanent reserve labour force of rural poor. Pakistani industrialists could thus benefit from the increasing poverty of the rural masses in yet another way, by holding wages just above those of the declining incomes of the bottom 40 per cent of the peasantry. As a result the 'industrial progress' of the past 20 years has left the average working-class family an income per person of 17 rupees monthly.[29]

Studies of the peasantry have confirmed similar trends: a decline of real income straining against increasing family size. Research into rural conditions carried out by Dacca University indicates a deterioration in the conditions of over 70 per cent of the population in East Bengal while the means of production increasingly accumulate in the hands of the remainder.[30] Another study places the figure for average *per capita* income at Rs. 10 a month.[31] Comparable findings have resulted from a number of other interviews and statistical investigations, all of which point to the same broad phenomenon: a decline in the real standard of living in the villages, aggravated by an increased polarization of what wealth remains. UN statistics reveal that calorie intake has deteriorated while another study indicates an ongoing shift towards a starvation diet of bulk starch.[32] After 20 years of scooping off something like one half of agricultural income, the rural areas of Pakistan have been

29. Azizur Rahman Khan, 'What Has Been Happening to Real Wages in Pakistan?', *Pakistan Development Review*, Autumn 1967.

30. Rehman Sobhan, *Basic Democracy Work Program and Rural Development in East Pakistan*, Dacca, 1968.

31. Swadesh R. Bose, 'Trend of Real Incomes of Rural Poor in East Pakistan', *Pakistan Development Review*, Autumn 1968.

32. Mohammad Irshad Khan, 'Aggregate Analysis of Food Consumption in Pakistan', *Pakistan Development Review*, Autumn 1968.

drained of resources: disinvestment, squalor, malnutrition, and eventually famine and epidemic are the inevitable consequences of an economy left without surplus.

The Colonial System in East Bengal

Hitherto we have analysed the economic structure which transfers the surplus of Pakistan's masses into the hands of the urban wealthy. It is now necessary to see how the relations of class were superimposed by those of colony when Islamabad and Karachi were viewed from the villages of East Bengal. For a double edifice of exploitation was built on the unique structure of two separate economies politically unified within a single pseudo-national state. Both the traditional forms of social and imperial exploitation were compressed in Bengal. The 'national state' characteristics of a common currency and import control system were employed to centralize East Bengal's wealth while the geographical and cultural distance separating the two wings of the country excluded it from the control of its distribution.

Throughout the history of Pakistan there persisted a constant discrimination in the allocation of import licences against East Bengal. West Pakistan's share of the vital industrial licences to import machinery and raw materials has averaged about 70 per cent while that of East Bengal comes to no more than 30 per cent.[33] In fact the share of East Bengal, with 55 per cent of the population, has been considerably less than that of Karachi with 2 per cent of the population! The distribution of all other important economic resources – commercial import licences, foreign aid, government development expenditure, military budget expenses – faithfully repeats these proportions: Bengal received less than one third of any specific resource, while the remainder went to West Pakistan (and the majority of that to the city of Karachi). The pattern of industrialization is nat-

33. Stephen Thomas, 'Import Licensing and Import Liberalization in Pakistan', *Pakistan Development Review*, Winter 1966, p. 534.

urally a direct consequence of such resource allocations. The data show that in 1960 East Bengal's contribution to value-added in Large Scale Manufacturing came to no more than 25 per cent while Karachi's share alone came to 29·7 per cent, and the whole of West Pakistan (including Karachi) came to 74·6 per cent.

These figures can be compared to those for total industrial employment in 1960: East Bengal, 30·9 per cent; Karachi, 23 per cent; and West Pakistan (including Karachi), 69·1 per cent.[34] Not only does East Bengal have pathetically less industry than West Pakistan but the ratios of value-added to employment show it to be of much lower technical quality.

Small though it is, this share of 25 per cent represented only the wealth *originating* in East Bengal industry: not all of this, however, stayed there. For the same bureaucracy that allocated resources has largely given over control of East Bengali industries to West Pakistani capital and entrepreneurs. Bengali Muslims owned less than 2·9 per cent of private industrial assets; the rest was owned by West Pakistanis or local Hindus.[35] Because of 'foreign control' little of the wealth created in East Bengali industry remained in the province: most of it found its way back to West Pakistan in the form of salaries, dividends, interest, and profits remitted home. Thus much of the most valuable source of capital accumulation in East Bengal was lost and with it the secondary multiplier effects of the initial investment. The financial and social links which tied East Bengal industry to the West made Eastern enterprises mere enclave extensions of the metropolitan economy of Karachi and the Punjab. Thus the East Bengal relation to the West was characterized by the classical contradictions of colonial 'development', where islands of technology rest in a swamp of agricultural stagnation.

The imperialist nature of the economic relations between the

34. Lewis, op. cit., p. 152.
35. Papanek, op. cit., p. 42.

two wings of Pakistan was by no means confined to the volume and control of industrial production: it determined the whole structure and flow of trade. East Bengal has consistently maintained a positive balance of trade with the rest of the world while West Pakistan has run a deficit. As we have seen, East Bengal earned foreign exchange through its sales abroad which was spent in West Pakistan on imports of industrial goods and luxuries. In fact, up to 1965 East Bengal had on average earned 60 per cent of foreign currency while receiving less than 33 per cent of imports.[36] The mechanisms of overvaluation and import licensing expropriate East Bengal's foreign exchange at two thirds of its value in order to finance West Pakistan's deficit. In other words, a major portion of the extortions described above as class transfers from the peasants to the capitalist shows up again as colonial transfers from East to West.

Trade between West and East Pakistan

The importance of these differential trade balances with the rest of the world acquires a further significance in the light of the flow of trade between the two wings themselves. At the time of Partition, West and East Pakistan had virtually no economic or trade relations whatsoever. Since then, trade has accelerated enormously and the East has suffered a constant deficit increasing from an annual average of 162·1 million rupees in the Pre-Plan Period to an annual average of 424·5 million rupees in the Second Plan Period. The nature of this trade may be easily surmised. The import-substitution industries of West Pakistan exported to the captive market of Bengal such products as cotton and woollen textiles, silk products, footwear, pharmaceuticals and cosmetics, rubber goods, cement, steel products, machine tools, and electrical equipment: in other words, the whole range of manufactures from light to

36. Lewis, op. cit., p. 142.

intermediary and producer goods. In return East Bengal shipped to the West tea, matches, paper, bananas, betel nuts, jute manufactures, pineapples and fish.[37] The combination of the three directions of trade produce a paradigm colonial triangle. The compulsory purchase of Western manufactures by the East led to a further wealth outflow, in payment of the inflated monopoly prices for Western goods. Thus just as the Empire once provided Britain with much of the liquidity and market for its industrial expansion, so East Bengal served the West. Perhaps the main difference is that its common nation-state institutions provided West Pakistan with various additional 'internal' forms of exploitation which the British in India never fully enjoyed.

The East Bengali worker and peasant was thus plundered by a double articulated structure of exploitation, built on class and imperial domination. All the forms of extortion practised by the ruling bloc in West Pakistan were magnified and intensified in East Bengal. While the West Pakistani peasant received 52 per cent of the international market price for his produce from 1950 to 1965, his counterpart in East Bengal received only 44 per cent.[38] Industrial wages in East Bengal were on average 25 per cent lower than those in West Pakistan, while working hours were longer. The Bengali consumer simultaneously paid prices between 10 per cent and 15 per cent higher than those prevailing in the West, while the rate of unemployment was

37. See M. A. Rahman, *Partition, Integration, Economic Growth and Inter-regional Trade*, Karachi, 1963. The balance of manufactures traded against primary commodities shifted eastward as the West-Pakistani-controlled industries (mainly jute manufacturing) expanded in East Bengal. However, this movement has more than been offset as West Pakistani industries (in the West) became in turn increasingly sophisticated in their exports to the East. So although East Bengal now exports manufactures (e.g. matches), the crucial balance of value-added remains favourable to Western exports (e.g. machine tools) in inter-regional trade.

38. Khan, op. cit., p. 332.

always greater as well.[39] It is not surprising that West Pakistan's *per capita* income grew at *five times* the rate of that of East Bengal after Partition, while *official* estimates admitted a sheer 60 per cent differential in the Provincial Average Income between the two.[40]

Recent Trends

The historical pattern delineated above is so stark that not even orthodox US economists can any longer ignore or conceal it today. However, in mitigation of the gross social and colonial exploitation of the West Pakistan ruling class, it is often argued that the last ten years have witnessed a significant improvement of the basic economic situation in Pakistan. Three main trends are singled out for praise. First, the very rapid growth of total agricultural output in the West during the sixties, consequent on the so-called 'Green Revolution'; secondly, the modest but apparently hopeful increase in aggregate agricultural production in East Bengal; thirdly, the expansion of manufactured exports, and the diversification of their markets. The combination of agricultural and manufacturing growth in the West is adduced to argue that the old structure of subsidies which siphoned off an 'undue' surplus from the rural sector in general, and East Bengal in particular, to West Pakistani industry was essentially a phenomenon of the fifties; which served its purpose in boosting the economy to the 'take-off point' but was then largely dismantled during the Second Plan Period, which

39. Abdul Ghafur, 'A Comparison of Inter-regional Purchasing Power of Industrial Wages in Pakistan', *Pakistan Development Review*, Winter 1967. The inter-regional disparity of industrial-wage purchasing power has increased greatly since the period covered in this study.

40. Manager of Publications, *Report of Panel of Economists on Proposals for the Fourth Five Year Plan*, Karachi, March 1971. Official estimates grossly underestimate the reality of regional income disparities which probably come to double this figure.

saw a more liberated and equitable flow of resources throughout Pakistan. The ostensible result is now that West Pakistani industry has both diversified its markets with an export drive and thereby started to generate its own foreign exchange; while growth in the Western agricultural sector has produced a substantial increase in purchasing power and hence the domestic market. Industry can therefore afford to view the peasant more as a consumer than as a source of concealed taxes. The implication of both of these arguments is that West Pakistani industry has become increasingly independent of East Bengal for market, materials and subsidies; and that as a consequence the old colonial pattern of the fifties has tended to pass away.

What are the realities behind these claims? In the fifties, as we have seen, overvaluation, forced procurement and distribution of PL 480 surplus were the principal instruments the government manipulated to hold down agricultural prices to the benefit of the urban sector. On the advice of the DAS, the government reversed part of this line in the early sixties to create improved rural market conditions in order to boost private investment and hence increased output. Rather than intervene to hold prices down, the state now acted to maintain a stable and high price for food products. The terms of trade between the two sectors in the West improved progressively for agriculture during the Second Plan Period from 0·56 to 0·64. The result was a rapid expansion of private investment in tubewells and water pumps at the rate of some 6,500 per annum; by the end of the Second Plan Period it was estimated that 31,500 tubewells had been sunk in West Pakistan.[41] The spread of fertilizer and improved varieties of seeds was equally impressive. The impact of the Green Revolution in West Pakistan has, in fact, been greater than in India, because concentrated in a smaller territory: agricultural output in the West

41. Gafur Mohammed, 'Private Tubewell Development and Cropping Patterns in West Pakistan', *Pakistan Development Review*, Spring 1965, pp. 1–53.

doubled between 1960 and 1970. However, this economic success takes on a very different aspect once it is set in its regional and class context. To begin with, the impact of the Green Revolution has been overwhelmingly located in Punjab, and within Punjab in the privileged Canal Colony Districts along the Indian border. 95 per cent of the tubewells and 80 per cent of the tractors whose advent was responsible for the sudden increase of yields in West Pakistan are sited in the Punjab. The result has been a massive increase in the polarization of wealth between the provinces *within* the West. Today, Punjab accounts for some 80 per cent of wheat, 70 per cent of cotton and sugar, and 50 per cent of rice output in West Pakistan. Its per capita wealth is now $2\frac{1}{2}$ times that of the other provinces of Sind, Baluchistan and the North-west Frontier. The beneficiaries of the rural boom in Punjab have been the large landowners-cum-kulaks. 80 per cent of all tubewells were sunk by cultivators with holdings of 25 acres or more: in other words, by the rural rich.[42] In Papanek's candid words: 'The ability to sink private tubewells differed greatly with the size of the holding ... The smaller peasant did not have enough cash to pay for the tubewells nor enough land to use them efficiently. Government or cooperative credit played only a small role in enabling poorer peasants to raise the capital for tubewells or in paying for privately distributed fertilizers.[43] The class character of the Green Revolution has thus perhaps nowhere been so patent as in West Pakistan, which provides a kind of magnifying glass for the more scattered but comparable changes occurring across the border in Indian Punjab, West UP, and Gujarat. Among the main social consequences is the displacement of the sharecropping peasantry, buying-out of the smallholder and the gradual transition to wage labour. Another is a rocketing domestic inflation, partly because of the sudden increase of landlord incomes; the work-

42. Ibid., cf. also Hamza Alavi, op. cit.
43. Papanek, op. cit., p. 177.

ing class and poor peasantry have paid the bill in escalating prices.[44] This inflation was one of the main single causes of the 1968–9 upheaval against the Ayub régime, when it coincided with bad harvests and the expensive aftermath of the Indo-Pak War; the dictatorship was gaily celebrating a 'Decade of Development' when the accumulated social hatreds of this same period exploded in full fury throughout the industrial centres of the West and the whole of the East.

The situation in East Bengal

The situation in East Bengal over the last decade has been very different. Pakistani officialdom has boasted of aggregate figures showing a 17 per cent increase in agricultural output during the Second Plan Period. But this figure conceals a significant and ominous shift in crop composition. A commodity breakdown reveals that rice output has grown by some 27·6 per cent while jute actually declined by 1·7 per cent.[45] The social meaning of this change is not in doubt: it represents a regression from

44. 'But the unequal distribution of the income from agriculture has brought about a manifold increase in the incomes of a small group of rich farmers and landlords in the Canal Colony Districts and the Rich Old Settled District of the Punjab. On the other hand, the incomes of small farmers in these districts, and especially of farmers in the other poorer regions, have failed to improve or have not improved in the same measure. The indirect consequences of the "Green Revolution" for the latter follow from the impact of the additional purchasing power in the hands of the former on the demand for and the prices of manufactured consumer goods. The main thrust of the inflationary pressure derives primarily from the greatly increased incomes of this class of rich farmers, for the weight of agricultural incomes in the total national income accounts is very large. A consequence of the Green Revolution, therefore, has been the generation of large inflationary pressures and the deterioration in the real incomes of those who have not directly benefited from it, and also an increased pressure on foreign exchange resources.' (Alavi, op. cit., pp. 27–9)

45. Griffin, op. cit., p. 603.

high-value to subsistence farming. However, the statistics themselves must be treated very cautiously. Western policy towards East Bengal has always been one of ritual gestures of reform in order to placate mass pressures of revolt in the province. The sixties produced a particularly elaborate healing ceremony entitled the Rural Works Programme, whose stated purpose was to redress Bengal's ailing agriculture. The RWP in fact proved to be as corrupt and inadequate as previous government placebos, and to conceal this, figures for paddy production eventually became a lively political football kicked about to show how healthy the East Bengali peasant really was. The figure of a 27·6 per cent increase in rice production therefore represents an official estimate derived from the lowest-level extension workers who were personally responsible for the implementation of the RWP project; these figures therefore are more likely to express their enthusiasm for the game than the realities of the rice. Independent surveys subsequently showed the government statistics to be overestimated by as much as 40 per cent.[46] However, quite apart from inflated official computations, the increase in rice production is in fact evidence, not of agricultural progress, but of the grim reality of rural disinvestment. The Bengali economist Rehman Sobhan has described the real forces operating behind the shift.[47] The transfers out of agriculture throughout the fifties increasingly left the villages without any investable resources. Let us see how this process worked.

The Bengali peasant's margin of surplus was remorselessly cut back for a full decade to finance West Pakistani industry. In any economy lack of surplus paralyses productivity, while usury becomes more profitable than investment in improved technique. The flight of Hindu moneylenders and landlords had allowed the peasant a brief spell of relief after Partition; but after the long depression of agricultural prices and the lack of

46. Sobhan, op. cit., p. 31.
47. Ibid., chapter 1, pp. 1–72.

any viable public credit institutions this respite came to an end. For while the market in good years allowed bare subsistence, in bad years the peasant was forced into debt. Given low prices, the surplus which escaped government extortion brought higher yields through exploitation of the peasant rather than the soil. As a result, the relatively egalitarian peasant society of the early period after Partition gradually polarized as the old forms of parasitism crept back. Class stratification deepened as the rich peasant and village usurer accumulated land, cattle and implements – in other words, the means of agriculture production. At the other end of the scale, about one third of peasant families clung to a fragment of land as the only protection against the market, middleman, moneylender and government agent. In the bad years, both poor and middle peasant were increasingly forced to liquidate their capital in order to stave off ruin.

The aggregate result, clearly documented by Sobhan, was a slow and sinister shift towards a survival economy: a movement away from cash and fibre crops to food grains; sluggish growth of the market; intense cropping of the land rather than capital investment. These were the real forces operating behind the actual (rather than official) increase in rice output in the Second Plan Period.[48] The spread of rice and the contraction of jute was the result of rural disinvestment as the peasant was increasingly driven to dissolve his capital in order to survive.

The resulting social formation is one of minifundia suspended in various forms of pre-capitalist decay, one in which the process of rural disinvestment and polarization continue simultaneously. N. K. Chandra characterizes East Bengal's productive mode as 'transitional': 'So far we have seen that

48. Comparison of agricultural output during the Third Plan Period (1965/6–1969/70) with that of the previous five years shows an increase of both raw and manufactured jute production. This movement modifies, but does not invalidate, the picture of East Bengal agriculture presented here.

rural rich (i) possess a good deal of land without being feudal lords of the classical type, (ii) hire permanent workers, as well as casual ones, to a significant extent, (iii) do save a good part of their income, but (iv) *make little productive investment to modernize agriculture and raise production.* Clearly the present phase is a watershed between feudalism and capitalism in agriculture.'[49] Extra-economic bonds of kin and community still cross-cut and retard the operation of the market. Although the propertied rest uneasily on an increasingly fluid undermass of the landless and uneconomic, these latter are still grafted to the rural polity through the patronage and factional networks operating independently of productive function. However, emergent Capitalism has yet to differentiate a fully landless proletariat.

Trade Balance

Let us now turn to the problems of the trade balance. The growth of manufactured exports, combined with the expansion of landlord–kulak incomes in the West, is sometimes cited to imply that West Pakistan's industry had diversified its markets and revenues to a point where the depressed economy of East Bengal appears as little more than a debit on the books. Those who advance this argument maintain that West Pakistani capitalism has matured beyond critical dependence on colonial exploitation. It is, of course, true that a dilemma presented itself to the Pakistani State when the nascent import substitution industries had saturated home demand and began pressing for markets abroad. Such was the case in the late fifties and early sixties when jute and cotton textiles had covered the domestic market. While eager to encourage sales of Pakistani manufactures abroad, the state could not do so without bringing the rupee down to some reasonable approximation of its world market prices. Yet to do this would wipe away in a sweep the

49. Chandra, op. cit., p. 24; emphasis mine.

meticulously constructed foundation of protection which supported West Pakistani industry. The predicament was a taxing one, but a solution was found that proved equal to it. The government instituted a new system designated the Export Bonus Voucher Scheme. Though too complex to describe at length here, its net effect was to maintain overvaluation and hence discrimination against traditional exports, while at the same time encouraging the new exports with further subsidies from agriculture. This was accomplished by intricate bureaucratic manipulation of a multiple pricing system for foreign exchange: certain lists of exporters (mainly, of course, manufacturers) were awarded Bonus Vouchers for goods sold abroad. These coupons were then turned in to the government in return for a price on foreign exchange almost twice as advantageous as that received by traditional exports. As is apparent to anyone who has noticed the back of a Rice Crispies packet, this scheme originated in the US and was suggested to the government by the DAS. So far from signifying a fundamental structural advance in the economy, the appearance of manufactured exports only confirmed the continuity of the old system, modified by ingenious loopholes which allowed industry to have its cake while eating it as well.[50] West Pakistani capitalists remained heavily dependent on agricultural subsidies.

Nor, however, did manufactured exports render West Pakistan in any way independent of its colonial market in Bengal. On the contrary, official data reveal that during the Second Plan Period East Bengal was still responsible for about 50 per cent or more of any given export category. Jute textiles alone accounted for approximately one half of the total growth in manufactured exports throughout the period. East Bengal's share of total Pakistani exports was almost 60 per cent. Thus, while aggregate exports have increased, East Bengal still ac-

50. There is a voluminous literature on the Bonus Voucher Scheme in the *Pakistan Development Review*; for the best summary, see Lewis, op. cit., chap. 5.

counts for the main share of them; and although manufactured exports have grown during the Second Plan Period, more than half of these again came from East Bengal.[51] West Pakistan's share of either total or manufactured exports has plainly not developed to a point where it could simply dispense with its traditional transfers of surplus from the East. West Pakistani capitalists are still dependent on the old forms of expropriation which put the wealth and foreign exchange earned in the East at their convenience.[52]

A last set of figures is fairly conclusive on this point. While West Pakistani industry has marginally expanded abroad in the last decade, *East Bengal's share of West Pakistan's total exports (foreign and inter-zonal) steadily increased from Partition right up to the end of the Second Plan Period.* In the Pre-Plan years, 25 per cent of West Pakistani exports went to East Bengal; during the First Plan Period, 48 per cent; in the Second Plan Period, 51 per cent.[53] In fiscal 1970, according to the *New York Times*, despite depression, disruption and inundations, East Bengal still claimed 40 per cent of West Pakistan's trade.[54] It scarcely needs to be added it would be optimistic to imagine that West Pakistan's adolescent industries could afford to relinquish their grip on two fifths to a half of their market without facing a significant political upheaval.

51. Ibid., pp. 12 and 20.

52. Although almost all jute textile industries are controlled by West Pakistani capital, provincial autonomy for East Bengal would still mean a heavy loss in the concealed subsidies and control over foreign exchange. In fact Sheik Mujib's 'Six Points' would have left West Pakistan capitalists nothing more than profits and salaries, a small share of their normal cut of the surplus.

53. Calculated from Lewis, op. cit., p. 143.

54. *New York Times*, 23 March 1971.

The Economic Structure of Pakistan and Bangladesh

The March Action: Origins and Consequences

The evidence is clear that Pakistan has suffered from a particularly stupid and myopic ruling class. The landlord–bourgeois oligarchy in the West learnt many of the techniques of exploitation from their former British masters: but Islamabad has remained utterly impervious to the nuances of 'indirect rule' brought to such a level of refinement by London. The uncompromising greed of the Western ruling class has drained East Bengal for 20 years and destroyed any possibility of a broadly based Eastern bourgeoise. The genocidal reaction of its military–bureaucratic state when confronted with the mass movement behind the Awami League's Six-Point Programme was not a sudden or unpredictable response. It cannot be attributed simply to the fanaticism of a few staff officers. It was, on the contrary, determined by the class-colonial logic inscribed in the whole structure of 'Pakistan' since Partition. It is no accident that every section of the Western ruling class and its political establishment applauded the massacre of 26 March and subsequent weeks. The political folly of the Army's action from the point of view of the long-term interests of the international bourgeoisie was merely a final, paroxysmic version of the crass stupidity of the degree of economic exploitation practised by the business class and its bureaucratic patrons. The war in Bangladesh was the continuation of traditional Pakistani politics, by other means.

Thus the Pakistani state machine which struck against the whole of East Bengal believed that it could not afford to let the province go. Once an effective resistance developed, however, it could no longer afford to keep it. For it takes foreign exchange to run a capitalist economy, not to mention a colonial war; and this is the one thing woefully lacking in Pakistan for some time. The economy had not really recovered since the great popular upsurge that brought the Ayub régime down between November 1968 and March 1969. The consequent slump in both manufactured and primary exports slashed growth in foreign exchange earnings to 1 per cent in fiscal 1969 – down from 9·4 per cent in the previous year. This fall in exports boosted the trade deficit to $366 million in fiscal 1970, which itself climbed atop an accumulated 3·5 million dollar external debt.[55]

Moreover, just before the military were turned loose, payments were falling due for Pakistan's 15-year free ride on the aid carousel. Indeed, scheduled dollar repayments in 1969–70 came to about 20 per cent of Pakistan's foreign exchange earnings. While the régime became yet more desperate for foreign aid, this backlog was taken as adequate cause by the Western powers to cut some of it off. Concerned over the economic deterioration of 1968–70, the eleven-nation consortium of Pakistan's underwriters cut back their offer of aid to $380 million for fiscal 1971; a very substantial drop from the year before. This move occurred well before the crisis in March. Their intention was to withhold dollars as a temporary threat in order to force Pakistan to devalue. Their action of course intensified the general malaise of the business community. By November the mercurial stream of foreign exchange had turned against Pakistan and from that time all events only accelerated its flow outwards. The threat of devaluation, political uncertainty following the elections, and even the damage in East Bengal caused by the December cyclone combined to paralyse investment. The stock market fell continuously, pulling down the general share index by some 18·7 percentage points between late November and 26 March.[56] Meanwhile prices rose by 50 per cent and according to official publications foreign reserves were slipping out of the country in the first half of the present fiscal year at four times the rate in the same period of the preceding year.[57] By January, a full month before the Army

55. *Christian Science Monitor*, 5 October 1970.

56. *Financial Times*, 1 May 1971.

57. Ibid., quoted from *Pakistan Economist* (Karachi).

was mobilized, reserves stood at $160 million, the lowest they had ever fallen in the decade.

Time of Crisis

The Bengali masses thus chose a particularly hazardous time of crisis in the Pakistani economy for their upsurge in the early months of 1971. When, after careful preparations, the Army finally struck in March to suppress the 'treason' of the Bengali population and expunge its political and cultural leadership, it simultaneously hit the rural economy during the planting season and devastated both Eastern markets and exports. The *Financial Times* estimated that within 45 days Pakistan lost Rs. 300 million in foreign exchange due to the stoppage in jute shipments alone.[58] Using non-Bengali labour Tikka Khan managed to squeeze a few boat-loads a week out of Chittagong. Major communications were reported to be irreparable for at least six months. At the same time the threat of terror, famine and epidemic compelled the peasant to plant subsistence rice wherever possible. It became apparent that the foreign markets lost during this period would never be recovered by the economy, no matter who controlled it. In no more than six months the liberation war leeched the vitality of the Pakistan economy: continued resistance promised to exhaust the economy to the point of near-collapse.

The Indo-Pakistani war of December 1971 thus came as an apparent *coup de grâce*. With the creation of Bangladesh, the Indian action sliced away 40 per cent of Pakistan's 'domestic' market, not to mention some $33 million in back credits due from the East. The clinical precision of the Indian fourteen-day operation was accepted by many as 'prudent' geopolitics, and an almost merciful euthanasia for an already debilitated Pakistani economy.

But within six months the whole tenor of expectation

58. Ibid.

changed. One year after the March action the first published trade figures revealed an astonishing improvement in the 1971–2 balance of payments position: exports had risen by $177 million, within $186 million of the United Pakistan figure for the previous year.

Rather than destroy the economy, the Bangladesh war had apparently amputated only the more cumbersome and gangrenous portions. Despite the waves of popular unrest, Pakistani business and official circles began to praise once again, in however subdued tones, the 'miracle' of the Pakistani economy.

Yet a probe behind the official figures reveals this – as is the case with most miracles – to be a product of wishful thinking. Even the official breakdown of exports disclosed the inability of the economy to find substitute markets for their former colony. The commerce ministry claimed $68 million of goods sold abroad were previously bought in East Pakistan. However, even these figures hardly justify the optimism expressed in business circles. For, again according to their calculations, only 54 per cent of the goods previously sent to the Bengali market is reckoned as 'divertible' – that is, to be marketed internationally – a figure which in terms of the international prices comes to about $127 million. Thus even of the divertible market, just over half managed to find buyers abroad. The remainder of Bengali trade is considered to be 'non-divertible' for various reasons: 18 per cent were mainly food products such as wheat, sugar, and oil seeds, while a 'difficult' category is composed of 'tobacco, cigarettes and machinery', whose style and quality were 'tailored to the particular market'; this class comes to about 15 per cent of the previous Bengali market. The remaining 13 per cent are classed as 'miscellaneous' and 'indifferent'.

Thus less than half of the previous West Pakistani exports to Bengal are considered 'divertible' to buyers abroad, while not much over half of that has yet been bought. One half to three quarters of Bengal's market will have to be either re-absorbed internally, or count as excess capacity resulting in further unemployment.

But even this $86 million of Bengal products sold abroad is considered evidence of the 'flexibility' of Pakistani capitalism and greeted as the insertion of a commercial wedge into the international market. The claim justified some doubt. First, the divertible products are composed of cotton yarn, rice and cement – equalling about $42 million of the $68 million figure. There is a good cash market for these products abroad, particularly for rice and cement. But Pakistan is heavily reliant on cotton goods and last year was an extraordinarily good season. The international price rose by 17 per cent, while the crop increased by 12 per cent. But the export gains from cotton sales were cancelled by import losses elsewhere as the increased cotton production resulted from a planning error which expanded cotton production at the cost of sugar cane! As a result Pakistan had to import $50 million worth of sugar.[59]

Pakistan's trade exports were therefore largely contingent on an exceptional crop situation which was unlikely to last. But even given increased production, last year's sales mark the limit rather than the first thrust of a militant commercial expansion. Grey cloth, their best product according to Pakistan officials, is severely hedged by quota restrictions in the UK and US as well as in the EEC; and these quotas have been filled already.

Turning away from the market in the industrialized world, Pakistan looks to North Africa. But if imperialists lock them out of the former, their Islamic brethren offer hardly a more cordial reception in the latter. Egypt produces better quality, while most of the countries in North Africa are setting up textile industries of their own. Where these countries have links with the EEC, Pakistan's task is more onerous yet. Needless to say this is not the time for the 'modernization' of Pakistani textiles industries, let alone 'expansion' in the African market. The export future is not bright. The most optimistic estimate

59. See Kevin Raferty, *Financial Times*, 24 August 1972.

for Pakistani export earnings is a steady increase reaching a plateau at $640–650 million.

These figures represent Pakistan's earning power only. The whole logic of this capitalist and import-substituting economy has made it dependent on foreign aid investment. Prior to the debt moratorium declared in May 1971, the country's foreign debt stood at the crushing total of $3,350 million with an annual servicing liability of $251 million. Compared with the figures above, Pakistan would spend over 30 per cent of export earnings to meet the interest, not to mention principal, of her foreign debt.

The truncated economy of Pakistan thus finds itself driven deeper into a foreign exchange crisis – one which can only be met within the framework of international capital through even more chronic dependence, now the 'captive market' in the East has escaped. Rather than liberating the dynamic West from the inert underdevelopment of the East, Pakistan finds itself all the more in need of short-term credits, long-term aid and debt rescheduling. But imperialism is exacting harsh terms before coming to bale out the economy. Over the past two years the Pakistan economy has resisted pressures to devalue and dismantle the protectionist import restrictions and foreign exchange controls that have made the upper classes rich. But, more vulnerable to international pressures than ever, she cannot avoid these measures, and they are now made conditions for IMF credits. Thus mid May was marked by devaluation, a dismantling of the 'bonus-voucher system' and an elimination of previous import restrictions. Less than a week following these measures, banking reforms were announced restricting credit by raising the reserve deposits and threatening a ceiling on loans. Within two weeks of these moves on the part of the Pakistan Government, the World Bank Aid Consortium ratified Bhutto's debt moratorium, rumoured an aid commitment of around $180 million and promised 'progress' on rescheduling of debts. The IMF then came forward with $108·6 million over a twelve month period to help meet Pakistan's international payments.[60]

Accommodation with her international creditors was reached but at far harsher terms than hoped for. The $200 million figure for aid represents a considerable decline from the $380 million of the previous year. While the impact of devaluation – a massive drop of 56·7 per cent to the dollar – will accelerate its aid needs in almost direct proportion. Imports will feel the burden of the new rates more than exports will benefit. The cost of foreign debt payments increases in proportion to the devaluation; while, in conjunction with the removal of all import restrictions, the largest increase in costs of imports will hit the capital goods front, which makes up 45 per cent of total imports. Under the protection of the bonus-voucher scheme capital goods came in at privileged rates. The loss of this advantage will have to be made up through the increased stimulus to exports. The exporters of manufactured goods used to get Rs. 9·5 per dollar under the bonus-voucher scheme; this amount has only been pushed up in accord with the value of the new exchange rate, an insignificant rise in comparison with the greater costs of capital goods. On balance the effects of Pakistan's post-war adjustments will profoundly weaken its position in the international market. Devaluation and removal of import restrictions raises the cost of former debts and the price of capital necessary to diversify production, while the trend towards an absolute decline in consortium aid, plus the quota and competitive limits on its markets abroad, undermine Pakistan's income and prospects of export earnings. The 1971–2 trade balance hardly signals a happy future for Pakistani capitalism. Rather, devaluation and credits allowed temporary

60. *Financial Times*, 12, 17, 19, and 26 May 1972. For the role of the IMF 'anti-inflationary programme' and loans in penetrating Third World protectionist barriers to international capital, cf. Cheryl Payer, 'The Perpetuation of Dependence: the IMF and the Third World', *Monthly Review*, vol. 23, no. 4, September 1971.

relief of the foreign exchange crisis at the long-term costs of economic diversification, modernization, and a competitive posture abroad.

The Bangladesh affair has thus exposed much of the framework underlying the meticulously constructed Pakistani economy. Beneath the imposing façade of economic growth is a crumbling edifice of national and class oppression constructed upon increasingly unstable economic foundations. The imposition of President's rule on Baluchistan and the North-west Frontier in early 1973 promises further costly political conflicts. Even before this, the chronic inflation, unemployment and recession which followed the war were ominous enough. And, as we have seen, these were not merely readjustments of a basically healthy system which simply needed time to find new markets. Only a small proportion of the goods formerly sold to East Bengal are 'divertible', while inability to sell the rest will produce further excess capacity, unemployment and recession. Thus the loss of East Bengal has brought to light the most vicious contradictions of Pakistani capitalism. And this time the action of oppressed classes and national groupings threatens to destroy the whole of the bizarre superstructure, along with its rococo élites and their garish profits.

Pakistan and Bangladesh: Results and Prospects

Tariq Ali

The disintegration of the state of Pakistan and the emergence of Bangladesh marked a watershed in the politics of the subcontinent. As a result of the disintegration both countries are beset by political and economic instability and a rising mass movement which can only be contained with difficulty by the existing order. To understand the real nature of this challenge and what it could mean for imperialist interests in South Asia, it is necessary to study the roots of the conflict which led to the creation of Bangladesh and the new dominance gained on the battlefield by the Indian bourgeoisie – a dominance which the imperialist powers wish to see stabilized politically in order to prevent further conflict in the region.

The struggle which took place in Bangladesh between the Bengali liberation forces and the armies of West Pakistan after 25 March 1971 represented both a continuation of the mass movement which erupted throughout Pakistan in 1968–9 and a qualitative break from it. In that sense we can say that the course which events took in East Bengal was not unpredictable.[1]

The war in Bangladesh has been an event of the greatest

1. In September 1970 I wrote: 'The national question, coupled with the combined and uneven development of political consciousness in the two parts of the country, could well lead to a situation where the revolution is successful in Bengal before it moves to the West. In this situation, revolutionary socialists will be faced with the possibility of protracted struggles in the East and the need to combat chauvinism in the West.' (T. Ali, 'Class Struggles in Pakistan', NLR 63, p. 52.)

international significance. Its immediate effects extend well beyond the frontiers of conflict and in the long term it may well be seen as a decisive phase of the Indian revolution. Together with the uprising in Ceylon, it signals the approaching demise of traditional bourgeois politics in the entire subcontinent.

There were two distinguishing features of politics in Eastern Bengal from the beginning of 1971: on the one hand, the enthusiastic participation of the common people in every level of an escalating social and national struggle; and on the other the political bankruptcy of the petty-bourgeois notables of the Awami League, whose whole tradition of compromise and manoeuvre rendered them completely incapable of providing leadership in a real independence movement. Even before the formal invasion took place on 25 March 1971, this tradition had led to the loss of hundreds of Bengali lives at the hands of the Army of General Yahya Khan. These earlier demonstrations of its power should have convinced the Awami League politicians of what was likely to follow unless they prepared the Bengali people for a protracted struggle. This they refused to do despite the evident desire of the mass movement, expressed in thunderous slogans at Awami League meetings, for a total break with Pakistan. The rising tide of popular political consciousness was already clear in the enormous meetings which took place throughout the province both before and after the General Election of 1970. At every stage the people assimilated the lessons of the past much more rapidly than their parliamentarist leaders and showed their willingness to fight the colonial state in East Bengal. At every stage they were checked by the visceral constitutionalism of the Awami League leadership. This conflict between the mass movement and the petty-bourgeois outlook of its official guides was all the more tragic in that the existing organizations of the revolutionary left were localized and in no position to influence the course of the struggle decisively. Just as the situation was beginning to alter in favour of the groups of the left and the creation of a National

Liberation Front was bringing them together, the Indian army intervened to prevent this development and to place the Awami League firmly in power.

The Awami League

The Awami League has been a party of reaction since birth. Its formative years were dominated by parliamentary manoeuvre and intrigue. Its main social roots have always been in the functionaries, teachers, petty traders and shopkeepers who proliferate in East Bengali society. Its founder, H. S. Suhrawardy, who for a short time succeeded in becoming Pakistan's Prime Minister, distinguished himself in 1956 by supporting the Anglo-French–Israeli invasion of Egypt. He became one of the most articulate defenders of imperialist interests in Pakistan and American policy in Asia as a whole.[2] Left-wing parties and organizations in East Pakistan who opposed these policies were physically attacked by Awami League 'volunteers' and had their meetings broken up with monotonous regularity. Suhrawardy's other notable achievement was to supervise the fusion of the provinces of Baluchistan, Sind and the Northwest Frontier into a single territorial unit dominated completely by Punjab. In this way he showed his respect for the 'autonomy' of the West Pakistani provinces. After 1958, Suhrawardy played a dissident role during the early years of the Ayub dictatorship and was imprisoned for a short time as a result; but his opposition was always limited to the bourgeois constitutionalist framework.

Suhrawardy's undoubted talents – he was a proficient lawyer, an artful political manipulator and a glib conversationalist – placed him head and shoulders above the rest of the Awami League leadership. His ambitions, however, were far removed from Bengali independence: his aim was to make

2. See T. Ali, *Pakistan, Military Rule or People's Power?*, Cape, London, 1970, pp. 66–7.

the Awami League an all-Pakistan electoral machine, capable of winning power as a 'national' party and thus catapulting himself into the highest possible office. His untimely death in 1963 put an end to this dream. His successor, Sheikh Mujibur Rahman, had won prominence as a party organizer and hatchet-man rather than as an astute politician. Under the new leadership the very idea of an Awami League disavowing the legacy of its dead leader was considered heresy of the worst sort.[3]

It is essential to recall this early history in order to understand the recent attitudes of the League. It continued to play an oppositional role during the remaining years of the Ayub dictatorship. Ayub himself more than once considered the idea of reaching some compromise with its leaders and incorporating them in the central government, but the gangster politicians from the East Pakistan underworld, on whom he had relied for so long to maintain 'law and order' in Bengal, constantly and successfully sabotaged this plan, as it would have meant the end of their own political careers. The Awami League was thus offered no choice but to continue as an oppositional force. It joined a multi-party alliance (Combined Opposition Parties) in 1964 to field a candidate against Ayub, but the elections were rigged by the Army and the Civil Service and the Field-Marshal was returned with a comfortable majority. In March 1965, the opposition tried to regroup and met in Lahore to hammer out a joint strategy. It was here that the Awami League, in the person of Mujibur, dropped a bombshell in the form of its famous Six-point Plan for regional autonomy. The West Pakistani leaders were so shocked that they accused the Ayub régime's most machiavellian civil servant, Altaf Gauhar,

3. Thus one of the Awami League's most sophisticated spokesmen, Rehman Sobhan, writing in his journal, *Forum* (6 December 1969), could argue that if Suhrawardy had remained alive his 'vision of national politics' would still have existed. The article is a good example of the League's preoccupation with constitutionalist politics.

of having drafted it in order to split the anti-Ayub opposition. This marked the beginning of the gulf between Bengali nationalism and the West Pakistani oppositional parties. The abyss was to widen in the coming years. It was transcended for a time during the mass upsurge against Ayub in 1968–9, but the absence of a strong revolutionary party meant that the division came to the forefront again as soon as the upsurge subsided.

There were two important reasons why the Awami League was able to win mass support and hegemonize the politics of East Bengal. The first was its success in grasping the importance of the national question. The second was the failure of the groups of the extreme Left, which had followed an extremely opportunist course during the Ayub dictatorship because of the latter's 'friendship' with China. Thus the Awami League could present itself as the only meaningful opposition force in the province. It constantly carried out propaganda in favour of its Six Points; it called for free elections and it organized demonstrations against the Ayub dictatorship. Some of its leaders, including Mujibur Rahman, were consequently arrested. The Maoist wing of the National Awami Party (NAP) had meanwhile shown complete blankness towards the national problem. Instead of joining popular agitation and deepening it by explaining that national and democratic problems can today only be solved within a socialist framework, and thus preparing the people for a long struggle, they entrenched themselves in sectarian isolation. In other words, they failed to see that uneven historical development would oblige Bengali revolutionaries to work out a strategy for their struggle independent of West Pakistan. Moreover, they insisted that the Ayub régime had 'certain anti-imperialist features' and was therefore in some ways to be preferred to bourgeois democracy.

In these conditions, the Awami League did not have much trouble in establishing itself as a powerful mass force. The stupidity of the Ayub régime in persecuting its leaders, manufacturing conspiracy cases against them and throwing them into gaol could only help this process. Thus when the anti-Ayub upsurge resulted in the fall of the dictator and his replacement by the Yahya junta in early 1969, it was hardly surprising that the Awami League reaped the benefits. Yet it still could not disavow its heritage. In the weeks before the army persuaded Ayub to retire, the Awami League eagerly participated in the 'constitutional' talks at the round table conferences called by Ayub to reach a compromise. It had fuelled the mass movement and witnessed the anger of Bengali peasants and workers; even so it remained tied to its parliamentarist past.

The Yahya military régime, unable to quell the mass up-heaval in both parts of the country, was forced to promise a general election on the basis of adult franchise. Its advisers evidently believed it could concede this as a diversionary tactic. They were confident that the bureaucracy, from long experi-ence in such matters, would be able to manipulate the results satisfactorily. To give the latter some time to prepare itself, the elections were postponed – ostensibly because of the cyclone disaster in late 1970, which claimed nearly a million Bengali lives. But the failure of the Army to provide any adequate flood relief only intensified the deep anger of the Bengali people. When the different Maoist factions in East Bengal decided to boycott the elections, the Awami League was given a free hand.

The result of the December General Election gave it a tidal victory. Of the 169 seats allocated to East Pakistan in the National Assembly, the League won 167, and it gained 291 out of the 343 seats in the Provincial Assembly. Its bloc in the National Assembly gave it an overall majority throughout the country and entitled it to form the central government. Such a prospect traumatized the West Pakistani ruling oligarchy. Given that the Awami League had fought the elections on the basis of the Six Points and had indeed on occasion surpassed them in its electoral rhetoric, it was clear that the Army would try to prevent a meeting of the Constituent Assembly.

The Six Point Programme

What did the Six Points represent? They were simply an attempt to reverse a situation which had existed ever since the partition of the subcontinent. The predominantly Hindu trader and landlord class of East Bengal migrated to West Bengal (India) in 1947, leaving their businesses and lands behind them. From the very start this vacuum was filled by Biharis and non-Bengali businessmen from the western portion of the country. The economic exploitation of East Bengal, which began immediately after Partition, led to an annual extraction of some 3,000 million rupees from the East by West Pakistani capital. The most important foreign exchange earner was jute, a crop produced in East Pakistan which accounted for over 50 per cent of exports. This money was spent on capital investment in West Pakistan. The sums granted for development projects by the central government offer an interesting case-study of discrimination. Between 1948 and 1951 a sum of 1,130 million rupees was sanctioned for development. Of this only 22·1 per cent went to East Pakistan. Over the period 1948–69 the value of the resources transferred from the East amounted to 2·6 billion dollars. The West Pakistan economy as a result has been heavily dependent on East Bengal, partly as a field for investment, but above all as a mine of subsidies and as a captive market. Thus the Six Points, which included both political and economic autonomy, directly threatened the immediate interests of West Pakistani capitalism. They demanded:

1. A federal system of government, parliamentary in nature and based on adult franchise.

2. Federal government to deal only with defence and foreign affairs. All other subjects to be dealt with by the federating state.

3. (a) Two separate, but freely convertible currencies for the

two parts of the country; or (b) one currency for the whole country. In this case effective constitutional measures to be taken to prevent flight of capital from East to West Pakistan.

4. Power of taxation and revenue collection to be vested in the federating units and not at the centre.

5. Separate accounts for foreign exchange earnings of the two parts of the country under control of the respective governments.

6. The setting up of a militia or para-military force for East Pakistan.

Immediately after the General Election I wrote:

Will the Pakistan Army and the capitalist barons of West Pakistan allow these demands to go through? The answer is quite clearly no. What will probably happen is that in the short-term Mujibur Rahman will be allowed to increase East Pakistan's percentage of import and export licences and will be allocated a larger share of foreign capital investment. These are the 'concessions' which the Army will be prepared to make in the coming few months. If Rahman accepts them, he will be allowed to stay in power. If not, it will be back to business as usual in the shape of the Army. Of course there is no doubt that in the event of another military coup there will be no holding back the immense grievances of Bengal and the desire for an independent Bengal will increase a hundredfold. What follows will depend on whether Bengali revolutionaries succeed in building a revolutionary organization to pose the question of state power. If the political leadership remains in the hands of the Awami League, the result will be yet another betrayal.[4]

The Six Points represented the charter of the aspirant Bengali bourgeoisie: it articulated the latter's desire to create its own regional state apparatus and to have an equal share of the capitalist cake. But this was precisely the reason why the dominant bloc in West Pakistan was opposed to these two fun-

4. 'Pakistan: After the December Election, what next?' the *Red Mole*, 1 January 1971, p. 10.

damental concessions. The Pakistani Army was organically hostile to the prospect of a Bengali civilian government because of the danger that it would reduce the lavish military apparatus which has been a built-in feature of the Islamabad régime since Ayub seized power in October 1958. Some idea of the enormous stake the Pakistani officer corps has in the present structure of the unitary state can be gathered from the fact that military expenditures have throughout the last decade absorbed no less than some 60 per cent of the total state budget. In the fiscal year of 1970 alone, some 625 million dollars were allocated for the armed forces. Awami League politicians had repeatedly denounced these colossal outlays on a military machine which was in its virtual totality non-Bengali. The Six Points meant the subtraction of Bengali taxes for its maintenance. Moreover, the Army was ideologically saturated from top to bottom with racist and religious chauvinism against the Bengalis, who had traditionally been regarded as dark, weak and infected with Hinduism. For its part, the Pakistani business class had its own extremely strong material reasons for resisting the Six Points. The complex economic system of interzonal exploitation in Pakistan is amply documented by Richard Nations elsewhere in this book. It is enough to stress here that while business interests in the West no longer regard the East as an optimal field of investment, Bengal remains of vital importance to them, both as a captive market and as a source of foreign exchange. In the late sixties, between 40 per cent and 50 per cent of West Pakistan's exports were taken by the East at monopoly prices. Where else could West Pakistani capitalism dispose of its high-cost manufactures?

Bhutto and the People's Party

The election results in West Pakistan had resulted in the emergence of Bhutto's Pakistan People's Party (PPP) as the largest western party in the new constituent assembly. But other smaller parties had also emerged with significant regional bases in Baluchistan and the North-west Frontier, and it was clear to Bhutto that at best he would be a junior partner in any coalition government at the Centre. If the Awami League chose to govern alone, he would be acknowledged only as the leader of West Pakistan. Bhutto had won the elections in Punjab and Sind after his party had campaigned on a platform of demagogic radicalism, land reform, extensive nationalization, an end to the economic power of the twenty-two families and other improbable promises. Because of the virtual eclipse of the extreme left, he was able to pose as a socialist. His party organization, however, was an improvised assemblage of feudalists, racketeers, lawyers and bandwagon petty bourgeois. Its electoral success owed a great deal to Bhutto's deals with powerful landlord cliques in the countryside (his pact with leading Sindhi feudalists was particularly notorious). However, the PPP also captured and confiscated the genuine popular aspirations for social change in the towns and villages. The extreme class tensions within Bhutto's electoral bloc and the hollowness of its party organization meant that the only ideological cement that could be used to hold it together was religious chauvinism (hence the meaningless slogan of the PPP: 'Socialism is our economy, democracy is our policy, Islam is our religion').

The overwhelming electoral success of the Awami League stunned Bhutto. It utterly upset his plans for taking power. He now emerged as the most vociferous defender of the traditional hegemony of West Pakistan, hysterically denounced the Six Points and after consulting with top army generals started to whip up an intensely chauvinistic atmosphere in Punjab. The Assembly was scheduled to meet three months after the election, on 3 March 1971. In collusion with the Army, Bhutto now threatened not to attend any Assembly unless Mujibur Rahman was willing to compromise on the Six Points. If the Assembly met without him, he would unleash a 'civil disobedience' movement in West Pakistan. Immediately after this announcement,

Yahya unilaterally decided, on 1 March 1971, to postpone indefinitely the meeting of the National Assembly. The result was predictable. There was a spectacular explosion of public anger in East Bengal and in the ensuing unrest the Army shot down hundreds of demonstrators in its major cities. Unarmed masses were called out on to the streets by the leaders of the Awami League. The latter then watched troops firing on them, entirely unable to offer any effective initiative. A continuous general strike brought the province to a standstill.

The Awami League was now forced to accept the logic of the situation and the result was a curious state of affairs which could be described as a kind of bourgeois caricature of dual power. The League was able to set up committees to take over the administration of key areas in the cities and countryside: only the Army cantonments were outside its control.[5] The Bengali section of the local bureaucracy aligned itself with the Awami League and the newly arrived military proconsul from Islamabad, General Tikka Khan, could not be sworn in as Governor because the Bengali Chief Justice of the High Court refused to administer the oath. But the committees were very definitely Awami League and had no autonomous popular character. They substituted a new authority for that of the Pakistani-controlled capitalist state in Bengal, but did not significantly alter its normal functions. 'Law and order' was preserved, no effort was made to mobilize or arm the people or prepare them for the confrontation that was plainly imminent. The Awami League leaders firmly refused to declare independence, at a time when the balance of forces was more

5. Even in the army cantonments the tension was felt very deeply. For instance, when the Awami League decided on 'non-cooperation' all the Bengali cooks, servants and laundrymen left the cantonments; in the food-markets the vendors refused to sell soldiers any food and Bengali cars visiting cantonments had their numbers published in the *Peoples* newspaper. At one stage the situation became so desperate that special nourishment for the officers had to be flown out from West Pakistan.

favourable than it was later to become. They had set their sights on autonomy within a federation and eagerly prepared to negotiate with the Yahya régime. In doing so they wanted to show themselves as a responsible party, concerned to preserve the existing social order. Addressing a mass meeting in Dacca on 7 March, Mujibur Rahman fulminated against intrigue, but rejected independence, much against the evident will of the people. Having won such a large majority he could not believe that the Army would crush it by force.[6]

The Military Coup of March

In Islamabad, however, the decision to intervene had been taken, no doubt after consultations with Bhutto. Staff plans were worked out to smash the Bengali national movement in a series of sharp and well-directed military blows. What the Army needed was time to dispatch troop reinforcements to ensure a speedy and successful surgical operation. The Awami League leadership, confident of a compromise settlement, was only too pleased to resume negotiations. Yahya therefore flew to Dacca where talks started on 15 March. Bhutto was also summoned and the Awami League politicians were lulled into believing that a deal was now virtually clinched. Yahya dragged out negotiations for ten days while extra troops were quietly flown in via Ceylon.[7] On 25 March the Awami League

6. In an interview with an AFP correspondent, Rahman was revealingly frank: 'Is the West Pakistan government not aware that I am the only one able to save East Pakistan from communism? If they take the decision to fight I shall be pushed out of power and the Naxalites will intervene in my name. If I make too many concessions, I shall lose my authority. I am in a very difficult situation.' (Le Monde, 31 March 1971)

7. Owing to a hijacking incident earlier in the year in which an Indian plane had been taken to Lahore by Kashmiri rebels and blown up, the Indian government had banned all Pakistani over-flights. The Bandaranaike régime, however, was only too willing to offer re-fuelling facilities at Colombo airport.

leaders were waiting for an announcement of the settlement.

It was to be a long wait. Yahya left for Rawalpindi with other West Pakistani politicians in the morning. That night the Army struck. Mujibur Rahman stayed at home and awaited his captors. Others could not afford the same luxury. Tikka Khan's first objective was a systematic effort to destroy the advanced elements of the Bengali working class and intelligentsia. The Army shelled Dacca University and wiped out all students and lecturers it could find; soldiers invaded the women's hostel, raping and killing its inmates. Artillery flattened working-class districts, while newspaper and trade-union offices were put to the fire: uncounted thousands were killed in the capital alone.

The people, unarmed and abandoned, attempted to fight back, without much success. Multitudes fled to the countryside. For two or three weeks after the attack of 16 March, scattered units of the East Pakistan Rifles and police force, under Awami League leadership, fought on. Their hopelessly incorrect policy of trying to fortify themselves in provincial towns, where they provided an easy target for mechanized expeditions by the Army, doomed them to rapid defeat and dispersal. By the second half of April, Tikka Khan was in command of all the main cities and only those combatants of the hastily formed Mukti Fouj (Liberation Army) who had taken to the countryside survived. Yahya's Army had scored every initial success; yet it had also signed and sealed the death warrant of Pakistan as a state. For it had crippled the only force which could have temporarily contained the rise of the mass movement – the Awami League. It thereby laid the future basis for a protracted armed struggle in Bengal, a prospect which has only marginally diminished since the establishment of Bangladesh.

Tariq Ali

Imperialistic Reactions

The utter inability of the League to grasp or deal with the dynamic turn of events should not be blamed on individual leaders. It was a result of the Party's inherent addiction to bourgeois constitutionalism. It was simply incapable of assimilating the lessons of March. Thus in both stages of the war (that is, both before and after the Indian intervention) the bulk of the surviving Awami League leadership, led by Tajudin Ahmed, sat in Calcutta relying on the international bourgeoisie for aid. The 'Provisional Government' of Bangladesh, namely the Awami League leadership, existed by courtesy of the Indian ruling class. Its 'ministers', all of them verbose parliamentarians, continued to behave in the same old way. They preached the politics of pressure: Awami League envoys were sent on world tours to persuade imperialist governments to halt aid to the Yahya régime.

To waste time, energy and resources in hoping that the USA would disarm the Pakistan Army – a vital component of its system for blocking social revolution in South Asia – was to harbour and create the most empty illusions. The West Pakistani state machine was and still remains, despite its defeat at the hands of its Indian counterpart, a tangible and reliable entity capable of guaranteeing imperialist interests and mediating them through those of the local landlord and capitalist classes. The Awami League, however pro-American the subjective sentiments of its leaders, has always been a woefully inadequate substitute for it as an objective vehicle of imperialist domination. Not only has the absence in Bengal of any solid pre-existent state apparatus, with a proper police and army, been a decisive deterrent to any real US backing for 'secessionism', but the Awami League, even as a party, has always fallen short of the qualities necessary to induce imperialism to entrust it with the responsibility of creating a new state. It is not a structured mass organization, with a genuine leadership system or party discipline. It is a shapeless collection of political notables and their followers, which has never proved that it can really handle the forces to its left and prevent their capture of its own rank-and-file.

Faced with a choice between Mujib and Yahya, the major imperialist powers naturally and unhesitatingly refused to gamble on the former, and concluded that they must continue to sustain the régime in Islamabad. Any doubts on this score were cleared up soon after the Indian intervention, when the Anderson papers were published in the United States and Nixon's leading adviser, Henry Kissinger, was quoted as saying at a top security meeting: 'I am getting hell every half hour from the President that we are not being tough enough on India. He has just called me again. He does not believe we are carrying out his wishes. He wants to tilt in favour of Pakistan.' Clearly, since Bangladesh is now an established fact, imperialism will do all in its power to maintain it as a client state. As we shall discuss below, a number of readjustments are already taking place which pose a serious challenge to the revolutionary movement.

Indian Intervention and its Consequences

As the war in Bangladesh unfolded it became more and more obvious that serious tensions were building up between the Awami League leaders based in Calcutta and the fighting units of the Mukti Bahini, engaged in a life and death struggle against the West Pakistani Army. The Mukti Bahini was a hybrid force composed essentially of three different elements: regular Bengali soldiers and policemen who had deserted the Pakistani state to fight for Bangladesh, Awami League supporters, and thousands of students, workers and peasants who were politically unaffiliated. It was the influence of the groups of the extreme Left on the latter that began seriously to concern the Awami League leaders in Calcutta. At this point their concerns coincided with those of the Indian ruling class. Both the 'Provisional Government' and Mrs Indira Gandhi understood perfectly well that it was impossible to fight a protracted armed struggle without the support of the people and that the only way to gain it was to begin the process of social revolution in the liberated areas. Once this had started it would have snow-balled and the Awami League would have been largely by-passed. That is why the prospect of an Indian invasion of East Bengal was always more congenial to the leaders of the Awami League than that of themselves organizing armed struggle for national liberation.

The failure of the Awami League to carry on without the Indian bourgeoisie is a terrible indictment of the ideology it espoused. Once again it confirms the fact that in this epoch the petty bourgeoisie is not capable of carrying through a real struggle for national independence. Moreover, the class limitations of the outlook of the League were compounded by the congenital defect of all such political formations on the Indian subcontinent: constitutionalism. This in turn reflects the low historical level of the struggle against the British. A recent commentator in the Indian press candidly noted this common element of Indo-Pakistani bourgeois politics, while expressing his sympathy for Sheikh Mujib:

The Awami League leadership in many ways corresponds to the leadership of our own Congress – a leadership which, with the backing of peaceful agitation, sought to arrive and ultimately succeeded in arriving at compromises with our colonialist masters. Our independence was the result of an understanding with the British masters. Sheikh Mujibur Rahman hoped to pull off a comparable deal with Islamabad. Like the Congress in India, the Awami League does not have the stomach for the type of war circumstances have forced Bangladesh to wage.[8]

These remarks unwittingly point, of course, to a very important difference between British and Pakistani colonialism in

8. Ranajit Roy, *Hindustan Standard*, 20 May 1971.

the subcontinent. British imperialism was able to grant a political decolonization because it nowhere meant the abandonment of its real *economic* empire, whose central segments were Malayan rubber and tin, Middle Eastern oil, South African gold, Indian plantations. But the loss of political control of East Bengal would have affected the vital interests of the impoverished and wretched sub-colonialism of Islamabad directly. For the weaker a colonial power, the more dependent it is on formal political possession of its subject territories.

Contemporary history has a striking lesson for us in this respect. The European imperialist nation which waged the longest and most stubborn war for the retention of its overseas possessions is not industrialized England, France or even Belgium. It is the small, backward and predominantly agrarian society of Portugal. For eleven years Lisbon fought a ferocious and unremitting campaign in Africa to keep Angola, Mozambique and Guinea, because of the enormous economic and ideological importance to it of these colonies. The sub-colonialism of Portugal, whose own economy is deeply penetrated by the capital investment of the advanced imperialist powers, might furnish an instructive comparison with that of Pakistan. Neither had much politico-economic room for manoeuvre: both were consequently driven in their different ways to extreme and unmediated measures of repression.

The intervention of the Indian army was, however, not a result of the 'humanitarian ideals' of Indira Gandhi or the Congress Party. There were two key reasons for it. In the first place, it was vital for India that the Awami League, and it alone, should exercise political power in Bangladesh. Secondly, Indian capital understood that a protracted war would begin to have an impact in West Bengal, where the political and economic situation has remained extremely unstable for the last decade. An Indian intervention thus not only solved the question of who held state power in Bangladesh, but also created a basis for defeating the Left in West Bengal.

The military success of the Indian army exceeded even its own expectations. In a two-week war Pakistan lost half its navy, a quarter of its air force, and nearly one third of its army. Undoubtedly one important reason for the speed of the Indian advance to Dacca was the collaboration of the Mukti Bahini and the information it supplied regarding Pakistani troop movements. Another factor was that the Pakistani Army decided not to fight and surrendered itself to the Indians. The Pakistani military commander, General Niazi, handed himself and 93,000 troops over to the Indians as prisoners-of-war and thus an important section of the military apparatus of the Pakistani bourgeoisie was transported wholesale to India, where it was to be preserved intact till a political settlement enabled it to be handed back to Pakistan.

The actual surrender of the Pakistan Army in Dacca was more reminiscent of scenes after a cricket match. Senior officers from both sides who had been trained in the same imperialist-sponsored military academies nostalgically exchanged anecdotes and barrack-room humour while consuming their whisky and soda in the army mess, much to the amusement of cynical British and American diplomats in Dacca. Forgotten were the atrocities committed by Pakistani troops in Dacca, such as the savage massacre of scores of Bengali intellectuals a few days before the final defeat; forgotten also were the large numbers of people and ordinary soldiers killed in this war. The generals and other senior officers of both armies thus displayed a certain class solidarity with each other and the victors consoled the defeated as they debated in the heart of a city where people were dying in the streets from starvation.

Once the Victory had been confirmed, the 'Provisional Government' returned home from Calcutta. It was flown home in an Indian air force plane, welcomed at Dacca airport by a guard of honour consisting of Indian troops, and packed into an Indian army truck and displayed to the people. Within the next few weeks the Awami League leader Mujibur Rahman, who had been held prisoner in West Pakistan, was released (by courtesy of the United States State Department) and allowed to return to Bangladesh. The scenario was complete and the Awami League was firmly installed in power. Despite the fact that the national struggle in Eastern Bengal was distorted by the Indian intervention, there can nevertheless be no doubt that Bangladesh is an independent bourgeois state. Notwithstanding its heavy dependence on India, its size and its political history will simply not allow it either to become an Indian protectorate like Sikkim and Bhutan or to be integrated into the Indian Union. Thus when the Indian civil servant in control of the Bangladesh desk in Delhi, a D. P. Dhar, visited Dacca in May 1972 he was greeted by demonstrators chanting: 'Neither Sikkim nor Bhutan, it is Bangladesh, Bangladesh!'

The decisive Indian role in the birth of Bangladesh by no means implies that its existence as an independent state is a pure fiction. Most régimes in the Third World have an independence which is seriously compromised by imperialist penetration of one sort or another without this meaning that they are simply colonial dependencies. An instructive parallel can, perhaps, be drawn with the circumstances whereby Cuba became an independent republic. In the late nineteenth century the Cubans waged a tenacious war against the Spanish for independence. However, during the course of the Spanish – American War of 1898 the US armed forces invaded and occupied Cuba, subsequently disarming the Cuban liberation fighters. The Cuban Republic was eventually set up by an act of the US Congress after four years of US military occupation. The other Spanish Caribbean island, Puerto Rico, became a US colony. The subsequent history of Cuba and Puerto Rico shows clearly enough that juridical independence can, under certain conditions, become a weapon which a genuine national liberation movement can use against imperialism.

Immediately after his return to Bangladesh Sheikh Mujibur Rahman set about the extremely difficult task of uniting the different factions in the Awami League, but has met only with limited success. The parliamentarians, most of whom fled to Calcutta and some of whom entered into a passive collaboration with the military, are rightly despised by those elements who fought in the ranks of the Mukti Bahini. Mujib's sympathies lie with the former. After all, he is of the same mould himself and preferred to surrender to the Pakistan Army rather than lead an armed struggle. This decision was no doubt tempered with the complacent understanding that he was far too important a figure for US imperialism to allow Yahya to execute him – a fact borne out by the speed with which Bhutto released the 'arch-traitor' after his return from New York and Washington.

Mujib thus established a new constitution modelled on the Acts by which British imperialism had governed India during the Raj, and the parliamentarians who had been elected before the invasions of Bengal were made Members of the Constituent Assembly (MCAs). A new general election would have produced a completely different result and that is precisely why it was avoided. But despite this fact the MCAs continue to be almost universally loathed: few serious observers in Bangladesh doubt that the majority of them are corrupt time-servers who are using their privileges to engage in black marketeering, smuggling, etc., and this at a time when the bulk of the nation needs food to survive.

Mujibur Rahman is beginning to realize that a combination of tears and rhetoric is no substitute for food and clothing, but his political character and the interests he represents make it impossible for him to undertake any radical solutions. His demagogy and constant references to 'socialism', far from pacifying the masses tend, on the contrary, to increase their disgust with the politicians in power. All the promises of a 'golden Bengal' created a mood of expectation among the people. They felt that after the colonial dominance of West Pakistan had been ended the entire pattern of their lives would change. But now they begin to understand that while formal political independence has been obtained, socially and economically they continue to remain part of the old system. The growth of anti-Indian and anti-Awami-League sentiment is directly related to the phenomenally high prices and the blatant corruption and smuggling which have haunted the country since its establishment. A special correspondent writing in the influential Bombay journal *Economic and Political Weekly* (10 June 1972, p. 1141) noted that:

The exploitation of Bangladesh by Pakistanis for years together, it may be mentioned, has made the people suspicious of anything which becomes a cause of their suffering. In this context a careful analysis needs to be made of the measures taken by the two governments which, directly or indirectly, have given rise to corrupt practices. A major factor responsible is the dependence on the bureaucracy. No doubt, smuggling was there before the liberation. And it was perhaps to be expected that it would grow after liberation in the absence of effective control of the frontier. The smugglers, of course, recognize no frontiers and it is their business to trade on the miseries of the people. They operate with the active patronage and connivance of social élites in both countries.

The smugglers operate within the legal framework as well as outside it. The recently concluded border trade pact with India makes it possible for the smugglers to operate under legal cover. The pact allows free trade within five miles of the border on both sides. Though there are restrictions on the quantity of goods that can be traded and on the number of trips that a trader can make and there is provision for check-posts, the pact is used by smugglers as a general cover for their activities. The smugglers take their goods within the 'free' zone from where the goods can be taken to the 'free' zone on the other side of the border. It is obviously not possible to post guards everywhere on this long frontier.

The dependence on India was inevitable given the role of the Indian Army in helping to establish and maintain an independent but bourgeois state in Eastern Bengal, but the barons of Indian capitalism will encounter growing hostility, as will their Awami League collaborators, if they simply try to replace the departed capitalists of West Pakistan. The Indian jute millionaires in particular are keen to control Bangladesh, which is their largest rival. An editorial in the *Economic Times* on 28 January 1972 (only a few weeks after the establishment of Bangladesh) indicates that Indian capitalists have not really understood the reasons why large numbers of people in Bangladesh gave up their lives to fight for national independence. Complaining about the new state selling jute to foreign buyers, the newspaper commented: 'India has reason to expect Bangladesh to meet our raw jute needs as a reciprocal gesture to what we have done to [*sic*] our neighbour.'

But while a struggle to assert the real independence of Bangladesh will undoubtedly resume at some stage, the Awami League, even within the present framework, has room to manoeuvre – and even more so now that relations with Pakistan are re-established and China is preparing to extend diplomatic recognition to the new régime. Internally, however, the situation continues to become more and more difficult for Mujibur Rahman. The Awami League is torn by internal dissention, and outside Dacca there is a continuous struggle for local power between the Mukti Bahini commanders and Awami League luminaries, the latter appointed without the former being consulted. In most of these rivalries it is the intervention of Mujib himself which has succeeded in maintaining some semblance of order, but even this trump card is losing its magic as the economic condition of the people continues to deteriorate. Even a journalist sympathetic to the Awami League was constrained to remark: 'Moreover, some Awami Leaguers have not only joined in the outright scramble for perks and patronage but have also, through their excessive sycophancy, clogged Mujib's channels of communication with the masses and tended to isolate him.' (Anthony Mascarenhas, *Sunday Times*, 11 June 1972)

The Revolutionary Left

The complete bankruptcy of the Awami League administration at every single level has opened up the possibility of a massive struggle for social liberation involving the workers, poor peasants and students. A struggle of this sort would involve, above all, armed organizations of the revolutionary Left. The Awami League has clearly been deeply discredited and weakened since the establishment of Bangladesh. Its catastrophic failures have decisively cleared the path for the assumption by the revolutionary Left of political leadership in the struggle for socialism. What is the current condition of, and what are the prospects for, the Left? It has been seen how, prior to the 1968–9 upsurge, the whole development of its numerically most significant sector – that under Maoist influence – was warped by the friendship proclaimed by the Chinese government for Ayub's military dictatorship in Pakistan. The effusive relationship between the two states had disastrous effects on the development of the Left throughout Pakistan: in particular it greatly facilitated the rise of the Awami League and the Pakistan People's Party.[9]

The bulk of the revolutionary Left in East Bengal learnt its lesson, however, during the great upheaval in 1968–9. The National Awami Party had traditionally functioned as an umbrella organization of the Left in East Bengal, under the dominance of a heteroclite pro-Peking majority. By 1969–70 the largest of the groups within this majority was the East Bengal Communist Party, led by Allaudin, Matin, Basar and Biswas.[10] It numbered perhaps 2,000 militants, its main re-

9. See *Pakistan: Military Rule or People's Power?*, pp. 133–44, for documentation and discussion of the effects of Chinese policy on the Pakistani Left.

10. This organization should not be confused with the reformist pro-Moscow party of the same name, led by Professor Ahmed, which has, as usual, been tail-ending the Awami League.

gional strongholds being the Rajshani, Chittagong and Pabna districts. Although it was by now too late to reverse in the short run the effects of previous opportunism (the influence of the Awami League was at its zenith in this period), this group made a decisive turn, in two ways.

First, it grasped the central importance of the national question and conducted agitation for a socialist solution to it. Second, it started to prepare its own cadres for a long-term armed struggle. In other words, the EBCP grasped the essential *specificity* of class struggle in East Bengal and rejected from the outset all electoralist illusions.

The three other pro-Chinese groups within the NAP gradually shifted in a similar direction, although with more hesitation. The Coordinating Committee for Communist Revolutionaries, whose leaders were Rashid Khan Menon and Kazi Zafar, was a smaller nucleus centred in Dacca itself. The veteran peasant leader Maulana Bhashani, himself no theoretician, was surrounded by a group of personal supporters who formed another current. Finally Muhammad Toha and Abdul Haq – the former an experienced trade-union militant who had once been Bhashani's secretary – formed the East Pakistan Communist Party (Marxist–Leninist). As its name suggests, this was the most rigidly 'orthodox' group, in that it alone rejected the Bengali right to self-determination and insisted on the necessity of preserving the unitary state of Pakistan (a theme to which China was, for reasons of its own, particularly attached). It, too, was the only group to reject united action in the developing crisis from 1968 onwards. The other tendencies cooperated in implementing the boycott strategy of the NAP in the December 1970 elections, and in radicalizing the demands of the base of the Awami League. However, it should be stressed that all four groups adopted an identical position in one fundamental respect. None of them harboured any illusions about either the capabilities of the Awami League[11] or the

11. In fact, many of the leftist groups felt that if the Awami League

intentions of Yahya Khan. By early March, their cadres were alerted and instructed to go underground, many of them leaving Dacca and heading for their respective bases in the countryside. Thus not many leftist cadres were eliminated by the military blitz of 25 March. The only important leader to be captured was the student spokesman in Dacca, Mahbubullah, a militant of the EBCP and one of the most talented Marxists in East Bengal. He had already been imprisoned in Dacca before the onslaught, but his comrades' fear that he had been killed was subsequently proved groundless.

Investigations in Bengal suggest that after the Army's attack the military tactics adopted by the guerrilla units of the revolutionary groups differed markedly from those of the regular soldiers and police enlisted under the banner of the Awami League. Thus an EBCP group in the Pabna area, led by Tipu Biswas, constantly harassed the Army garrison in Pabna, drew it out of its cantonment and after a week-long battle destroyed it. The guerrillas then occupied the city, ignored the hostility of the local Awami League, seized the arsenal and distributed arms to the local population. They did not dig in and establish positions, but thereafter left the city. Such an experience was in evident contrast with the positional warfare employed by the League-dominated Mukti Fouj in early April 1971, which led to its utter rout in the cities.

But it would be a serious mistake to exaggerate the size of the small detachments of the revolutionary Left which struggled during the military occupation to entrench themselves among the waterways and hills of East Bengal. No *mass* organization of the Left existed prior to March 1971 and it was impossible to create one overnight. As a result the Left was confined to attacking and disrupting the Pakistan Army communications and installations in their own localities – the

---

had come to power, they would have had to confront immediate persecution anyway.

EBCP in the Rajshani–Pabna zone, to the north-east of Bang-ladesh, the EPCP(M-L) in the Noakhali district in the Ganges delta (Toha's home territory). They were under-trained and under-equipped, and discovered that the terrain was not uni-formly hospitable to guerrilla warfare. The flat plains of the east do not afford extensive cover, and water transport can increase army mobility. The hill country in the West, behind Chittagong, Comilla and Sylhet, is more intractable.[12]

However, despite their size, the left groups were beginning to increase their weight inside the liberation movement and sections of the extreme Left were starting to collaborate with local units of the Mukti Bahini and were influencing the politi-cal direction of the latter. This led to a new series of splits within the extreme Left: the EBCP split into two factions which today exist as the Banglar Communist Party and the EBCP(M-L); and a split took place between Toha and Abdul Haq as the latter continued to support the existence of a united Pakistan and Toha's faction dropped East Pakistan from the name of their party. The Toha–Haq split reflected another split in near-by West Bengal between Charu Mazumdar and Ashim Chatterji in the CPI(M-L) on precisely the same issue. Chatterji and Haq assumed identical positions and the former's views were broadcast on Radio Peking and Radio Tirana; in addition a number of intellectuals led by Badrudin Omar with-drew from Toha's group, citing as a reason his inability to understand the national question. An already splintered Left thus continued to splinter yet further: a situation beneficial above all to the Awami League government.

Since Sheikh Mujibur Rahman and his followers were

12. The North-east of the province, in the region of Sylhet and Mymensingh, was the epicentre of the great Tebhaga peasant rising for rent reductions in 1945–7, the most militant social revolt of the rural poor in the subcontinent to that date. Its tradition will cer-tainly not have disappeared. For a good discussion of the Tebhaga rebellions, see Hamza Alavi's essay 'Peasants and Revolution' in the *Socialist Register*, 1965, pp. 265–8.

placed in power by the Indian Army, the government has unleashed a wave of repression directed against the forces of the
extreme Left. Special para-military units trained by the CIA
and the Indian Army and known as the Mujib Bahini systematically terrorize and intimidate striking workers, Communists and, in fact, anyone who dares question the policies of the
Awami League régime. The Left in its turn has begun to pose
the question of unity and some form of reunification is being
discussed by the larger groups of the extreme Left. However an
important weakness which still remains in the Left is the failure to make a self-critical analysis of its past.

Toha, in particular, has chosen to do the exact opposite. In
the first public statement of the Toha group since the establishment of Bangladesh they opted for the old Stalinist trick of
rewriting their own history. In a statement entitled 'On the Present Situation' Toha claimed that his group had favoured the
establishment of an independent Bengal as far back as 1967
and had instigated and led the anti-Ayub movement. History of
course tells a different story, and it is no secret in Bangladesh
what the role of the Maoists was during the years of the Ayub
dictatorship, when they not only refused to participate in the
anti-Ayub struggle, but held that the Ayub régime was anti-
imperialist because of its 'friendship with China'.

A failure to understand and explain its own past often serves
as the tombstone of a party which claims to be revolutionary. In
addition the traditional Maoist mistakes of defining the Soviet
Union as 'social-imperialist' and of continuing to maintain the
theory of revolution by stages (i.e. of a 'people's democratic
revolution'[13]) reveal the weaknesses of a section of the extreme
Left. These weaknesses have not only allowed the Awami
League to get away with murder (in the literal sense of the
word), but have also permitted the development of a strong

13. We are never told which forces accomplish this revolution, and
the class nature of the state after it is neither explained nor understood.

pro-Moscow Communist Party and enabled it to establish itself as the strongest force in the universities, traditionally the barometers of Bengali politics.

Of course, the pro-Moscow currents slavishly follow behind the Awami League, make no criticisms even when it bans strikes and kills communist workers, and invite Sheikh Mujibur Rahman to speak at their meetings and conferences. But this reflects more than anything else a certain disillusionment with China and those who have supported it uncritically inside East Bengal. The question of China can therefore no longer be avoided and unless the Maoist, semi-Maoist and ex-Maoist groups offer a coherent and cohesive analysis of the subject, the pro-Moscow revisionists will continue to gain ground.

The Bangladesh elections of March 1973 underlined both the repressive character of Awami League rule and the hopeless inadequacy of the existing Left forces. The election campaign itself was marked by a wave of intimidation of all opposition candidates and opposition parties. In the course of the campaign at least one hundred political murders were committed by supporters of the Awami League. In other cases meetings were broken up and opposition candidates were prevented from filing their nomination papers. Thus *The Times* for 7 February reported the following typical incidents which occurred during the pre-election period:

> The Bangladesh election campaign, already marked by violence, became more involved today when the opposition leader, Mr Asm Rab, charged that in various constituencies his party's nominees had been kidnapped. Mr Rab, general secretary of the National Socialist Party ... accused Awami League supporters last night of 'physically preventing' 17 nominees from filing their nomination papers. Yesterday the opposition newspaper *Ganakhanta* reported that 100 pro-government 'gangsters' opened fire on Major M. A. Jalil, the President of the National Socialist Party, as he left his launch at Bhola Island to address a public meeting ... In a report today, *Ganakhanta* said that 50 people

were killed and 150 injured on Sunday night in a labour camp at a jute mill at Sitakunda, an industrial town near Chittagong. According to official figures last night 12 died and 31 were injured.

One mysterious feature of the terrorization of the opposition was the fact that right from the beginning of the election campaign it was clear that the Awami League was going to win overwhelmingly. The various Left forces were in evident disarray and clearly incapable of winning more than a few seats. In the event the Awami League won 294 seats out of 300 with three going to 'Independents' and three to the Left parties. These included the National Socialist Party, a group of former Awami League members who had been disgusted by Government corruption and repression but had no clear programme of their own; the pro-Moscow National Awami Party, weakened by the support it had given to the Government in the first year of Independence; and finally the group around Maulana Bhashani which entered an electoral agreement with a reactionary and communalist Muslim Party. The defeat of these parties should open a period of profound political self-examination for all the groupings on the Left since it is clear that none of them is as yet capable of mounting a serious challenge to the Awami League government.

The Role of China

If the pro-Peking currents were actively involved in the armed struggle, they fought despite the positions adopted by the Chinese government, and without its help, moral or material. The Chinese leaders gave unconditional and blanket approval to the Yahya régime in its attempt to crush the Bengali resistance. Their support extended far beyond state diplomacy; it faithfully echoed the ideological justifications offered by the Islamabad military clique for its genocide in Bengal. Yahya claimed that the whole upheaval was the result of a handful of

separatist leaders of the Awami League conspiring in concert
with the Indian government. The official West Pakistan propaganda machine presented the revolt of an entire people as
'Indian interference'. The Chinese government had publicly
endorsed this myth. In a fulsome personal letter to Yahya
Khan, Premier Chou En-Lai openly accepted and defended the
right of the Pakistani Army to trample on the aspirations of an
oppressed people.[14] The Chinese government thus deliberately
aligned itself with a murderously reactionary capitalist state
against a mass popular upsurge, which included many supporters of the Chinese Revolution.

The Chinese justification that they were upholding the
'unity and sovereignty' of Pakistan is grotesque. The Pakistani
state, as every socialist militant must be aware, was a uniquely
reactionary and anti-national construct. It was, in fact, one of
the only two confessional states in the world: the other is Israel.
The People's Republic of China now apparently maintains that
the sacred ties of religion are indissoluble. In fact, of course, the
basic right of national self-determination, a fundamental principle of Marxism and Leninism, has scarcely ever belonged so
unequivocally to a people as to the oppressed masses of East
Bengal – who are not only ethnically, historically, linguistically
and culturally a distinct community, but who constitute the
majority of the population of 'Pakistan' anyway. The class
nature of the state machine which attempted to enforce the
unity of Pakistan was equally plain: it was and remains the
repressive weapon of the landlord–capitalist ruling class
against millions of poor peasants and workers. The Pakistani
Army is a shock force of imperialist-trained and Pentagon-
backed coercion, which has not only tyrannized its own country

14. The full text of Chou En-lai's letter, printed as Appendix 2 to
this book, was published as the lead story on the front page of the
government newspaper *Pakistan Times* on 13 April 1971. For other
Chinese statements on Pakistan, see *Peking Review*, 9 and 15 April
1971.

for the past twelve years. It has been an integral component of CENTO and SEATO, has provided officers and troops for the feudal despotism of Oman against the popular revolt in Dhofar,[15] and advised and assisted King Hussein in maintaining the monarchy in Jordan.

China has by no means limited itself merely to verbal support for this Army and its dictatorship in Pakistan. Its military and economic assistance has been crucial to the Yahya régime. The tanks used to raze workers' districts in Dacca were Chinese-made. The fighter-bombers which bombed Bengali villages were Chinese-constructed. When Islamabad confronted a grave economic crisis because of its war, Peking stepped into the breach with a generous loan of 100 million dollars, delivered to Yahya free of interest.[16] Meanwhile, the newly opened four-lane highway which links Sinkiang with North-west Pakistan across the Karakorum, from Sufu to Gilgit, became a constant conduit for both military and civilian supplies to the Pakistani régime throughout the crisis. Already in early March 1971, when the general strike in East Bengal halted shipments of paper to the West, Chinese trucks were bringing newsprint south to keep the official presses running in Pakistan.[17] Later, when the war itself had started, a hundred lorries a day were reported to be doing the run to Gilgit, with military supplies for the ordnance depots in Peshawar and Rawalpindi.[18] There can be no doubt that this assistance has been of direct benefit to the cause of counter-revolution in Pakistan.

15. For documentation of the Pakistani military role in Muscat and Oman, see Fred Halliday's reportage in the *Black Dwarf*, 6 April 1970.

16. See the *Financial Times*, 14 May and 17 June 1971.

17. The *New York Times*, 27 April 1971.

18. The *Daily Telegraph*, 28 April 1971. The credibility of this information cannot be discounted merely because it was printed in the bourgeois press. In fact, it is clear that it was supplied to reporters by sources within the Pakistan Government itself, and had an official character. It reveals nothing that Peking had not declared to be Chinese state policy anyway.

Tariq Ali

In addition the position adopted by the Chinese government seriously impeded the development of the revolutionary movement in Bangladesh. Because the extreme Left groups were so closely associated with China, the Awami League and the pro-Moscow groups used this fact to isolate them and at the same time to discredit revolutionary ideas in general. That is why we have constantly insisted that for the revolutionary movement to develop in Bangladesh a clear break with the opportunist line of China is absolutely vital. (cf. a number of articles on China published in the *Red Mole* and reprinted in the Bengali weekly *Holiday* on 12 March and 25 March 1972.)

Of course, by now it should have become clear to even the most religious of Maoist apologists that Chinese policy in relation to Bangladesh was not an unfortunate or isolated mistake. It is part of a complete turn in Chinese policy since the Cultural Revolution, manifested in Chinese support for the repressive Bandaranaike régime in Ceylon, Nimeiry in the Sudan, Haile Selassie in Ethiopia and Reza Pehlavi in Iran, and crowned by Nixon's visit to Peking. There is qualitatively no difference today between the Chinese and Soviet brands of peaceful coexistence, as revolutionaries in Asia and elsewhere who have hitherto supported the Maoists are already discovering to their cost.

The Consequences of Bangladesh

The establishment of Bangladesh and the continuing crisis which haunts its bourgeois government cannot be isolated within Bangladesh alone. Its echoes are being heard in both West Pakistan and West Bengal. The defeat of the Pakistan Army has seriously affected the credibility of the West Pakistani ruling class and engulfed the country in a serious political and economic crisis. While the discrediting of the Army has forced it to move to the background, this is only a temporary step, and a new military take-over cannot be ruled out in the near future.

I. WEST PAKISTAN

The Army's oft-repeated claim that it is independent of 'vested interests' has finally been exposed. Indeed, the whole historical role of the military and bureaucratic state apparatus which Pakistan 'inherited' from British rule in India has now emerged into the light of day for many young Pakistanis. This role was in many ways a peculiarly central and concentrated one in Pakistan, setting it off from most other Asian and African countries, despite the formal similarities of the military régimes which exist in them today. During the Second World War Japanese invasion and occupation temporarily smashed the old colonial apparatus of government – which had anyway never had a very large indigenous quotient – in Burma, Indonesia and elsewhere. After the War, there was little chance for the imperialist powers to reconstitute these, and considerable sections of the armed forces and civil service which emerged in the post-independence period had often participated in a national liberation struggle against either Japanese or European oppressors. In Africa, on the other hand, the colonial administrations were usually staffed so completely by the colonizing power itself that a civilian bureaucracy and – above all – an army had to be built up virtually from scratch after 'independence' had been granted.

On the Indian subcontinent, however, neither of these two patterns prevailed. There, a large and locally recruited civil service was an absolute necessity, since the British could not hope themselves to staff the bulk of the administrative system necessary to control its immense population. The same situation obliged them simultaneously to create an extremely large Indian Army, whose junior and some senior officers were recruited from the feudal aristocracy of the subcontinent.[19] These troops did sterling service for their imperialist masters both in the First and Second World Wars, and in constant domestic repression at home. No other colonial power could boast of such a capacious sepoy force. A precondition of it was, of course, the ethnic heterogeneity of India, which allowed the British to recruit their mercenary Army from selected 'martial races' – mainly Punjabis, Sikhs, Pathans, Rajputs, Jats and Dogras – who could be relied on to keep down the other subject nationalities of the Empire. However, in India the Congress Party led a strong bourgeois independence movement from the twenties onwards, which built a mass organization in the countryside, and succeeded in levering Britain out of its imperial suzerainty after it had been fatally weakened by the Second World War. The Congress Party was then able itself to knit the state together and dominate a parliamentary system that has survived ever since.

The scenario in Pakistan was very different. The Muslim League was always an extremely weak organization by comparison. Originally created by Islamic princes and nobles in 1906 'to foster a sense of loyalty to the British government among the Muslims of India' (to quote from its statement of aims), it was captured by the educated Muslim middle class led by Jinnah in the 1930s and for a brief period was in alliance with the Congress Party. However, its main thrust was always anti-Hindu rather than anti-British. It collaborated with the Raj during the Second World War and received a separate state

19. Lord Curzon's Memorandum on Army Commissions for Indians stated in 1900 that indigenous officers 'should be confined to the small class of nobility or gentry ... [and] should rest upon aristocracy of birth'. Such an officer corps would serve 'to gratify legitimate ambitions, and to attach the higher ranks of Indian society, and more especially the old aristocratic families, to the British Government by closer and more cordial ties'. See *Select Documents on the History of India and Pakistan*, Vol. IV, pp. 518–20, ed. C. H. Phillips, London, 1962.

from it in 1947, without having seriously struggled for independence. Jinnah became the Governor-General of Pakistan without having ever created a substantial party organization, let alone one of a mass character. The Uttar Pradesh, one of the main regions of the Muslim bourgeoisie he represented, was not included in the new state. Largely a stranger to the present provinces of West Pakistan, he simply confirmed the provincial landlords and feudalists in power as the representatives of his party there. The result was that the ruling class in Pakistan never possessed a reliable political party capable of mystifying or controlling the masses. The Muslim League was discredited permanently when it became merely a clutch of corrupt and quarrelsome caciques.

Pakistan was thus from the outset firmly dominated by its civilian bureaucracy and army, both of which had faithfully served the British. The top echelons of each were composed of an exclusive upper-class élite, handpicked and trained for its tasks by British imperialism. In the first decade after Partition the civilian bureaucracy exercised political domination in Pakistan. The CSP – Civil Service of Pakistan – comprised a closed oligarchy of 500 functionaries commanding the state. Indeed, the two masterful Heads of state of this period, Ghulam Mohammed and Iskander Mirza, were coopted directly from its ranks. They manipulated the token parliamentarism of the time until it became so discredited that in 1958 a military coup was engineered which brought Ayub Khan to the presidency. This change was itself stage-managed by the bureaucracy, which initially wielded most of the real power. Once in the saddle, however, Ayub surrounded himself with a clique of cronies and increasingly made his régime into a personal dictatorship – although not yet a corporate dictatorship of the Army as such. There were, for example, no military ministers in the Cabinet.

A decade later, Ayub's régime had in its turn become so immensely unpopular that it provoked the largest social upheaval in the history of the country. It was henceforward useless to the ruling class. Thus, in the emergency of early 1969, with the people on the streets in Rawalpindi, Lahore, Karachi, Dacca and Chittagong, and continuous strikes and riots in both East and West, the Army dislodged Ayub and finally assumed direct political command. The Yahya régime represented the end of a slow shift in the intra-state complex of power from the civilian to the military apparatus. Naturally, the CSP remains very influential within the present government: key civilian bureaucrats still concern themselves with those manifold problems of running the state machine and the economy which were beyond the competence of the military. But the Army is now the senior partner.

*

The Pakistani Army is a force of 300,000 troops, mostly recruited from those sections of the Punjabi and Pathan peasantry who traditionally provided infantry for the British. 93,000 of them were deployed in Bengal. The officer corps, from the critical rank of lieutenant-colonel upwards, is a select élite screened with the utmost care for its class background and political outlook. The generals, brigadiers and colonels of the Pakistani Army are scions of the feudal aristocracy and gentry of Punjab and the North-west Frontier, with a sprinkling of wealthy immigrants from Uttar Pradesh, Gujerat and Hyderabad. The impeccable social credentials and English accents of this group, which so entrance British journalists, reveal their past. They were trained as mercenary thugs for imperialism in Sandhurst or Dehra Dun. So much so, that the first commander-in-chief of the Pakistan Army *after* Independence was actually the British General Gracey, whose 20th Indian Division seized Saigon and thereby started the Indo-China War in 1945.[20] The Punjabi regiments which engaged in re-

20. See the account in Donald Lancaster, *The Emancipation of French Indochina*, pp. 129–34, London, 1962.

pression in Bengal thus included units who once practised their trade in Vietnam. Tikka Khan, the butcher of Dacca, is a veteran of Montgomery's army in the North African campaign.

During the repression in Bengal and during the war, supreme power in Islamabad was exercised by a small circle of these military officers, flanked by a few civilian advisers and accomplices. Yahya Khan himself was a dim and slothful figurehead. The clique which ruled behind him included some five generals: Hamid, the Deputy C.-in-C. of the Army; Umar Khan, the Chairman of the National Security Council; Akbar Khan, the Chief of the Inter-Services Intelligence Committee; Pirzada, the Deputy Chief Martial Law Administrator; and Tikka Khan, now C.-in-C. of the Pakistan Army.[21] To these should be added the régime's top civilian bureaucrat, Muzaffar Mohammed Ahmed, Chairman of the Planning Commission and heir to the tradition of Ghulam Mohammed and Iskander Mirza in an earlier epoch. The strength of this group lay in the very intensity of the social conflicts unleashed in Pakistan since 1968–9.

Like all political expressions of class rule, the Pakistani Army and civil bureaucracy have always enjoyed a certain relative autonomy from the landlords and businessmen of West Pakistan.[22] But unfortunately for the West Pakistani ruling

21. The similarity to the sinister generals' clique in Indonesia is striking. But Yahya by no means possessed the authority of Suharto.

22. In his very valuable essay 'Bangladesh and the Crisis of Pakistan', *Socialist Register*, 1971, Hamza Alavi stresses this autonomy of the Army from the local landlord and bourgeois classes and the imperialist powers. This emphasis is essentially correct, but there are two weaknesses in the way he argues the case. Firstly, he presents the Pakistani state as a typical example of a state machine in a 'post-colonial' society. Yet as we have argued above, the peculiar history of the establishment of Pakistan lends it certain quite specific features. Our own account of this specificity has been necessarily brief and the subject can do with further discussion. But unless a real attempt is made to grasp the special features of the military and civilian apparatus in Pakistan, no properly scientific account can be given of the

class, the converse does not hold. Since the mass upsurge of 1968–9, the oligarchy in the West has become more and more acutely aware of its dependence on the continued strength of the military and civilian state machine. *The Army and its cohesion is thus needed as a political rallying-point over and above its purely repressive functions.* The Six Points of March 1971 thus struck at the heart of oligarchic rule in the West. This is what explains the refusal to compromise with the Awami League, the ferocity of the action against the East, and the remarkable degree of unanimity in West Pakistani ruling circles in immediately supporting the coup of 25 March. It is also

---

reasons for the Army's action on 25 March, and resort has to be made to impressionistic speculations about the psychology of Army 'hawks', a dubious category of political analysis.

Secondly, it should be pointed out that the notion that the state or political level has a certain 'relative autonomy' is not a novel one, as Alavi appears to believe. The writings of both Lenin and Trotsky made it clear long ago that such a relative autonomy is a general law of all capitalist social formations, not just underdeveloped ones. For a recent statement on this question, consider the following: 'When Marx designated Bonapartism as the "religion of the bourgeoisie", in other words as characteristic of *all* forms of the capitalist state, he showed that this state can only truly serve the ruling class in so far as it is relatively autonomous from the diverse fractions of this class, precisely in order to organize the hegemony of the whole of this class.' (Nicos Poulantzas, 'The Problem of the Capitalist State', *New Left Review* 58, p. 74.) Marxists have further maintained that the ruling classes of the backward capitalist countries are, if anything, even more inclined to this particular 'religion of the bourgeoisie'. As we put it above, the Army or Civil Service may be *relatively* independent of the Pakistani landlord and business classes, but the Pakistani ruling classes are highly dependent on them. Indeed the very specificity of Pakistan throws this whole question into still sharper relief. The Pakistani ruling class has attempted to go one step further than the French bourgeoisie in the time of Louis Bonaparte: not only does it make the state its religion, but it has sought to make religion into the organizing principle of its state. That it may now in certain respects have become the victim of the irrationality it sought to exploit only confirms the essential teachings of Marxist class analysis.

what explains the fidelity of the United States and Britain to the military régime, despite the fact that it jeopardized 'stability' in Bengal.

At the same time, however, the USA attempted to deflect the Pakistani dictatorship towards 'moderation', while shoring it up otherwise. Economic pressure was undoubtedly applied to induce a more understanding attitude to the international interests of world capitalism, which Yahya had sacrificed to defend a narrow national egoism. Since Yahya's feeble intelligence and inertia were a constant embarrassment to imperialists, they chose to remove him after the defeat of the Army and give the Pakistani régime a fresher look. This was done in collusion with the leader of the People's Party, Zulfiquar Ali Bhutto, who went to the United Nations as Yahya's envoy, was approved by the luminaries of the State Department, and was summoned back to replace Yahya and give the military régime a civilian head. The military defeat convinced the more conscious elements in the Army that it was impossible for them to govern through a blatant and discredited military dictatorship. Thus immediately after assuming power as 'Chief Martial Law Administrator' Bhutto ordered the dismissal of several leading generals associated with Yahya Khan and placed the latter under house arrest: Hamid, Umar, Akbar and Pirzada were all dismissed.

To understand this turn we have to appreciate that, within the Army itself, a whole wave of junior officers were revolted by the behaviour of the High Command, which they characterized as bankrupt and consisting of drunkards. The crack armoured division was on the verge of open mutiny soon after the war. A large number of junior officers met and decided to lead their division into Islamabad and overthrow Yahya forcibly, despite the risk of civil war. This situation was avoided only by the intervention of General Karim, the senior officer of the division. He persuaded the officers to postpone their projected action, went to Islamabad, and made it clear that unless

Yahya and the generals closest to him were ousted, the country would be engulfed in a civil war. At a stormy meeting of senior officers, General Hamid (an old Yahya stooge) was abused and almost physically assaulted. It was agreed to send for Bhutto, as a new military leader would not have been welcome at that particular moment.

Bhutto's take-over of the country was thus to enjoy the full support of the Army, but he rightly felt uneasy at being appointed president by General Gul Hassan, an officer well known for his political ambitions, and a Pathan inhabitant of the North-west Frontier Province to boot.

The continuing unrest in the country, particularly the strike by the police force, created a tense situation in which it was becoming clear that the intervention of the Army might be necessary. Gul Hassan, we now learn, refused to allow the Army to be used to crush the police strike and was, as a result, removed from his post and given an ambassadorial job in Europe. In addition the Air Force chief, A. Rahim Khan, and six senior Air Force officers were also removed. In announcing their dismissal, Bhutto pledged in a typically demagogic fashion to wipe out all 'Bonapartist influences' from the armed forces. The removal of the Air Force chiefs was undoubtedly related to growing unrest in the ranks. For instance in January 1972 hundreds of members of the Air Force marched in the streets of Karachi against their officers. They declared that the officers were totally redundant and that the rank-and-file pilots were entirely capable of running the air bases on their own!

The Bhutto purge was meant to show his strength in relation to the Army, but the man appointed as Gul Hassan's successor was none other than General Tikka Khan who had been entrusted with the task of subjugating Bengal. Tikka is a ruthless soldier but is considered to be extremely simple-minded politically. He is also a Punjabi. These factors make him a more pliable element when compared to the extremely clever Pathan whom he has replaced. Nevertheless his appointment was also a veiled warning to nationalist elements in the Frontier and Baluchistan provinces, where Bhutto's own party is in a minority and power is largely in the hands of the National Awami Party. The NAP is led by Wali Khan and supported by the pro-Moscow Communists, though their influence is marginal in the two provinces where the NAP has its real strength.

On the political front Bhutto announced the withdrawal of martial law, called a meeting of the National Assembly, appointed provincial governments and promulgated a series of political and economic 'reforms'. It is necessary to recall that the war in Bangladesh badly shook the Pakistani economy, which had been depressed in any case since 1968. During the war foreign exchange dwindled drastically, while prices and unemployment mounted rapidly. Jute exports collapsed, precipitating a steep decline on the Karachi stock exchange. The main reason for this was the cost of the expeditionary force in Bengal which was estimated at something approaching 2 million dollars a day – a massive burden when added to West Pakistan's chronic import deficit of 140 million dollars a month. The military régime was thus faced with a domestic squeeze it had not bargained for when it embarked on its genocidal operations in March 1971. It was forced unilaterally to suspend payments on foreign debts and to rely even more on imperialist aid to ward off bankruptcy.

Since the conclusion of the war and the establishment of Bangladesh, the Pakistani bourgeoisie's problems have mounted tenfold. *Pakistan Forum*, a journal of radical Pakistanis in North America, published the following estimate of the situation by its editor, Feroz Ahmed, in March 1972:

The major economic consequences of the separation of East Bengal for West Pakistan are:

1. Reduction of at least 45 per cent in GNP (Gross National Product), not counting the downward economic trend in West Pakistan itself.

2. At least a 50 per cent reduction in export earning, again not counting the reduced capacity for earning foreign exchange in West Pakistan. This would mean a drastic (at least 40 per cent) reduction in the foreign exchange available for the importation of capital goods and industrial raw materials. West Pakistan earned, at the most, 50 per cent of united Pakistan's foreign exchange and spent, at least, 70 per cent of it.

3. Loss of markets for Rs. 1·7 billion (one Pakistani rupee equals US $0·21) worth of West Pakistani goods annually, including approximately 40 per cent of West Pakistan's manufactured goods. Even if alternative markets are found in the Middle East, there will be no incentive to expand industries such as cotton textiles.

4. It will be necessary to spend Rs. 550 million annually in foreign exchange to purchase tea, jute and paper, assuming that no foreign exchange is spent on Rs. 200 million worth of other commodities which were purchased every year from East Bengal.

5. Repayment of nearly $5 billion, owed foreign creditors, from West Pakistan's resources alone.

6. Bearing a tremendous burden of military expenditure; the defence budget of undivided Pakistan being roughly 5 per cent higher than the total revenues of West Pakistan.

7. It will be necessary to absorb the surplus (about 50 per cent) West Pakistani civil service personnel in the central government who were employed in a ratio of more than 4 to 1 as compared to East Pakistanis.

Given the deteriorating economic situation, Bhutto's 'reforms' amount to a confidence trick against the Pakistani people. The land reforms have not affected in any way the grip of the landlords over the Pakistani countryside – indeed if they had done so the social base of Bhutto in Sind, where his main support is from his fellow landlords, would have been destroyed – and in certain cases will allow landlords to control even more land than they do at present. Thus comments on the 'land reforms', even in the tame Pakistani press, have been fairly cynical. Writing in the Karachi newspaper *Dawn* a writer prudently signing himself 'Observer' noted that the effective land ceiling had been reduced from 36,000 produce index units to 18,000, and while this appeared to suggest radical change the important fact to be understood was that 'the key unit in determining the ceiling of land to be owned by an individual *is not* the acreage but the produce index unit. Produce index is a measurement for determining the gross product of various classes of lands and is calculated at the time of the land settlement.' Since land settlements can only be revised after a period of forty years the produce index unit calculations are completely out of date. The last settlement was made during the mid thirties, a period of depression, and it was at this time that the existing unit was established. As 'Observer' wisely noted:

How the produce index is likely to defeat the objective of the Reforms can be judged from the fact that the value of an acre in terms of produce index units ranges from 10 units to 110 units. Where an acre is equivalent to 100 units, 18,000 units will form 180 acres, but where it is equivalent to 10 units the ceiling will come to 1,800 acres. And this difference will not reflect the difference in productivity of the two but only their status in the mid-thirties. In actual fact, the former may be less productive to-day than the latter. Hence the effective ceiling may not be 150 acres of irrigated land and 300 acres of un-irrigated land, as is the intention of the President, but anything up to 1,800 acres or even more. (*Dawn*, 6 March 1972)

Any meaningful land reforms would have included the following measures:

1. The abolition of feudalism by expropriating the estates of the landlords without compensation.

2. The giving of all land to the tillers: the complete abolition of sharecropping and the giving of ownership of the land to the peasants engaged in this medieval practice.

3. The immediate annulment of all peasant debts.

4. The maximum landholding fixed at 25 acres of cultivated land.

5. The fixing of a minimum wage for rural proletarians and the restriction of their working hours to 40 per week with a compulsory day of rest. The extension to rural workers of full trade-union rights.

6. The expropriated surplus land from the big landlords used to resettle landless peasants and the rural unemployed in a system of cooperative farming.

7. The control of all marketing facilities by the state.

8. The rationalization of the water supply by placing tube-wells under the direct control of elected peasant committees to ensure an equitable water supply for all.

9. The outlawing of moneylending by private individuals, and state-instituted cheap rural credit at low rates of interest.

10. The stopping of the auction of state lands, and their distribution among the landless peasants. The immediate confiscation and distribution among poor peasants of all land given as reward for services rendered to civil servants, army officers.

11. The distribution of all chemical fertilizers and seeds only through cooperative societies at cheap prices.

12. The allotment of at least one school and one medical centre to every village, and of one hospital and technical college to every sixty villages. The increase of the number of agricultural universities available.

These are the only measures which would destroy the grip of landlordism in Pakistan, and Mr Bhutto's 'reforms' do not even approach them. This is not surprising as any real agrarian reform would also challenge the power of the bourgeoisie and the Army. The 'land reforms' of the Bhutto régime are a complete sham designed to deceive the people and must be recognized as such. However, given the rhetoric employed by the People's Party, the total failure of these reforms could well lay the foundation for a revolutionary movement among the Pakistani peasantry. If the latter were successfully mobilized the entire structure of the Pakistani oligarchy would be very seriously challenged.

Reforms in other fields amounted to similar demagogic tricks designed to conceal the basic fact that the country was being run in exactly the same way as before. Thus, despite the fact that Bhutto's speech on May Day 1972 made references to the 'spirit of the Paris Commune' and May Day was declared a public holiday, in the following month at least thirty workers were shot down by armed policemen in the streets of Karachi. The murdered workers were part of a gigantic popular upsurge in protest against rising prices, inflation and attempts to outlaw strikes. This upsurge culminated in a general strike in Karachi and despite the calls of 'Left' trade-union leaders the strike remained solid for a number of weeks. In October 1972 the whole tragedy was re-enacted and another fifteen workers who had occupied factories in the Landi industrial estate were attacked by police and army units and defeated *militarily*.

In the two border provinces of Baluchistan and the North Western Frontier province (NWFP) the NAP-dominated governments were soon to discover the extreme reluctance of Bhutto to share his monopoly of power. Both governments were summarily dismissed and, while in the NWFP the reaction was muted, in Baluchistan the dismissed government leaders Bizenjo (Governor) and Mengal (Chief Minister) were arrested together with the chief of the Marri tribe, Khair Baksh (Chairman of the Baluchistan NAP). Their supporters took to the hills and since the beginning of 1973 have been waging a guerrilla war against the Pakistan Army, whose units have been trying, unsuccessfully till now, to suppress the uprising. The struggle in Baluchistan has not created a serious crisis for the régime so far, but all the indications suggest that it could develop a certain dynamic unless Bhutto negotiates a rapid settlement with the NAP leaders, who are constitutionalists to the core and desperate to conclude a rapid peace. Baluchistan

337

is the smallest and most rugged of Pakistan's provinces and its population is well below the million mark. As such, on its own it is unlikely to develop into a Bangladesh-type situation, and up till now has had no real impact on workers and peasants in other parts of the country. However, it is diminishing still further the credibility of the Pakistan army, since the latter's casualties have been comparatively high (between 200 and 300) and the Baluchi guerrillas are both growing in numbers and moving leftwards.

The tragedy of the situation was and remains the extremely low political level of the revolutionary Left. There is no understanding of the concept of dual power, of the importance of creating organs of the working class as a counter to the bourgeois state and of laying the foundations of a workers' militia. Thus, despite the fact that Bhutto's demagogy is beginning to wear a bit thin and there are grave dissensions within his own People's Party, the weakness of the revolutionary movement makes it impossible to take advantage of the extremely favourable objective conditions.

The pro-Peking National Awami Party has split into three factions: the Pakistan Socialist Party under the leadership of veterans C. R. Aslam and A. Minto follows a more or less centrist course but has disowned Peking; the Pakistan Workers' Party is a smaller organization led by an old trade-union activist, Mirza Ibrahim, and by Sardar Shaukat Ali; and the Mazdoor-Kissan Party led by Mohammed Ishaq and Afzal Bangash is probably the largest of the extreme Left organizations. But the last of these is still deeply influenced by orthodox Stalinist concepts and refuses to combat chauvinism within the Left. On the contrary it uses chauvinistic and reactionary religious mythology in its appeals to the people and in its political programme.

The débâcle of the Left is in no small measure due to the opportunist role of Peking in relation to the Ayub and Yahya dictatorships. Only recently Bhutto informed a private gathering of People's Party members of parliament that Chou En-lai had told him that all talk of socialist revolution in Pakistan was Utopian. It is possible that Chou En-lai actually believes this, but for the revolutionary movement in Pakistan the task of building a party still remains the key to the present crisis. The creation of a serious revolutionary formation would have to be based on an understanding of the following key problems:

1. The formation of an independent political force of the urban and rural proletariat and of combating the ideological influence of the urban and rural bourgeoisie within the proletarian movement.

2. If the occasion arises, the giving of critical support to any real anti-imperialist move by the local ruling class (similar to the nationalization of Mexican oil, Suez Canal, Bolivian tin, foreign banks, etc.), while constantly explaining the limitations of the bourgeoisie which is compelled owing to its inner contradictions to carry out these policies.

3. The representation of the most radical and energetic force within the anti-imperialist movement, not only by actions of solidarity with the struggles for national liberation in the three continents, but by linking these struggles to the revolutionary movement against one's own bourgeois class, whatever verbal stance it might have adopted.

4. The alerting of the working masses to the fact that a struggle against the bourgeoisie and upper petty bourgeoisie is essential for an overthrow of the existing social structure, and that the latter are incapable of mobilizing the masses against imperialism.

5. Fighting on these political lines for the hegemony of the proletariat in the revolution. In concrete terms this means the victory of the proletarian party in gaining the leadership of workers in both town and countryside and leading them to overthrow the bourgeois state and establish the new socialist order.

Up till now the revolutionary Left in Pakistan has been

unable to understand these problems, and its ability to do so will to a large extent be determined by its willingness to assess its own past and that of the international 'communist' movement of which it has been a part.

2. WEST BENGAL

A protracted struggle in Bangladesh could well have had extremely critical repercussions in West Bengal. It has been the Achilles heel of the Indian Union and only the inadequacy, both theoretical and practical, of the forces on the extreme Left has postponed a serious revolutionary explosion. A different outcome in Bangladesh, however, could have shown a new road to militants in the West, and this factor is of great importance in understanding first Indira Gandhi's response to the events in East Bengal and later the military intervention by the Indian Army. Nevertheless, despite their precautionary measures the Indian bourgeoisie will find that even a Bangladesh controlled by the Awami League is not the same as a Bangladesh under direct Indian control, and that a development of serious armed force will overflow into West Bengal.

Over the last decade the most effective political force in West Bengal has undoubtedly been the CPI(M), with its tens of thousands of militants and millions of supporters. But this party has been in a dilemma ever since it split from the orthodox pro-Moscow CPI in 1964, and while it has offered a more radical-sounding rhetoric, particularly in the sphere of its foreign policy, its day-to-day practice has clearly revealed its centrist limitations. Thus its entire political strategy has been dominated up till now by parliamentarism and the formation of coalition governments with bourgeois parties. It has constantly sought to avoid a decisive confrontation with the Indian state and imagined that its massive size and strength was a semi-permanent guarantee of its continued influence.

In the past, Indian Communism subordinated itself to the diplomatic manoeuvres of the bureaucratized workers' states, the

Soviet Union and China. The CPI(M) has partially broken with Peking and Moscow, but retains a bureaucratic and Stalinist conception of the class struggle. The leadership of this party cannot understand that only a revolutionary democracy based on the workers and peasants is capable of carrying through the formidable and urgent task of destroying the Indian bourgeois state machine.

Because of the party's vacillations and its inability to understand the nature of the bourgeois state, the Indian government was able to take advantage of Bangladesh and the Naxalite–CPI(M) rivalry (which extended to physical annihilation of each other's cadres) to reassert its hegemony in West Bengal through the Congress Party. Thus the 1972 election in West Bengal resulted in a crushing defeat for the CPI(M). The total number of seats won by it amounted to 14, compared to 113 it had obtained in the election held only a year before. The Congress Party thus succeeded in something which it had been trying to achieve ever since 1967.

The result of the West Bengal election should under no circumstances be underestimated. The province has been in a pre-revolutionary crisis for several years and thus presented a constant threat to the efforts of the Congress Party to try to stabilize the political situation throughout India. There were elements in the Indian ruling class who would have looked for stronger solutions and were even toying with the idea of a military-style régime if the sore of West Bengal continued to fester. In that sense, therefore, the Congress victory has won that party and the parliamentary system it favours a new lease of life.

The tragedy of West Bengal is not so much that the Congress has won, but the fact that the organizations of the Left are in a state of disintegration. The ultra-leftism of the Naxalites and the opportunism of the CPI(M) have created a situation where hundreds of political militants can be killed both inside and outside the state prisons without evoking any serious response from the workers' organizations.

There is also a tendency to blame the defeat of the CPI(M) on the gangster tactics employed by the Congress, but this is a dangerous over-simplification as it prevents the development of any serious analysis of the CPI(M) and of its mistakes both in the past and at the present moment. Of course the bourgeoisie and its political party, the Congress, used gangsterism to try and win more seats. No one can deny the fact that the election took place at a time when there were between 16,000 and 20,000 people in prison without trial, that there had been 2,000 political murders in 1971 and 1972, and that the Congress used repressive laws to gag the opposition. Nor can any observer deny the reports which appeared in the left-wing Calcutta weekly, *Frontier*, one of which described rather graphically Congress tactics for the election:

To conduct free and fair elections the state Government fielded in West Bengal a strength which, Governor Dias boasted, surpassed that of the Army in any sector during the 1965 Indo-Pak war. This was in addition to the police and armed police, national volunteer forces and home guards. To conduct this free and fair poll, 6,000 leftist election workers were arrested without trial last week, which took the total of people arrested in the state to 32,600. Four thousand leftist election workers and their families were externed from the localities by the local roughs. The CPM could not appoint polling agents in 96 centres out of 171 because it feared that the agents would be killed by either the police or the roughs or both.

Mrs Gandhi came to the state on a whistle-stop campaign and addressed a score of gatherings. At the Tallah gathering PWD [Public and Works Department] workers worked for 10 days to prepare for the election meeting and that cost the state exchequer 1·5 hundred thousand rupees [one Indian rupee equals US $0·137]. Rs. 44,000 was spent for the Chinsurah meeting, Rs. 50,000 for a North Bengal meeting. The cost of these was borne by the state Government, because of the principle that any visit and meeting of the Prime Minister is the charge of the government.

All this is undoubtedly correct, but is not sufficient to explain the extremely sharp electoral decline of the CPI(M). We would suggest that there were two key reasons for this. In the first place the CPI(M), despite its decision to part company with the CPI, never broke from the Stalinist concepts of the latter and thus completely failed to understand the class nature of the state. This led them to a typically popular-frontist strategy which, far from destroying the state machine of the bourgeoisie, instead attempted to utilize it, on occasion against the extreme Left in the shape of the split-away Maoists, referred to as Naxalites. The ultra-leftism of the latter and their refusal to understand the importance of always relating the activity of the revolutionary organization to the activity of the people is a direct result of the CPI(M)'s opportunism. When in government the CPI(M), despite its demagogy, was not qualitatively different from preceding bourgeois governments, and its two periods of governmental power had the effect of demoralizing its own social base in the working class and the peasantry.

Secondly, the political strategy of the CPI(M) was based entirely on parliamentary manoeuvres. Instead of building a strong extra-parliamentary force and using parliament simply to strengthen the former they did the exact opposite. They used their mass organizations largely as pawns which enabled them to manoeuvre in Parliament. Coupled with this weakness was the total inability of the CPI(M) to propagandize on the necessity of the armed struggle and the need to build and develop armed units of the party together with peasants' and workers' militia. We are not arguing that the CPI(M) should have launched the armed struggle, but merely that unless it educated its own cadres and the mass organizations it dominated in the ultimate necessity of waging such a struggle it would be paralysing itself. The killing of many CPI(M) militants in West Bengal by Congress hoodlums illustrates this weakness in an even more striking way.

There are indications that since its defeat sections of

Tariq Ali

CPI(M) militants are beginning to discuss and analyse their past, but unless the party does this as a whole by frank and free internal discussions on a number of interrelated questions – Stalinism, the class nature of the Soviet Union and China, popular frontism, armed struggle, the need to develop organs of revolutionary democracy, etc., – they will not be able to recover and sections of the party will simply desert to the CPI.

It has to be understood that the objective conditions in West Bengal today are such that the Congress government will *not* be able to bring any real change in the situation. But what the defeat in West Bengal has done is to give the Congress Party a few more years to rule India on behalf of the bourgeoisie before the latter look for tougher solutions.

It is obvious that any strategy for West Bengal has to take into account the existence of Bangladesh and the struggle of the Left in that country. The right of the Bengali people to national self-determination cannot simply be confined to East Bengal and therefore a strategy has to be developed in terms of a united socialist Bengal and a coordinated struggle.

Whatever form it took, a Red Bengal would sound the death-knell of imperialist domination over the Indian subcontinent and that is why the Indo-Pak ruling classes will wage a bitter struggle to prevent such a possibility.[23] Bengal, historically in

23. The prospect of a Red Bengal is viewed with lively alarm by imperialism, as may be inferred from the following editorial which appeared in the *New York Times*, entitled 'Bengal is the Spark'. The occasion for it was apparently some reflections of mine reported from Calcutta: 'Mr Ali's radical vision of chaos on the Indian subcontinent cannot be taken lightly ... A prolonged guerrilla conflict in East Pakistan would have profound repercussions in the neighbouring vio-lence-prone Indian state of West Bengal, already shaken by the influx of more than three million refugees from the Pakistani Army's cam-paign of terror. Prime Minister Indira Gandhi is under mounting pressure to intervene to try to check this threat to India's own internal peace and integrity. It is obviously in no one's interest to allow the Bengali "spark" to explode into a major international conflict, one which might speedily involve the major powers. Nor is it wise to

the vanguard of the anti-British-imperialist struggle, the area which gave birth to the Indian revolutionary movement, may once again play a pilot role. The first shots have already been fired in a struggle to liberate a small portion of the peninsula. Whether those who fired them realize it or not, those shots may herald the beginning of a long process which would decisively change the map of the world – the subcontinental revolution.

A revolution in the Indian subcontinent, despite its uneven development, would also mark the end of imperialist domination of Asia. That is why the USA has modified its old strategy in relation to the People's Republic of China. Nixon's visit to China has clarified Chinese policy in relation to South Asia and has brought the régime of Mao Tse-tung into line with the policies of Brezhnev and Nixon. The three major powers are agreed that the situation in the Indian subcontinent is far too unstable and that henceforth the 'stability and peace of Asia' depend on the preservation of the status quo in South Asia. Hence a *rapprochement* between the Chinese government and the Indian bourgeoisie is the order of the day. The USA is determined above all to prevent any repetition of the Indo-Pakistan war which would weaken its global interests. Hence American strategy is designed to unify the military power of the bourgeoisie in the subcontinent in such a way that it cannot fight internally. That is why Bhutto and Indira Gandhi engage in

---

permit the situation in East Pakistan to continue to fester, inviting the gradual political disintegration of the entire subcontinent. To deprive Tariq Ali and his like of their "big opportunity" it is essential that Pakistan's President Yahya Khan come to terms speedily with the more moderate Sheik Mujibur Rahman and his Awami League, which won an overwhelming popular mandate in last December's national and state elections. Such an accommodation with East Pakistan's elected representatives should be a pre-requisite for the resumption of US aid, except for relief assistance, to Pakistan.' (*New York Times*, 2 June 1971.)

'summit talks' and will continue to do so as far as the USA is concerned. For the latter now believes that the main threat is not an external one (i.e. the China bogey should now be discarded) but is situated within the subcontinent, being the mass movement. It therefore wants to formalize the alliance which helped Bandaranaike crush the JVP in Ceylon, and wants all the bourgeois leaders in the subcontinent to unite against the potential threat of a mass revolutionary movement.

It is of course understandable why US imperialism is worried. The success of the struggle in Indo-China and the ultimate withdrawal of American troops from South-east Asia would leave the subcontinent as the largest Asian land mass still to be liberated from the tyranny of the capitalist world market.

The continuous rise of mass movements and the establishment of liberated areas in this region would therefore mark the beginning of the end for imperialism in Asia. A successful seizure of power in India would change the map of Asia overnight and the revolutionary wave would engulf other areas of struggle such as the Middle East. A socialist revolution in India would also greatly alter the balance of forces between the Chinese bureaucracy and the Chinese masses in favour of the latter. Hence the unanimity of views between Nixon, Chou En-lai and Brezhnev as far as South Asia is concerned. This formidable alliance was seen in operation in Ceylon, where it helped to suppress the militants of the JVP (Janatha Vimukthi Peramuna – People's Liberation Front).

The enormous strategic significance of the Indian subcontinent – the fact that after Indo-China it is imperialism's weakest link in Asia today – necessitates on the part of the revolutionary movement in the Indian subcontinent and abroad an understanding of the problems that South Asian revolutionaries will confront and the areas where success is most likely.

Within this weakest link there are further weaknesses and we have tried to show that these are Pakistan, Bangladesh and

West Bengal, but, as Fred Halliday argues elsewhere, Ceylon is an equally unstable situation.

The sad fact is that the revolutionary movement is today extremely weak in relation to the tasks that confront it, both politically and numerically. If the experience of Ceylon and Bangladesh is to be utilized properly, then the question of building independent revolutionary Marxist organizations linked to each other and to the revolutionary movement in the rest of the world becomes a prime task. We would argue that the Fourth International established by Leon Trotsky and other Leninists in 1938 has provided a programmatic continuity to the principles of Marxism and Leninism, and that the growth of this embryonic International in Europe and Latin America shows its capacity to intervene in and lead revolutionary struggles. Furthermore it is the only Marxist organization which revives the spirit of internationalism concretely (by organizing itself as an international organization), and offers the only real answers to the bureaucratic degeneration in both China and the Soviet Union and the problems being confronted and created by their followers on a world scale. The construction of sections of this International in the subcontinent becomes absolutely vital for the Indian revolution and the world revolution.

Appendix 1
Declaration of the Fourth International on the Struggle in Bangladesh

As the Pakistani armies continue their effort to crush the independence movement of the people of Eastern Bengal, it becomes clear that the Yahya military clique failed to secure the quick victory it sought. Despite the brutalities and the mass killings, it has been unable to terrorize the Bengali people into submission.

Incensed by the wholesale slaughter of unarmed people, the Bengali masses are certain to continue their resistance against the colonial régime ruling their country. But the whole question of revolutionary leadership and revolutionary strategy is posed with the utmost sharpness. The Bengali people are united as never in the past. However their current leadership is completely inadequate. Far from preparing the workers and peasants for the decisive prolonged struggle for independence, Sheikh Mujibur Rahman did all in his power to arrive at a compromise with Yahya Khan. The Awami League opposed independence and set its sights instead on autonomy. Mujibur engaged in discussions with Yahya Khan while the dictator placed his military forces in position. The Mujib leadership now flounders and hopes for help from the United Nations and the international bourgeoisie, starting with the Indian capitalists. Its real line was clearly expressed in Sheikh Mujibur Rahman's declaration to the *Agence France Presse*: 'Is the West Pakistan government not aware that I am the only one able to save East Pakistan from communism? If they take the decision to fight I shall be pushed out of power and the Naxalites will intervene in my name. If I make too many concessions, I shall lose my authority. I am in a very difficult position.' (*Le Monde*, 31 March 1971.)

The Fourth International, while declaring its complete solidarity with the struggle of the Bengali masses against national oppression, reaffirms its view that the development of a revolutionary leadership is essential to win the struggle. This victory will only be achieved by the Bengali workers, peasants and students organized and led by a revolutionary proletarian leadership. This party will have the task of continuing the revolutionary struggle by all means necessary and thus begin the task of smashing the old structures of the Bengali countryside and cities and laying the basis to establish a workers' and peasants' government, which will start building a socialist society. This task can only be impeded by any intervention of the Indian bourgeoisie, which is interested only in preserving the status quo and preventing the struggle in Bangladesh from overflowing into West Bengal. The Fourth International is opposed to intervention by the Indian bourgeoisie which would be designed to hinder the development of the Bengali struggle rather than to help it. Once more the counter-revolutionary nature of Indira Gandhi's policies and of the bourgeois state of India has been confirmed by her government's aid, side by side with the Yahya Khan clique, to the Ceylon Army's repression of the revolutionary forces in that country.

The Fourth International condemns the treachery of the Maoist government in publicly supporting the Yahya dictatorship and thus helping it to maintain its ruthless exploitation and oppression of the Bengali people. In the guise of combating Indira Gandhi's 'interference', the Mao régime stands today as direct accomplice to the massacre. Chou En-lai's message to Yahya Khan on 12 April is a brazen attempt to cover up Peking's approval of the massacre of the Bengalis: 'We believe that through consultations and the efforts of Your Excellency and leaders of various quarters in Pakistan, Pakistan will certainly be restored to normal. In our opinion unification of Pakistan and unity of the peoples of East and West Pakistan are basic guarantees for Pakistan to attain prosperity and strength.'

Mao's subsequent personal message to Yahya Khan repeats the same idea in even stronger language. The 'unity' of Pakistan is the 'unity' of a monstrosity sponsored by British and world imperialism against the unity of the workers and peasants of the Indian subcontinent. It is a 'unity' that strengthens the grip of a tiny group of semi-feudal landlords, comprador capitalists and Generals over millions of super-exploited and starving peasants, agricultural and industrial workers. It is a 'unity' that showed callousness to the most elementary needs of the Bengali people by failing to take precautionary measures in advance of last year's tornado and by doing nothing for the victims afterwards. It is a fundamental revision of the elementary principles of Marxism–Leninism to speak about the Pakistani 'state' and the Pakistan Army without clearly specifying its class character: a state defending the interests of a coalition of semi-feudal landlords, rapacious compradors and monopoly capitalists (22 families of robber barons control two thirds of the industrial assets of the country). The army is a reactionary bourgeois army formed and trained by imperialism and ready to join similar armies in Iran and Afghanistan in forming an anti-communist *cordon sanitaire* in Central Asia in the direct service of world imperialism. These are the forces approved by Mao to preserve 'unity'.

The support given to Yahya Khan by the Chinese bureaucracy represents an open betrayal of the class interests of the workers and poor peasants who had died in the struggle for national self-determination, who are struggling today against the Pakistan Army and who will tomorrow continue the struggle for a socialist Bengal. It is obvious that the Maoist leaders, far from learning the lessons of the Indonesian defeat or the lessons of their unprincipled support for Yahya's predecessor, Ayub Khan, continue on the same opportunist road.

Their course weakens the socialist forces in Bangladesh and strengthens right-wing elements that utilize Peking's support of Yahya to discredit 'communism'. Mao's support to Yahya Khan weakens and harms the advance of the Chinese Revolution: the only substantial bulwark against the threat of imperialist aggression from the Indian peninsula against the People's Republic of China is a strong and powerful revolutionary mass movement moving towards the overthrow of the reactionary states of India and Pakistan, towards a victorious workers' and peasants' revolution in the whole subcontinent. If the mass uprising in East Bengal is smashed, this will strengthen reaction in the whole peninsula and the very same reactionary army that Mao and Chou flatter today, would be ready tomorrow to support aggression against the Chinese Revolution.

Those communists on a world scale who have chosen to support the Chinese leadership in the Sino-Soviet dispute on the grounds that it acts in a more revolutionary and militant way against imperialism must say today where they stand on this issue. Silence would amount to complicity.

The various Western imperialist powers have, while deploring the mass slaughter, supported in various ways the status quo. The United States in particular has manipulated the distribution of its stocks of food to favour Yahya Khan, knowing full well that starvation is a key weapon in his armoury. Moreover most of the arms used by Yahya were supplied by the Pentagon and will be replaced from the same source as they are used up in putting down the population.

The Fourth International appeals to the international workers' movement to render all possible assistance to the freedom fighters of Bangladesh, to carry out solidarity actions with the Bengali masses and to demonstrate unconditional support of the Bengali struggle for national self-determination. The Fourth International calls upon all socialists to oppose any interference by capitalism and imperialist forces designed to maintain neo-colonialism's grip on the whole Indian sub-continent. In particular military aid and especially assistance to Yahya Khan's forces in transit must be opposed by all means necessary. Revolutionaries should put the maximum pressure on the Maoist leadership to end its shameful support to Yahya Khan's dictatorship. It is also a vital task to expose the Soviet military aid which helped build up the West Pakis-tan counter-revolutionary army. The Left should be on its guard against the possibility of a massive intervention spon-sored by US imperialism to prevent any spread of the revolutionary struggle in Asia. The Fourth International calls upon the workers, peasants, students and revolutionary in-tellectuals in West Pakistan to break with all chauvinistic anti-Bengali sentiments, to understand that the murderous Generals now trying to smother the uprising of the Bengali people in a bloodbath are their old oppressors. The struggle against the colonial war unleashed by Yahya Khan in Eastern Bengal is not only their internationalist duty, but is also in their own class interests. To defeat the West Pakistan Army in Bengal will speed the liberation of the West Pakistani masses from the yoke of their exploiters.

The Fourth International is confident that despite temporary setbacks, the Bengali masses will finally triumph over the armed might of West Pakistani capital and thus pave the way for a united socialist Bengal which in turn will give powerful impetus to the liberation of the entire subcontinent from the yoke of imperialism and landlordism.

Victory to Bangladesh!

For a Socialist Bangladesh!

For a United Socialist Bengal!

(United Secreriat of the Fourth International, 18 April 1971)

Appendix 2
Defend the Ceylonese Revolution!

The government of Ceylon has declared a state of emergency and imposed a curfew throughout the island; they have suspended all democratic rights, imposed a strict press censorship, and arrested hundreds of militants of the Janatha Vimukthi Peramuna (the People's Liberation Front – JVP). They have proscribed the JVP and have started shooting prisoners without trial.

The leaders of the coalition government have used their monopoly of the communication media to lie about the JVP, misrepresenting them as a 'fascist' and right-wing organization. At the same time the government has not dared to inform the public that it has sought and received aid from the imperialist governments of the United States and Britain; that it is using Indian and Pakistani gunboats and helicopters; that it has expelled the North Korean diplomats from Ceylon.

The Bandaranaike popular front government came to power in May 1970 by promising the masses that it would usher in a 'new era' and build a socialist Ceylon. One pro-Moscow Stalinist and three renegades of the reformist Lanka Sama Samaja party (LSSP) were included in the cabinet in order to bolster up the 'socialist' image. However, despite all the rhetoric, the coalition government has demonstrated that its real role is to maintain capitalist property relations and preserve the imperialist stranglehold on the Ceylonese economy.

During its ten months in power, the coalition government increased the police force by 55 per cent and set up an anti-revolutionary committee in the army. 'Socialism' of the Bandaranaike variety means the denial of such basic democratic rights as joining or forming a trade union, as shown in the cases of the Velona factory, Dawasa Publishing House, and the Norwood Tea Estate. Workers who resort to strike action in struggling for union rights face bullets from the 'people's' police.

The first budget of the coalition government submitted by N. M. Perera offered precious little to the masses. The budget demonstrated to the local and foreign capitalists that they need not have any fears or anxieties about the Bandaranaike government or its 'Marxist' ministers. Of course they explained that they had not forgotten about socialism, but right now it was not 'practical' and socialism had to wait. Neither the' 'save the country fund' nor the autumn budget could help the government avert the deep financial crisis it faced. Ceylon already owed the World Bank more than $50,000,000 and has been unable even to pay the interest on it. And yet it desperately needed more hard currency to pay for even the most essential imports. The World Bank would not grant any further loans until the government agreed to follow a course of 'austerity'. This meant the imposition of further burdens on the masses, such as withdrawal of the rice subsidy, pruning of social services, and the imposition of a wage freeze. The coalition government accepted the strictures. These developments have confirmed the position of the Lanka Sama Samaja party (Revolutionary) [LSSP(R)] that the coalition led by the Sri Lanka Freedom party [SLFP] is a capitalist government dependent on imperialism for its survival.

Under these conditions the government had no alternative but to impose more and more burdens on the masses. The masses rapidly became disillusioned with the coalition government. The government had failed even to project any solutions to the problems of rising prices and constant erosion of the masses' living standards. Unfortunately for the coalition leaders, they now had to contend with another factor: the emergence of a revolutionary united front between the JVP and the LSSP(R), the Ceylon section of the Fourth International, and the newly formed revolutionary nucleus in the tea plantations, the Young Socialist Front. This united front rapidly gathered momentum, and the disillusioned masses were attracted to it. The Bandaranaike régime realized that the movement stood in the way of their 'austerity' course.

*

On 6 February, 10,000 people held a rally in Colombo sponsored by the JVP, the LSSP(R), and the Ceylon Mercantile Union (CMU), the most important trade union of the Ceylonese urban working class. The gathering condemned setting up a US imperialist base in the Indian Ocean, called for Ceylon to immediately leave the British Commonwealth, demanded nationalization of the banks, plantations, and foreign trade, and appealed for defence of the masses' standard of living by an all-out war on unemployment and rising prices.

Faced with this situation, the government decided to try to isolate this political movement and to destroy it before the masses mobilized. The immediate aim was to destroy the JVP. After alerting the army and the police, the government staged a provocation on 6 March. This provocation was a petrol bomb attack on the US embassy by an unknown organization called the 'Mao Youth Front.' The government attributed this action to the JVP despite its denial of responsibility, and invoked special powers under the Public Security Act. The government then imposed emergency regulations, and began to arrest all known militants and leaders of the JVP.

The JVP realized that they were faced with a critical situation. Rather than being decimated without a fight, they decided to resist the government repression. The clashes that followed between the JVP and the security forces were thus the direct consequence of the government action. The government miscalculated. They did not expect the JVP to resist. They did not realize that the JVP and its allies would have such solid mass support.

Appendices

The Fourth International recognizes that the struggle broke out before all the sections of the oppressed masses, particularly the urban and plantation workers and the Tamil minority, had become politically united so that they were in a position to meet the bourgeois government's provocation adequately and settle accounts with the capitalist state and class.

The Fourth International calls upon revolutionists everywhere to break the conspiracy of silence covering the repression in Ceylon. It declares its full support to the repressed and persecuted Ceylon revolutionary militants. It calls upon the international working class, all working class and anti-imperialist organizations to do everything possible to block the shipment of military supplies, and all workers' states to immediately stop sending military aid and equipment to the Ceylon government, which is used only to murder and terrorize its own people. It calls upon the international working class not to be taken in by the 'left' pretences of the Bandaranaike government, and to recognize the basic capitalist nature of the régime and pro-imperialist nature of its repression. The state of emergency proclamation was approved by all parties in parliament, including the reactionary United National Party (UNP). The Bandaranaike government opened Ceylon's airfields to the use of the Pakistani government in transporting troops and supplies to suppress the rising of the peoples of East Bengal. Lieutenant Colonel Ranatunga of the Ceylon army, in a press conference 18 April, justified the execution of JVP prisoners without a trial by saying: 'We have learnt too many lessons from Vietnam and Malaysia. We must destroy them completely.' (The London *Times*, 19 April 1971.)

Indian workers and anti-imperialist militants: oppose Indira Gandhi's shameful pact with the butcher Yahya Khan and the British and US imperialists in support of the Bandaranaike régime's civil war against the Ceylon working class, peasant, and student youth!

Down with the traitorous Kenemans, N. M. Pereas,

Colvin R. de Silvas, and Leslie Goonewardenes, who, like their forerunner Noske, now arm reaction, let a bourgeois army murder revolutionists, support the murders or participate in the suppression of the masses of their country, and help suppress all democratic freedoms for the workers.

Freedom for Rohan Wijeweera and all the other arrested JVP and revolutionary leaders!

Not one dollar, not one gun to the bourgeois army and state of Ceylon!

Long live the Ceylon socialist revolution!

(United Secretariat of the Fourth International, 19 April 1971.)

Appendix 3
Chou En-lai's Message To
Yahya Khan

I have read Your Excellency's letter and Ambassador Chang Tung's report on Your Excellency's conversation with him. I am grateful to Your Excellency for your trust in the Chinese Government. China and Pakistan are friendly neighbours. The Chinese Government and people are following with close concern the development of the present situation in Pakistan.

Your Excellency and leaders of various quarters in Pakistan have done a lot of useful work to uphold the unification of Pakistan and to prevent it from moving towards a split. We believe that through the wise consultations and efforts of Your Excellency and leaders of various quarters in Pakistan, the situation in Pakistan will certainly be restored to normal. In our opinion, the unification of Pakistan and the unity of the people of East and West Pakistan are the basic guarantees for Pakistan to attain prosperity and strength. Here it is most important to differentiate the broad masses of the people from a handful of persons who want to sabotage the unification of Pakistan. As a genuine friend of Pakistan, we would like to present these views for Your Excellency's reference.

At the same time, we have noted that of late the Indian government has been carrying out gross interference in the internal affairs of Pakistan by exploiting the internal problems of your country. The Soviet Union and the United States are doing the same, one after the other. The Chinese Press is carrying reports to expose such unreasonable interference and has published Your Excellency's letter of reply to Podgorny.

The Chinese Government holds that what is happening in

Pakistan at present is purely an internal affair of Pakistan, which can only be settled by the Pakistan people themselves and which brooks no foreign interference whatsoever. Your Excellency may rest assured that should the Indian expansionists dare to launch aggression against Pakistan, the Chinese Government and people will, as always, firmly support the Pakistan Government and people in their just struggle to safeguard state sovereignty and national independence.

Pakistan Times, 13 April 1971

Appendix 4
Chou En-lai's Message To Sirimavo Bandaranaike

Below is the complete text of Chou En-lai's letter to Sirimavo Bandaranaike, dated 26 April 1971 and officially published by the Ceylonese Government a month later. The Chinese Government has not questioned the version released in Colombo.

I am grateful to Your Excellency and the Ceylon Government for your trust in the Chinese Government and your friendly sentiments towards the Chinese people. The friendship between China and Ceylon is in the fundamental interests of the two people and can stand tests. The Chinese Government and people highly treasure the friendship between our two countries and no one with ulterior motives will ever succeed in trying to sow discord and sabotage our friendly relations.

Following Chairman Mao Tse-tung's teaching the Chinese people have all along opposed ultra 'left' and right opportunism in their protracted revolutionary struggles. We are glad to see that thanks to the efforts of Your Excellency and the Ceylon Government, the chaotic situation created by a handful of persons who style themselves 'Guevarists' and into whose ranks foreign spies have sneaked has been brought under control. We believe that as a result of Your Excellency's leadership and the cooperation and support of the Ceylonese people these acts of rebellion plotted by reactionaries at home and abroad for the purpose of undermining the interests of the Ceylonese people are bound to fail.

We fully agree to the correct position of defending state

sovereignty and guarding against foreign interference as referred to by Your Excellency. The Chinese Government and people admire this and firmly support Ceylon in her just struggle towards this end. As Your Excellency is deeply aware the Chinese Government has consistently abided by the Five Principles of Peaceful Co-existence, has never interfered in the internal affairs of other countries, and is also firmly opposed to any country interfering in other countries' internal affairs, and particularly to foreign reactionaries taking advantage of the opportunity to carry out armed intervention. I would like once again to reaffirm this unshakeable stand of the Chinese Government.

In the interests of the friendship between China and Ceylon and in consideration of the needs of the Ceylon Government, the Chinese Government in compliance with the request of the Ceylon Government, agrees to provide it with a long-term interest-free loan of 150 million rupees in convertible foreign exchange. We would like to hear any views which Your Excellency might have on this matter. We are prepared to deliver a portion of the loan in May and sign a document on it. As for other material assistance, please let us know if it is needed.

Ceylon Daily News, 27 May 1971

Appendix 5

Text of Secret Documents on Top-level US Discussions of Indian-Pakistani War[1]

The *New York Times*, Thursday 6 January 1972
Special to the *New York Times*

WASHINGTON, Jan. 5 – Following are the texts of three secret documents made public today by the columnist Jack Anderson describing meetings of the national Security Council's Washington Special Action Group on the crisis between India and Pakistan:

MEMO ON DEC 3 MEETING

Secret Sensitive
ASSISTANT SECRETARY OF DEFENSE
   WASHINGTON, DC 20301
International Security Affairs
   Refer to: I–29643/71 Memorandum for Record

  SUBJECT
WSAG meeting on India/Pakistan
   PARTICIPANTS
Assistant to the President for national security affairs – Henry A. Kissinger
Under Secretary of State – John N. Irwin
Deputy Secretary of Defense – David Packard
Director, Central Intelligence Agency – Richard M. Helms
Deputy Administrator (AID) – Maurice J. Williams
Chairman, Joint Chiefs of Staff – Adm. Thomas H. Moorer

  1. A key to the initials used will be found at the end of this appendix.

Assistant Secretary of State (NEEAR) – Joseph J. Sisco
Assistant Secretary of Defense (ISA) – G. Warren Nutter
Assistant Secretary of State (IO) – Samuel De Palma
Principal Deputy Assistant Secretary of Defense (ISA) – Armistead I. Selden Jr.
Assistant Administrator (AID/NESA)–Donald G. MacDonald

TIME AND PLACE

3 December 1971, 1100 hours, Situation Room, White House

SUMMARY

Reviewed conflicting reports about major actions in the west wing. CIA agreed to produce map showing areas of East Pakistan occupied by India. The President orders hold on issuance of additional irrevocable letters of credit involving $99 million, and a hold on further action implementing the $72 million PL 480 credit. Convening of Security Council meeting planned contingent on discussion with Pak Ambassador this afternoon plus further clarification of actual situation in West Pakistan. Kissinger asked for clarification of secret special interpretation of March, 1959, bilateral US agreement with Pakistan.

KISSINGER: I am getting hell every half-hour from the President that we are not being tough enough on India. He has just called me again. He does not believe we are carrying out his wishes. He wants to tilt in favor of Pakistan. He feels everything we do comes out otherwise.

HELMS: Concerning the reported action in the west wing, there are conflicting reports from both sides and the only common ground is the Pak attacks on the Amritsar, Pathankat and Srinagar airports. The Paks say the Indians are attacking all along the border; but the Indian officials say this is a lie. In the east wing the action is becoming larger and the Paks claim there are now seven separate fronts involved.

KISSINGER: Are the Indians seizing territory?

HELMS: Yes; small bits of territory, definitely.

SISCO: It would help if you could provide a map with a shading of the areas occupied by India. What is happening in the West – is a full-scale attack likely?

MOORER: The present pattern is puzzling in that the Paks

have only struck at three small airfields which do not house significant numbers of Indian combat aircraft.

HELMS: Mrs Gandhi's speech at 1.30 may well announce recognition of Bangladesh.

MOORER: The Pak attack is not credible. It has been made during late afternoon, which doesn't make sense. We do not seem to have sufficient facts on this yet.

KISSINGER: Is it possible that the Indians attacked first and the Paks simply did what they could before dark in response?

MOORER: This is certainly possible.

KISSINGER: The President wants no more irrevocable letters of credit issued under the $99-million credit. He wants the $72-million PL 480 credit also held.

WILLIAMS: Word will soon get around when we do this. Does the President understand that?

KISSINGER: That is his order, but I will check with the President again. If asked, we can say we are reviewing our whole economic program and that the granting of fresh aid is being suspended in view of conditions on the subcontinent. The next issue is the UN.

IRWIN: The Secretary is calling in the Pak Ambassador this afternoon, and the Secretary leans toward making a US move in the UN soon.

KISSINGER: The President is in favor of this as soon as we have some confirmation of this large-scale new action. If the UN can't operate in this kind of situation effectively, its utility has come to an end and it is useless to think of UN guarantees in the Middle East.

SISCO: We will have a recommendation for you this afternoon, after the meeting with the Ambassador. In order to give the Ambassador time to wire home, we could tentatively plan to convene the Security Council tomorrow.

KISSINGER: We have to take action. The President is blaming me, but you people are in the clear.

SISCO: That's ideal!

KISSINGER: The earlier draft for Bush is too even-handed.

SISCO: To recapitulate, after we have seen the Pak Ambassador, the Secretary will report to you. We will update the draft speech for Bush.

KISSINGER: We can say we favor political accommodation but the real job of the Security Council is to prevent military action.

SISCO: We have never had a reply either from Kosygin or Mrs Gandhi.

WILLIAMS: Are we to take economic steps with Pakistan also?

KISSINGER: Wait until I talk with the President. He hasn't addressed this problem in connection with Pakistan yet.

SISCO: If we act on the Indian side, we can say we are keeping the Pakistan situation 'under review'.

KISSINGER: It's hard to tilt toward Pakistan if we have to match every Indian step with a Pakistan step. If you wait until Monday, I can get a Presidential decision.

PACKARD: It should be easy for us to inform the banks involved to defer action inasmuch as we are so near the weekend.

KISSINGER: We need a WSAG in the morning. We need to think about our treaty obligations. I remember a letter or memo interpreting our existing treaty with a special India tilt. When I visited Pakistan in January 1962 I was briefed on a secret document or oral understanding about contingencies arising in other than the SEATO context. Perhaps it was a Presidential letter. This was a special interpretation of the March 1959 bilateral agreement.

Prepared by:

[Signed initials]

James M. Noyes

Deputy Assistant Secretary for Near Eastern, African and South Asian Affairs Approved:

[illegible signature]

For G. Warren Nutter, Assistant Secretary of Defense for International Security Affairs.

Distribution: Secdef, Depsecdef, CJCS, ASD(ISA), PDASD(ISA), DASD: NEASA & PPNSCA, Dep Dir: NSCC & PPNSCA, CSD files, R&C files, NESA.

ACCOUNT OF DEC. 4 MEETING

Covering Memorandum
THE JOINT CHIEFS OF STAFF
WASHINGTON, DC 20301
Secret Sensitive
Memorandum for:
Chief of Staff, US Army
Chief of Staff, US Air Force
Chief of Naval Operations
Commandant of the Marine Corps

SUBJECT
Washington Special Action Group meeting on Indo/Pakistan
hostilities; 4 December 1971

1. Attached for your information is a memorandum for record concerning subject meeting.
2. In view of the sensitivity of information in the NSC system and the detailed nature of this memorandum, it is requested that access to it be limited to a strict need-to-know basis.

For the Chairman, JCS:
A. K. Knoizen
Captain, US Navy
Executive assistant to the Chairman, Joint Chiefs of Staff

REPORT ON THE MEETING
Secret Sensitive
THE JOINT CHIEFS OF STAFF
WASHINGTON, DC 20301
5 December 1971

MEMORANDUM FOR RECORD
SUBJECT
Washington Special Action Group meeting on Indo-Pakistan
hostilities; 4 December 1971.

1. The NSC Washington Special Action Group met in the Situation Room, the White House, at 1100, Saturday,

4 December, to consider the Indo-Pakistan situation. The meeting was chaired by Dr Kissinger.

2. Attendees

A. Principals:
Dr Henry Kissinger
Dr John Hannah, AID
Mr Richard Helms, CIA
Dr G. Warren Nutter, Defense Admiral Elmo Zumwalt, JCS
Mr Christopher Van Hollen, State

B. Others:
Mr James Noyes, Defense
Mr Armistead Selden, Defense
Rear Adm. Robert Welander, OJCS
Capt. Howard Kay, OJCS
Mr Harold Saunders, NSC
Col. Richard Kennedy, NSC
Mr Samuel Hoskanson, NSC
Mr Donald MacDonald, AID
Mr Maurice Williams, AID
Mr John Waller, CIA
Mr Samuel De Palma, State
Mr Bruce Lanigen, State
Mr David Schneider, State

3. Summary. It was decided that the US would request an immediate meeting of the Security Council. The US resolution would be introduced in a speech by Ambassador Bush as soon as possible. The USG–UN approach would be tilted toward the Paks. Economic aid for Pakistan currently in effect will not be terminated. No requirements were levied on the JCS.

4. Mr Helms opened the meeting by indicating that the Indians were currently engaged in a no holds barred attack of East Pakistan and that they had crossed the border on all sides this morning. While India had attacked eight Pak airfields there were still no indications of any ground attacks in the West. Although not decreeing a formal declaration of war, President Yahya has stated that 'the final war with India is upon us,'

to which Mrs Gandhi had responded that the Pak announcement of war constituted the ultimate folly. The Indians, however, had made it a point not to declare war. The Indian attacks have hit a major POL area in Karachi resulting in a major fire which will likely be blazing for a considerable length of time, thus providing a fine target for the India air force. Mr Helms indicated that the Soviet assessment is that there is not much chance of a great power confrontation in the current crisis.

5. Dr Kissinger remarked that if the Indians have announced a full scale invasion, this fact must be reflected in our UN statement.

6. Mr Helms indicated that we do not know who started the current action, nor do we know why the Paks hit the four small airfields yesterday.

7. Dr Kissinger requested that by Monday the CIA prepare an account of who did what to whom and when.

8. Mr De Palma suggested that if we refer to the India declaration in our discussion in the UN, that we almost certainly will have to refer to remarks by Yahya.

9. Dr Kissinger replied that he was under specific instructions from the President, and either someone in the bureaucracy would have to prepare this statement along the lines indicated or that it would be done in the White House.

10. Mr Helms referred to the 'no holds barred' remark in the official India statement and similar remarks that were being made from the Pak side.

11. Dr Kissinger asked whether the Indians have stated anything to the effect that they were in an all-out war.

12. Mr Helms said that the terminology was 'no holds barred'.

13. Dr Kissinger asked what the Paks have said. Mr Helms said the terminology was 'final war with India'. Dr Kissinger suggested this was not an objectionable term. It did not seem outrageous to say that they (the Paks) were trying to defend themselves.

14. Dr Kissinger then asked what was happening in the UN, to which Mr De Palma responded that the UK, Belgium, Japan and possibly France were joining for a call for a Security

Council meeting. The Japanese preferred a blander formulation. We have not, however, reacted to the Japanese.

15. Dr Kissinger asked to see the letter and requested that it be promulgated in announcing our move in the UN, to which Mr De Palma responded affirmatively.

16. Dr Kissinger stated that while he had no strong view on the letter, our position must be clearly stated in the announcement.

17. Dr Kissinger stated he did not care how third parties might react, so long as Ambassador Bush understands what he should say.

18. Dr Kissinger said that whoever was putting out background information relative to the current situation is provoking Presidential wrath. The President is under the 'illusion' that he is giving instructions: not that he is merely being kept apprised of affairs as they progress. Dr Kissinger asked that this be kept in mind.

19. Mr De Palma indicated that he did not yet know whether the Security Council would be convened in the afternoon or evening (this date). However, the first statements at the meeting would likely be those by the Indians and Paks. He suggested that Ambassador Bush should be one of the first speakers immediately following the presentation by the two contesting nations. He felt that the impact of our statement would be clearer if it were made early. Dr Kissinger voiced no objections.

20. Mr De Palma asked whether we wanted to get others lined up with our resolution before we introduced it. This, however, would take time. Dr Kissinger suggested rather than follow this course, we had better submit the resolution as quickly as possible, alone if necessary. According to Dr Kissinger the only move left for us at the present time is to make clear our position relative to our greater strategy. Everyone knows how all this will come out and everyone knows that India will ultimately occupy East Pakistan. We must, therefore, make clear our position, table our resolution. We want a resolution which will be introduced with a speech by Ambassador Bush. If others desire to come along with us, fine; but in any event we will table the resolution with a speech by Ambassador Bush.

21. Dr Kissinger continued that it was important that we register our position. The exercise in the UN is likely to be an exercise in futility, inasmuch as the Soviets can be expected to veto. The UN itself, will in all probability do little to terminate the war. He summarized the foregoing by saying that he assumed that our resolution in the UN will be introduced by a speech and there will be no delay. We will go along in general terms with reference to political accommodation in East Pakistan but we will certainly not imply or suggest any specifics, such as the release of Mujib.

22. Dr Kissinger asked how long the Indians could delay action in the Council. Mr De Palma said they could make long speeches or question our purpose. Mr Van Hollen said that they would draw out as long as possible which would allow them to concentrate on the situation in East Pakistan. Mr De Palma said that they could shilly-shally for three or four days which, Mr Helms stated, would be long enough for them to occupy East Pakistan. Mr De Palma stated that we could always try to force a vote. Dr Kissinger reiterated that there was no chance in getting anything useful in the UN.

23. Mr De Palma suggested that in all likelihood one side or the other will veto.

24. Concerning the matter of economic aid, Dr Kissinger stated that the President had directed that cutoff was to be directed at India only. He indicated, however, that he wanted to read the announcement to the President, so that the latter would know exactly what he might be getting into. At this point Mr Williams asked whether some mention should be made in the statement explaining why aid for Pakistan is not being cut off. Dr Kissinger said that information would be kept for background only.

25. Mr Williams said that the Department of Agriculture indicated that the price of vegetable oil was weakening in the United States; thus cutting off this PL 480 commodity to India could have repercussions on the domestic market. He asked, therefore, whether oil could be shipped in place of wheat. Dr Kissinger said that he will have the answer to that by the opening of business Monday.

26. Dr Kissinger then asked for a brief rundown on the military situation. Admiral Zumwalt responded that he thought the Paks could hold the line in East Pakistan for approximately one or two weeks before the logistics problems became overriding. He expected the Soviets to cement their position in India and to push for permanent usage of the naval base at Visag. He anticipated that the Soviets' immediate short range objective would be to gain military advantage through their current relationship with India.

27. Dr Kissinger indicated that the next meeting will convene Monday morning (Dec. 6).

[signed] H. N. Kay
Captain, USN
South Asia/MAP Branch, J5
Extension 72400

MEMO ON DEC. 6 MEETING

THE JOINT CHIEFS OF STAFF
WASHINGTON, DC 20301
6 December 1971

MEMORANDUM FOR RECORD
SUBJECT
Washington Special Action Group meeting on Indo-Pakistan hostilities; 6 December 1971.

1. The NSC Washington Special Action Group met in the Situation Room, the White House, at 1100, Monday, 6 December, to consider the Indo-Pakistan situation. The meeting was chaired by Dr Kissinger.

2. Attendees
A. Principals:
Dr Henry Kissinger
Mr David Packard, Defense
Ambassador U. Alexis Johnson, State
Gen. William Westmoreland, JCS
Mr Richard Helms, CIA
Mr Donald MacDonald, AID

B. Others:

Mr Christopher Van Hollen, State
Mr Samuel De Palma, State
Mr Bruce Lanigen, State
Mr Joseph Sisco, State
Mr Armistead Selden, Defense
Mr James Noyes, Defense
Mr John Waller, CIA
Mr Samuel Hoskanson, NSC
Col. Richard Kennedy, NSC
Mr Harold Saunders, NSC
Rear Adm. Robert Welander, OJCS
Capt. Howard Kay, OJCS
Mr Maurice Williams, AID

3. Summary. Discussion was devoted to the massive problems facing Bangladesh as a nation. Dr Kissinger indicated that the problem should be studied now. The subject of possible military aid to Pakistan is also to be examined, but on a very close hold basis. The matter of Indian redeployment from East to West was considered as was the legality of the current sea 'blockade' by India.

4. Mr Helms opened the meeting by briefing the current situation. He stated that the Indians had recognized Bangladesh and the Paks had broken diplomatic ties with India. Major fighting continued in the East but India is engaged in a holding action in the West. Mr Helms felt that the Indians will attempt to force a decision in the East within the next 10 days. The Indians have almost total air superiority now in the East where they can employ approximately a hundred of their aircraft against Pak ground forces and logistic areas. The Indians, however, have not yet broken through on the ground in East Pakistan. Major thrust of the Indian effort in East Pakistan is in the north-west corner of the province. The airfield at Dacca is all but closed. The Indians are registering only minor gains in the Jessore area, but they claim to have taken Kamalpur. In the West, Indian activity is essentially limited to air attacks. The Paks appear to be on the offensive on the ground and have launched air strikes in

Punjab. Overall, the Paks claim 61 Indian aircraft destroyed; the Indians claim 47 Pak planes. In naval action one Pak destroyer has been sunk by the Indians and another claimed sunked [*sic*]. The Indians also claim the sinking of one Pak submarine in eastern waters. Moscow is increasingly vocal in its support of India and is not supporting any UN moves to halt the fighting. The Chinese press made its strongest attack on India this morning.

5. Dr Kissinger then asked for a military assessment, questioning how long the Paks might be able to hold out in the East. General Westmoreland responded that it might be as much as three weeks.

6. Dr Kissinger asked what is to be done with Bangladesh. Mr Helms stated that for all practical purposes it is now an independent country, recognized by India.

7. Ambassador Johnson suggested that the Pak armed forces now in East Pakistan could be held hostage. General Westmoreland re-inforced this by noting there was no means of evacuating West Pak forces from the east wing, particularly in view of Indian naval superiority.

8. Dr Kissinger stated that the next state of play will involve determining our attitude toward the state of Bangladesh.

9. Mr Williams referred to the one and a half million Urdu speaking (Bihari) people in East Pakistan who could also be held hostage.

10. Dr Kissinger asked if there had already been some massacre of these people. Mr Williams said that he certainly thinks there will be. Dr Kissinger asked if we could do anything, to which Mr Williams stated that perhaps an international humanitarian effort could be launched on their behalf. Dr Kissinger asked whether we should be calling attention to the plight of these people now. Mr Williams said that most of these people were, in fact, centered around the rail centers; that they are urban dwellers and that some efforts on their behalf might well be started through the UN. Dr Kissinger suggested that this be done quickly in order to prevent a bloodbath. Mr Sisco stated that while the UN cannot do anything on the ground

at this time, public attention could be focused on this situation through the General Assembly.

11. Mr Williams referred to the 300,000 Bengalis in West Pakistan, and that they too were in some jeopardy. Mr Sisco said that this humanitarian issue could be a very attractive one for the General Assembly and that we would begin to focus on Assembly action. Mr MacDonald cited as a possible precedent the mass movement of population from North Vietnam in 1954.

12. Returning to the military picture, Mr Williams stated that he felt that the primary thrust of the Indian Army would be to interdict Chittagong and cut off any supply capability still existing for the Paks in the East. He said that he felt that the major thrust of the Indian Army in the East would be to destroy the Pak regular forces. He felt that a major job would be to restore order within the East inasmuch as it will be faced with a massacre as great as any we have faced in the 20th century.

13. General Westmoreland suggested that the Indians would probably need three or four divisions to continue to work with the Mukti Bahini; the remainder could be pulled out to assist the Indian forces in the West.

14. Mr Sisco opined that the Indians would pull out most of their troops once the Pak forces are disarmed, inasmuch as the Indians will be working with a very friendly population; thus, they will turn the military efforts over to the Mukti Bahini as quickly as possible. He felt that the extent and timing of Indian withdrawal from East Pakistan would depend to a large degree on developments in the West.

15. In response to a question, General Westmoreland stated that Indian transportation capabilities were limited from West to East, and that it would probably take at least a week to move one infantry division. It might take as much as a month to move all or most of the Indian forces from the East to the West.

16. Mr Sisco said that the long term presence of Indian forces in Bangladesh would have to be addressed. Mr Van Hollen remarked that should the Indian Army remain more than two

or three weeks after the situation in East Pakistan is wrapped up they would, in fact, become a Hindu army of occupation in the eyes of the Bengalis.

17. Mr Van Hollen raised the problem of the return of the refugees from India. Inasmuch as Bangladesh is predominantly Moslem, the return of 10 million refugees, most of whom are Hindu, would present another critical problem.

18. General Westmoreland suggested that the Indian position in the West was not unadvantageous. He briefly discussed the order of battle in West Pakistan and suggested that the Indians were in relatively good shape. He said that he expected the major Pak effort to be toward Kashmir and the Punjab. The Indians, he felt, will be striking toward Hyderabad so as to cut the main LOC to Karachi. He did not think that the Indians necessarily plan to drive all the way to Karachi. He also suggested that the current Indian move in that direction could very well be diversionary in order to force the Paks to pull reserves back from the Kashmir area.

19. Mr Packard asked about the POL supply situation, for Pakistan. Mr Helms said that at the present time it looked very bad. The overland LOC's from Iran, for example, were very tenuous.

20. Mr Williams suggested that the reason for the Indian thrust to the south was essentially political. Inasmuch as the Indians do not want to fight on the border they will have to give ground in Kashmir. In order to ward off parliamentary criticism, Mrs Gandhi may be going for some Pak real estate in the south.

21. Dr Kissinger then asked about UN initiatives. Mr Sisco said that we are now reviewing the situation with Ambassador Bush. Two Security Council resolutions have been vetoed by the Soviets. However, there is a ground-swell building in New York for an emergency session by the General Assembly to be convened under the provisions of the 'threat to peace' mechanism. The crisis could be moved into the Assembly through a simple majority vote.

22. Dr Kissinger and Mr Sisco agreed that any resolution introduced into the General Assembly must retain two key

elements: Cease fire and withdrawal of military forces. Dr Kissinger agreed that our UN delegation has handled the situation extremely well to date. Mr Sisco said that although it is very likely that the crisis will be introduced in the General Assembly, we must remember that there are 136 countries represented therein and we can expect all sorts of pressure to be generated. Mr De Palma suggested that when the resolution is introduced in the Assembly there will be a new twist, i.e.: the Indians will be no longer terribly interested in political accommodation. By that time that issue will have ceased to be a problem.

23. Mr De Palma said that a Council meeting was scheduled for 3.30 today and at that time we could try to get the Council to let go of the issue in order to transfer it to the Assembly, it being quite obvious that we are not going to get a cease-fire through the Security Council.

24. Dr Kissinger asked if we could expect the General Assembly to get the issue by the end of the day, to which Mr De Palma replied that hopefully this was the case.

25. Dr Kissinger said that we will go with essentially the same speech in the General Assembly as was made in the Security Council, but he would like something put in about refugees and the text of our resolution.

26. Dr Kissinger also directed that henceforth we show a certain coolness to the Indians; the Indian Ambassador is not to be treated at too high a level.

27. Dr Kissinger then asked about a legal position concerning the current Indian naval 'blockade'. Mr Sisco stated that we have protested both incidents in which American ships have been involved. However, no formal proclamation apparently has been made in terms of a declaration of a war, that it is essentially still an undeclared war, with the Indians claiming power to exercise their rights of belligerency. State would, however, prepare a paper on the legal aspects of the issue. Ambassador Johnson said that so far as he was concerned the Indians had no legal position to assert a blockade.

28. Dr Kissinger asked that a draft protest be drawn up. If we considered it illegal, we will make a formal diplomatic

protest. Mr Sisco said that he would prepare such a protest.

29. Dr Kissinger then asked whether we have the right to authorize Jordan or Saudi Arabia to transfer military equipment to Pakistan. Mr Van Hollen stated the United States cannot permit a third country to transfer arms which we have provided them when we, ourselves, do not authorize sale direct to the ultimate recipient, such as Pakistan. As of last January we made a legislative decision not to sell to Pakistan. Mr Sisco said that the Jordanians would be weakening their own position by such a transfer and would probably be grateful if we could get them off the hook. Mr Sisco went on to say that as the Paks increasingly feel the heat we will be getting emergency requests from them.

30. Dr Kissinger said that the President may want to honor those requests. The matter has not been brought to Presidential attention but it is quite obvious that the President is not inclined to let the Paks be defeated. Mr Packard then said that we should look at what could be done. Mr Sisco agreed but said it should be done very quietly. Dr Kissinger indicated he would like a paper by tomorrow (7 Dec.).

31. Mr Sisco suggested that what we are really interested in are what supplies and equipment could be made available, and the modes of delivery of this equipment. He stated that from a political point of view our efforts would have to be directed at keeping the Indians from 'extinguishing' West Pakistan.

32. Dr Kissinger turned to the matter of aid and requested that henceforth letters of credit not be made irrevocable. Mr Williams stated that we have suspended general economic aid, not formally committed, to India which reduces the level to $10 million. He suggested that what we have done for Pakistan in the same category does not become contentious inasmuch as the Indians are now mobilizing all development aid for use in the war effort, whereas remaining aid for East Pakistan is essentially earmarked for fertilizer and humanitarian relief. A case can be made technically, politically and legally that there is a difference between the aid given India and that given to Pakistan.

33. Dr Kissinger said to make sure that when talking about

cutoff of aid for India to emphasize what is cut off and not on what is being continued.

34. Dr Kissinger then asked about evacuation. Mr Sisco said that the Dacca evacuation had been aborted.

35. Dr Kissinger inquired about a possible famine in East Pakistan. Mr Williams said that we will not have a massive problem at this time, but by next spring this will quite likely be the case. Dr Kissinger asked whether we will be appealed to bail out Bangladesh. Mr Williams said that the problem would not be terribly great if we could continue to funnel 140 tons of food a month through Chittagong, but at this time nothing is moving. He further suggested that Bangladesh will need all kinds of help in the future, to which Ambassador Johnson added that Bangladesh will be an 'international basket case.' Dr Kissinger said, however, it will not necessarily be our basket case. Mr Williams said there is going to be need of massive assistance and resettling of refugees, transfers of population and feeding the population. Dr Kissinger suggested that we ought to start studying this problem right now.

36. Mr Williams suggested that the Indians had consistently requested refugee aid in cash. The Indians in turn will provide the food and support for the refugees. This has provided India with a reservoir of foreign currency. Dr Kissinger also asked that this problem be looked at by tomorrow to determine whether we could provide commodities in lieu of cash. We do not want to cut off humanitarian aid. We would like to provide material rather than cash.

37. The meeting was then adjourned.

[signed] H. N. Kay
H. N. Kay
Captain, USN
South Asia/MAP Branch, J5
Extension 72400

TERMS USED IN THE TEXT

AID – Agency for International Development

ASD (ISA) – Assistant Secretary of Defense, International Security Affairs

CIA – Central Intelligence Agency

CJCS – Chairman, Joint Chiefs of Staff

DASD – NEASA and **– PPNSCA** – Deputy Assistant Secretary of Defense, Near Eastern, African and South Asian Affairs; Deputy Assistant Secretary of Defense, Policy Plans and National Security Council Affairs

Dep Dir: NSCC & PPNSCA – Deputy Director, Policy Plans and National Security Council Affairs

Depsecdef – Deputy Secretary of Defense

ISA – International Security Affairs of Defense Department

JCS – Joint Chiefs of Staff

LOC – Line(s) of communication

MAP – Military Assistance Program

NEA – Near Eastern Affairs, Section of State Department

NESA – Near East and South Asia

NSC – National Security Council

OJCS – Office of Joint Chiefs of Staff

OSD Files – Office of Secretary of Defense Files

Paks – Pakistanis

PDASD (ISA) – Principal Deputy Assistant Secretary of Defense, International Security Affairs

POL – petroleum, oil and lubricants

PL – public law

R & C Files – Records and Control Files

Secdef – Secretary of Defense

USG – United States Government

WSAG – Washington Special Action Group, arm of National Security Council

More about Penguins and Pelicans

Penguinews, which appears every month, contains details of all the new books issued by Penguins as they are published. From time to time it is supplemented by *Penguins in Print*, which is a complete list of all titles available. (There are some five thousand of these.)

A specimen copy of *Penguinews* will be sent to you free on request. For a year's issues (including the complete lists) please send 50p if you live in the British Isles, or 75p if you live elsewhere. Just write to Dept EP, Penguin Books Ltd, Harmondsworth, Middlesex, enclosing a cheque or postal order, and your name will be added to the mailing list.

In the U.S.A.: For a complete list of books available from Penguin in the United States write to Dept CS, Penguin Books Inc., 7110 Ambassador Road, Baltimore, Maryland 21207.

In Canada: For a complete list of books available from Penguin in Canada write to Penguin Books Canada Ltd, 41 Steelcase Road West, Markham, Ontario.

India's China War

Neville Maxwell

This is one of those rare books that puts an
entirely new light on a chapter of history[1], and it
must be read by anyone concerned with
international affairs[2]. Although cool and scholarly[3]
it unrolls like a fascinating thriller[4]. It is an
important work of revisionist history and a
gruesome case study of the way in which wars
start[5], superbly documented (largely from official
Indian sources but also from secret Indian
papers)[6] and beautifully sustained[7]. By showing
how India led the world up the garden path[8] it
demolishes and throws to the wind a pillar of the
'contain China' doctrine – the belief that in 1962
India was the victim of unprovoked Chinese
aggression[9]. Maxwell's book is magnificent on
every count, an historical achievement of the
first rank[10].

This Pelican edition includes a Postscript
specially written by the author to cover new
material on the Sino-Indian dispute.

1. *Sunday Oregonian*. 2. *Foreign Affairs*. 3. Michael
Edwardes, *Encounter*. 4. *Military Review* (USA).
5. Michael Howard, *Sunday Times*. 6. Bernard Nossiter,
Book World. 7. Charles Elliott, *Life*. 8. Rohan Rivett,
Herald (Melbourne). 9. John K. Fairbank, *New York
Review of Books*. 10. A. J. P. Taylor, *Observer*.

For copyright reasons this edition is not for sale in the U.S.A.